# Contemporary Public Speaking

# Contemporary Public Speaking

## PAT GEHRKE
University of South Carolina

## MEGAN FOLEY
Independent Scholar

**W. W. NORTON & COMPANY**
*Celebrating a Century of Independent Publishing*

**W. W. Norton & Company** has been independent since its founding in 1923, when William Warder Norton and Mary D. Herter Norton first published lectures delivered at the People's Institute, the adult education division of New York City's Cooper Union. The firm soon expanded its program beyond the Institute, publishing books by celebrated academics from America and abroad. By midcentury, the two major pillars of Norton's publishing program—trade books and college texts—were firmly established. In the 1950s, the Norton family transferred control of the company to its employees, and today—with a staff of five hundred and hundreds of trade, college, and professional titles published each year—W. W. Norton & Company stands as the largest and oldest publishing house owned wholly by its employees.

Editors: Elizabeth Pieslor, Pete Simon
Developmental Editor and Project Editor: Michael Fauver
Assistant Editor: Olivia Atmore
Associate Editor: Katie Pak
Media Editor: Joy Cranshaw
Associate Media Editor: Jessica Awad
Media Editorial Assistants: Juliet Godwin, Maria Qureshi
Managing Editor, College: Marian Johnson
Managing Editor, College Digital Media: Kim Yi
Media Project Editor: Sarah McGinnis
Production Manager: Jane Searle
Photo Editor: Ted Szczepanski
Design Director: Rubina Yeh
Designer: Jen Montgomery
Permissions Manager: Joshua Garvin
Market Research and Strategy Manager, Communication and Media: Trevor Penland
Sales and Market Development Specialists, Humanities: Heidi Balas, Ryan Schwab, Sarah Purnell
Ebook Producer: Sophia Purut
Copy Editor: Laura Sewell
Proofreader: Jennifer Greenstein
Indexer: Maureen Johnson
Interns: Anouck Dussaud, Felicia Jarrin, Nora Martinez, Letty Mundt, Kiran Pandey, Leif Wood
Composition: Brad Walrod/Kenoza Type, Inc.
Art Studio: Graphic World
Manufacturing: Transcontinental—Beauceville

W. W. Norton & Company, Inc., 500 Fifth Avenue, New York, NY 10110
wwnorton.com
W. W. Norton & Company, Ltd., 15 Carlisle Street, London W1D 3BS

1 2 3 4 5 6 7 8 9 0

*This book is dedicated to the memory of Malachy Jerome Foley and David Kendall Walker, lifelong learners, teachers, and storytellers who saw the best in everyone.*

# Praise for
# *Contemporary Public Speaking*

*"This textbook is a modern, inclusive, engaging way to teach public speaking. It is a long-overdue update and breath of fresh air. The material is interesting and integrates many timely examples that will resonate with students. I am very excited that the textbook includes direction for creating contemporary assignments like podcasts and live-stream videos."*
—Jill Underhill, *Marshall University*

*"This book is conceptually brilliant and its justification utterly compelling. It is overdue, and I hope will lead to a culture change in public speaking pedagogy."*
—Charles Morris III, *Syracuse University*

*"Totally revolutionary and engaging way of teaching public speaking today. Absolutely representative of inclusivity and social justice."*
—Allison Brenneise, *University of Minnesota*

*"Frankly, this is a great book. While it is hard to make standpoint and strengths-based styles easily graspable and 'actionable,' this book does a great job of doing so. It teaches sound research, organization, and persuasion while also covering delivery and incorporating digital and online speaking as more than an afterthought. The writing is clear, it meets students where they are without trying to pander, and it uses good examples."*
—Donovan Bisbee, *Baruch College*

*"This is a relevant text, one that will provide the diversity and digital approach to public communication our students and discipline need."*
—Lisa Katrina Hill, *Harrisburg Area Community College*

*"Hits all the necessary topics but with much deeper appreciation for identity difference and digital speech, and an unusually strong chapter on delivery."*
—Bonny McDonald, *Louisiana State University*

# About the Authors

## Pat Gehrke (he/him)

Pat Gehrke is a professor in the Speech, Communication, and Rhetoric Program and the Department of English at the University of South Carolina. He has more than twenty years of experience teaching and directing public speaking courses. He has taught over fifteen different undergraduate courses, including public speaking, online public communication, small group communication, political communication, civic engagement, argumentation, rhetoric, and communication ethics. He also designed and teaches USC's unique and innovative online public speaking course. He is the author or editor of six books, including *The Ethics and Politics of Speech* (2009), *A Century of Communication Studies* (with William Keith, 2014), and *Teaching First-Year Communication Courses* (2017). He served as editor of *Review of Communication* from 2013 to 2016 and has twice received the National Communication Association's presidential citation for service to the discipline. He is widely recognized as a leading authority on the history of communication studies in the United States and an innovator in online public speaking pedagogy. He holds a PhD in communication from the Pennsylvania State University.

## Megan Foley (they/them)

Megan Foley is the curator of standpointadvocacy.org, a digital resource for advocates, activists, and educators committed to social justice. They have fifteen years of college teaching experience and have taught more than a dozen different undergraduate courses, including public speaking, intercultural communication, gender and communication, persuasion, small group communication, nonverbal communication, interpersonal communication, communication theory, and rhetorical theory. They have published award-winning research in *Communication & Critical/Cultural Studies, Critical Studies in Media Communication, Rhetoric & Public Affairs, Philosophy & Rhetoric,* the *Quarterly Journal of Speech,* and the *Journal of Communication Studies.* They have served on the editorial boards of the *Quarterly Journal of Speech* and *Women's Studies in Communication* as well as on the National Communication Association's Leadership Development Board. They hold a PhD in communication studies from the University of Iowa.

# Brief Contents

# Contents

**Marley Dias**
YOUTH LITERACY ACTIVIST

**Mariale Marrero**
BEAUTY INFLUENCER
AND LATINX ADVOCATE

**Jazz Jennings**
LGBTQ+ ACTIVIST

**Deja Foxx**
COMMUNITY ORGANIZER
AND POLITICAL STRATEGIST

**Jahmal Cole**
NONPROFIT FOUNDER AND
COMMUNITY LEADER

**Joshua Wong**
PRO-DEMOCRACY ACTIVIST
AND MOVEMENT LEADER

**Edna Chavez**
YOUTH LEADER AND
IMMIGRATION ACTIVIST

## 8  RESEARCH AND CITATION   155

**Blair Imani**
SOCIAL JUSTICE EDUCATOR
AND INFLUENCER

**Thandiwe Abdullah**
BLACK LIVES MATTER ACTIVIST

**Stella Young**
COMEDIAN AND DISABILITY
RIGHTS ADVOCATE

**Xiuhtezcatl
Martinez**
ENVIRONMENTAL ACTIVIST
AND HIP-HOP ARTIST

**Jordan
Raskopoulos**
COMEDIAN AND WEB
CONTENT CREATOR

**John Leguizamo**
ACTOR AND STAGE
PERFORMER

# 14 ONLINE AND MEDIATED PRESENTATIONS  317

**Danielle Desir**
PODCASTER AND
COMMUNITY ORGANIZER

**Hyeonseo Lee**
POLITICAL REFUGEE
AND ACTIVIST

**Melati and Isabel Wijsen**
ENVIRONMENTAL ACTIVISTS AND YOUTH ORGANIZERS

**Amanda Gorman**
POET AND ACTIVIST

**Lights for Liberty**
IMMIGRATION ACTIVISTS
AND ORGANIZERS

# Instructors' Overview

As a public speaking teacher or basic course director, you touch the lives of hundreds—even thousands—of students. You give young people the skills and the confidence they need to advocate for themselves, both professionally and politically. You know what it feels like to watch your students come into their own over the course of a semester. You know what it means to empower your students.

And you know that today's college students are facing new challenges. As professionals, they're entering a workforce that requires increasingly complex digital speaking skills. As citizens, they're entering a divisive political climate where our basic human rights have become hotly contested. Your work as a public speaking educator has never been more important.

We wrote *Contemporary Public Speaking* to equip you with the resources to help your students share their voices in today's diverse and digital world. This book will give your students the tools they need to embrace their unique strengths, think critically about their intersectional standpoints as speakers, and make their voices heard both in person and online.

## Starting from Student Strengths

*Contemporary Public Speaking* invites each student to explore and develop their one-of-a-kind strengths as a speaker. From the very first chapter, **"Your Standpoint and Strengths,"** we encourage each student to speak from their unique constellation of experiences, knowledge, values, and identities. **Chapter 3, "Ethics and Credibility,"** explains how making a unique contribution is a crucial part of establishing your credibility, and **Chapter 7, "Evidence and Reasoning,"** emphasizes direct observation, demonstration, and personal testimony as important forms of evidence and expertise. **Chapter 6, "Topic and Purpose,"** starts by asking students what specific interests, passions, or values are calling them to speak, and **Chapter 2, "Confidence and Anxiety,"** teaches students practical strategies for reframing their public speaking anxieties as strengths. **Chapter 11, "Language and Style,"** gives students tools for cultivating a signature speaking style from their everyday speech, and **Chapter 12, "Vocal and Physical Delivery,"** helps students select and adapt performance techniques to best fit their own style and abilities.

## Celebrating Diverse Intersectional Identities

*Contemporary Public Speaking* celebrates diverse forms of eloquence, grounded in each speaker's own unique intersection of experiences and identities. For example, **Chapter 1, "Your Standpoint and Strengths,"** encourages students to reflect on the intersecting identities that inform their standpoints as speakers. **Chapter 3, "Ethics and Credibility,"** addresses critical issues of inequality and privilege that many speakers face, and **Chapter 4, "Listening and Responding,"** explains how to recognize the limits of your own standpoint and create space for others to share their perspectives. **Chapter 5, "Audiences and Publics,"** explains how to earn support and build consensus across different values and beliefs. **Chapter 12, "Vocal and Physical Delivery,"** emphasizes that community norms for delivery—like pronunciation, gesture, and attire—are culturally particular, and **Chapter 11, "Language and Style,"** underscores the importance of valuing all speech communities equally. We also emphasize accessibility—not only in the chapters on delivery, presentation aids, and digital media, but in the book's dyslexic-friendly font and high-contrast design.

## Building Speaking Skills In Person and Online

*Contemporary Public Speaking* gives students the tools they need to actively participate in today's digital culture. We discuss examples of online speaking in every chapter of the book—from podcasts to explainer videos to digital town hall meetings—and each chapter offers actionable strategies for digital speaking.

For example, **Chapter 8, "Research and Citation,"** provides updated methods for evaluating online sources and spotting misinformation, and **Chapter 13, "Presentation Aids and Slides,"** explains how to navigate media credits and copyrights. In **Chapter 10, "Emotion and Narrative,"** we discuss ways to handle emotional contagion and hate speech online, and **Chapter 4, "Listening and Responding,"** describes how to avoid digital echo chambers and filter bubbles that silence dissenting voices. **Chapter 14, "Online and Mediated Presentations,"** focuses entirely on developing digital speaking skills, like recording audio and video and delivering live online speeches. Plus, we have created a library of video tutorials to help students master the technical skills they need to share their message online—making digital technology accessible for students and instructors with any level of experience.

# What's in the Book

*Contemporary Public Speaking* encourages students to recognize their unique strengths as speakers and to actively engage the ideas and strategies they're learning. Students will see speakers like themselves represented throughout the book: a diverse range of young, contemporary speakers sharing their own standpoints and strengths. We encourage students to actively engage with the course material by showing them how to apply their new skills in everyday speaking situations, by asking them questions that promote critical thinking, and by encouraging them to use insights from their own experiences to critically evaluate ideas presented in the text.

## CHAPTER OPENERS

Each of the eighteen chapters opens with an exemplary speaker who illustrates the importance of the skills students will learn in that chapter. These chapter openers demonstrate how speakers use their unique strengths and standpoints to adapt to a variety of speaking situations. Just flipping through the opening pages of each chapter, students will see speakers with a range of intersecting identities, including race, class, gender, sexuality, disability, nationality, indigeneity, size, and age, as well as transgender and English-as-a-second-language speakers. These introductions show students how each chapter will help them build skills as a speaker and give them diverse models for successful speaking.

## SPEAKER SPOTLIGHTS

Each chapter also features Speaker Spotlight breakout boxes that illustrate how a speaker has applied specific techniques and concepts from the chapter. These Speaker Spotlights focus on current events and contemporary issues—like climate change, gun violence, racism, policing, gender equity, LGBTQ+ rights, and body positivity. Each Speaker Spotlight is accompanied by web search terms to help students locate video footage of the speech, and the Norton Teaching Tools instructor resource site provides instructors direct links to those videos and questions for class discussion and analysis.

## "SPEAK OUT" STRATEGIES

Every chapter includes a "Speak Out" feature that shows students step-by-step strategies for applying their new skills in everyday speaking situations. These "Speak Out" strategies focus on informal, spontaneous speaking challenges—for example, how to respond when you hear someone using stereotypes or how to avoid linguistic appropriation when using idioms and expressions from other cultures. These "Speak Out" strategies make great impromptu exercises and encourage students to transfer their public speaking skills into a wide variety of communication contexts.

## CRITICAL THINKING CHECKS

To encourage active learning, each major section ends with questions designed to encourage critical thinking. These Critical Thinking Checks ask students to consider ethical issues, evaluate concepts, and discern which techniques to use in different speaking situations. With no single "right" answer, these open-ended questions encourage students to exercise their own critical judgment.

## STANDPOINT REFLECTIONS

At the end of each chapter, we also include a series of questions that invite students to reflect on their standpoints and apply their own experiences, knowledge, and values to the concepts and strategies in the text. These questions encourage students to think beyond the ways that we, as authors, present the information from our own limited standpoints. These Standpoint Reflections empower students to critically interrogate the text and recognize the value of their own perspectives and ideas.

## PATHWAYS

To make navigating the book easier, we provide Pathways boxes in the margins that link key ideas to relevant tools and techniques in other chapters. These Pathways boxes encourage students to make conceptual connections—reinforcing strategies they've learned in previous chapters and pointing them to future chapters where they can dive deeper into new concepts. Pathways boxes make it easy for instructors to assign the chapters in this book in any order.

# Digital Resources for Students and Teachers

*Contemporary Public Speaking* includes a large collection of digital resources to support both students and teachers. For students, we provide resources that promote active learning, self-reflection, and deeper understanding of the skills taught in the text. The searchable Norton Teaching Tools site provides additional teaching materials to help instructors shine in both brick-and-mortar classrooms and online classes. Our goal is to give students everything they need to explore their own strengths and become skilled speakers—and to provide both new and experienced teachers resources for helping their students succeed.

## RESOURCES FOR STUDENTS

*Contemporary Public Speaking* gives students a variety of digital resources: from hands-on worksheets that guide them through each step of creating and delivering a speech to audiovisual tutorials on reducing anxiety and creating online media. These resources can be integrated directly into your learning management system and are available for students to access on their own online.

**"Try This" Exercises**   Every chapter is accompanied by multiple exercises and worksheets that help students apply the public speaking principles they've just learned. These are practical and detailed downloadable resources to help students prepare and practice their speeches. Students can use these exercises on their own, or instructors can assign them as homework or for in-class activities. Many of these exercises work effectively to facilitate collaborative learning in small student groups. For example, **Chapter 1, "Your Standpoint and Strengths,"** includes a Strengths Inventory Worksheet, a Reclaiming Strengths

Reflection, and a Speaking Situation Analysis Worksheet. **Chapter 6, "Topic and Purpose,"** includes a Finding Your Topic Worksheet, a Purpose Statement Worksheet, and a Thesis Statement Checklist. We include a list of the relevant exercises at the end of each chapter, and the full list of exercises can be found on the inside front and back covers of the print textbook.

## "Learn More" Tutorials

Many chapters are also accompanied by video or audio tutorials that provide students with more detailed instruction. Most of these are focused on technical skills, online platforms, and software relevant to public speaking—everything from using online surveys and library databases to creating digital presentations. For example, **Chapter 13, "Presentation Aids and Slides,"** contains videos on how to create presentation slides, use digital whiteboards online, and implement universal design principles. And **Chapter 14, "Online and Mediated Presentations,"** includes an extensive suite of tutorials on preparing and delivering live video presentations, as well as creating and editing audio and video recordings. These tutorials help students build skills at their own pace and reduce the burden on instructors who may not have the time or lab space to demonstrate technical skills during class.

## InQuizitive

Included with all new copies of *Contemporary Public Speaking*, InQuizitive provides interactive questions that give students a low-stakes way to check their comprehension and practice applying key concepts. When they answer a question, students receive immediate feedback with links to relevant pages from the text for support. Students can keep working to increase their score, giving them additional practice in the areas where they need more help. By assigning InQuizitive, you can ensure students are reading the book—while also building their confidence and preparing them to use principles and practices from the text in their own speeches.

## MLA and APA Style Guides

Sourced from the best-selling *Little Seagull Handbook*, MLA and APA documentation guides are also available online to support *Contemporary Public Speaking*. These guides complement the in-depth discussion of citations and style guidelines found in **Chapter 8, "Research and Citation."**

## Plagiarism Tutorial

Norton's Plagiarism Tutorial can be assigned alongside the discussion of plagiarism and citations found in *Contemporary Public*

*Speaking.* The Plagiarism Tutorial explains why plagiarism matters, what counts as plagiarism, and how to avoid it—with activities and short quizzes to assess what students learned. You can see your students' scores, how much time they spent working, and when they finished in your Class Activity Report, which can also record scores into the gradebook in most learning management systems.

## RESOURCES FOR INSTRUCTORS

All of the above resources for students can be used as teaching tools for instructors, especially the "Try This" exercises. Instructors teaching online or incorporating digital speaking assignments into their brick-and-mortar classes may also find the "Learn More" tutorials helpful for developing online lectures and audio-visual assignments. Many additional resources are also available in the searchable Norton Teaching Tools site for the book, including speech videos; sample assignments, rubrics, and syllabi; a test bank; and presentation slides.

### Real-World Speech Videos
Our resources for instructors include video links to the presentations featured in the chapter openers and Speaker Spotlights. In addition to featuring a diverse range of speakers, these speeches include a mix of in-person and online presentations. Along with each video link, we provide a backup method to locate the video using web search terms, plus discussion questions that can be used to analyze the speech either in class or in an online forum.

### Sample Assignments and Rubrics
We include a variety of sample assignments designed for both in-person and online public speaking classes. These include assignments for informative, persuasive, and connective (that is, ceremonial or special occasion) speeches. Each sample assignment is accompanied by a rubric designed to reflect the same values of inclusion and accessibility emphasized in the book. We also provide recommendations for how to use the assignment and rubric in different kinds of public speaking courses.

### Sample Syllabi
You will also find complete sample syllabi for both in-person and online public speaking classes. These take a modular format that allows you to swap in different assignments from the provided samples to build the course that best suits your students, your institution, and your own strengths as a teacher. We have designed these syllabi to be compliant with Quality Matters

standards—they are easy for new instructors to implement or for more experienced instructors to customize.

**TestMaker Test Bank**   The test bank features a wide range of questions for each chapter, designed to support a seamless transition to this textbook. The Norton TestMaker test builder makes it easy to create and export assessments online, allowing you to search and filter test bank questions by chapter, type, difficulty, learning objectives, and other key criteria. You can customize the questions and answer choices to fit your course, then export your finished test to Microsoft Word or Common Cartridge files for your campus learning management system.

**Presentation Slides**   Our fully editable and ADA-compliant PowerPoint slides can serve as a quick and easy starting point for your class lectures. If you prefer to create your own lecture slides, all the images in the book are available in both .jpg and PowerPoint format.

# Acknowledgments

This book would not have been possible without the extraordinary efforts of extraordinary people. First and foremost, we want to thank the brilliant editorial team at Norton. Our editor Elizabeth Pieslor has made major contributions to this project both on the page and behind the scenes. Without her insights and encouragement, this book might have never been completed. Michael Fauver, our developmental editor, not only enhanced the clarity and usability of this book, but also deepened its commitment to inclusion, diversity, equity, and accessibility. He has been an invaluable ally in our mission to create a culture where every voice matters. Olivia Atmore gave us rich feedback throughout the project that helped us take the perspective of both faculty and student readers. Pete Simon, who originally commissioned this book, was an indispensable advocate for this project in its early days.

We also had a remarkable team of people helping us with the media and design of this book. Joy Cranshaw, Jessica Awad, Maria Qureshi, and Juliet Godwin helped us create an extensive library of digital media and instructor's resources. Allison Brenneise provided invaluable guidance to ensure the accessibility and inclusivity of our sample assignments and rubrics. She, along with Joshua

Young, Charles Ecenbarger, Sorin Nastasia, and Janessa Bauer, created many of the excellent instructional materials and online resources found in the Norton Teaching Tools. Mary Fratini designed an amazing set of interactive questions for the InQuizitive test bank. Many thanks to our copy editor Laura Sewell and proofreader Jennifer Greenstein for their superhuman attention to detail. Rubina Yeh and Jen Montgomery created a brilliant design for the book around the theme of intersectionality, and Brad Walrod executed it to perfection. Jane Searle managed the complex production schedule, ensuring we publish this book beautifully and that all its many components arrive on time. Angie Quintanilla Coates designed a showstopping cover that truly captures the spirit of the book. We're grateful to Debra Morton Hoyt for finding Angie and to Ted Szczepanski and all the media and permissions crew at Norton who spent countless hours helping us locate and create images for the book.

This textbook would never be able to accomplish its mission of empowering students without the support of the dedicated people who get it into the hands of faculty. We're thankful to Trevor Penland, Heidi Balas, Ryan Schwab, Sarah Purnell, the Norton Communication Ambassadors, and all the wonderful sales representatives at Norton for everything they do to provide this book as an option to faculty who share our commitment to inclusion, diversity, equity, and accessibility.

So many of our students and colleagues over the years have contributed to our thinking about inclusive pedagogy and public speaking that it would be impossible to even begin to list them all. We are especially grateful to the many people who served as reviewers for select chapters or the full manuscript. Without the insights and advice of these generous colleagues, this book would only be a shadow of its current form. Our thanks to:

Jennifer Bender, *Tuskegee University*
Donovan Bisbee, *Baruch College (City University of New York)*
Mardia J. Bishop, *University of Illinois–Urbana, Champaign*
Allison D. Brenneise, *University of Minnesota–Twin Cities*
James L. Cherney, *University of Nevada–Reno*
Kevin Ells, *Texas A&M University–Texarkana*
D. Leland Fecher, *Clemson University*
Jacob S. Ford, *Baylor University*

Joshua D. Hill, *Pennsylvania College of Technology*

Lisa Katrina Hill, *Harrisburg Area Community College*

Steve Hill, *University of Wisconsin–Stevens Point*

Sherry Lowell-Lewis, *University of Texas at El Paso*

Sara M. Mathis, *George Mason University*

Bonny McDonald, *Louisiana State University (now Southern University Baton Rouge)*

Ben Medeiros, *SUNY Plattsburgh*

Sarah Meinen Jedd, *University of Wisconsin–Madison*

Juliane Mora, *Gonzaga University*

Charles E. Morris III, *Syracuse University*

Stevie M. Munz, *Utah Valley University*

Suzy Prentiss, *University of Tennessee*

Maggie Price, *Maysville Community and Technical College*

Brandi A. Quesenberry, *Virginia Tech*

Tracey Quigley Holden, *University of Delaware*

Anand Rao, *University of Mary Washington*

Dawn Pfeifer Reitz, *Pennsylvania State University, Berks College*

Jane Pierce Saulnier, *Emerson College*

Julie L. Snyder-Yuly, *Marshall University*

Michael J. Stutz, *Three Rivers Community College*

Jill C. Underhill, *Marshall University*

Kim Weismann, *Williston State College*

Finally, we want to thank you for considering *Contemporary Public Speaking*. While no book can meet the unique needs of every faculty member, department, or institution, we endeavor to make this book a valuable asset for any public speaking instructor who values inclusion, diversity, equity, and accessibility. We all best understand social, political, and pedagogical issues when we listen to people from a wide range of backgrounds, social locations, and experiences. So please get in touch and let us know what you think about this book—especially if you see something we could or should be doing better. With your help, we look forward to making this an even more inclusive and empowering textbook with every future edition.

# For Students

Hello!

We're pleasantly surprised that you're reading this letter. When we were in college, we never—not once—read the letter from the authors at the beginning of our textbooks. So, we have to assume that either (a) you're smarter and more dedicated than we were back in the day, or (b) you have some time to kill. Probably both.

Since you're one of the select few who went the extra mile to read this, we'll let you in on a little secret. A lot of people just starting out think they have to become someone they're not to give a good speech. They think they have to pretend to care about things that don't interest them. Or use gestures that feel unnatural. Or throw out a bunch of four-dollar words that they'd never use in everyday conversation.

But here's the secret: you don't need a personality transplant to be a great public speaker. In fact, you can't be a great public speaker if you're hiding who you are and what matters to you most. We guarantee that your speeches will be way more interesting if you show up as yourself, with all your quirks, passions, and imperfections.

It can feel risky to show people what's unique about you—to let them see what makes you different. But building a relationship with your audience is just like any relationship: they can't love you unless you show them who you are. This book will help you do that.

Best of luck this semester,
Pat and Megan

YOUTH LITERACY
ACTIVIST  Marley Dias

# 1 Your Standpoint and Strengths

Teen activist Marley Dias has spoken at the White House and the United Nations, has appeared on *The Today Show*, *Ellen*, and *The View*, and has even hosted her own Netflix show *Bookmarks: Celebrating Black Voices*—all before graduating high school. Her success as a public speaker started with her passion for reading and her disappointment that the "classics" she was assigned in school—books like *Shiloh*, *Old Yeller*, and *Where the Red Fern Grows*—didn't feature characters like her.

Dias explains how schools and communities often fail to account for the places where multiple identities intersect: "They're thinking that 'because you're Black and because you're a woman, we are trying to create a system that supports you.' But they're not thinking about the intersection between the two, where I'm a mix of both."[1]

To advocate for more diverse representation on reading lists, she launched the #1000Black GirlBooks campaign, with the goal of collecting 1,000 books featuring Black female main characters. So far, she has collected over 13,000 books for schools in the United States, Jamaica, and Ghana.

She explains that she wants to create "mirrors and windows" for kids all over the world: "When I say mirrors, I mean I want these stories to be reflected for the Black girls who are reading them, so they can see themselves and identify themselves and learn about their history. When I say windows, I mean open up to people who are different, to understand and to see and grow from those things we don't understand."[2] By speaking from her own experiences and sharing her unique strengths, Dias has become a powerful advocate for diversity and inclusion.

## LEARNING OBJECTIVES

**After completing this chapter, you will be able to**

- Define public speaking
- Identify different types of publics
- Discover your signature strengths as a speaker
- Analyze the elements of your speaking situation

Drawing her passion and purpose from the intersection of her identities, Marley Dias demonstrates the secret to great public speaking. When you speak from your own identities and experiences, you unlock your full potential as a public speaker. You give people who share your experience a mirror that reflects and affirms who they are, and you give people from different backgrounds a window into your way of seeing the world. Sharing who you are is the key to public speaking—to finding your purpose, connecting with your audience, and changing the world around you.

## What Is Public Speaking?

People have gathered to hear others speak in nearly every culture for thousands of years. The ancient Greek and Roman speakers may be the most well known, but the art of public speaking arose even earlier in Africa and Asia.[3] Public speaking and principles of effective speech are found in ancient Mayan and Aztec traditions.[4] The Navajo, Cherokee, and Nahua peoples likewise have rich histories of public speaking.[5] While each culture has its own practices of engaging, effective, and ethical public speech, those practices share many common themes: appealing to audiences, holding their attention, evoking their emotions, reasoning with them, and earning their trust.

Even in contemporary American culture, filled with text and technology, public speaking remains one of our most powerful tools. We use it to inspire and promote causes in fund-raising campaigns and political speeches, at rallies and protests. We use it to sell products and services in launch presentations, sales pitches, and crowdfunding videos. We use it to teach and share ideas in classrooms, training seminars, instructional videos, and podcasts. Across many parts of our lives and through a variety of media, public speaking shapes our world and gives each of us an opportunity to make an impact.

As communication technologies have evolved, the scope and shape of public speaking has changed. Today, you can reach a global audience without leaving your home, thanks to online platforms like YouTube, TikTok, and Zoom. These days, public speaking goes far beyond delivering prepared remarks behind a podium. So, what is public speaking? To answer this question, let's define two key terms: *speaking* and *public*.

# WHAT IS SPEAKING?

Understanding what speech is and what makes some speech public is the first step to becoming an effective public speaker. Every speaker has a unique background, style, and set of strengths. As a speaker, you bring your unique abilities and perspective to the act of speaking. **Speaking** is any action that is embodied, communicative, and addressed.

- **EMBODIED.** Speaking can be auditory, visual, or both, but it cannot be separated from the speaker's body. When we see a speaker, everything about their physical presence—their gestures, posture, facial expression, and appearance—shapes our experience of their speech. When we can hear speakers but not see them—as in radio or podcasting—we still hear their bodies through their voices. For example, listeners can hear a smile in a speaker's voice, and they can tell the difference between a smile of joy and a smile of embarrassment.[6]

- **COMMUNICATIVE.** When a listener or viewer interprets a speaker's actions, they draw meaning from them. Speaking can evoke emotions, generate ideas, convey information, and change beliefs. When a speaker creates a message and their audience interprets it, they share in the process of communication.

- **ADDRESSED.** Speaking requires an audience. When we speak, we speak *to* someone. In other words, we direct our message toward some individual or group. That person or group may not always respond the way we expect or even pay attention, but we are still addressing them when we speak.

You might notice that we haven't mentioned the vocal cords. That's because many effective public speakers express themselves in other ways. Speakers can give presentations without uttering a sound by using sign language or speech-generating devices controlled by toe taps, cheek muscles, or other small gestures. Physicist Stephen Hawking is probably the most famous example of such a speaker, but certainly not the only one. Whether through sign language, speech-generating devices, or vocal delivery, speaking is an embodied act that addresses and communicates with others.

**speaking**
embodied action that addresses and communicates with others

---

## Pathways

To learn more about the role that listening plays in the communication process and how we listen through multiple senses, see **Chapter 4, Listening and Responding**.

---

Many speakers communicate through sign language and speech-generating devices.

## WHAT MAKES PUBLIC SPEAKING PUBLIC?

**public speaking**
embodied action
that addresses and
communicates to a
public

While all speaking is embodied, communicative, and addressed, **public speaking** is an action that is embodied, communicative, and addressed *to a public*. Sometimes people assume that public speaking is just speaking that happens in public. But public speaking is not defined by your setting; it's determined by your audience. Speaking becomes public speaking when you speak *to* a public—regardless of whether you are speaking *in* public.

For example, there might be a public park in your town that's often empty during the day. If you practiced a speech there, you would be speaking in public, but there would be no public there for you to address. Until people arrive and you address them as a group, no public speaking has occurred. On the other hand, you could set up a camera in your room, record your speech, and distribute the recording to a public via YouTube or Instagram. Even if no one else was physically present when you recorded it, and even though you recorded it in the privacy of your home, that speech would still count as public speaking. Your speech becomes public speaking when you share it with a public—regardless of how or whether that public responds.

Some of the most memorable public speeches by US presidents in the past forty years were delivered on television, with no audience in the room except the recording crew and the president's communications team. But you do not need to address an entire nation to address a public. In fact, public speaking can't address everyone—there is no such thing as "the public at large." Instead, public speaking addresses one of the many publics that exist. These publics form in three main ways: as identity groups, immediate audiences, and media audiences (see Table 1.1).[7]

- **IDENTITY GROUPS.** When a group of people identify with a shared social, cultural, or political membership, they form a public. For example, you might address Americans or Nebraskans or Bostonians as residents of their nation, state, or city. You might address members of ethnic groups like Pacific Islanders, civic groups like Rotary International, or religious groups like your local church, synagogue, or mosque. Even less formal identity associations like professions or hobbies can also constitute publics.

- **IMMEDIATE AUDIENCES.** A public can also form when a group of people assemble to hear you speak. Sometimes, this audience is defined by physical space, such as a stadium, a theater, or a classroom. Other times, it takes the form of a festival, political protest, professional conference, or even a crowd of onlookers at a spectacle. Any group of people gathered together in a specific place, at a particular time, can be addressed as a public.

- **MEDIA AUDIENCES.** Groups of people who share what they read, watch, or listen to can form publics, too. They might be subscribers to a podcast or an

## Pathways

To learn more about how to address your audience as a unified public, see **Chapter 5, Audiences and Publics**.

Left: US Space Force Brigadier General Jody Merritt speaks via live video to members of the 278th Air Expeditionary Wing of the US Air Force, a public based on their shared professional identity. Right: At the New York Comic Convention, actress Gillian Anderson addresses fans of *The X-Files*, a public based on their shared media consumption.

Instagram feed. They might be *Game of Thrones* fans, *Vogue* readers, or *Minecraft* players. Any shared media consumption can form a public. Even readers of this textbook could be addressed as a public, as we are addressing you now—hello there!

So a **public** is a group of people connected by shared identity, assembly, or media consumption. While they may or may not interact with each other directly, they are linked together indirectly by their shared connection to an identity, an event, or a message. But whichever kind of public you address, if you're addressing them through speech, you are engaged in public speaking.

| Identity groups | Immediate audiences | Media audiences |
| --- | --- | --- |
| Californians | Attendees at a festival | *The Expanse* viewers |
| Environmental lawyers | Conference participants | Followers of Imani Barbarin |
| Hispanic Americans | Crowd at a disaster site | *Serial* podcast listeners |
| Marshall University students | Protestors at a march | Los Angeles Sparks fans |
| People with disabilities | Spectators at a sports event | Megan Thee Stallion fans |
| Republican voters | Students attending a class | *Candy Crush* players |
| NAACP members | Supporters at a political rally | Reddit users |
| Veterans | Visitors to a museum | |

**TABLE 1.1** Identity groups, immediate audiences, and media audiences can all form publics.

## ✓ Critical Thinking Check

1. Why is it important to expand our definition of speaking to include more than just the sounds people make with their vocal cords? What—and who—would we leave out with such a narrow understanding of speech?

2. If a video presentation posted on YouTube has zero views, would it count as public speaking? Why or why not? How about a face-to-face presentation to a group of coworkers all scrolling on their phones—would that count as public speaking? Why or why not?

# Identifying Your Strengths as a Speaker

Sharing who you are is the key to connecting with the publics you address. We recommend that you always start with yourself—where you are, as you are. One of the quickest ways to lose an audience is to pretend to be someone you're not. Audiences want their connection with you to be genuine. That desire to make a genuine connection has become even stronger as Instagram, TikTok, YouTube, Twitter, Reddit, and other online platforms feed us photoshopped images, fabricated stories, and fake lives. Your identity, experiences, and perspective are unique, and they are your most powerful asset as a speaker.

Understanding your unique standpoint allows you to share a perspective that can only come from you. Your **standpoint** is more than just your point of view; it is your critical awareness of your location in a social context. When you understand your standpoint, you know where you're speaking from. This position within a social context is called your **social location**. No two people have the exact same social location. Our social locations are unique because they are **intersectional**: defined by a complex interconnection of multiple identities and experiences, including gender, race, age, socioeconomic status, sexual orientation, disability, education, ethnicity, nationality, religion, profession, family, and many more (see Figure 1.1).[8]

All our different identities and experiences combine to make us who we are, and no single part of our identity defines us. For example, think about regional identity in the southeastern United States. Southern identity and culture will mean something different for a seventy-year-old gay white man in rural Mississippi, a Catholic high school student in Houston whose parents

**standpoint**
your critical awareness of your social location

**social location**
your position in a social context

**intersectionality**
the complex interconnection of different identities and experiences that form your social location

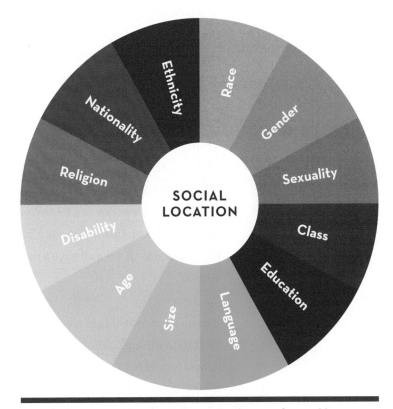

FIGURE 1.1 Your standpoint as a speaker is informed by your experiences at the intersection of multiple identities.

When you are speaking to a group or individual who sees the world from a different standpoint than your own, these steps can help you give them a window into your way of looking at the world:

1. **START WITH THE RELEVANT IDENTITIES THAT INFORM YOUR PERSPECTIVE.** For example: "As a bisexual woman . . ." or "As someone who grew up in poverty . . ."

2. **SHARE HOW THAT SOCIAL LOCATION HAS SHAPED YOUR EXPERIENCE.** For example: "I know what it's like when people assume my sexual orientation is just a phase." Or, "I know what it's like to rely on the free lunch program in the school cafeteria."

3. **EXPLAIN HOW THAT EXPERIENCE HAS INFORMED YOUR UNDERSTANDING AND VALUES.** For example: "That is why I believe that every person has the right to define who they are." Or, "That is why I support more funding for food services in our school district."

immigrated from Mexico, and a Black professional woman from a small town in Georgia working in New York City. We might share some elements of our identity and experience with others, but ultimately, we each live at a unique intersection of overlapping and interlocking identities.

## Pathways

To learn more about how inequality and privilege affect your standpoint, see **Chapter 3, Ethics and Credibility**.

Those intersecting identities position each of us within a web of different communities and cultures that shape our experience of the world. And because our intersecting identities shape our experiences, they also shape our knowledge, values, and beliefs. Since no two people have exactly the same intersection of identities and experiences, no two people see the world in exactly the same way. On the one hand, this means each person's perspective is limited. On the other hand, it means that we all have a one-of-a-kind contribution to share with others.[9]

Each of us can see things from our own standpoint that others do not see from theirs. For example, Marley Dias's intersectional standpoint as young, Black, and female helped her to see the lack of diverse voices in the assigned reading at her school. By speaking out and sharing her experience, she helped other people see it too. Just like Marley Dias's standpoint, your intersectional standpoint gives you unique strengths as a public speaker: your own unique combination of experiences, knowledge, values, and identities.

- **EXPERIENCES.** You have experienced the world in a way that no one else has. Although sharing a memorable moment from your life—say, a trip to Antarctica—can make a speech interesting, your everyday experiences might be even more powerful and illuminating for someone from a different social location. Experiences that seem commonplace to you—like the steps you take to walk home safely after dark or the way you change your speech patterns to be taken seriously by authority figures—can open your audience's eyes to issues they had never considered before.

- **KNOWLEDGE AND SKILLS.** We typically think about knowledge and skills as coming from study and practice, such as playing the piano, mastering a second language, or solving complex equations. But they can also come from your social location. For many people, families are a key source of social and cultural knowledge, teaching us about social roles, work, dress, language, values, and money. Our friendships, clubs or groups, schools, workplaces, and larger community likewise reflect and shape our views of the world. Sharing knowledge and skills from your unique standpoint can help others better understand the social world and even make them rethink their own place within it.

- **VALUES AND PASSIONS.** Your experiences, knowledge, and social location allow you to recognize value and meaning in places that other people may take for granted. Experiencing a scarcity of food, water, money, love, medical care, security, or any other basic need can strengthen your commitment to ensuring access and support for everyone. Witnessing the generosity, inventiveness, and kindness of others can inspire you to pursue your passions. By sharing your standpoint, you can help others discover the significance of ideas, issues, and causes that are important to you.

- **SELF-PRESENTATION AND IDENTITY.** Your intersectional identity shapes the way you present yourself. Your choice of words, gestures, posture, facial expressions, clothing, and even your body itself all work together to perform your identity. Sharing your identity—simply showing others who you are—can expand and transform your audience's worldview. As a speaker, you have the opportunity to share your identity in every aspect of your

 **TRY THIS**

To discover your own unique strengths as a speaker, try the **Strengths Inventory Worksheet** and the **Reclaiming Strengths Reflection**.

# Greta Thunberg's Climate Activism

In 2019, Swedish activist Greta Thunberg gained international acclaim for her speeches on global climate change. She started protesting at age fifteen, with just a sign, a short leaflet, and her personal Twitter account. Within a year she was speaking at the European Parliament, the United Nations, and the World Economic Forum. Her work has inspired the "Skolstrejk för Klimatet/School Strike for Climate" and "Fridays for Future" protest movement, with branches in over thirty countries. How did she become such a powerful speaker? She turned two perceived weaknesses into powerful strengths.

As a teenager, Thunberg might have been perceived as too young to have a voice in global politics. Instead, she has used her age as a strength. She frequently challenges policymakers to protect the future of today's children. She explains that young people have the right to demand change because they are the ones who will bear the true costs of future climate change. She often says that policymakers are "not mature enough to tell the truth"—a statement made even more powerful coming from a youth activist.

Thunberg attributes her direct, courageous, and assertive style to her Asperger's syndrome—another strength that others often see as a weakness. Asperger's is considered a "developmental disability" and classified as part of the autism spectrum.[10] People with Asperger's tend to focus intensely on presentation: from the way you dress, talk, and move, to the ideas, emotions, and arguments you present to your audience.

## Pathways

To learn more about reclaiming your anxiety as a strength, see **Chapter 2, Confidence and Anxiety**.

Our experiences, knowledge, values, and identities give each of us unique strengths as public speakers. But there is one major source of strength that most of us overlook: our weaknesses. Beginning public speakers often focus on fixing the areas where they believe they fall short, rather than embracing the vulnerabilities that make them relatable. For example, almost all speakers feel anxious about giving presentations, and people new to public speaking often see that anxiety as a weakness. But as the next chapter will show you, anxiety can be harnessed as a powerful strength for a public speaker. In fact, any quality, habit, or challenge you have can be reclaimed as a strength you can use in your presentations. What we see as our weaknesses are really just our differences—and our differences are the source of our unique strengths as public speakers.

a single topic for long periods of time and process social cues differently than people without autism. Both abilities are major strengths for someone who is committed to a complex and controversial issue like climate change. Thunberg began studying climate change at the age of eight and has maintained her commitment to the topic since. When she was viciously targeted by some politicians and media pundits on Twitter, she replied, "When haters go after your looks and differences, it means they have nowhere left to go. And then you know you're winning."[11]

You can find a video of her 2019 United Nations speech by doing a web search for: Thunberg United Nations 2019 speech. The video is approximately 4:30 in length.

Greta Thunberg, speaking to the United Nations in 2019, turned what others may have considered weaknesses into strengths. She used her youth and assertive style to chastise world leaders for failing to act on climate change.

## ✓ Critical Thinking Check

1. What different identities make up your social location? What can you see from the intersection of these identities that might not be obvious to someone from a different social location?
2. What are some attributes or behaviors that people commonly think of as weaknesses in public speaking? How could each of those serve as a potential source of strength?

# Adapting to Your Speaking Situation

While your standpoint as a speaker gives you unique strengths, you can find additional opportunities and advantages in your speaking situation. The **speaking situation** is the set of resources you have available to build your

**speaking situation**
the set of resources available to build your speech, including speaker, audience, context, and purpose

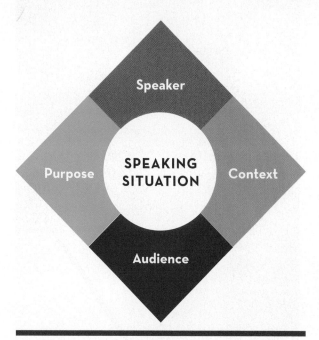

**FIGURE 1.2** The four elements of the speaking situation are the speaker, audience, context, and purpose.

speech.[12] You can think about your speaking situation like the ingredients you have on hand to prepare your message. Those ingredients are the *speaker*, *audience*, *context*, and *purpose* (see Figure 1.2). These elements will shape every part of your speech, from your first topic ideas to your final delivery.

## SPEAKER

As the speaker, your strengths will be the cornerstone of every speech you give. You can, however, choose which of your strengths to highlight in each speech. You can strategically emphasize the experiences, knowledge, passions, and identities that will best fit your purpose, your audience, and your context. For example, if you invited the authors of this book to give speeches to your class on how they got interested in public speaking, Pat would emphasize his experience as a first-generation college student who found a sense of belonging on his community college's debate team, while Megan would focus on their experience watching a classmate at an all-women's college give a powerful speech on sexual assault.

## AUDIENCE

Your **audience** is the group of people who will listen to you speak. Just as your intersectional standpoint gives you many different identities and experiences, your audience has a wide variety of common memberships, attitudes, experiences, and interests that you can use to address them as a public. For example, you may be able to address the same college class in many ways: as students concerned with the rising costs of education, as drivers who have issues with campus parking, or as eligible voters in your next state election. You can activate any connection that your audience shares and use it to appeal to them as a public.

**audience**
the people who will listen to you speak

**context**
the setting and circumstances that frame your speech

## CONTEXT

Your **context** is the setting and circumstances that frame your speech. Often, the most obvious setting is your physical environment—including your background,

# Barack Obama's Mic Drop

For his 2016 speech at the White House Correspondents' Association dinner, President Barack Obama and his speechwriters faced a speaking situation with many fixed factors.[13] In keeping with the event's decades-long tradition, the president would be the main speaker. Although different presidents have used this opportunity for different purposes, there is an expectation that the president's speech will use humor to relieve tension and strengthen the relationship between the White House and the media. The primary audience that President Obama would address were the three thousand attendees of the dinner, including reporters, media executives, politicians, and their guests. The event was also televised and streamed online to a broader audience, with sound bites featured in news reports, social media, and late-night TV monologues. The most important element of the context was that this was Obama's last year as president and his last time to speak at the correspondents' dinner.

Obama and his speechwriters leveraged this context as the starting point and the foundation for the speech. He walked onstage to the song "Cups" ("You're gonna miss me when I'm gone"). Then he made a series of self-deprecating jokes about his "lame duck" year in office. He roasted the up-and-coming presidential candidates in the audience, sticking to short jokes and one-liners that could easily be circulated afterward as clips or quotations. At the end of his speech, Obama marked the end of his time as president with an iconic "Obama Out" mic drop, which was replayed

President Barack Obama used the context of his speaking situation for humorous effect by ending with "Obama out" and dropping the microphone, a play on basketball star Kobe Bryant's "Mamba Out" retirement speech from two weeks earlier (32:25).

on every major news outlet and circulated as a GIF on social media. This memorable moment was a riff on current events and the president's love of basketball, mirroring Kobe Bryant's "Mamba Out" retirement speech given just two weeks earlier. Starting with the context—his last year as president—Obama drew on his unique strengths as a speaker, addressed both his immediate audience and his media audience, and fulfilled the speech's purpose to entertain and connect with the press and his constituents.

You can find a video of his 2016 White House Correspondents' Association dinner speech by doing a web search for: Obama remarks 2016 White House Correspondents. The video is approximately 33:08 in length.

lighting, ambient noise, and the arrangement of any furniture or other objects in the space. When speaking online, the setting also includes the web platform where your audio or video appears. Social circumstances and cultural events are also part of the context that frames your message. For example, you could contextualize your speech as a response to a recent event, an upcoming holiday, a major news story, a special occasion, or even a time of year.

## PURPOSE

**purpose**
the impact you want your presentation to have on your audience

Your **purpose** is the impact you want your presentation to have on your audience—to inform them, persuade them, or connect with them. In most speeches you give, your purpose will be even more specific—to toast the couple at a wedding, to rally support for a cause, to sell a product to customers, or to share an idea with colleagues. Often, your purpose will be guided by your context or your audience, but it is most powerful when it connects with your strengths as a speaker.

## Pathways

To learn more about finding a purpose in your own unique strengths, see **Chapter 6, Topic and Purpose**.

# Analyzing Your Speaking Situation

Before you begin preparing your first speech, make an inventory of what you know about your speaking situation: your audience, your context, your purpose, and your own strengths as a speaker. How will you respond to this speaking situation? How will you use the resources it provides? The following three-step process can help you take advantage of the opportunities and overcome the challenges in your speaking situation.

## 1 Identify the Fixed Factors

**📋 TRY THIS**

To identify the key elements of your public speaking situation anytime you give a presentation, see the **Speaking Situation Analysis Worksheet**.

Certain dimensions of the speaking situation will be determined for you. You might be assigned to speak to a specific group of coworkers, classmates, or colleagues. The place and timing of your speech might be set by a teacher, supervisor, client, or event organizer. You might be asked to speak on a specific topic, for a specific reason, or to fulfill a specific assignment. These fixed factors limit your options, but they also serve as a foundation for developing your speech. For example, if your professor asked you to give a two- to three-minute speech of self-introduction to your class, then you would already know your purpose and your audience, as well as the time you have available for your speech.

Different speaking situations call for different approaches. Left: Jonathan Paik of the Korean Resource Center speaks at a rally in support of the DREAM Act. Right: Mayor Quinton Lucas of Kansas City, Missouri, speaks at the US Conference of Mayors.

## 2 Choose a Starting Point

Once you have identified the fixed factors of the speaking situation, select one of those factors to serve as a springboard for the rest of your speech. Is there already a clear purpose to guide your message? Does this context call for a certain kind of response? Is there something that this audience wants or needs to hear? Do you have a strength that would shine in this situation? Choose one standout element as the foundation for your speech. For example, in a speech of introduction to your public speaking class, you might decide to start with your purpose—sharing who you are—since you don't know much yet about your classmates as an audience.

## 3 Elaborate the Elements One by One

Once you have identified a key element of your speaking situation as a starting point, build the rest of your strategy around it. Elaborate each of the elements in the speaking situation with greater detail. While someone else may have selected you as the speaker, you can choose which of your strengths will best reinforce your message. Even if the group of people you will address has been chosen for you, you can choose the way you address them and band them together as a public. The location and timing of your speech may already be decided, but you can still decide the way you frame your message within a broader context. Although you may have been given an assignment or a topic to discuss, you can still shape, refine, and target that purpose to give it more meaning and impact.

**Pathways**

To learn more about crafting speeches of introduction, see **Chapter 17, Connecting and Celebrating**.

For example, in a short speech of self-introduction, you would want to narrow down the broad topic of who you are and focus on sharing things about yourself that best fit your context, audience, and strengths as a speaker. You might contextualize your speech by focusing on what starting a new semester is like for you, or by talking about an upcoming event that you're excited about. You might connect with your audience by talking about your experience as a college student, or how you feel about trying public speaking for the first time. And you can emphasize your strengths by brainstorming the unique experiences, knowledge, values, and identities that you have to share.

When you are finished, each element of your analysis should fit together into a coherent plan for your speech. Check to make sure that every element—speaker, audience, context, and purpose—supports all the others. If they don't, work on reframing the elements so that they all fit together into a unified whole. By analyzing and framing these different elements, you will have a road map for developing a speech that makes the most of the opportunities and challenges in your speaking situation.

## ✓ Critical Thinking Check

1. Why is the speaker an important part of any speaking situation? How can considering your own standpoint and strengths within a particular situation make your presentations more effective?
2. Before giving your first speech to your class, what would you like to know about your audience? Your purpose? Your context? How would having that information help you develop a better presentation?

# Next Steps

From identifying your strengths to analyzing your speaking situation, this chapter has given you the foundations to begin your training as a public speaker. Your strengths and standpoint as a speaker can help you respond to any speaking situation you encounter. We encourage you to complete the Strengths Inventory Worksheet, the Reclaiming Strengths Reflection, and the Speaking Situation Analysis Worksheet, and return to them whenever you are working on a presentation.

As you continue reading, you will learn more about crafting messages for a wide range of audiences, contexts, and purposes, helping you better understand and adapt to a wide range of speaking situations. You will find examples drawn from face-to-face presentations, televised speeches, and online public speaking. The principles and skills you will learn will be equally valuable whether you're standing in front of a crowd or sitting at a microphone.

The chapters that follow contain strategies and ideas that you can incorporate into your analysis of other speakers and your own presentations. Not every idea in this book will work in every speaking situation, and not every suggestion will work with your unique set of strengths. But the more of them that you try, the more you will find the right techniques to spotlight your standpoint, amplify your strengths, and raise your unique voice.

# Standpoint Reflection

- Does your standpoint position you to understand public speaking differently from the way it has been described in this chapter? How so?

- What unique public speaking strengths does your intersectional identity give you?

- Do you expect to face any public speaking challenges based on your social location? Why or why not?

- How can you adapt the public speaking strategies presented in this chapter to best fit your own strengths and challenges?

## Key Terms

# Resources for Your Standpoint and Strengths

##  "Try This" Exercises

Access the "Try This" exercises as directed by your instructor or online at digital.wwnorton.com/chapterexercises-conpubspeak

- To discover your unique strengths as a speaker, see the **Strengths Inventory Worksheet**.

- To reframe your perceived weaknesses as strengths, see the **Reclaiming Strengths Reflection**.

- To identify the key elements of any speaking situation, see the **Speaking Situation Analysis Worksheet**.

---

**Want to practice these skills to prepare for your next speech? Go to INQUIZITIVE to review and apply concepts from this chapter and get personalized feedback along the way.**

BEAUTY INFLUENCER AND LATINX ADVOCATE Mariale Marrero

# 2 Confidence and Anxiety

With over 18 million followers on YouTube and millions more on other social media sites, Venezuelan influencer Mariale Marrero looks like one of the most confident public speakers on the planet. But she actually started making online videos to help get over her fear of public speaking: "When I was in college I was terrified of public speaking! I was really worried because I knew when I graduated I would have to stand in front of a bunch of people to present my thesis, so I knew I had to improve. I thought maybe talking to a camera would help out with that."[1]

Marrero found her voice by bringing her standpoint and strengths to a topic she was excited about. She started posting makeup tutorials in Spanish "because I followed a lot of English beauty channels, but they weren't using products I could find and didn't speak my language."[2] Today, she creates videos in both Spanish and English that not only provide makeup tips, but also discuss the importance of including a more diverse range of voices—and bodies—in the fashion and beauty industries.

Asked what makes her channel so popular, she says, "I'm just me being silly. I don't feel like there's anything special about me. I mess up, and I show them that. I'm not perfect.... But sometimes I feel like that's why people follow me—because I'm me, I'm real."[3] Rather than striving for an impossible image of perfection, Marrero shows that facing your fears and embracing your vulnerabilities can help you connect with your audience.

## LEARNING OBJECTIVES

**After completing this chapter, you will be able to**

- Explain how anxiety can strengthen your public speaking

- Recognize and define the three dimensions of anxiety

- Use affective, cognitive, and behavioral strategies for managing anxiety

- Develop a personal model of resilience for overcoming challenges

Like Mariale Marrero, almost everyone experiences some degree of anxiety when making a speech or giving a presentation. No matter how anxious you feel about public speaking, there are strategies you can use to harness that anxiety and transform it into a strength. Even if you already feel reasonably confident as a public speaker, these techniques can help you focus your energy and channel your strengths for maximum effect. Our experiences of anxiety are highly individual, so not every technique will work for every speaker. Try all of them at least once to see what works best for you. The goal is to find the right set of tools for your particular standpoint, strengths, and situation.

## Reclaiming Anxiety as a Strength

You might be surprised to learn that many famous speakers—from Abraham Lincoln to Mahatma Gandhi—have admitted to feeling anxious about public speaking.[4] Even though speakers like these often feel anxious during their presentations, they still appear calm and confident to us. Communication researchers have consistently found that audiences perceive speakers to be much less anxious than those speakers actually feel.[5] Just as you may look at other speakers and admire their confidence, others watching you probably see you as confident—even when you're not.

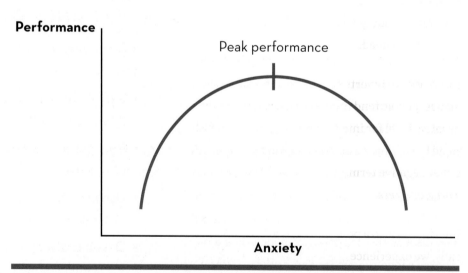

**FIGURE 2.1** The Inverted-U Model shows that a moderate amount of anxiety can improve performance.

When you're feeling anxious during a speech—especially when you're worried that your anxiety might be outwardly visible to others—these steps can help you use that anxiety to show your audience how important your topic is to you:

1. **START BY SHARING SOME OF YOUR ANXIETY SYMPTOMS.** For example: "My mind is racing and my hands are shaking" or "My heart is beating a mile a minute right now."

2. **THEN, TURN TOWARD THE SIGNIFICANCE OF YOUR TOPIC.** For example: "But I didn't want to miss this chance to say how much Andrea means to me" or "But I can't stay silent on an issue as important as human trafficking."

Because most public speakers don't appear anxious from the outside, we tend to see our own internal anxieties about public speaking as personal weaknesses. But anxiety can actually be a powerful asset in public speaking. Why? Because it can give you the energy and motivation you need to become an effective speaker.

While very strong feelings of anxiety can make public speaking challenging, too little anxiety can also impair your performance. Researchers call this the **Inverted-U Model**, illustrated in Figure 2.1.[6] The lowest levels of performance occur not only with very high anxiety, but also with very low anxiety. Your peak performance levels occur at the midpoint, where you experience a moderate amount of anxiety.[7] So our goal is not to eliminate anxiety, but to manage and channel it instead.

Although the Inverted-U Model shows that moderate anxiety improves performance, people tend to frame any amount of anxiety as a problem. **Anxiety** is a negative label for intense physiological and psychological stimulation, such as rapid breathing, racing heart, butterflies in the stomach, and runaway thoughts. Other negative terms frequently used to describe these sensations are *fear*, *worry*, or *stress*.

But there is also a positive label for these same sensations: **excitement**. Physically, we experience anxiety and excitement in similar ways. The key difference is how we interpret and act on those sensations. So, ask yourself: Am I anxious? Or am I just excited to share my message?

**Inverted-U Model**
peak performance levels occur at a midrange of anxiety, while the lowest levels of performance occur at both very high and very low anxiety

**anxiety**
a negative label for intense physiological and psychological stimulation

**excitement**
a positive label for intense physiological and psychological stimulation

# Luvvie Ajayi Jones Overcomes Fear with Purpose

Luvvie Ajayi Jones is a podcaster, blogger, public speaker, best-selling author, and self-proclaimed "professional troublemaker." But she isn't fearless. In her 2018 TED talk, she explains that people who speak up often speak despite their fear: "We're not fearless. We're not unafraid of the consequences or the sacrifices we have to make by speaking truth to power."[8] She compares her experience with public speaking to the fear she felt going sky-diving: "I feel like every day that I'm speaking truth against institutions and people who are bigger than me, and forces that are more powerful than me, I feel like I'm falling out of that plane."

But for Jones, speaking up is a defining part of her standpoint, her mission, and her values. As she explains, "Being yourself can be a revolution-ary act." As a Black woman born in Nigeria, she explains that she has often experienced pressures to keep quiet and not make trouble. But to live by her core values of honesty, integrity, and justice, she feels a duty to speak, especially when it's scary. Jones uses three questions to help her know when she needs to speak up: "Do I mean it? Can I defend it? And can I say it with love?" If the answer to all three is yes, she knows it aligns with her values and purpose. By sharing her truth, her purpose, and her standpoint, she has sparked conversations on

At the 2017 TEDWomen conference, Luvvie Ajayi Jones explained that once she focused on her pur-pose, she stopped letting her fears hold her back and accomplished her goals (3:25).

important social and political controversies, and inspired hundreds of thousands of followers to speak up—especially when it's difficult.

You can find a video of her 2017 TEDWomen speech by doing a web search for: Luvvie Jones 2017 TED. The video is approximately 10:54 in length.

When you start to feel sensations associated with anxiety, you can identify those sensations and frame them in a positive way. For example:

- I've got butterflies in my stomach—I must be really excited about my speech.

- My mind is racing—I've got so many great ideas.

- My heart is pounding—it's go time!

Reframing anxiety as excitement turns it into a strength.[9] Excitement will motivate you to prepare a better speech. Excitement will make your delivery more animated and engaging. Excitement will come through in your voice, your gestures, and your facial expressions. Use your excitement to share your passion with your audience.

Few people experience too little public speaking anxiety, but if you are one of them, focus on increasing your excitement and commitment to your presentation. Is there a way you could change your approach—your purpose, your public, or the strengths you use—to increase your passion and excitement about your speech? Showing that you care about your audience, your purpose, and your message is easier when you have connected your speech to your own unique standpoint, values, and strengths.

## Your Experience of Anxiety

Because we all have unique standpoints, we all have different experiences of anxiety. The first step to mastering speech anxiety is understanding what kind of anxiety you have. There are three dimensions of anxiety: affective, behavioral, and cognitive.[10]

- **Affective anxiety** includes physical sensations and emotions, such as an upset stomach, a pounding heart, a general sense of fear or dread, and feeling on edge, tired, and jittery.

- **Behavioral anxiety** includes outward expressions of anxiety, such as trembling, pacing, sweating, and using verbal fillers like "umm" or "uhh."

- **Cognitive anxiety** includes negative thoughts and images, such as worries, predicting negative events, and negative beliefs about yourself.

**Pathways**
To learn how to choose a topic that's exciting and meaningful to you, see **Chapter 6, Topic and Purpose**.

**affective anxiety**
physical feelings of anxiety, including rapid breathing, increased heart rate, fatigue, and upset stomach

**behavioral anxiety**
outward expressions of anxiety, including trembling, pacing, sweating, and using verbal fillers

**cognitive anxiety**
negative mental images and thoughts, including worry, predicting negative events, and negative beliefs about oneself

# Is It More than Public Speaking Anxiety?

The strategies in this chapter will help you work with common experiences of public speaking anxiety, manage them, and even use them productively. However, if your experience of anxiety—either about public speaking or in general—feels overwhelming, please contact a counselor, mental health provider, or counseling center. The differences between the anxiety most people feel around public speaking and a **clinical anxiety disorder** are the persistence of the feeling, the difficulty in controlling that feeling, and the severity of the impact that feeling has on a person's life.[11]

About 19 percent of adults each year experience severe anxiety, and roughly a third of us have experiences that qualify as an anxiety disorder at some point in our lives.[12] A trained professional can help you manage and treat a clinical anxiety disorder. Many colleges and universities have a counseling center that can help you find resources and support. A clinical anxiety disorder may also qualify for learning accommodations through the student accessibility or disability center on your campus. You can also find support online, including anonymous online support groups, through the Anxiety and Depression Association of America at www.adaa.org.

**clinical anxiety disorder**
anxiety that is persistent, difficult to control, and severe enough to interfere with a person's everyday life

Most of us experience a combination of all three dimensions, since each dimension of anxiety interacts with the others. For example, cognitive worries—"Did I do enough to prepare?"—can create a physical response, like an increased heart rate, which might then spur a particular behavior, like bouncing or pacing. Noticing an anxious behavior (like talking too fast) may lead to predicting a negative outcome—"I'll get a bad grade!"—which sparks an emotional reaction, like fear or stress. One type of anxiety can create a chain reaction that increases your experience of the other types (see Figure 2.2).

Fortunately, you can use this chain reaction to your advantage. When you calm your cognitive anxiety by reducing your worries, it also calms your affective and behavioral anxiety. When you soothe your affective anxiety by relaxing your body, you also reduce your cognitive and behavioral anxieties. By using the right combination of strategies for your personal experience of anxiety, you can turn a negative cycle into a positive one.

1. Why do you think public speakers perform better with moderate anxiety than with very high anxiety? Why do you think public speakers perform better with moderate anxiety than with no anxiety at all?

2. What's the difference between public speaking anxiety and a clinical anxiety disorder? How do you know when to seek support services and learning accommodations for anxiety?

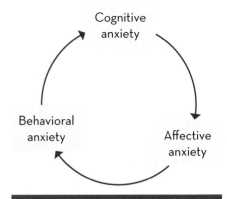

**FIGURE 2.2** An increase or decrease in one type of anxiety can start a chain reaction that further increases or decreases the other types.

# Strategies for Harnessing Speech Anxiety

When you have a moderate amount of anxiety, it's easy to reclaim your nervous energy as enthusiasm that can boost your performance. But when your anxious feelings are running high, you may need to reduce your anxiety levels before you can transform that energy into a strength. Mindfulness techniques can help you gain more perspective and mastery over your experience of anxiety.

**Mindfulness** is the practice of cultivating both awareness and detachment from your current experience.[13] One of the simplest techniques of mindfulness is observing and naming what you are experiencing. If you feel anxious, simply watch and describe your experience: "This is my heart beating." "This is worry." "This is pacing the room." This self-observation creates psychological distance between yourself and the experience so you can examine it without being caught up in it.

**mindfulness**
the practice of cultivating both awareness and detachment from what you are experiencing

With mindful awareness, you can begin to understand your own experience of anxiety. By becoming more aware of your personal experience, you can choose the anxiety-reduction techniques that will work best for you. Whether your experience is affective, behavioral, cognitive, or some combination, there are several techniques you can use to get your energy back into the optimal range.

## AFFECTIVE STRATEGIES

Muscle tension, rapid or shallow breathing, racing heart, upset stomach, and sweating are some of the most common sensations of anxiety reported by public

 **TRY THIS**

To identify the affective, behavioral, and cognitive strategies that will work best for you, try the **Speech Anxiety Reflection**.

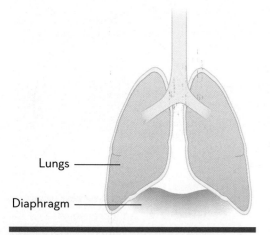

**FIGURE 2.3** Deep breathing uses the diaphragm, a muscle below the lungs.

Lungs

Diaphragm

▶ **LEARN MORE**

Learn to relax by breathing into your diaphragm with the **Deep Breathing Video**.

▶ **LEARN MORE**

Learn how to relieve anxiety by reducing muscle tension with the **Progressive Muscle Relaxation Audio**.

speakers. Affective relaxation strategies like deep breathing, progressive muscle relaxation, and physical movement can reduce anxious feelings by working directly on these physical sensations.

**Deep Breathing** One of the most powerful ways to calm the body is through deep breathing. It's even used by Navy SEALs to help them stay calm in combat situations.[14] To get the maximum relaxation from breathing exercises, breathe with your diaphragm, the dome-shaped muscle at the base of your lungs (see Figure 2.3). Start by placing one hand on your belly. Take a slow, deep breath in through your nose, pushing your belly out as you inhale. Then breathe out through your mouth, letting your belly gently fall as you exhale. Empty your lungs fully when you exhale, making your out-breaths last slightly longer than your in-breaths.

**Progressive Muscle Relaxation** You can enhance the effectiveness of breathing exercises by combining them with progressive muscle relaxation. This technique involves tensing and relaxing groups of muscles throughout your body. Sit or lie down in a comfortable position. Start by taking a deep breath into your belly while tightly clenching the muscles in your feet. Keep the muscles tight for at least four seconds while holding your breath in. Then exhale and let your muscles relax. Pause briefly, and then repeat the process, gradually tensing and releasing muscles throughout your body. Move upward through your ankles, calves, knees, thighs, lower back, stomach, upper back, shoulders, upper arms, lower arms, hands, and face.

**Physical Movement** Many types of movement can help control anxiety and relax the body. While extensive research demonstrates the benefits of regular exercise for reducing feelings of anxiety, even a short walk can ease both your mind and body.[15] You don't have to go to the gym or do strenuous exercise to help your body relax. Rhythmic movement like dancing or shaking out the arms and legs can help you to literally "shake off" anxiety. If your anxiety includes significant tension in the body, you may also find it helpful to stretch. Yoga poses can help reduce anxiety and increase energy levels, but so can any ten-minute stretching session that includes the upper and lower body.[16] It doesn't take a lot of movement—or any particular kind of movement—to lower your anxiety.

## COGNITIVE STRATEGIES

While releasing anxiety from our bodies almost always helps, sometimes the root of that anxiety starts in our minds. If you are thinking negative thoughts or imagining worst-case scenarios, these cognitive strategies can help you build confidence.

**Recognize Your Inner Critic**  When you're anxious, it can feel like there's a voice in your head saying you can't do it, something will go wrong, or you're not good enough. To distance yourself from this inner critic, try giving it a name based on someone or something it reminds you of. People name their inner critics after childhood bullies, critical parents, unkind teachers, or even historical figures and fictional characters. Choose any person or character that resonates with you. Then, whenever you hear that negative inner voice, you can talk back to it: "Thank you for your concern, Inner Critic. I know you are afraid, so I will be sure to give myself plenty of time to prepare and practice my speech. You don't have to worry; I know that I can do this." This dialogue diminishes the power of your inner critic, separating you from its negative thoughts and soothing the worries that come from this inner voice.[17]

**Create Empowering Beliefs**  You can create a more empowering inner dialogue with affirmations, what researchers call "positive self-talk."[18] **Affirmations** are positive statements that you tell yourself about yourself. Start with the negative statements of your inner critic and write down a positive statement to counteract each one. If your inner critic says: "I don't have anything interesting to talk about," you might write: "I have interesting and unique knowledge and experiences."

**affirmations**
positive statements that you tell yourself about yourself

Affirmations can change your views of yourself and your abilities, but they cannot change others or the external world. So, focus on present-tense statements about your own feelings and behavior: "I feel calm and confident when I speak" or "I make eye contact when giving a presentation." The present tense gives affirmations more power, describing what you can already do rather than imagining a hypothetical future.

Recite your affirmations to yourself at least once a day. Some people record their affirmations and listen to them while working out, driving, or walking. Some even write their affirmations as "you" statements—like "You've got this"—and recite them while looking in the mirror. Years of research shows that doing this just once a day for a few weeks can increase confidence, reduce anxious feelings, and improve performance.[19]

**▣ LEARN MORE**

Learn how to mentally rehearse giving a successful speech with the **Guided Visualization Audio**.

### Positive Visualization

In addition to reversing negative beliefs, you can replace negative mental imagery with positive visualization. The term *visualization* is just a metaphor—positive visualization is a practice of imagination that can include any and all of your senses. Olympic athletes, musicians, actors, and many others have been using positive visualization for decades, and research demonstrates that it helps public speakers control anxiety and feel more confident.[20]

Begin by imagining a scenario or event where you want to build confidence, and then imagine yourself acting with strength, poise, and effectiveness. You might imagine giving your whole speech successfully, or you might focus on a particular aspect of the presentation that is worrying you. You can handle any situation with grace and confidence if you have already practiced it in your mind. This mental rehearsal simultaneously improves your performance and reduces your anxiety.

## BEHAVIORAL STRATEGIES

If you've tried the affective and cognitive strategies above, you may have already reduced anxious behaviors like fidgeting, pacing, and talking too fast. But there are also behavioral strategies you can use to ease your anxiety: reducing environmental stress, seeking support, and practicing your speech ahead of time.

### Reduce Environmental Stress

Anxiety is cumulative. We often experience stress from multiple sources at once: work, school, family, friends, current events, health concerns, social media—the list goes on. This stress can add up, making new events—like an upcoming presentation—more challenging.

**distress tolerance**
the ability to manage stressful or anxiety-producing events

**Distress tolerance** is the ability to manage stressful or anxiety-producing

# Emma Watson's Public Speaking Anxiety

Even people who have been in the public spotlight for years can get nervous before an important presentation. Emma Watson—famous for playing Hermione Granger in the Harry Potter movies—has done countless interviews, press conferences, and public events. But when she was invited to speak on gender equity at the United Nations, she said she was "utterly terrified."[21] Watson explained that she often struggles with insecurity and anxiety, just like everyone else: "I'm just as human as you are. I'm just as insecure as you are."[22] When she spoke at the UN, she was feeling especially anxious: "I really didn't think I had it in me to do that speech."[23]

Watson has used several anxiety management techniques to overcome her fear of public speaking. She meditates to help calm her mind and keep her grounded. She also practices yoga, combining deep breathing and stretching exercises to relieve physical tension.[24] When faced with high-pressure situations like her UN speech, Watson relies on friends, inspiring figures, and her own values to help her overcome anxiety and fear.

Before her UN speech, she called a friend who gave her a pep talk and helped build her confidence. She thought about women who inspire her and what they might do in her situation. And she connected to her own values and purpose, asking herself, "If not me, who? If not now, when?"[25] By

Emma Watson was nervous to speak at the United Nations in 2014, but you can see her relax and gain confidence when she begins to speak from her own standpoint and about her own experiences with gender stereotypes (0:28).

reducing her anxiety, seeking support, and remembering her mission, Emma Watson delivered a speech that launched her role as a United Nations Goodwill Ambassador and a vocal advocate for global feminism and transgender rights.[26]

You can find a video of her 2014 United Nations speech by doing a web search for: Watson HeForShe 2014 United Nations. The video is approximately 11:47 in length.

**TRY THIS**

Reduce your environmental stress by setting boundaries with the **Boundary-Setting Activity**.

events. We each have different levels of distress tolerance, and tolerance for different kinds of stress. Reducing or eliminating other sources of stress will help you manage your anxiety about public speaking. Take good care of yourself before your presentation: eat well and get enough sleep. If you can, avoid other appointments or deadlines on your presentation day. Set boundaries with others to protect your time, energy, and attention. The better you manage your overall stress, the easier it is to manage public speaking anxiety.

**Seek Support** Don't hesitate to reach out for resources and support when you're preparing a presentation. At most colleges, there are teams of people available to support you. Librarians can jump-start your research and help you develop a plan for finding the information you need. Your campus may have a speaking center or writing center that can help you with everything from composing your presentation to practicing your delivery. There may also be class tutors or a student success center that can provide support for specific assignments. And of course, your teacher is an excellent source of support, so ask questions and request feedback as early as you can and as often as you need to. You may be surprised by how many people are waiting for an opportunity to help you.

**Prepare and Practice** Sometimes, people feel anxious because they aren't sure what to expect when speaking. Starting your preparations early and practicing at least a handful of times before your presentation can help you feel ready. If you're overwhelmed and having trouble getting started, just focus on one small thing you can do. It could be as simple as rereading the assignment or doing a web search to get ideas about your topic. Every small move forward can help you build momentum.

Whenever possible, practice your speech with the same technology you will use and in the venue where you will deliver it.

When you can, practice your speech the same way you will present it. If you will present standing, stand when you practice. If you're anxious about being at the front of your classroom, try to get some practice speaking from there. If you will present via videoconference, practice on the videoconference platform you will use. If you feel anxious about being on camera, try a test recording so you can get used to the equipment. If you have specific worries about making a flub or having a technical difficulty, practice how you would recover if that happened. The more you practice, the less you have to worry about.

## ✓ Critical Thinking Check

1. How do cognitive strategies like affirmations and positive visualization work to manage anxiety? Do these cognitive strategies only work for cognitive anxiety, or can they help reduce affective and behavioral anxiety, too?
2. What's the difference between affective strategies—like deep breathing, progressive muscle relaxation, and physical movement—and behavioral strategies—like reducing environmental stress, seeking support, and preparing and practicing your speech?

# Developing Your Personal Model of Resilience

In addition to the affective, behavioral, and cognitive strategies presented above, your standpoint and strengths give you a range of resources to help with your anxiety. Remember: strengths are not just what you are good at. Strengths are experiences, knowledge, values, and identities that help you feel strong. If you feel strong when thinking about an idea, talking about a passion, or participating in an activity, then that strength can help you feel more confident in your presentations.

For example, a cause or interest you feel strongly about can help shape your purpose. Your passion can be contagious, building audience enthusiasm and helping you feel more confident as a speaker. Sharing an aspect of your identity or experience can give your message more impact. The more you bring your personal strengths into your presentations, the more confident you will feel.

We each have our own personal strategies that help us overcome challenges and succeed in the face of adversity. This is called a **personal model of resilience**: the set of strengths and strategies an individual uses to face and manage life

**personal model of resilience**
the set of strengths and strategies an individual uses to face and manage life events

events.[27] Each of us has these strategies, but most of us are unaware of them. Once you discover your own personal model of resilience, you can use it to help you face any situation—including public speaking. The personal model of resilience has three parts: strengths, strategies, and symbols.

📋 **TRY THIS**

To identify your unique strategies for overcoming challenges, try the **Personal Model of Resilience Worksheet**.

1. **STRENGTHS**. Return to the Strengths Inventory Worksheet you did in Chapter 1. Reflect on how you have used those strengths to help you through a challenging event. What experiences, knowledge, values, and identities helped you overcome that challenge? You might even discover more strengths you didn't write down the first time.

2. **STRATEGIES**. Review your list and turn each strength you have used in the past into a strategy you can use in the future. What did you say, do, or think to help you through that experience? This might include talking to a friend or relative, focusing on a task for an extended period, or waiting for the right moment to act—everybody's list will be different.

3. **SYMBOLS**. For each strategy, create an image or metaphor that symbolizes your own strengths and strategies for working through challenges. For example, if family support is an important way you handle challenges, you might use the metaphor of redwood trees connecting their roots together to support each other. Choose a symbol that resonates with you and captures your personal feeling of strength.

Whatever your own strategies and symbols, your personal strengths will give you the tools you need to succeed at public speaking. By developing your personal model of resilience and reclaiming your anxiety as a strength, you can improve both your confidence and your performance as a speaker.

## ✓ Critical Thinking Check

1. What's the difference between a strength and a strategy? How can turning your strengths into strategies help you use them in a wider range of situations?
2. What's the value of using a symbol to represent your strengths? How can developing an image or metaphor to represent your strengths help you find creative ways to deal with challenges?

# Next Steps

This chapter has given you a wide range of tools for improving your confidence and harnessing your anxiety as a strength. To better understand your experience of public speaking anxiety, take some time to complete the Speech Anxiety Reflection and the Personal Model of Resilience Worksheet. Then, use what you learn to identify the affective, behavioral, and cognitive strategies that will help you the most. Experiment with these strategies to create a confidence-building toolbox best suited to your own experiences and strengths. The Deep Breathing Video, Progressive Muscle Relaxation Audio, and Guided Visualization Audio will guide you through some of the most common and helpful anxiety management techniques.

Speaking from your own strengths is the key to mastering public speaking anxiety. You don't have to be perfect—you just have to be yourself to make a genuine connection with your audience. Remember: your audience is on your side. They want you to succeed. When you focus on making your speech a great experience for them, public speaking will be a great experience for you.

# Standpoint Reflection

- Does the description of anxiety in this chapter fit with your own experience? How is it the same as or different from the experiences you have had?

- Do you agree that a moderate amount of anxiety can help you become a better public speaker? Why or why not?

- Do you face any unique challenges with public speaking anxiety based on your standpoint? How might other elements of your standpoint and strengths help you overcome those challenges?

- Which of the various affective, cognitive, and behavioral strategies in this chapter do you find most helpful for managing your own experience of anxiety? Do you have any other personal anxiety management strategies you would add?

## Key Terms

**affective anxiety**, p. 27

**affirmations**, p. 31

**anxiety**, p. 25

**behavioral anxiety**, p. 27

**clinical anxiety disorder**, p. 28

**cognitive anxiety**, p. 27

**distress tolerance**, p. 32

**excitement**, p. 25

**Inverted-U Model**, p. 25

**mindfulness**, p. 29

**personal model of resilience**, p. 35

# Resources for Confidence and Anxiety

## 📋 "Try This" Exercises

Access the "Try This" exercises as directed by your instructor or online at digital.wwnorton.com/chapterexercises-conpubspeak

- To identify the affective, behavioral, and cognitive strategies that will work best for you, try the **Speech Anxiety Reflection**.

- Reduce your environmental stress by setting boundaries with the **Boundary-Setting Activity**.

- Identify your best strategies for overcoming challenges with the **Personal Model of Resilience Worksheet**.

## 🎬 "Learn More" Tutorials

Access the "Learn More" tutorials as directed by your instructor or online at digital.wwnorton.com/videos-conpubspeak

- Learn to relax by breathing into your diaphragm with the **Deep Breathing Video**.

- Learn how to relieve anxiety by reducing muscle tension with the **Progressive Muscle Relaxation Audio**.

- Learn how to mentally rehearse giving a successful speech with the **Guided Visualization Audio**.

---

 Want to practice these skills to prepare for your next speech? Go to INQUIZITIVE to review and apply concepts from this chapter and get personalized feedback along the way.

LGBTQ+ RIGHTS ACTIVIST

Jazz Jennings

# 3 Ethics and Credibility

Jazz Jennings uses her voice to speak her truth, spread acceptance, and advocate for the rights of transgender youth. She is a public speaker, a popular YouTuber, the cofounder of the TransKids Purple Rainbow Foundation, the author of two books, and the subject of TLC's long-running reality show *I Am Jazz*. She has been educating audiences about what it's like to be transgender in America since her first television interview when she was only six years old. As a lifelong advocate for gender-affirming health care, she shows just how important it is to love yourself for who you are.[1]

Jennings has established credibility with millions of viewers by grounding her message in her own experiences. Her reality show, YouTube channel, and public presentations are open about everything from challenges with school administrators to the details of her gender-affirming surgery. When criticized for sharing too much, she replied: "How are we going to learn if someone doesn't step up to the plate and share their story and personal details?"[2] By speaking openly about her own struggles and successes, she helps her audience understand who she is and why she cares about transgender rights.

Jennings shows that a speaker's credibility is closely tied to both their experience and their ethics. She sees speaking up as an ethical calling: "I tell myself, in sharing my story, it's not about me, it's about the message. It's not just about changing lives, it's about saving lives."[3] She repeatedly emphasizes values like love, acceptance, and embracing difference, encouraging others to "stay authentic" and "be yourself." She explains, "We're all beautiful and unique, and we just have to learn to embrace that."[4] By sharing her unique standpoint and strengths, Jennings demonstrates the integrity that public speakers need to build trust with their audiences.

## LEARNING OBJECTIVES

### After completing this chapter, you will be able to

- Identify and refine your personal ethics
- Explain how privilege and marginalization affect your credibility
- Develop credibility by sharing your ethics
- Restore your credibility in response to ethical challenges

As a public speaker, your greatest strength is who you are. Your standpoint is a powerful resource you can draw on to make a connection with your audience and a contribution to the world. Your standpoint gives you credibility. **Credibility** is your audience's trust that you have the relevant experience, knowledge, values, and identities to speak on a particular topic. As Jazz Jennings shows, you can build credibility with your audience by embracing your best self and sharing who you truly are. But what does it mean to embrace your best self? Reflecting on your ethics can help you find the answer.

# Reflecting on Your Personal Ethics

*Ethics* is a slippery term. We sometimes talk about whether or not something is ethical—as if there were some universal standard we could use to judge everyone's behavior. But it's more accurate to think of ethics as part of an individual's own standpoint. The word *ethics* comes from the ancient Greek word *ethos*, meaning both character and habit.[5] Your character and your habits are linked because you become what you repeatedly do. Your habits create your character; your character, in turn, guides your habits. How you act determines who you are, and who you are determines how you act (see Figure 3.1). **Ethics** are the habits and principles that guide an individual's actions.

Contemporary research in neuroscience supports this ancient Greek idea that what you do makes you who you are. Our brains are constantly changing to incorporate new experiences. Neuroscientists call this **brain plasticity**.[6] The more often you take a particular action, the more the brain adapts to make it easier to repeat that action. This is how we develop skills—and how we develop our ethics, values, and personalities. Every action you take is training you to be the kind of person who takes that action.

This means that your actions, your habits, and your character are not set in stone. Rather than having fixed habits and abilities, you are constantly growing. Each action you take is an opportunity to shape yourself into the person you want to be. The way you act, the way you speak, and the way you present yourself to others all shape who you become. That's why reflecting on and communicating your own ethics is the key to both your credibility and your growth as a speaker.

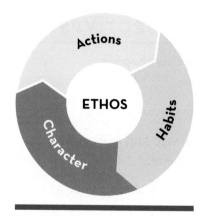

**FIGURE 3.1** Your credibility, or *ethos*, comes from a circular relationship between your actions, habits, and character.

Many of our behaviors come from habits or cultural norms we have not consciously chosen. **Implicit ethics** are the unquestioned beliefs and ingrained habits that we did not consciously choose, but instead learned from our family, culture, or social groups. Implicit ethics are often invisible to the people who live by them, who may assume them to be facts of life or human nature. But even when speakers are unaware of them, their implicit ethics can have a big impact on their credibility.

Reflecting on your beliefs and habits can make you more aware of your implicit ethics. Reflecting on your ethics allows you to begin making intentional choices about your behavior and beliefs, making your implicit ethics explicit. While implicit ethics are things we do and believe without thinking, **explicit ethics** are principles that we have consciously chosen to live by. When you reflect on your ethics, you can choose whether to reject, adapt, or more fully embrace your existing habits and beliefs.

- **REJECT.** For example, when one of our students reflected on his habit of making jokes about women, thinking about his younger sister helped him realize just how harmful his jokes might be.

- **ADAPT.** Considering people with limited educational opportunities helped another student expand her beliefs about the range of valuable gifts that people have to share.

- **EMBRACE.** Reflecting on their habit of saying "y'all," several of our students embraced it as a more gender-inclusive way of addressing groups than "you guys" or even "ladies and gentlemen."

The decision to reject, adapt, or embrace a habit or belief is up to you. The crucial factor is not which choice you make, but that you make a choice—rather than passively accepting beliefs and behaviors that you have not consciously chosen. Your choices become the foundation for how you present yourself to others, build connections, and establish credibility. Reflecting on your ethics can help you navigate the complexities of your standpoint by intentionally deciding how you want to live and who you want to be.

Your standpoint exists at the intersection of multiple identities and experiences, and every aspect of your standpoint can influence your ethics. Different

**implicit ethics**
unquestioned beliefs and ingrained habits that we did not consciously choose

**explicit ethics**
principles that we have consciously chosen to live by

📋 **TRY THIS**

To identify your implicit ethics and make explicit ethical decisions, use the **Personal Ethics Reflection**.

facets of our identities often challenge us with competing pressures and contradictory expectations. For example, many people who identify as LGBTQ+ are raised in religious communities that believe that homosexuality and gender non-conformity are sinful. When you are a member of multiple identity groups with competing beliefs, reflecting on your ethics can empower you to choose the beliefs you want to live by.

## SELF-DEFINITION: CHALLENGING STEREOTYPES

As you reflect on your ethics, you are likely to encounter lots of social expectations about yourself and your standpoint, messages that say you must think or act in a particular way because you are a member of a particular group. For example, you may have encountered messages like: "Real men don't cry" or "I thought all Asian people were good at math." These messages are **stereotypes**: simplistic generalizations about groups of people. Stereotypes fail to respect the richness of your intersectional standpoint by totalizing and essentializing your identity.

**Totalizing** is defining a person's whole identity based on a single aspect of their identity or experience—as if it were the sum total of who they are.[7] For example, it would be totalizing to treat a gay person as if their sexuality were their entire identity, or treat a deaf person as if their disability were all they are. Totalizing diminishes a person's humanity by reducing their intersectional standpoint down to a single dimension.

**Essentializing** is assuming that some characteristic or set of characteristics defines the intrinsic nature—or essence—of all members of a group.[8] For example, it would be essentializing to say that all women are emotional or that all white Southerners are racist. Characterizing a group in terms of their supposedly essential traits both disregards and misrepresents the diverse spectrum of their experiences.

Totalizing and essentializing messages are especially damaging when they are motivated by hate. **Hate speech** is any communication that attacks, dismisses, or demeans a person or a group based on who they are, including their religion, ethnicity, nationality, race, gender, sexual orientation, disability, or any other

---

**stereotypes**
simplistic generalizations about groups of people

**totalizing**
defining a person's whole identity based on a single aspect of their identity or experience

**essentializing**
assuming that some characteristic or set of characteristics defines the intrinsic nature of all members of a group

**hate speech**
any communication that attacks, dismisses, or demeans a person or a group based on who they are, including religion, ethnicity, nationality, race, color, gender, sexual orientation, disability, or any other aspect of their identity

When you hear someone making overgeneralizations about groups of people, these steps can help you expand their perspective without raising their defenses:

1. **SHARE PERSONAL CONNECTION.** Start by describing a relationship you have with a member of the group being stereotyped. For example: "A Korean family lives right next door us . . ." or "My favorite uncle is gay . . ."

2. **CHALLENGE THE STEREOTYPE WITH A STORY.** Then, share a specific, positive anecdote as a counterpoint to the overgeneralization. For example: "Our kids always play tag and hide-and-seek together, and . . ." or "He always brings back the coolest souvenirs from his work trips, like . . ."

aspect of their identity.[9] As an attack on a person or group of people, hate speech disrespects the fundamental dignity that every human being has the right to expect.

But stereotypes are harmful even when they are not rooted in hate. So-called "positive" stereotypes—like "Black people are good at sports" or "Indigenous people are spiritual"—still misrepresent people by reducing their identities to a single dimension and assuming that every member of the group is the same. All essentializing and totalizing messages—even stereotypes about positive traits—ignore the complex interplay of identities and experiences that makes each person unique.

Only you can decide how to best navigate the intersecting identities that make you who you are. Only you can define your experience, and only you can tell your story. Reflecting on stereotypes can help you challenge any implicit biases that your audience may hold about you—and help you spot potential bias in your own implicit habits and beliefs.

## SELF-REFLECTION: QUESTIONING PRIVILEGE

Our standpoints give each of us an irreplaceable and unreproducible way of looking at the world. You see the world in a way that no one else does. But that also means that other people see things you don't. While our standpoints make our perspectives unique, they also limit our field of vision. Questioning the limits of

# Linguistic Stereotypes and Inclusive Language

You can avoid stereotyping by using inclusive language. **Inclusive language** uses person-centered and identity-neutral terms to avoid excluding or marginalizing others. **Person-centered language** refers to the humanness of an individual, while recognizing relevant identity traits as qualities of that person. For example, referring to people as "queers" or "the unemployed" dehumanizes them, while person-centered terms like "queer people" or "unemployed people" emphasize their personhood. Person-centered terms offer a way to recognize an identity trait important to a discussion while affirming someone's humanity.

When a person's identity is unknown or irrelevant to a discussion, identity-neutral language is more inclusive. **Identity-neutral language** refers to a person or persons without marking them according to their actual or possible identity traits. For example, don't modify professional titles like "professor," "doctor," "senator," "lawyer," or "electrician" by referring to the person's race, gender, sexual orientation, or other identity markers, unless there is a specific reason that trait is important to the discussion.

Identity-neutral language avoids implicit stereotypes—such as the gender of nurses, doctors, plumbers, carpenters, and other professions. When talking generally about what a lawyer or a flight attendant might do, inclusive language uses "they" rather than "she" or "he." You can also use "they" to refer to a specific individual when their gender is irrelevant to the discussion or they have indicated that they prefer "they" as their personal pronoun. Almost all major language authorities and style guides not only accept but strongly recommend these uses of the singular form of "they."[10]

our standpoints can help us become more ethical and effective public speakers. Acknowledging the gaps in our own experience can help us to connect with audiences who experience the world in different ways.

The gaps in our experience and understanding are widened by **social inequality**: the uneven distribution of power and resources in society. Unequal power is distributed across a wide spectrum of identities: race, ethnicity, sexual orientation, gender expression, economic class, religion, citizenship, language, and many more. Social inequality creates **privilege**: unearned social, political, and economic advantages granted to certain groups (see Figure 3.2).[11] People with privileged identities have greater access to power and resources than people with marginalized identities.

Social inequality limits our understanding because privileged identities are **normalized**: their needs, values, and culture are treated as the standard for everyone.[12] For example, in the United States, the English language is treated as a standard. If you are a fluent English speaker, you have the privilege of meeting workplace requirements and reading legal documents without learning another language. For people with privileged identities, these "standard" social expectations can seem normal and natural, making it easy to take the privilege they experience for granted. Because their own experience is treated as the norm, the needs, values, and culture of marginalized identity groups can easily become invisible to people with privileged identities.

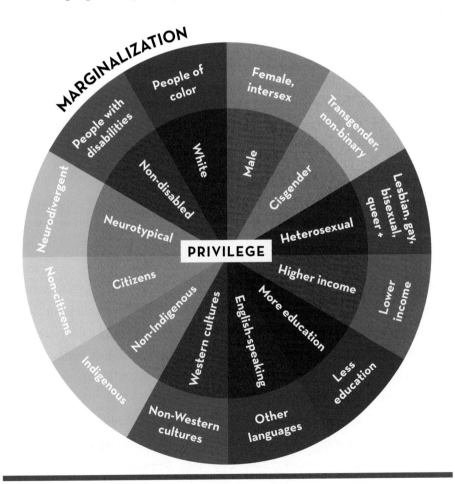

**FIGURE 3.2** Unequal power is distributed across a range of different intersecting identities in US culture.

**inclusive language**
language that uses person-centered and identity-neutral terms to avoid excluding, marginalizing, or stereotyping people

**person-centered language**
language that refers to the humanness of an individual, while recognizing relevant identity traits as qualities of that person

**identity-neutral language**
language that refers to a person or persons without marking them according to their actual or possible identity traits

**social inequality**
the uneven distribution of power and resources in society

**privilege**
unearned social, political, and economic advantages granted to certain groups in a society

**normalization**
treating the needs, values, and culture of a privileged group as the standard

**double vision**
marginalized groups'
understanding of the
needs, values, and
culture of the privileged
identity group as well as
their own

At the same time, this normalization requires people with marginalized identities to cultivate **double vision**—to understand the "standard" needs, values, and culture of the privileged identity group as well as their own—in order to navigate a social world that wasn't built for them.[13] For this reason, people with marginalized identities often have more complete and complex understandings of social dynamics than people in more privileged positions. For example, in the United States, people of color usually know much more about white culture than most white people know about other racial and ethnic cultures because "mainstream" media, workplace expectations, and laws still predominantly represent and are created by white people.

Because our standpoints are complex and intersectional, so are the dynamics of privilege and marginalization. Your standpoint may include both identities that are privileged and identities that are marginalized in our society. For example, we—the authors of this textbook—have standpoints that include both marginalized and privileged identities:

📋 **TRY THIS**

To recognize the
unearned advantages
you experience
and build solidarity
with people
who experience
marginalization
in ways different
than you, try the
**Questioning Your
Privilege Reflection**.

- As an autistic person, Pat was misdiagnosed by a school counselor as "mentally retarded" and had to pursue alternative schooling. But as a cisgender man, he does not experience the same pressure to conform to social expectations of politeness that many autistic women and girls face.

- As a genderqueer person, Megan has experienced workplace harassment and been refused service by health-care providers. But as a white person, they do not experience the same police violence and housing discrimination that target queer and trans people of color.

When different forms of social inequality intersect, they compound and change shape.[14] Someone whose standpoint includes multiple marginalized identities will likely encounter even more discrimination than they would if only one aspect of their identity were marginalized. More than having just double vision, a person with multiple marginalized identities might have triple or quadruple vision. As the Black feminist philosopher Audre Lorde explains: "Within the lesbian community I am Black; and within the Black community I am a lesbian. . . . I cannot afford the luxury of fighting one form of oppression only."[15] Because our intersectional standpoints are made up of overlapping and interlocking identities, we experience overlapping and interlocking forms of inequality and privilege.

# Michael Render's Double Vision

In the wake of nationwide protests against the murder of George Floyd by Minneapolis police, Atlanta mayor Keisha Lance Bottoms invited community leaders and activists to speak at an extended press conference. Michael "Killer Mike" Render stood out for his powerful call for justice and peaceful political action.[16] Known to most members of the community as a rapper, activist, and local business owner, Render began his speech by adding that he is also the son of an Atlanta city police officer. Using his double vision as the son of a police officer and as an activist for racial justice, he expressed both "love and respect for police officers" and how it "tore your heart out" to watch a white officer assassinate a Black man.

Standing with the mayor and police chief behind him, he delivered his speech wearing a T-shirt that read "Kill Your Masters"—a reference to the last track on his album *Run the Jewels 3*, which calls for dramatic change in the structures and power dynamics that enable violent policing.[17] He unflinchingly described the long history of racism and violence against Black Americans, while praising the progress Atlanta has made over the past decades. He called for protestors "not to burn your own house down," but instead to "plot, plan, strategize, organize, and mobilize." Throughout, he challenged people to do their part to organize, to vote, to be counted through the census, and to stay politically active. His complex standpoint

Michael Render combined his own standpoint, the history of civil rights in Georgia, and his family history to acknowledge the monstrosity of George Floyd's murder while calling on protestors not to "burn your own house down," but to organize for change (7:42).

gave him exceptional credibility to simultaneously address both the protestors for racial justice and the officials who represent the systems they were protesting.

You can find a video of the press conference, including Render's speech, by doing a web search for: Atlanta Press Conference Protest 5-29-2020. The video is approximately 29:06 in length, and Render's speech runs from approximately 6:30 to 14:51.

Recognizing how different forms of privilege may limit your knowledge and experience can help you connect with others and avoid alienating your audience. For example, we have seen white students give speeches against affirmative action and male students give speeches against abortion rights without considering how their privilege might limit their understanding of those issues. When you speak about an issue or policy that affects a group of people that you are not a part of, you can lose your audience's trust if you fail to acknowledge the standpoint you are speaking from.

So, ask yourself: Am I speaking about people who have experiences, values, and identities different from my own? Or am I speaking from my own experiences, values, and identities? Our standpoints give each of us a unique place from which to speak. Reflecting on your standpoint—understanding both your strengths and the limits of your experience—is vital for building and maintaining credibility with your audience.

## ✓ Critical Thinking Check

1. How does defining your own ethics and identity make you a better public speaker?
2. Take another look at the forms of privilege and marginalization represented in Figure 3.2. What would you add or change?
3. Is it ever acceptable to speak for a group of people that you are not a part of? If so, when? If not, why not?

# Credibility: Communicating Your Ethics

No matter what you share with an audience, a single public speaking event can only give them a partial view of your standpoint. Even if you spoke for an hour, it would barely scratch the surface of who you are. In any speaking situation, you will want to consider which parts of your story are most important to share. Which dimensions of your standpoint do you want to highlight?

We're all constantly shifting aspects of ourselves into the foreground or the background. For example, when you're on a date, you might emphasize your gender and sexuality in ways that you wouldn't when you're at a family reunion. When you're in a job interview, you might emphasize your educational achievements in ways that you wouldn't when you're hanging out with friends. While we each still have our own unique and complete intersectional standpoints, we emphasize different aspects of ourselves for different purposes, in different places, with different people. Why? Because different situations call for different strengths.

Emphasizing the strengths that best fit your purpose, your context, and your audience can help you build credibility. Your **initial credibility** is your audience's impression of you before your speech begins; your **terminal credibility** is the lasting impression you leave on your audience when your speech is over. You can enhance your credibility over the course of your speech by sharing your unique gifts and building a relationship with your audience. When selecting which strengths to foreground, aim to make both a contribution and a connection to your audience.

## CONTRIBUTION: SHARING YOUR GIFTS

First, decide what contribution you can make in your speaking situation. Your **contribution** is a unique perspective that you as a speaker can offer to this audience, on this topic, in this context. If you don't offer a clear contribution, your audience will wonder why they are listening to you. The key to making a contribution is sharing something new and different—either information or an interpretation that your audience hasn't heard before.

Making a contribution does not require any special credential or degree. As Jazz Jennings shows, you can make a contribution simply by sharing your unique standpoint. Even with highly technical and complex topics, a wide range of people have important insights to share. Everyday people affected by climate change, HIV/AIDS, and nuclear power have made essential contributions to research and policy debates.[18] While your contribution might come from specialized knowledge or training, it might also come from personal experiences that make abstract issues more meaningful or bring overlooked problems to light. Your contribution might come from offering an outsider's perspective or a beginner's view of a topic. The key to contribution is uniqueness, and expertise is only one way of being unique.

Each unique element of your standpoint is a potential resource to contribute, and every element of your speaking situation shapes the contribution you can make.

**📋 TRY THIS**

To identify which of your strengths to highlight in a particular speaking situation, use the **Contribution and Identification Worksheet**.

**initial credibility**
your audience's impression of you before your speech begins

**terminal credibility**
the lasting impression you leave on your audience after your speech

**contribution**
a unique perspective that a speaker offers to a particular audience, on a particular topic, in a particular context

To highlight your contribution, emphasize the differences between your standpoint and your speaking situation:

- **AUDIENCE.** Show how your point of view diverges from your audience's. Are you a farmer speaking to a group of city-dwellers? A Jewish person speaking to a group of Christians? A soldier speaking to a group of civilians?

- **CONTEXT.** Demonstrate how your standpoint provides a different perspective on your context. Are you an environmental activist speaking at a hazardous waste site? A divorced person giving a toast at a wedding? A Vietnamese American speaking at the Vietnam Veterans Memorial?

- **PURPOSE.** Explain how your standpoint gives you unexpected reasons for your purpose. Are you a young person advocating for retirement benefits? A small business owner advocating for tax increases? A hunter advocating for animal rights?

## IDENTIFICATION: CONNECTING WITH YOUR AUDIENCE

While your contribution will highlight your differences from your audience, you will also want to emphasize aspects of your standpoint that help your audience connect with you. Communicating shared identities, experiences, and values is called **identification**.[19] If an audience can identify with you, they are more likely to trust you and more likely to believe that your contribution has value. The easiest way to establish identification is finding an element of your standpoint that your audience shares:

**identification**
communicating shared identities, experiences, and values

- **IDENTITIES.** Highlight aspects of your identity that you share with your audience. Did you all grow up in rural Montana? Are you all gay Republicans? Are you all mothers of adopted children?

## Pathways

To learn how to gather information about your audience's identities, values, and experiences, see **Chapter 5, Audiences and Publics**.

- **EXPERIENCES.** Let your audience know that you share their experiences. Did you all run track in high school? Have you all struggled with clinical depression? Did you all just drive through heavy rain to get to your talk?

- **VALUES.** Even if you do not have the same identities or experiences as your audience, you can still emphasize the values that you share. Do you all value the freedom to be yourself? Do you all put family first? Do you all believe in reparations as a path to restorative justice?

Helping an audience see the identities, experiences, and values you have in common can reduce the distance between you and make them more receptive to your contribution (see Figure 3.3). Look for the points of identification that will be most compelling to your audience, for your purpose, and in your context. When you know what you have in common, you can connect with your audience by sharing a part of your own story. Remember: communicating your *ethos*—your identities, experiences, and values—is the key to your credibility.

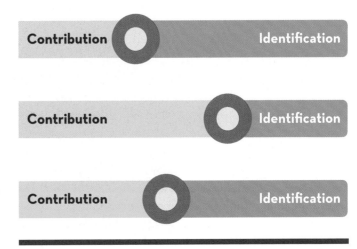

**FIGURE 3.3** By emphasizing your differences or similarities, you can adjust the balance of contribution and identification to fit your speaking situation.

## ✓ Critical Thinking Check

1. Why do you need to highlight both your similarities and your differences to establish your credibility with an audience?
2. What kinds of audiences, purposes, and contexts might call for more focus on your contribution? What kinds of audiences, purposes, and contexts might call for more focus on identification?

# Restoring Your Credibility

By sharing your experiences, knowledge, values, and identities, you can make genuine connections and important contributions to the audiences you address. But sometimes, public speakers make mistakes and express biases that damage their connection to their audiences. And sometimes, audiences bring their own assumptions and biases to their judgments about a speaker's credibility. When bias threatens your connection with your audience, you may need to restore your credibility during your speech, in a question-and-answer session after your speech, or in a later statement or presentation. You can do this with a genuine apology, a transformation story, or a transcendence story.

## APOLOGIES

Despite our best intentions, we all sometimes act in ways that violate our own values and the values of our communities. While you can't take back words or actions you regret, you can use those moments as opportunities to grow—and

Delivering public apologies can be an important skill for maintaining your credibility as a speaker. Left: Soccer player Samuel Eto'o apologizes for mocking his former team Real Madrid after a win. Right: Former CIA director and retired US General David Petraeus apologizes for the extramarital affair that ended his political career.

maybe even strengthen your bond with an audience. When your words or actions are out of step with your values, the best response is a sincere apology:

1. **ACCEPT RESPONSIBILITY.** Avoid the temptation to excuse your mistake as unintentional, emphasize your good qualities, or downplay the harm. These strategies alienate your audience by delegitimizing their concerns. Instead, take responsibility for your mistake. For example: "I accept full responsibility for the stereotypes about homeless people that I used in my speech on housing policy."

2. **SHOW YOU UNDERSTAND THE PROBLEM AND ITS SIGNIFICANCE.** Demonstrate that you recognize the magnitude of the harm done and the values that are at stake. For example: "I now understand that those stereotypes are dehumanizing and that dehumanizing homeless people keeps us from finding workable solutions to the housing crisis."

3. **TAKE CORRECTIVE ACTION.** Describe what you will do to remedy the harm done and the steps you will take to prevent this problem in the future. For example: "I am working to better educate myself on housing inequality so that I can be a more effective ally for unsheltered people."

## TRANSFORMATION STORIES

Transformation stories help to resolve a tension between who you used to be and who you are now. Since our standpoints are fluid and we all change over time, most of us will tell multiple transformation stories throughout our lives. Owning your past mistakes and showing how you have changed can set a powerful example for others to grow. Transformation stories offer a three-step narrative of your personal growth:

1. **PRESENT AN IMAGE OF YOUR PAST SELF.** Describe the actions, habits, and values you used to hold that you do not hold anymore. For example: "Until a year ago, I never thought about public bathrooms. Men on one side; women on the other."

2. **DESCRIBE A TRANSFORMATIONAL EVENT OR EXPERIENCE.** Tell your audience how the experience made you feel, what it made you realize, and how it changed you. For example: "But then when my brother came out as trans, I realized how dangerous gender-assigned bathrooms can be for trans and non-binary people. He's been hassled a couple of times, and it's really opened my eyes."

3. **OFFER AN IMAGE OF YOUR TRANSFORMED SELF.** Tell your audience how your beliefs and values have changed and show them how your recent actions and new habits reflect this transformation. For example: "I started talking with some people in student government about providing gender-neutral bathrooms on our campus. Now our school has gender-neutral bathrooms in almost half the buildings."

## TRANSCENDENCE STORIES

While apologies and transformation stories can help restore your credibility when you express bias or stereotype others, stories of transcendence can restore your credibility when your audience stereotypes you. Audiences sometimes make assumptions about a speaker based on only a partial understanding of the speaker's standpoint. Our standpoints are complex, and we might surprise, confuse, or even upset people when we show them an unfamiliar side of ourselves. If you are sharing aspects of your standpoint that might challenge your audience's expectations about you, a transcendence story can weave familiar and unfamiliar aspects of your standpoint together:

1. **ACKNOWLEDGE THEIR EXPECTATIONS.** Start by recognizing a familiar aspect of your standpoint and the expectations it might create. For

example: "You might look at me and see my wheelchair first. You might wonder what someone like me could possibly have to teach you about exercise."

2. **CHALLENGE THEIR ASSUMPTIONS.** Introduce an unfamiliar aspect of your standpoint, and acknowledge how it might challenge their assumptions about you. For example: "You might be surprised to learn that I'm a weightlifter. I can bench-press one and a half times my body weight, which is pretty respectable for a non-competitive lifter."

3. **SHARE YOUR STORY.** Tell a personal story that shows how you live both aspects of your standpoint simultaneously, navigating the challenges and embracing the gifts of each. For example: "I wish I could tell you some rah-rah inspiring story about how I started lifting to empower myself, but the truth is I started lifting because I needed a way to channel my anger about my injuries."

4. **INTEGRATE THE FAMILIAR AND UNFAMILIAR.** Identify an overarching value, principle, or identity that connects the two different aspects of your standpoint. For example: "For me, being an athlete and an amputee is all about working out my anger. And I'm here to tell you that exercise is the best free therapy you can get."

## ✓ Critical Thinking Check

1. Why do you think people hesitate to admit their mistakes? Why is acknowledging your mistakes a necessary part of an apology or transformation story?
2. As a speaker, do you think it's your responsibility to educate your audience when they have stereotypical assumptions about you? Why or why not?

# Next Steps

Every one of us is a complex person, with a unique history, who grows and changes over time. Each of us has our own values and habits—our own ethics—born from our histories and standpoints. You can get started thinking about your own ethics by trying out the Personal Ethics Reflection and the Questioning Your Privilege Reflection. You can then use those insights to highlight your strengths and build your credibility with the Contribution and Identification Worksheet.

Public speaking is an opportunity to decide who you want to be and how you want to share your story with others. Whether we are giving a presentation on a stage or speaking to a group online, public speaking allows us to share our ethics, showcase our strengths, and build connections with others. By sharing our stories and listening to the stories of others, we can embrace what is beautiful and unique in each one of us.

# Standpoint Reflection

- What are some important ways that your ethics have changed over time? What decisions and experiences sparked those changes? How have those changes affected the way you present yourself to others?

- What stereotyping messages have you received about your standpoint? Have other people made assumptions about your credibility based on your membership in an identity group? How did those stereotypical expectations affect you? How did you respond to them?

- What aspects of your strengths and standpoint can you use to build identification with your classmates this semester? What aspects of your strengths and standpoint can you use to share a unique contribution with them? Will identification or contribution be more important for establishing your credibility with this audience?

- As the authors, we want to acknowledge our own privilege as people who are white, middle-class, and fluent English speakers in America. How do you think these privileged aspects of our standpoints might shape or limit our understanding of ethics and credibility? Is there anything that you can see from your own standpoint and experience that we have missed?

## Key Terms

# Resources for Ethics and Credibility

## 📋 "Try This" Exercises

Access the "Try This" exercises as directed by your instructor or online at digital.wwnorton.com/chapterexercises-conpubspeak

- To identify your implicit ethics and make explicit ethical decisions, use the **Personal Ethics Reflection**.

- To recognize the unearned advantages you experience and build solidarity with people who experience marginalization in ways different than you, try the **Questioning Your Privilege Reflection**.

- To identify which of your strengths to highlight in a particular speaking situation, use the **Contribution and Identification Worksheet**.

Want to practice these skills to prepare for your next speech? Go to INQUIZITIVE to review and apply concepts from this chapter and get personalized feedback along the way.

COMMUNITY ORGANIZER
AND POLITICAL STRATEGIST    Deja Foxx

# 4 Listening and Responding

**D**eja Foxx is an activist, a digital strategist, and the youngest full-time staffer to ever work on a US presidential campaign. As a first-generation college student who grew up in poverty and experienced homelessness as a teenager, she works to help people in power listen to a broader range of perspectives.

Foxx explains that real listening requires us to seek out a range of different viewpoints and foster inclusive environments that encourage everyone to contribute. She advises political leaders to listen to "diverse perspectives, both at the very top...to the very bottom, to make space and time for constituents and their stories."[1] Foxx says she seeks to create the kind of environments that really welcome and can help diverse leaders from interesting perspectives thrive."[2]

To young people who want to make a difference, Foxx recommends starting small with something that is personally meaningful to you. Build communities and networks where people genuinely listen to each other, and encourage people you know to speak and share their stories. This "relational organizing" unites people who care about you and each other enough to make a difference.[3]

She explains that we get better outcomes when we invite more people to participate in the conversation: "If we put collaboration over competition, we can all do better. Our success is truly tied to one another."[4] By listening to each other and making space for others to speak, we all enrich our understanding of the issues and create greater opportunities for change.

## LEARNING OBJECTIVES

**After completing this chapter, you will be able to**

- Explain the definition and benefits of listening

- Create listening environments that welcome diverse voices

- Build your speaking skills by listening to other public speakers

- Respond to audience feedback and facilitate discussion

Listening offers profound benefits to the listener, to the speaker, and to the community they share. Listening validates other people's experiences and affirms the inherent value of their standpoints. When you listen, you step outside the limited window of your own experience and develop a more panoramic perspective. Your understanding of the social world becomes both more complex and more complete. By listening to speakers from different standpoints, you can improve your own speaking skills and learn new ways to express your views to others. Listening is simply the best way to grow as a speaker.

# Creating a Context for Listening

Regardless of our experience or expertise, all of us can improve our understanding of the world by listening to people who speak from different standpoints. **Listening** is the intentional act of giving your attention to a speaker and interpreting their message.[5] Listening is much more than what you hear with your ears. Just as public speaking can happen through channels other than the voice, you can apply listening skills—active attention and interpretation—to speakers you hear, see, or experience through other senses. Much more than hearing, **active listening** means suspending judgment and striving to understand other people.

Your listening skills can help build a culture that recognizes the importance of diverse contributions. Listening actively shows respect to other speakers, even when you disagree. The act of listening can de-escalate conflict, turning a disagreement into an opportunity for dialogue and collaboration. Without a context where all voices are valued, respected, and heard, it can take enormous courage to speak up about potentially sensitive or controversial issues. So whether you're a speaker or an audience member, it is crucial to foster an environment that welcomes a diverse range of perspectives.

We all encounter moments when we feel less welcome to share our experiences, knowledge, values, and identities. You might worry that your family, friends, classmates, or coworkers will disapprove of your ideas or beliefs—or even who you are. To avoid negative judgment, we often stay silent on certain issues when we believe the people around us do not share our views. Ironically, others who *do* share our views might also stay silent because they too think they are alone. This effect—where the silence of each person reinforces the silence of others—is called the **spiral of silence** (see Figure 4.1).[6]

**listening**
the intentional act of giving your attention to a speaker and interpreting their message

**active listening**
suspending judgment and striving to understand others

**spiral of silence**
the effect where the silence of each person reinforces the silence of others

Over time, this fear of negative social judgment can create an **echo chamber**, where we only encounter views similar to our own.[7] In an echo chamber, people primarily associate with people like themselves. Social media sites and search engines intensify the problem, using our history, browsing behavior, mobile app usage, and other activity to filter and rank what we see. By presenting us only with content we will enjoy and engage with, web-based platforms place each of us into personalized echo chambers known as **filter bubbles**.[8]

But here's the good news: there are practical steps you can take to prevent the spiral of silence, step out of your echo chamber, and burst filter bubbles. As both a speaker and audience member, you can contribute to a context that encourages different standpoints, diverse beliefs, and dissenting perspectives. You can help create a context where all speakers are affirmed, heard, and valued—even when they disagree.

**FIGURE 4.1** When one person decides to stay silent, it creates a vacuum of support that leads other people to stay silent as well.

## 1 Acknowledge the Limits of Your Own Standpoint

Our knowledge is always limited because each of us can only see a portion of any given issue. Because we each approach the world from our own backgrounds and values, our interpretations always contain some bias. Recognize that you need input from others to gain a more complete perspective. For example: "As someone who has only held work-study jobs on campus, I realize that my understanding of minimum-wage policy might be limited. That's why I've connected with people who work a range of different minimum-wage jobs to ask them about their experiences."

## 2 Invite Contributions from Diverse Standpoints

Rather than waiting for a courageous person to voice a dissenting opinion, encourage people to share viewpoints that haven't already been expressed by the group. You never know who might have a different perspective, so address your invitation to the whole group rather than putting anyone on the spot. For example: "So far, I've gotten a lot of questions from people who agree with me about cancel culture. I'd love to hear from someone who has a different point of view."

**echo chamber**
a context where people only encounter others who express similar views

**filter bubbles**
personalized echo chambers where web-based platforms only present us with content we will enjoy and engage with

### 3 Thank Speakers Who Share Dissenting Views

When someone does voice an opinion different from the majority, publicly thank them for their willingness to speak, even if you disagree with their position. It takes courage to express an unpopular view. Often, dissenting perspectives reveal limitations or drawbacks overlooked when everyone is agreeing. Sometimes an unpopular opinion is the one we most need to hear to understand an issue or find a solution. For example: "Thank you for sharing your logistical concerns about reparations with us. While I still believe reparations are necessary, I think you've raised some important issues for us to consider as we move forward."

### 4 Respect the Person and Engage Their Position

Willingness to engage someone in dialogue is a sign of respect. You can affirm someone as a person even while strongly disagreeing with what they say. Attacking, belittling, or dismissing a person or group of people shuts listening down, leaving all of us with less information, poorer decisions, and lost opportunities to grow. So, keep your disagreement focused on the issue, not the individual. For example: "I admire you for standing up for what you believe in, but the statistics you're citing don't line up with the data that I've seen. Can you tell me more about where that information is coming from?"

I reflected on it and I thought 'oh man'

Sometimes an organization or special event can help people with different standpoints and opinions listen to each other. The Living Room Conversations project facilitates dialogue among people with diverse views and values, such as in this online discussion about forgiveness and responsibility (2:07).

### 5 Speak Up When You See Others Being Silenced

If you see someone silencing others, especially by attacking or demeaning them, say something. Likewise, if you notice that a group or organization favors certain voices over others, let the members of that group know that you value everyone's voices and contributions. In some cases, you might even propose changes to procedures, rules, or policies to help ensure that everyone has the opportunity to speak. For example: "I am noticing a tone to this discussion that I'm not comfortable with. Elena has made some really important points, but it seems like she keeps getting interrupted. I'd like to give her the floor so that she can fully explain her ideas."

# *We're Here's* Small-Town Community Organizing

The HBO series *We're Here* fosters inclusive environments in rural communities across America. In each episode, drag entertainers Shangela, Bob the Drag Queen, and Eureka travel to small towns—like Branson, Missouri; Ruston, Louisiana; and Twin Falls, Idaho—where they partner with local residents to put on a community drag performance. They feature residents from a wide range of standpoints and backgrounds, listening to stories of living in rural America as an LGBTQ+ person, stories that intersect with disability, race and ethnicity, class and economic precarity, religious faith, and mental health. Host Shangela Wadley explains, "If you really want to be heard, you have to go in there willing to listen."[9]

By staging an event that includes drag performances, speeches on LGBTQ+ issues, and community organizing, the local residents and the show's hosts foster a safe space for people who feel invisible and silenced in the broader community. "What's so special about the show is that it's giving voices to people who don't normally get heard," says host Eureka O'Hara.[10] Although the event is one night only, it creates lasting change by breaking the spiral of silence. By bringing together a large and vocal group of LGBTQ+ people and their allies, the events reveal that there was already strong community support in places where it seemed like none existed. As one journalist explains, the show has "taken real strides toward

In the Farmington, New Mexico episode of *We're Here*, Nate's drag performance spoke to the intersectional experience of Indigenous LGBTQ+ people. In a short speech after his performance, he called for the creation of more places and events in which the Indigenous community and the LGBTQ+ community can affirm and support one another (46:26).

increasing queer visibility in rural communities nationwide" by "breaking down gender stereotypes and providing queer safe spaces long after the HBO crew packs up."[11]

You can find episodes of *We're Here* on HBO Max or view clips by doing a web search for: HBO #werehere. To see a clip of Nate's performance search for: We're Here Nate's Performance. The clip is approximately 1:41 in length.

65

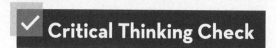
1. What are some of the risks involved in breaking the spiral of silence? What are the potential rewards?
2. When someone expresses stereotypical or even hateful views, is it still a good idea to respect the person and engage their position? Why or why not?

# Listening to Understand

Listening can help you understand people who have experiences, knowledge, values, and identities different from your own. The better you listen, the better you can engage other people, learn from their unique standpoints, and enrich your understanding of important issues and ideas. The following listening strategies can help you expand your understanding by stepping outside your own familiar views.

## 1 Recognize Your Assumptions

There is always more to learn about any issue, and this speaker may see something that you don't. Ask yourself what biases you might have about the topic and the speaker. Both positive and negative biases can shape your interpretation of a speaker or their message. For example, if you have strong feelings about gun control, don't automatically assume that you don't have anything in common with a speaker advocating for gun rights—you might both have a deep interest in the safety of your families. Recognizing the experiences, knowledge, values, and identities you bring to an issue can help you recognize the different experiences, knowledge, values, and identities that inform other speakers' perspectives.

## 2 Reserve Judgment

Set your assumptions aside and give your attention to the speaker and their message. Hear them out and keep an open mind. Resist the temptation to come up with any responses or objections before you fully understand their message. If you have a question or concern, you can always write it down and return to it once you've listened to the whole message. For example, if a speaker is sharing their experience of getting an abortion, you might be tempted to tune them out if your religious faith considers abortion wrong. But by reserving judgment and hearing the speaker out, you might learn something important about the circumstances that cause women to seek abortions in the first place.

### 3 Take Their Perspective

**Perspective taking** is considering an experience from another person's standpoint.[12] You can take another speaker's perspective by imagining what you might think, feel, say, and do if you were in their shoes. For example, if you are listening to a speech about underage drinking from a speaker who has lost a sibling due to drunk driving, you might consider how you would feel and what you would think about this issue if someone you love had been hurt by a drunk driver. Ask yourself: How might this issue look different from this speaker's standpoint? Even if your answer is "I don't know," recognizing the gap between your standpoint and theirs can help you realize the limits of your current understanding.

## REDUCING EXTERNAL DISTRACTIONS

Keeping your attention on a speaker and working to understand their message isn't always easy. There are always distractions in our external environment and in our own minds that can make it difficult to understand others. Listening is easier if you have active strategies for avoiding these distractions.

External distractions include sounds, sights, smells, and even physical sensations in your environment that make listening difficult. Loud noises, flashing lights, or uncomfortable temperatures can make it hard to focus. External distractions can pull your attention away from a speaker, and even affect your interpretation of their message.

When your brain receives sensory input—such as sight, sound, and touch—it fuses those sensations together to create your experience. This is why it's easier to understand what someone says aloud if you can see their lips moving. Your brain combines what the eyes see with what the ears hear to create

Cell phones have become a ubiquitous distraction. To listen more effectively, be sure your phone is set to Do Not Disturb so that neither sounds nor vibrations interrupt your focus, and place it out of sight, such as in your pocket or bag.

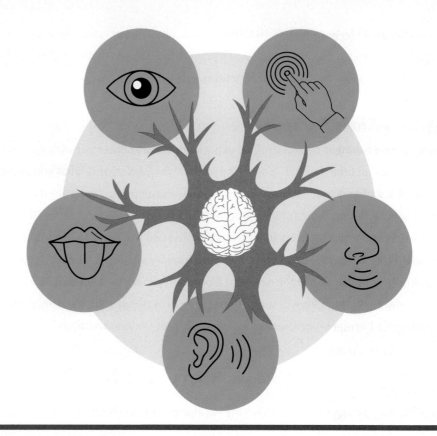

**FIGURE 4.2** Your brain processes multisensory information as a single, integrated experience.

**cross-modal perception** blending the spectrum of sensory inputs into a unified whole to create experience

your experience of someone's speech. This combination of sensation to create experience is called **cross-modal perception** (see Figure 4.2).[13] Because our perception blends the spectrum of sensory inputs into a unified whole, external distractions can both interfere with our attention and distort our experience of a message.

To reduce the impact of external distractions, you can both amplify the sensory input you want to focus on and de-amplify the unwanted sensory input in your environment.

## 1 Choose Your Position

If you are in a room with the speaker, find a spot that lets you see and hear them clearly. Reducing the number of windows and other people in your field of view, sitting away from sources of distracting sounds, and finding a comfortable place to sit or stand can all make listening easier.

## 2 Request Accommodation

If you have difficulty hearing and need to sit closer, don't hesitate to ask for accommodation either from another audience member or the host of the event. If a microphone is available, you can ask the speaker to use it to ensure that you and everyone else can hear. Similarly, if you need the speaker to face toward the audience so you can see their lips when they speak, let the speaker or event host know before the presentation. A surprising number of speakers look away from the audience when speaking, especially if they are presenting slides.

## 3 Create Full-Screen Focus

When viewing a public speaker online, you can eliminate distractions by closing other tabs, windows, and applications. Use full-screen or "theater mode" to hide distracting sidebars, ads, and pop-ups. Try positioning your screen somewhere with limited distractions around or behind it. Headphones or earbuds can help reduce audio distractions. To focus your attention, pause or turn off any notifications from email, text messages, and other apps. There are even applications that can help you focus by temporarily blocking distractions on your device, such as Freedom and FocusMe.

## 4 Avoid Multitasking

Some people believe they can effectively listen while doing another task. **Multitasking** is the attempt to perform more than one activity simultaneously. Nearly every study of multitasking comes to the same conclusion: multitasking for cognitive tasks makes people less productive, reduces understanding, and

**multitasking**
the attempt to perform more than one activity simultaneously

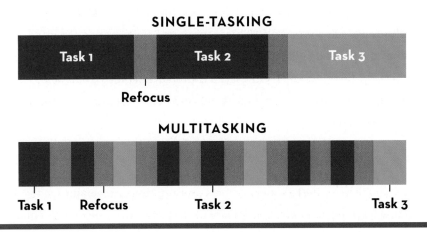

**FIGURE 4.3** When you attempt to perform multiple tasks simultaneously, you spend most of your time refocusing between one task and another.

increases errors.[14] When you multitask, what your brain actually does is switch back and forth between the two tasks. Your brain is still only capable of paying attention to one task at any given moment. Plus, your brain takes extra time and attention to switch between tasks—time when you cannot focus on *either* task (see Figure 4.3).

## REDUCING INTERNAL DISTRACTIONS

While external sensations can be distracting, your internal experience—thoughts, emotions, and moods—can also distract you. Unrelated thoughts and intense emotions can make it difficult to focus when you're listening to other speakers or receiving feedback on your own presentations. To reduce these internal distractions, focus on the present moment and engage with the presentation or feedback as fully as you can.

**Pathways**

Many of the anxiety management strategies you learned in **Chapter 2, Confidence and Anxiety**, can also help you reduce internal distractions when you're listening.

### 1 Breathe Mindfully

Sometimes listeners are distracted by strong emotions, which may or may not be related to the presentation or feedback they are receiving. Mindful breathing can help calm these overwhelming emotions. Take a slow, deep breath in through your nose, and hold it for a couple seconds. Then exhale through your mouth and wait for a couple seconds after the exhale. This slow, deep breathing lowers your stress levels and reduces intense emotional reactions.[15]

### 2 Name Internal Distractions

Many people find it helpful to acknowledge and name their distracting thoughts and emotions. If you have distracting thoughts, you can observe them and label them "thinking." Say to yourself, "This is thinking." If you have distracting emotions, examine and name the feeling: "This is anger" or "This is excitement." By observing your thoughts and feelings, you gain some distance from them. This detachment can help you return your attention to the presentation or the feedback you are receiving.

### 3 Take Notes

Whether you're listening to someone else's presentation or receiving feedback on your own, taking notes can help you focus. Note-taking immerses you in the other person's ideas, activating portions of your brain that are dormant when you listen passively. When taking notes, try to paraphrase the key points and major themes, rather than trying to write their presentation or feedback down word for word. You don't even need to save the notes to benefit from note-taking. For listening, your objective is simply to engage the portions of your brain that facilitate interpretation.

## ✓ Critical Thinking Check

1. Is it possible to fully understand someone else's perspective? Why or why not? If so, how? If not, is it still valuable to try?
2. Why do you think people multitask? How does contemporary American culture encourage people to divide their attention?

# Listening to Improve Your Speaking Skills

Great public speakers are excellent at listening to other speakers and learning from them. Barack Obama often made references in his speeches to the speeches of Dr. Martin Luther King Jr., Abraham Lincoln, and Franklin Roosevelt.[16] Personal finance speaker Suze Orman credits Oprah Winfrey as one of the major influences on her speaking style.[17] Even motivational speaker Tony Robbins learned from watching his mentor Jim Rohn.[18] Anytime you are listening to a presentation, you can learn techniques and strategies to use in your own presentations. Likewise, listening to feedback from others can accelerate your learning and develop your speaking skills.

## LISTENING TO PUBLIC SPEAKERS

You can always learn something when listening to another speaker. More than just learning about their topic, you can also learn their techniques for crafting and presenting a speech. Sometimes, you might also provide them with helpful feedback. To get the best public speaking ideas and give the best public speaking advice, follow these steps when you listen to other speakers.

### 1 Consider the Speaking Situation

Remember that the speaker is responding to a speaking situation. That situation includes the speaker's unique standpoint, the purpose of the presentation, the audience being addressed, and the surrounding context. Few universal rules apply to all speaking situations, and what you might say from your standpoint or in a different situation might not work for this speaker in this situation. For example, a seventy-year-old woman with glaucoma might gain credibility in a town hall debate on drug policy by revealing that she uses marijuana. But a similar appeal to personal experience with marijuana might damage the credibility of a third-grade teacher making a drug policy presentation to the school board.

## 2 Identify the Speaker's Strengths

How is the speaker using their strengths in the presentation? Could you use similar strategies in your own presentations? For example, if you saw a classmate build a connection with your class by sharing embarrassing high school yearbook photos, you might think about ways you could likewise use humor and vulnerability to bond with your audience. But remember: adapt their strategies to your own strengths—don't just bring in your own yearbook photos. The goal is not to turn yourself into a copy of another speaker, but to see what you can learn from them that fits your own strengths and standpoint.

## 3 Pinpoint Speaking Strategies

Throughout this course, you will learn many speaking strategies—how to demonstrate credibility, how to stir emotions, how to give reasoned arguments, and more. As you watch other speakers, try to identify moments when they use one of the strategies you have learned. Observing the range of ways that speakers adapt established techniques to their own strengths can help you make those techniques your own. For example, if you notice a classmate telling a transformation story, listen for the ways they use their own experiences to fill in each step of the narrative process.

## 4 Focus on Specific Examples

When you listen to a presentation, it's tempting to react to it as a whole. But you can learn more by focusing on specific moments where something worked especially well, or perhaps fell flat. Rather than giving a general evaluation—like "Good job establishing competence and credibility"—point to a specific statement or approach the speaker used to create that effect—like "Showed thorough research by citing several scientific experiments." Specific examples make other speakers' strategies easier to adapt to your own presentations, and they offer more useful feedback to the speaker.

## 5 When Asked, Offer Actionable Suggestions

If you are asked to provide feedback, offer action-oriented, strengths-based recommendations for improvement. If part of the presentation doesn't work, consider how the speaker could more effectively use their strengths in this speaking situation. Give the speaker concrete actions they can take to improve, using their strengths as the foundation for your suggestions. For example, if you are asked to give peer feedback to a classmate, a comment like "You had a really strong opening—you might try modeling your conclusion after that" would be much more helpful than "Conclusion needs improvement."

## LISTENING TO FEEDBACK AND CRITICISM

Listening to feedback can significantly improve your public speaking skills. That feedback includes not only written and spoken comments you receive from your classmates and instructor, but also nonverbal feedback you receive from your audience while you are giving your presentation. Are they showing interest and agreement with positive facial expressions, eye contact, and an open posture? Or are they expressing disinterest or disagreement by frowning, looking away, or crossing their arms? Even when feedback isn't clearly stated, there are still ways to listen and learn from it. With good listening skills, even the most unpleasant feedback can be an opportunity to grow as a speaker.

A student debate society in Chennai, India, prepares feedback on a teammate's speech.

## 1 Avoid Defensive Reactions

When people give us negative feedback, sometimes it can feel like we're being attacked. If you notice yourself reacting to feedback defensively, reserve judgment, breathe mindfully, and observe your emotional reactions. Even when feedback is misguided or offensive, it's an opportunity to learn. It may show you something about your audience you didn't know or reveal a misunderstanding you can prevent by making your point differently. There's something to learn from any response to your presentation—what is this feedback here to teach you?

## 2 Ask for Clarification

Feedback is sometimes given quickly—or even automatically, in the case of nonverbal feedback—and it may not be very specific or actionable. Asking for more detailed suggestions can transform that feedback into something valuable. You might ask the person who gave you the initial feedback, or you might seek clarification from other audience members. If you get vague feedback, ask for an example of what didn't work and concrete steps you can take to improve.

## 3 Remember Your Strengths

Learning from feedback can sometimes feel like you're being pushed to change who you are. It's helpful to consider the standpoint of the person giving the feedback. What works for them may not work for you. Taking the perspective of the person offering the feedback can help you understand where their response is coming from. Once you understand their perspective, focus on strategies for improvement grounded in your own standpoint and strengths. For example, if someone tells you to dress in a way that doesn't fit with your identity—to take off your hijab, remove your nose ring, or wear a skirt—that might say more about their biases than it does about your outfit. You could respond by showcasing how your clothes connect to your identity in your next speech.

## LISTENING TO QUESTIONS AND DISCUSSION

In some speaking situations, you will have the opportunity to listen and interact with your audience during your presentation. This discussion or question-and-answer (Q&A) session is just as important to the success of your

If you receive hostile or emotionally charged questions during a discussion, these steps can help you keep your cool and maintain your credibility:

1. **STAY CALM AND ACKNOWLEDGE THE EMOTIONAL REGISTER OF THE QUESTION.** For example: "I can tell that this is really important to you" or "It seems like our discussion is getting a little heated."

2. **RESTATE THE QUESTION IN LESS EMOTIONALLY CHARGED TERMS.** For example, if someone asks, "How can you tell us to buy organic food when it's so ridiculously expensive?" you could rephrase the question as: "I'm hearing you ask about the cost of organic food."

3. **CHALLENGE THE PREMISE OF LOADED QUESTIONS.** For example, if someone asks, "How could you support an economic policy that will put thousands of people out of work?" you could respond: "I don't agree that this policy will put people out of work—in fact, it will create jobs."

4. **CLARIFY YOUR POSITION.** For example, if someone asks, "Who will be there to protect us if you defund the police?" explain the misunderstanding: "When I say defund the police, I mean redirecting a portion of the police budget to help fund social services, not eliminating the police entirely."

5. **PIVOT FROM THE INDIVIDUAL ASKING THE QUESTION TO ADDRESS THE AUDIENCE AS A WHOLE.** For example: "Does anyone else have a question?" or "Let's open this up and make sure everyone gets a chance to participate."

presentation as your planned remarks. Fortunately, you already know a lot of skills that can help you welcome diverse contributions, listen for understanding, and receive feedback gracefully. With just a little preparation and a few additional techniques, you can ensure that your Q&A goes smoothly.

## 1 Anticipate Audience Responses

Part of preparing a good presentation is thinking about how your audience will respond. When preparing your presentation, list questions or responses you think that different stakeholders might raise. A **stakeholder** is anyone who has an interest—or a "stake"—in an issue or an outcome. Try to understand the different experiences, values, and identities of different stakeholder groups, and consider what questions or concerns they might have. Then practice responses that address those questions and concerns.

 **TRY THIS**

To understand an issue from multiple perspectives and anticipate a range of different responses from your audience, use the **Stakeholder Analysis Worksheet**.

**stakeholder**
someone who has an interest in an issue or an outcome

## Pathways

To learn more about tailoring your presentations to your audience's attitudes and values, see **Chapter 5, Audiences and Publics**.

## 2 Prepare Questions for Your Audience

Sometimes an audience has trouble getting a discussion period started, and sometimes discussion slows down before it's scheduled to end. You can get things rolling by coming prepared with questions to ask the audience. Offer two or three questions of your own to break the ice or revive the conversation if it tapers off too early. Avoid questions that are vague or overly simplistic, like: "So, what do you think?" or "Do you agree?" Instead, aim for questions that connect your topic to the unique perspectives and experiences of your audience members. For example, "What are your experiences with airport security?" or "How does voter suppression affect people in your community?"

## 3 Explain Format and Timing

Before your presentation, let the audience know if there will be a Q&A or discussion period, when it will happen, and how long it will last. Such periods are almost always at the end of the presentation, but sometimes they occur in breaks throughout a presentation. When the Q&A or discussion period begins, let the audience know how to participate. Should they raise their hands to speak? Will they line up behind a microphone? Do they submit written questions to a

At large events it can be important to provide audience members with a microphone during a Q&A both so that everyone can hear the questions and so the Q&A is accessible for people who cannot speak loudly. Here, an audience member asks a question of Senator John McCain during a 2008 town hall in Denver, Colorado.

# Anthony Fauci's COVID-19 Town Hall

During the COVID-19 pandemic, Healthline hosted a live town hall event featuring Dr. Anthony Fauci, director of the National Institute of Allergy and Infectious Diseases.[19] Fielding questions about the virus, available medications, and vaccine development, Fauci listened carefully to each question, often emphasizing the question's importance and giving substantive answers. At one point, however, Dr. Elaine Hahn Le asked Fauci about the risk of the United States ending up in a kind of "cold war," competing with other countries in "a race for medications and vaccines." Fauci responded by saying, "You know, I can't address that, Hahn, because that's not what I do. I test them [medications and vaccines] to see if they work."

Fauci enhanced his credibility by acknowledging the limits of his expertise and declining to comment on international politics and diplomacy. Attendees watching the live event via Facebook expressed appreciation for Fauci's "transparency, humility, and intelligence," his "acknowledgment of uncertainty," and the "nuances" he added to the discussion. By both giving knowledgeable

When Dr. Elaine Hanh Le interviewed Dr. Anthony Fauci in 2020, she asked him about the risk of countries competing for limited supplies of medications. Fauci replied that his expertise is in testing whether they work, not in their distribution. By admitting the limits of his knowledge, he increased his credibility and gained audience trust (24:49).

responses and admitting the limits of his knowledge, Fauci demonstrated why he is one of America's most trusted leaders on the COVID-19 pandemic.[20]

To watch a recording of the town hall event, do a web search for: Healthline town hall Fauci video. The video is approximately 51:00 in length.

moderator? When the Q&A is nearly finished, announce that there is only time for one more question or only five minutes left for discussion. This avoids the perception that the final question or comment caused the discussion period to end. When it does conclude, thank the audience for their participation.

## 4 Listen to the Full Question

Speakers are often both well versed on their subject and anxious about interacting with an audience. The result is that sometimes a speaker leaps into an answer before the question is finished. Stay calm and listen closely to each question—in full—to be sure you understand what is being asked. Audiences perceive speakers who interrupt before the question is finished as less confident and less respectful of the audience. By giving each question your undivided attention, you communicate interest, build trust, and bolster your rapport with the audience.

## 5 Repeat and Rephrase the Question

When an audience member asks a question or makes a comment, begin your response by rephrasing the question to acknowledge what you hear them asking. In a large space where audience members may not hear each other, this will help everyone understand your response. Even when audience members *can* hear each other, restating the question helps to validate the person asking it and reflects your own understanding of what they are asking.

## 6 Give Substantive Answers

Providing meaningful answers to your audience's questions demonstrates your competence and credibility on your topic. To get the biggest credibility boost from your Q&A, share your knowledge and understanding in answers that are clear, brief, and helpful. Offer examples, information, or stories to illustrate or support the points you are making. Stay on topic and stick to the question that the person asked.

## 7 Admit Your Limits

Sometimes you simply do not have a substantive answer, or the question raises issues that are not yet resolved. In these cases, the worst thing you can do is pretend to know the answer and bluff your way through it. Instead, say what you do know and admit your uncertainty about the rest. Depending on the topic and your role, you can either promise to report back to the audience when you do know the answer, or you can open the question up to the audience and ask them for ideas and suggestions.

## ✓ Critical Thinking Check

1. What's the difference between a stakeholder and a public? Is every public a stakeholder? Is every stakeholder a public?
2. Why is it important to admit when you don't know the answer to a question? Does admitting what you don't know help or hurt your credibility as a speaker?

# Next Steps

Listening—giving your attention to others and striving to understand their meaning—can help you develop any skill, but it is especially important for public speakers. By listening to others, you can both enrich your understanding of different standpoints and improve your own speaking abilities. To start practicing your listening skills, try the Perspective Taking Reflection and the Stakeholder Analysis Worksheet.

Every person's standpoint gives them unique strengths, and listening allows you to learn from the strengths of others. While we are always listening from our own standpoints, our experiences, knowledge, values, and identities can change, develop, and grow over time. Every time you listen, you can look beyond the limits of your standpoint, learn from others, and help build a culture in which all voices can be heard.

# Standpoint Reflection

- Have you ever felt unwelcome to share your views because you were worried that others would disapprove of your beliefs and opinions? What would have helped you feel more comfortable speaking up in that situation?

- Take a look at your social media feeds. Do you think you might be in a filter bubble? What kinds of attitudes, values, and standpoints are reflected in your feeds? What attitudes, values, and standpoints are filtered out?

- Listening and responding to feedback can be difficult, especially when that feedback is negative. How do you tell the difference between constructive criticism and unwarranted negativity? Is there value in listening and responding to negative feedback when it is unjustified or malicious?

- Why is it important to acknowledge the limits of your standpoint? What makes it difficult to acknowledge your limits? How do you react when other people admit the limits of their experience and understanding?

## Key Terms

# Resources for Listening and Responding

 **"Try This" Exercises**

Access the "Try This" exercises as directed by your instructor or online at digital.wwnorton.com/chapterexercises-conpubspeak

- To better understand speakers who have different experiences, knowledge, values, and identities than you do, use the **Perspective Taking Reflection**.

- To understand an issue from multiple perspectives and anticipate a range of different responses from your audience, use the **Stakeholder Analysis Worksheet**.

---

**Want to practice these skills to prepare for your next speech? Go to INQUIZITIVE to review and apply concepts from this chapter and get personalized feedback along the way.**

NONPROFIT FOUNDER
AND COMMUNITY LEADER    Jahmal Cole

# 5 Audiences and Publics

As the founder and leader of one of Chicago's fastest-growing nonprofit organizations, Jahmal Cole speaks to many different audiences: politicians, donors, community leaders, media professionals, and high school students. To pursue his mission of achieving a more equitable Chicago, Cole knows he needs to adapt his presentations to each of these different audiences—and that isn't always easy. Politicians and donors with more privileged standpoints may find it difficult to relate to the experiences of the young people that he mentors.

When Cole received Chicago's Champion of Freedom Award, he gave a speech that helped bridge the gap between his audience at the awards breakfast and the inner-city youth he helps. To gain his audience's interest and support, he needed to tailor his message to both expand and connect with their existing worldviews.

To do that, Cole gave vivid descriptions of the everyday challenges faced by people living in Chicago's most economically marginalized neighborhoods: "It's not regular for German shepherds to be sniffing kids on 79th Street.

It's not regular for helicopters to be landing on top of people's houses at night. It's not regular to have to order your breakfast through bulletproof glass windows every day."[1]

He then asked his audience to take the perspectives of the people who live in his neighborhood: "If you all just ate your quiche through a bulletproof glass window right now, you'd be traumatized." By helping his audience connect with the experiences of the community he serves, Cole helps them understand why his mission is so important to their city.

## LEARNING OBJECTIVES

**After completing this chapter, you will be able to**

- Understand your audience's values, attitudes, and behaviors

- Gather and analyze relevant information about your audience

- Address your audience as a unified public

- Adapt to your audience to increase their interest and gain their support

Audiences are as complex, diverse, and unique as the individuals who form them. Like Jahmal Cole, you can draw on different aspects of your experiences, knowledge, values, and identities to tailor your message to a diverse range of audiences. You can adapt your presentations to address the values, attitudes, and behaviors that are most important to them. Audience research and analysis can help you connect with your audiences by learning more about who they are.

# Analyzing Your Audience

Your **audience** is the group of people who will listen to you speak. Your audience does not include everyone who might hear your speech, but those who will listen—those who will be attentive and receptive to your presentation. That includes people already willing to listen, and people you can motivate to be attentive and receptive. Even when you have a group of people sitting in front of you, they don't truly become your audience until you earn their attention. To do that, you must understand who they are and what they care about.

**audience**
the people who will listen to you speak

**common ground**
values, attitudes, and behaviors that your audience shares

**values**
what people consider both good and important

**value priorities**
the relative importance of some values over others

**attitudes**
particular beliefs about someone or something

**behaviors**
actions and habits that outwardly express a person's values and attitudes

Just like you, each member of your audience has a unique intersectional standpoint, a one-of-a-kind combination of experiences, knowledge, values, and identities. Because each person is so complex, addressing the full range and specificity of every individual audience member's standpoint would be impossible. So instead of addressing an audience as separate individuals, public speakers must look for **common ground**: values, attitudes, and behaviors that their audience shares.

- **VALUES.** Each of us holds certain beliefs about what is good and bad, important and unimportant. **Values** are what people consider both good and important.[2] It's likely that your audience will hold a wide range of values. Not all values will be equally important to all your audience members. **Value priorities** are the relative importance of some values over others.[3]

- **ATTITUDES.** While values are abstract beliefs about what is good and important, **attitudes** are particular beliefs about someone or something. Your audience's attitudes may include beliefs about your topic and context, their perceptions of themselves, and even their knowledge or assumptions about you.

- **BEHAVIORS. Behaviors** are the actions and habits that outwardly express a person's values and attitudes. Often, what people do is a more reliable

| Values | Attitudes | Behaviors |
|--------|-----------|-----------|
| Community | People are better when they work together and share a sense of belonging. | Inviting others to share in projects or activities |
| Fairness | It's not right that some people have billions of dollars while others are starving. | Voting for representatives who will increase taxes on billionaires |
| Faith | My religion calls for people to gather for worship and fellowship. | Participating in religious ceremonies or services |
| Happiness | Happiness comes from looking inward and knowing oneself. | A daily practice of meditation |
| Knowledge | Books help me learn new things and build new skills. | Reading as a hobby or for personal development |

**TABLE 5.1** An audience's values, attitudes, and behaviors are often linked.

indicator of their beliefs than what they say. Analyzing an audience's behaviors can even reveal their **unconscious beliefs**: attitudes and values they hold without being aware of them.

**unconscious beliefs**
attitudes and values people hold without being aware of them

Our values, attitudes, and behaviors are often connected (see Table 5.1). For example, if your physical health is very important to you, that would be a high-priority value. If you believe that cross-country running is the best way to maintain your health, that would be an attitude. And if you actually wake up and go for a run every morning, that would be a behavior. But our values, attitudes, and behaviors are not always aligned. For example, it would be possible to hold attitudes about what is healthy without valuing your health. And it would be possible to value your health without taking any action to maintain it.

When you understand your audience's values, attitudes, and behaviors, you can tailor a presentation to them. For example, if your audience believes that running would be good for them even though they don't run regularly, you could focus on motivating them to lace up their shoes and get out the door. But if your audience is already a group of daily runners, they might benefit more from a speech on

**audience analysis**
the process of gathering and interpreting information about your audience's values, attitudes, and behaviors

**psychographic information**
data that describes your audience members' values, attitudes, and behaviors

**demographic information**
data that categorizes your audience members' identities

avoiding injuries or improving their endurance. And if your audience has health, ability, or safety concerns about running, you might encourage them to try a different form of exercise altogether. When you know what your audience cares about, what they believe, and how they act, you can meet them where they are. The process of gathering and interpreting information about your audience's values, attitudes, and behaviors is called **audience analysis**.

## GATHERING INFORMATION ABOUT YOUR AUDIENCE

Gathering information is the first step to better understanding your audience. There are two basic types of information you can collect: demographic and psychographic. We encourage you to focus on **psychographic information**: data that describes your audience members' values, attitudes, and behaviors. Psychographic information provides a more ethical and effective approach to audience analysis than **demographic information**: data that categorizes your audience members' identities, including their race, age, gender, sexual orientation, socioeconomic status, ethnicity, nationality, religion, profession, marital status, education level, and more.

## Pathways

For a reminder about the dangers of stereotyping, see **Chapter 3, Ethics and Credibility**.

Be careful to avoid making assumptions about your audience's values, attitudes, and behaviors based solely on demographic information. Understanding your audience members' identities is important—especially when you recognize how those identities intersect to shape each person's unique standpoint. But generalizing about people's characteristics based on identity categories is the very definition of stereotyping. Fortunately, there are several strategies you can use to discover the values, attitudes, and behaviors that are important to your audience without resorting to generalizations and assumptions.

**Informal Conversations** If you know little to nothing about your audience, one of the most effective ways to learn about them is through informal conversations with the event organizer, host, group leader, or potential audience members. The following steps can help you make the most out of those conversations:

1. INITIATE A LIVE CONVERSATION WHEN POSSIBLE. Real-time interactions—in person, by phone, or via video chat—often provide richer

information than emails or text chains, and they give you a better chance to ask additional questions.

2. **USE QUESTIONS THAT INVITE IN-DEPTH DESCRIPTIONS. Open-ended questions**—like "why," "how," or "what"—ask the other person to give extended answers in their own words. For example: "What can you tell me about my audience?" or "How did your group choose me to speak at this event?" (see Table 5.2).

3. **ASK FOR MORE DETAILS.** Ask **follow-up questions** that encourage the other person to elaborate on their responses. For example: "You mentioned several local chefs will be there. Do you have an idea of what they'll be hoping to get out of my presentation?"

4. **REQUEST ADDITIONAL RESOURCES.** Event organizers and potential audience members can often point you toward other sources of information

Informal conversations with event organizers and potential audience members can be a quick and easy way to learn more about your audience and their expectations.

**open-ended questions** questions that invite respondents to answer in their own words

**follow-up questions** questions that encourage respondents to elaborate on their previous answers

| Open-ended questions | Closed-ended questions |
|---|---|
| How do you feel about your current job? | On a scale of 1–5, with 1 being very unsatisfied and 5 being very satisfied, how satisfied are you with your current job? |
| Why will you be attending this seminar? | Which of the following is the most important thing you hope to gain by attending this seminar? Check one. <br> ___ Greater confidence    ___ Lower anxiety <br> ___ A sense of purpose    ___ Self-acceptance |
| What experiences have you had with living or traveling outside the United States? | Have you ever been to a country outside the United States? <br> ___ Yes  ___ No |
| How do you use Instagram? | How often do you use Instagram? <br> ___ Every day   ___ 1–6 days a week <br> ___ Less than once a week   ___ Never |

**TABLE 5.2** Open-ended questions invite people to respond in their own words. Closed-ended questions require them to choose from limited response options.

about the group you'll be addressing. For example: "Does the group I'll be speaking to have an online presence?" or "Do you mind if I look at some of the publicity materials you're using?"

**Audience Surveys** While one-on-one conversations can give you in-depth information about your audience, surveys allow you to collect responses from a greater number of audience members. A **survey** is a planned series of questions designed to gather information from your audience. The following steps can help you get useful responses from a survey:

**⊡ LEARN MORE**

To learn more about how to build and distribute a survey to your audience, see the **Creating Online Surveys Video Series**.

**survey**
a planned series of questions designed to gather information from your audience

**closed-ended questions**
questions that require respondents to pick from a set list of options

1. **DECIDE HOW TO DISTRIBUTE YOUR SURVEY.** If you have access to your audience in person—say, in a classroom or workplace—you can distribute your survey as a handout. If you can reach your audience through email or social media, you can use an online platform like Google Forms or Survey Monkey.

2. **INTRODUCE YOUR QUESTIONS.** Explain who you are and why you are asking for input. Let your respondents know that their participation is voluntary, and their responses will remain confidential.

3. **ASK QUESTIONS WITH A SET LIST OF OPTIONS. Closed-ended questions**—like "how often," "how much," and "which one"—ask for responses that are quick for audience members to make and easy for you to interpret. Multiple choice, checkboxes, rankings, and ratings scales are all examples of closed-ended questions (see Table 5.2).

4. **CONCLUDE WITH AN OPEN-ENDED QUESTION.** Try to capture any important information that your other questions may have left out. For example: "What previous experiences have you had with [your topic]?" or "Overall, how do you feel about [your topic]?"

## Pathways

To learn how to evaluate the reliability of information posted on social media and other online sources, see **Chapter 8, Research and Citation**.

**Online Presence** If you are speaking to a club, social group, business, or other organization, looking at their online presence can help you assess how the organization sees itself and presents itself to others. The following steps can help you analyze a group's web content:

1. **SEARCH FOR THE ORGANIZATION'S WEBSITE.** Look for mission statements and "About" pages that share their attitudes and values, as well as event calendars and newsletters that describe their behavior as a group.

# About GoFundMe

There's a part of every one of us that dreams of a better world. That spark of inspiration to help a person, fix a neighborhood, or even change a nation. At GoFundMe, we believe your inspiration should be shared with everyone. Because that is how change happens.

That's why we make it easy to inspire the world and turn compassion into action. By giving people the tools they need to capture and share their story far and wide, we have built a community of more than 50 million donors and helped organizers raise over $5 billion—and we are just getting started.

---

The "About" page of GoFundMe.com contains clues about the values you might use when speaking to people at the organization. Note the repetition of "inspiration" and "inspire" and the focus on change, fixing, and making the world better.

2. **SEARCH FOR THE ORGANIZATION'S SOCIAL MEDIA ACCOUNTS.** Even organizations without a website often have a Facebook page, a Twitter handle, or a YouTube channel. Their social media feeds might reference media they like, figures they admire, and causes or issues that matter to them.

3. **LOOK FOR THEMES.** Are there key words or phrases they use often—like slogans, mottoes, or quotations? Do they use clusters of words and phrases that express a similar meaning—like "justice," "equality," "fairness," and "rights"? Do they regularly participate in similar kinds of activities or events—like an annual blood drive or Karaoke Fridays? Those patterns can reveal important group values, attitudes, and behaviors.

**Publicity Materials** Event organizers or hosts may distribute publicity materials to attract an audience to your presentation. Examining those materials can help you understand what your audience will expect of you. The following steps can help you learn more about what's drawing people to attend:

1. **REQUEST MATERIALS.** Ask to see copies of any flyers, web pages, social media posts, or other promotional materials for your presentation—and ask where and how those materials are being distributed. You might even offer to help publicize the event through your own social networks.

> **▶ LEARN MORE**
>
> To learn more about how to create printable flyers and digital announcements, see the **Event Promotion Video Series**.

When you want to attract a larger audience to your presentation, you can use both online and offline strategies to spread the word:

1. **DECIDE WHO YOU WANT TO ATTEND YOUR PRESENTATION.** Are they local people attending in person? People from across the country attending online? Do they share specific interests or concerns, like hiking, climate change, or computer programming? Do you hope to attract people who can take a specific action, such as donating money to a cause, purchasing a product, or voting for a candidate? Start collecting information about their values, attitudes, and behaviors.

2. **LOOK FOR PLACES THEY GATHER, BOTH ONLINE AND IN PERSON.** For example, people interested in city politics might attend town hall meetings or visit your city's forum on Reddit. People who are avid hikers might frequent a local sporting goods shop or participate in a local hiking Facebook group.

3. **CREATE ANNOUNCEMENTS TAILORED TO YOUR DESIRED AUDIENCE AND THE PLACES THEY GATHER.** For example, if your audience has diverse political views and hangs out at a local bookstore, you might create a paper flyer using nonpartisan language to post in that bookstore. A free account at a service like Canva makes it easy to create both printable flyers and social media announcements.

4. **REQUEST PERMISSION TO POST YOUR ANNOUNCEMENT.** Online communities have moderators. Stores, offices, and public spaces have managers. Show them what you would like to post in advance so they don't take down your announcement or block you from posting in the future. You can also ask the people in charge of these venues about other ways to reach your audience.

2. **LOOK FOR VALUE TERMS THAT CREATE EXPECTATIONS.** For example, do the promotional materials describe your presentation as "important," "exciting," "informative," or "compelling?" Do they frame it as a presentation about a value like community, health, family, or success? What do they say attendees will get out of your presentation?

3. **WATCH FOR REACTIONS ON SOCIAL MEDIA.** If your presentation is promoted on a site like Instagram, TikTok, or Twitter, you can read people's responses to the announcement and see where it gets reposted or shared. Those responses often communicate potential audience members'

**PG James**
@PGJames_Media

• • •

We're excited to offer this free event to the public!

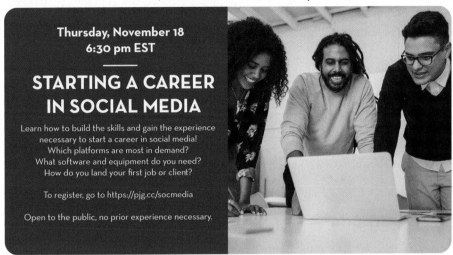

> **Thursday, November 18**
> **6:30 pm EST**
> ———
> **STARTING A CAREER IN SOCIAL MEDIA**
>
> Learn how to build the skills and gain the experience necessary to start a career in social media! Which platforms are most in demand? What software and equipment do you need? How do you land your first job or client?
>
> To register, go to https://pjg.cc/socmedia
>
> Open to the public, no prior experience necessary.

10:26 AM · Nov 4, 2022

---

**27** Retweets  **74** Likes

---

💬          ↻          ♡          ↑

---

**Aden Kodi** @akodi3 · Nov 4, 2022                              • • •

So excited for this! I have been trying to figure this out on my own but need help!

💬          ↻                    ♡ 14          ↑

**Gaines Schuyler** @gainesyskies04 · Nov 4, 2022          • • •

Will you cover how to build your own following or is this for people to run a company's social media account?

💬 1          ↻                    ♡ 2          ↑

**SkylarCasen** @skylarincase4 · Nov 4, 2022                  • • •

I've been doing a little social media gig work for a year and could really use help getting my career to the next level.

💬          ↻                    ♡ 9          ↑

---

This Twitter announcement promises specific content in the presentation and welcomes attendees with no prior knowledge of the topic. The replies indicate interest in different types of social media careers and varying levels of experience.[4]

# Cathrin Manning Analyzes Her YouTube Audience

At heart, successful YouTubers follow a simple rule: make more of what your audience wants to watch. But knowing what your audience wants can be tricky. Fortunately, YouTube's built-in analytics offer content creators data about what attracts their audience, what their audience watches, and what turns them away. Cathrin Manning built a YouTube channel with over four hundred thousand subscribers by paying close attention to what attracts people to her videos and how they respond.

Manning recommends creators start by looking at clickthrough rate—how often someone clicks on a title or thumbnail to watch a video. She focuses on what kinds of thumbnail images and titles gain the highest and lowest clickthrough for her videos, using this to guide not only the topics she speaks about but the titles and thumbnails she uses for future videos.

Next, she looks at audience retention—the percentage of a video that people watch before clicking away. She can often see exactly where in a video people stop watching by looking at its audience retention as a percentage of the video's length. This helps her find what might be turning people away.

Manning also looks at audience engagement—viewers' commenting on, sharing, or liking a video. The more likes, comments, and shares, the better, but the content of the comments is also important. Viewers will tell you what they liked, didn't like, own expectations and motivations for attending your presentation. You can even look at the profiles of people who liked, commented on, or shared the materials to get a sense of the people most interested in your talk.

**Social Media Analytics** You can learn a great deal about an audience by looking at their online behavior. **Social media analytics** is the collection and analysis of user behavior on social media sites like Twitter, Instagram, TikTok, and YouTube. If you run your own channel or account, you can use the social media platform's built-in analytics tools to learn more about who views your content and how they interact with it. You can use social media listening

**social media analytics**
the collection and analysis of user behavior on social media platforms

and what they want from future videos. Reading user comments offers a lot of insight about audiences' values, attitudes, and behaviors.

Finally, she looks at traffic sources—the different places viewers see links to her videos and click on them. In particular, Manning focuses on traffic from search engines and the keywords that lead her audience to her videos. Viewers' search terms are direct expressions of their needs and desires, which make them excellent guides to your audience's attitudes and behaviors.

To watch Manning's video explaining how to use YouTube's social media analytics, do a web search for: Manning understanding YouTube algorithm 2020. The video is approximately 15:55 in length.

In a 2020 video presentation, Cathrin Manning explains YouTube's algorithm and how to use analytics to attract an audience. She emphasizes three techniques for increasing views and subscribers: using the right keywords so your videos appear in search results, choosing titles and thumbnails that get people to watch those videos, and producing quality content that people will engage with (5:44).

services—like Audiense or Meltwater Buzz—to learn about audiences who follow other accounts. Whether you are gathering information about your own social media followers or about another audience, the following steps can guide you:

1. **SELECT YOUR ANALYTICS TOOL.** If you're gathering information about your own online followers or subscribers, do a web search for your social media platform's analytics tool. For social media listening services, check if your school, employer, or library provides access. If not, some social media listening services, such as Audiense, provide a limited free account.

▣ **LEARN MORE**

To learn more about how to use social media analytics tools, see the **Social Media Analytics Video Series**.

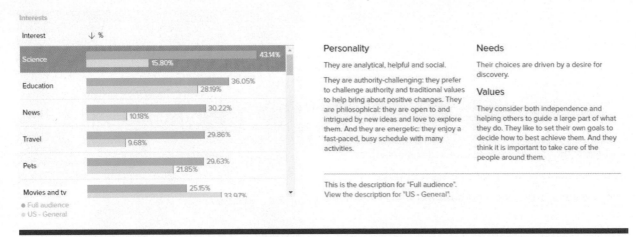

These "Interests" and "Personality" profiles from Audiense reflect data about the people who follow the National Communication Association's Twitter account.

2. **LOOK FOR TUTORIALS.** Search the web for tutorial videos on how to use the analytics tool you have selected. YouTube has numerous tutorials for almost all the major social media analytics and listening tools.

3. **RESEARCH YOUR AUDIENCE.** When looking at analytics about your own account or channel, you will see which of your posts and videos they like or comment on and how they interact with your account. When looking at analytics about another account, you may also learn about their interests, values, and media consumption.

4. **FOCUS ON DATA ABOUT YOUR ACTUAL AUDIENCE.** For example, if you're going to post a video to your YouTube channel, focus on the values, attitudes, and behaviors of your subscribers—rather than data about YouTube viewers in general. If you're giving a presentation to the members of an organization, focus on followers of their Twitter account—rather than a cross-section of people with similar interests or demographic characteristics. Remember that generalizations based on demographic information don't offer reliable insights about your audience.

## INTERPRETING INFORMATION ABOUT YOUR AUDIENCE

When you've finished your audience research, you're ready to interpret the information you've gathered. The following steps can help you build a profile of the values, attitudes, and behaviors that are most important to your audience in your speaking situation:

1. **LIST ALL THE VALUES, ATTITUDES, AND BEHAVIORS YOU FOUND IN YOUR AUDIENCE RESEARCH.** Include everything you found to ensure you don't overlook something important.

2. **NARROW YOUR LIST TO FOCUS ON THE VALUES, ATTITUDES, AND BEHAVIORS THAT ARE RELEVANT TO YOUR PRESENTATION.** Identify the habits and beliefs that might shape your audience's view of your topic or your credibility as a speaker.

3. **DIVIDE YOUR LIST INTO ASSETS AND CHALLENGES.** Which of their values, attitudes, and behaviors support your purpose and which oppose it? Which align with your own standpoint and values and which don't?

4. **ASSESS HOW STRONGLY YOUR AUDIENCE HOLDS THOSE VALUES, ATTITUDES, AND BEHAVIORS.** For example, do they say they "like" something or "love" it? Do they describe something as "bad" or "horrendous"? This gives you a clue to the intensity of their support or opposition.

5. **DETERMINE HOW WIDELY YOUR AUDIENCE HOLDS THOSE VALUES, ATTITUDES, AND BEHAVIORS.** You may notice that many of the audience members you spoke with, surveyed, or observed online expressed similar ideas or used similar terms. These repetitions indicate a greater consensus among your audience members.

When you are done, you will have a map of the psychographic information that will help you reach your audience. You will know which of their values, attitudes, and behaviors give you the strongest and widest support and which might create disinterest, opposition, or division. Use your list of assets to help you craft

**📋 TRY THIS**

To gather information about your audience and use it to discover assets and challenges for your presentation, see the **Audience Analysis Worksheet**.

a message that connects your own purpose, standpoint, and context to your audience's values, attitudes, and behaviors. Use your list of challenges to identify potential sources of resistance you will need to address in your presentation.

## ✓ Critical Thinking Check

1. Why might people who hold the same values have different attitudes and behaviors? For example, why might people who all value fairness have different attitudes about what is fair and different behaviors related to fairness?

2. Think of a group or community you are a part of, such as a club, online community, or religious organization. Which techniques would you use if you wanted to gather more information about their values, attitudes, and behavior? Why would those work better than other techniques?

# Addressing Your Audience as a Public

**public**
a group of people connected by shared identity, assembly, or media consumption

When you've completed your audience analysis, you will understand the shared values, attitudes, and behaviors that bring your audience members together to listen to your presentation. Rather than speaking to them as separate individuals, you will be able to address them as a **public**: a group of people connected by shared identity, assembly, or media consumption. Addressing your audience as a public means finding the common ground that unites them with each other and with you. Focus on the interests that your audience members share, and then zero in on what connects them together in your specific speaking situation:

- What values, attitudes, and behaviors bring your audience together as a public?

- Which values, attitudes, and behaviors are most relevant to your context?

- Which values, attitudes, and behaviors best support your purpose?

- How can you connect their common interests to your own standpoint and strengths as a speaker?

Remember: the same audience may gather for different reasons in different speaking situations. For example, a group of students gathered to participate in a graduation ceremony would be a different public than a group of students gathered to protest a school dress code. A skilled public speaker understands which shared values, attitudes, and behaviors are bringing their public together for a particular purpose in a particular moment.

In Chapter 1, we talked about the different ways that publics form: through shared identity, media consumption, or immediate co-presence. Now, you can use those categories to address your own audience as a public: as an identity public, a media public, an immediate public, or a complex public (see Table 5.3, p. 101).

## IDENTITY PUBLICS

Shared identity can create a powerful bond. **Identity publics** are defined by membership in a social, cultural, or political group. Although the members of an identity public will not share every aspect of their intersectional identities, they do share at least one aspect of their identity that they see as important in a particular situation. That identity will shape their values, define their attitudes, and guide their behaviors. When a group unites around a shared identity, that identity becomes a lens that frames their interpretation of your speech.

**identity publics**
groups defined by shared social, cultural, or political membership

Has your audience gathered because they share a social, cultural, or political identity? Maybe you are addressing members of a club, business, or organization, like students in ROTC or employees at your workplace. Maybe you are addressing people who gather around a shared religious or ethnic identity, like worshippers at a synagogue or members of a Latinx Student Association. Maybe your audience has come together as supporters of a political cause, like #MeToo activists or Black Lives Matter protestors. Or maybe your audience has come together as citizens of a locality, state, or nation—as Chicagoans, Californians, or Colombians. Audiences also gather around their professional identities and hobbies, such as doctors, plumbers, guitar players, or hikers. Social roles can also become identities, with audiences identifying as grandparents, friends, or allies.

To appeal to an identity public effectively, you must first understand how they see themselves within your speaking situation. Just because an aspect of someone's identity is important to them does not mean it will be relevant to every context or purpose. For example, a group of working mothers may expect to be addressed as moms at a school board meeting—but they may not appreciate being addressed as moms in the middle of a business negotiation. Appealing to

**TRY THIS**

To build audience support by validating their self-perception, see the **Affirming Audience Identity Worksheet**.

Identity publics come together on the basis of shared group membership. Left: A Jewish congregation in Rostock, Germany, gathers for a synagogue service. Right: Arizona State University basketball players listen to a pep talk from their coach before tipoff.

identities that are not relevant to your purpose or context will miss the mark with your audience and may even alienate them.

## MEDIA PUBLICS

**media publics**
groups defined by their shared consumption of a media text, artist, or genre

Shared media can also produce a strong bond. **Media publics** are defined by their shared consumption of a media text, artist, or genre. Has your audience gathered in this speaking situation because they watch the same TV shows or movies? Do they read the same books, magazines, or blogs? Listen to the same music or podcasts? Play the same video games? Participate in the same online communities?

Maybe they are fans of the Harry Potter books attending a PotterCon convention. Maybe they are subscribers to a YouTube channel, like How to Cook That, gathering online for an event. Or maybe they are followers of a particular musical artist, like Lizzo, Ariana Grande, or Lil Nas X. They might even be brought together as fans of a sport, like WWE wrestling, or a sports team, like the Seattle Storm. Sometimes the media they share may be more broadly defined, such as with Netflix viewers, nonfiction book readers, or anime fans.

If your public is defined by shared media, address them with appeals to the media text, artist, or genre that binds them together in your speaking situation. Almost every media message has values and attitudes embedded in it. Media messages also contain recognizable language, stories, and inside jokes that fans bond over.

For example, most Harry Potter fans have interpreted the books to support the value of equality and the attitude that young people can accomplish things adults fail to act upon.[5] And the stories offer fans a variety of terms they use metaphorically or to invoke value lessons, such as "boggart," "muggle," "Mirror of Erised," or "mischief managed." Fans likewise often sort themselves into the various houses of the Hogwarts school to express their identities. But be careful: insider terms and values may fall flat with an audience that did not come together because of a shared interest in the media you are referencing.

**📋 TRY THIS**

To use your audience's own language preferences and key terms to build identification and evoke emotion, see the **Media and Magic Words Worksheet**.

## IMMEDIATE PUBLICS

Perhaps the most loosely connected kind of public, **immediate publics** are defined simply by sharing a physical or virtual space. For whatever reason, they are present and listening in the time and place where you are presenting. Although any audience you address as a group becomes an immediate public, this category typically refers to audiences that have not gathered based on shared identity or media consumption.

**immediate publics** groups defined simply by sharing the physical or virtual space of your presentation

The challenge and opportunity of addressing immediate publics is crafting a collective identity or shared interest that unites them as a cohesive group. By the end of your presentation, you want your immediate audience to see themselves as a more strongly bonded public. At the beginning of your presentation, the only thing that binds them together is that they are here listening to you. You can address your immediate audience members as a unified public by appealing to this common experience.

What has brought them together at this particular moment? Does their simple act of showing up in this place and time point to common interests or a common identity? Look for the unrecognized or underemphasized values, attitudes, and behaviors that your audience members share. This common ground can serve as a foundation for creating a stronger bond between your audience members—and between your audience and yourself. For example, if your classmates were your immediate audience, you may discover they share similar attitudes about job opportunities, or prioritize friendship as a value, or all watch the same streaming service. Depending on the other elements of your speaking situation, you might be able to use any one of these to unify them as a public.

# COMPLEX PUBLICS

**complex publics**
a combination of two or more types of publics

In many public speaking situations, your audience will be a combination of two or more types of publics (see Figure 5.1). These are called **complex publics**. Such an audience may gather both because they are members of a shared identity group and because they share a media interest. For example, they may be both students at your university and viewers of your college women's basketball team. Sometimes, a group's connection as a media public may be so strong that it has created an identity for them—like die-hard *Star Trek* fans who identify as Trekkers, or Lady Gaga fans who call themselves Little Monsters. An identity public may also create shared media—for example, political and religious groups often create books, television shows, and radio programs that help bond their members together.

Complex publics offer you more opportunities to address your audience based on their shared interests, and more avenues for analyzing their values, attitudes, and behaviors. With complex publics, you must determine which of their shared identities and media interests are most relevant to your context and purpose. For example, your audience may identify as autistic—an identity public—and be subscribers to the Autistic Self-Advocacy Network (ASAN) newsletter—a media public. If your presentation is specifically about ASAN, you may want to focus on what they share as newsletter readers. But if you are speaking about the support services available to autistic people, you might focus on their bond as an identity public.

Because they are bonded in multiple ways, complex publics usually have firmer boundaries regarding the acceptable values, attitudes, and behaviors within their group. When speaking to a complex public, take extra care with your audience research to make sure you represent their interests accurately. For example, in gathering information about ASAN members you would find they generally prefer the term "autistic people" instead of "people with autism" because the phrase "with autism" makes their identity sound like a disease.

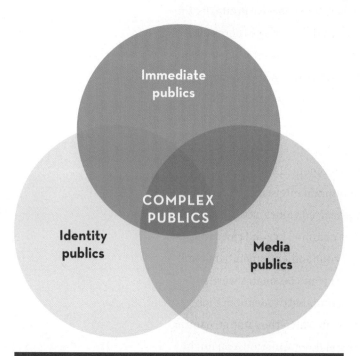

**FIGURE 5.1** Identity groups, immediate audiences, and media audiences can overlap to form complex publics.

| Type of public | Strategies |
|---|---|
| Identity public | • Understand how they see themselves in your speaking situation.<br><br>• Focus on values, attitudes, and behaviors connected to their perception of their shared identity. |
| Media public | • Use appeals to the media text, artist, or genre that binds them together in your speaking situation.<br><br>• Connect your presentation to shared values and insider terms that come from their shared media. |
| Immediate public | • Help them see each other as a more strongly bonded public.<br><br>• Look for unrecognized or underemphasized values, attitudes, and behaviors that your audience members share. |
| Complex public | • Determine which of their shared identities or media interests are most relevant to your context and purpose.<br><br>• Use the strategies for that type of public (above). |

**TABLE 5.3** Speakers use different strategies to address different kinds of publics.

# Adapting to Your Audience

Public speaking would be easy if your audience always found your topic relevant, supported your purpose, and shared a consensus with both you and each other. However, those audiences are rare. Usually, you will need to help them see the importance of your purpose, overcome their resistance, and build common ground across a range of different beliefs and priorities.

## INCREASING RELEVANCE, OVERCOMING DISINTEREST

If your audience does not already see the relevance of your topic to their values, attitudes, and behaviors, you can help them make that connection. You may discover their disinterest in your topic as part of your initial audience research, or you may recognize it when your audience appears inattentive during your presentation. Their disinterest may come across as a lack of eye contact, slouching in their seats, or a blank facial expression. Connecting your topic to something they care about will increase their interest in your presentation. There are several strategies you can use to connect their priorities to your purpose:

- **CAUSE-EFFECT.** Describe your purpose as the cause, and their value as the effect: "By [fulfilling my purpose], you will [achieve something you value]." For example: "By supporting the Freedom to Vote Act, you can help preserve American democracy."

- **IF-THEN.** Challenge your audience's commitment to their values, then call for your purpose: "If you believe in [your attitudes and values], then [fulfill my purpose]." For example: "If you believe in American democracy, then support the Freedom to Vote Act."

- **EITHER-OR.** Ask your audience to choose between your purpose and a negative outcome for their values: "Either [fulfill my purpose] or [face a threat to your values]." For example: "Either we support the Freedom to Vote Act, or we give up on American democracy."

The cause-effect statement focuses on what the audience can gain. The if-then statement hints at what the audience can lose, and the either-or statement focuses on that loss even more directly. More negative framing makes a stronger case because it puts the audience's values in jeopardy. But be careful—your audience might associate that negativity with their impression of you.

If these approaches do not seem to work, maybe the audience does not care as much about that value, attitude, or behavior as you initially thought. In that case, you can ask the audience directly about their commitments, starting with something as simple as a show of hands: "Raise your hand if you want more . . . in your life" or "By a show of hands, how many people here believe . . . ?" This will create active commitment from the audience, and their physical participation by raising their hands will increase their engagement.

A young audience member loses interest and falls asleep during a town hall meeting in Montana.

# INCREASING SUPPORT, OVERCOMING RESISTANCE

An audience's opposition may come from their beliefs about your topic or from their assumptions about you as a speaker. You might uncover these opposing views during your audience research, or you might notice your audience displaying disagreement through nonverbal behaviors like shaking their head, frowning, or crossing their arms. You might not completely change their minds or eliminate their biases in one presentation, but you can follow these steps to reduce their resistance:

1. **ACKNOWLEDGE THE OPPOSITION WITHOUT JUDGMENT OR CONDEMNATION.** Show them that you understand and respect their position. For example:
   - "I recognize you and I may not share the same views on . . ."
   - "You may be wondering what someone like me might know about . . ."

2. **CONCEDE THE DIFFICULTY OF DISCUSSING THE ISSUE AT HAND.** This builds a connection with your audience by making the opposition a shared problem you will face together. For example:
   - "Talking about controversial issues like this can be uncomfortable."
   - "I know that our differences might make it difficult for us to discuss this topic."

3. **PRAISE THE AUDIENCE FOR THEIR WILLINGNESS TO LISTEN.** You can praise them for any quality that will make them more attentive and receptive, but make sure it fits with how they see themselves. For example:
   - "Thank you for being kind enough to listen to my story."
   - "Tackling a controversy like this shows real courage."

4. **ACKNOWLEDGE THE LIMITS OF YOUR OWN PERSPECTIVE.** Disarm any defensive reactions by openly recognizing your need for their help, input, and contribution. For example:
   - "I know that I don't have all the answers."
   - "I know that I can learn a lot from your experience with . . ."

5. **TURN TO THE LARGER STAKES OR COMMON VALUES YOU SHARE WITH THE AUDIENCE.** Find a point of identification that outweighs your differences. For example:

# Jon Stewart Addresses Multiple Publics in Congressional Testimony

In 2019, Jon Stewart, former host of *The Daily Show*, spoke before a committee of the US House of Representatives.[6] He admonished them for not providing 9/11 first responders ongoing support for serious health problems caused by exposure to the World Trade Center attacks. In his powerful and often emotional presentation, he addressed multiple publics who experienced his speech from different perspectives and through different media. He opened his remarks noting a contrast between two different publics and how they served as a metaphor for the problem: "Behind me, a filled room of 9/11 first responders, and in front of me, a nearly empty Congress."

To connect with the identity public of 9/11 first responders and their advocates, Stewart referred to some by name and mentioned details of their medical treatments. He shared stories of the first responders he worked with in his decade of advocating for them, sometimes stopping to compose himself to keep from crying. He then directly addressed the Congress members, both present and absent. He reminded them that after 9/11 they all tweeted comments like "never forget the heroes of 9/11"—and yet they failed to show up on the day when those first responders came to speak and needed their support.

While formally addressing the first responders and members of Congress, his words also spoke to a wider American public who would hear his

Jon Stewart testified before the Judiciary Committee of the US House of Representatives in 2019. He opened by rebuking representatives who failed to attend the hearing, calling it shameful and decrying the lack of accountability in Congress (0:54).

remarks in the news. Stewart's speech made headlines—it was replayed on news channels across the country, and it went viral on social media. A little over a month after Stewart's presentation and eighteen years after 9/11, the House and Senate finally passed a bill to provide permanent funding to first responders affected by the 9/11 attacks.

To watch Stewart's speech, do a web search for: Stewart slams Congress over benefits. The video is approximately 9:12 in length.

- "We must come together to overcome this challenge because…"
- "This problem is simply too important to ignore."

The more you can adapt these five steps to connect with the attitudes and values of your specific audience, the better you can transform their opposition into a commitment to engage with you and your presentation.

## INCREASING CONSENSUS, OVERCOMING DIVISION

Audiences sometimes hold diverse values, attitudes, and behaviors. Different segments of your audience might prioritize different values or hold different attitudes about your topic. You may discover this in your initial research or in widely diverging responses to your presentation. If part of your audience is crossing their arms and frowning, while another part is leaning forward and nodding in agreement, you likely have a division to overcome. You can use parallel address to acknowledge their differences, and then appeal to overarching beliefs to unify them.

1. **PARALLEL ADDRESS**. First, acknowledge the identities, values, or attitudes that divide your audience, then suggest that both positions lead to the same conclusion.

   - "Whether you believe … or …, we can all agree that …"
   - "Whether you are …,…, or …, we all deserve …"

   To succeed, your parallel address must accurately reflect relevant divisions that exist in your audience. Only address differences that matter to your audience, or you risk creating division rather than acknowledging it.

2. **OVERARCHING PRIORITIES**. Then, you can create identification in a divided audience the same way you create identification between an audience and yourself: appealing to shared values, attitudes, and behaviors. While your audience may be divided at one level, you can bring them together by identifying a higher-priority value, attitude, or behavior they all hold. Your goal is to find a shared priority that transcends their differences, unites them as a public, and connects them to your purpose. For

**Pathways**

For more on techniques to create identification, see **Chapter 3, Ethics and Credibility**.

example, audience members may have different attitudes about the frequency of cheating in college classes, but they may all highly value fairness. Appealing to that value could gain their support for a fairer way of handling accusations of cheating, transcending the attitudes about how often such cheating occurs.

## ✓ Critical Thinking Check

1. Why does addressing an identity public call for different strategies than addressing a media public? Could you combine those strategies when addressing a complex public? Why or why not?

2. Can you recall a time when you were not interested in a topic or issue, and someone else overcame your disinterest? How did they do it? How might you use a similar approach in your own presentations?

3. Why would acknowledging opposition without judgment be an important part of overcoming resistance? What are the risks in doing this?

## Next Steps

Just as you speak from a unique standpoint, each audience member will listen and interpret your presentation from their own particular social location. Your audience members will both differ from you and differ from one another. Respecting the diversity of their perspectives will help your audience listen to your own views and engage with you as a speaker. Maintaining that respect requires each of us to examine our own assumptions and find bridges between our views and those of our audience members.

You can learn more about tools for researching your audience in the Creating Online Surveys Video Series and the Social Media Analytics Video Series. And the Event Promotion Video Series will show you how to create materials to promote your presentations. To better understand your audience, try the Audience Analysis Worksheet. Once you have a sense of who you are trying to reach, you can use the Affirming Audience Identity Worksheet and the Media and Magic Words Worksheet to help you build identification and goodwill.

Regardless of what kind of public they are, what they value, believe, and do, or how they view you and your topic, adapting to your audience is essential.

Understanding your audience will help you choose the right purpose for your presentation, reason with them, and connect with their emotions. It can also help you understand which aspects of your own standpoint and strengths to feature in your presentation and how to tailor your speaking style to your situation. With effective adaptation, you can turn even the toughest audience into a unified, engaged public.

# Standpoint Reflection

- What publics—identity publics, media publics, immediate publics, or complex publics—do you participate in?

- What values, attitudes, or behaviors connect you to these publics? How might those same priorities help you connect with audiences you address?

- Which of the different audience research strategies are the best match for your own personal strengths? Why?

- Remember a time when you faced a challenging audience. What strategies did you use? How well did they work? Would any of the audience adaptation strategies in this chapter have helped you in that situation?

## Key Terms

attitudes, p. 84
audience, p. 84
audience analysis, p. 86
behaviors, p. 84
closed-ended questions, p. 88
common ground, p. 84
complex publics, p. 100
demographic information, p. 86
follow-up questions, p. 87
identity publics, p. 97

immediate publics, p. 99
media publics, p. 98
open-ended questions, p. 87
psychographic information, p. 86
public, p. 96
social media analytics, p.92
survey, p. 88
unconscious beliefs, p. 85
value priorities, p. 84
values, p. 84

# Resources for Audiences and Publics

## "Try This" Exercises

Access the "Try This" exercises as directed by your instructor or online at digital.wwnorton.com/chapterexercises-conpubspeak

- To gather information about your audience and use it to discover assets and challenges for your presentation, see the **Audience Analysis Worksheet**.

- To build audience support by giving them the gift of fulfilling their values and becoming who they want to be, see the **Affirming Audience Identity Worksheet**.

- To use your audience's own language preferences and key terms to build identification and evoke emotion, see the **Media and Magic Words Worksheet**.

## "Learn More" Tutorials

Access the "Learn More" tutorials as directed by your instructor or online at digital.wwnorton.com/videos-conpubspeak

- To learn more about how to build and distribute a survey to your audience, see the **Creating Online Surveys Video Series**.

- To learn more about how to create flyers and online announcements, see the **Event Promotion Video Series**.

- To learn more about how to use social media analytics tools, see the **Social Media Analytics Video Series**.

---

Want to practice these skills to prepare for your next speech? Go to INQUIZITIVE to review and apply concepts from this chapter and get personalized feedback along the way.

PRO-DEMOCRACY ACTIVIST
AND MOVEMENT LEADER

Joshua Wong

# 6 Topic and Purpose

Since he was a teenager, Joshua Wong has been a vocal activist for democracy in his home of Hong Kong. A self-described "nerdy kid" mostly interested in video games, Wong found his calling when his government proposed a mandatory high school class on "moral and national education."[1] Wong saw the new course as an attempt at indoctrination by the Chinese Communist Party, which had been suppressing democracy and free speech in Hong Kong since gaining control over the region a few years earlier.

Along with fellow high school students, Wong founded an organization called Scholarism to oppose the new curriculum. It quickly gained thousands of followers and international media attention. After their protests succeeded in getting the course suspended, Wong and his fellow protestors grew the organization into a pro-democracy political party.[2]

In just a handful of years, Wong has become internationally renowned as the "face of Hong Kong's protest movement."[3] British, French, and American news media have recognized him as a major political leader, and a US government commission has nominated him for the Nobel Peace Prize.

Although the Hong Kong government has imprisoned him multiple times for his political statements and protests, he continues to advocate for his mission: "I will be sent to prison, but I do not regret it at all, and I will still keep fighting for democracy."[4]

What began as a student protest has blossomed into a pro-democracy movement that has inspired hundreds of thousands of people. Wong's commitment to his cause demonstrates how a meaningful purpose can help a public speaker spark major change.

## LEARNING OBJECTIVES

**After completing this chapter, you will be able to**

- Identify the key exigences in your speaking situation

- Select topics connected to your standpoint, audience, and context

- Develop a meaningful and achievable purpose for any presentation

- Craft complete, concise, and clear thesis statements

**purpose**
the impact you want your presentation to have on your audience

**exigence**
a call to speak to a particular audience in a particular context

Like Joshua Wong, we all want our speech to have an impact. You might want to help people take an action, reconsider an opinion, understand a topic, or celebrate an event. Your **purpose** is the impact you want your presentation to have on your audience. As a speaker, your purpose is your opportunity to make a difference—and the North Star that will guide you as you prepare the rest of your speech. Having a clearly defined purpose will show you the best way to address your audience, respond to your context, and speak from your own strengths and standpoint.

# Exigence: Your Call to Speak

To determine the impact you want to make, begin by asking yourself: Why am I going to speak? What is it about this speaking situation that is inspiring me to say something? Your **exigence** is the reason you are called to speak to a particular audience in a particular context.[5] Exigences can come from:

- **YOUR STRENGTHS AND STANDPOINT.** Do you have interests, passions, or values that are calling you to speak?

- **YOUR AUDIENCE.** Does your audience have needs, desires, or problems that are calling you to speak?

- **YOUR CONTEXT.** Does this context present a challenge, an event, or an occasion that is calling you to speak?

Most speaking situations present multiple exigences. For example, presentations assigned for a classroom or workplace usually call for you to accomplish at least two things: first, to inform, persuade, or connect with your audience; and second, to receive a high evaluation from your instructor or boss. Ideally, the multiple exigences you face will be compatible. If not, you must decide which of those exigences are most important in your speaking situation.

To identify the exigences in your speaking situation, answer three questions: Why you? Why them? And why now? Considering these questions will help you identify the outcome you want to achieve and select the best strategies for achieving it.

When your own passions and values are calling you to speak up, these steps can help you get other people invested in the issues and concerns that are important to you:

1. **MAKE YOUR ISSUE OR CONCERN RELEVANT TO THE CONTEXT.** For example: "Now that you mention it..." or "You've probably been hearing a lot about..."

2. **CONNECT THE ISSUE OR CONCERN TO THE VALUES, ATTITUDES, AND BEHAVIORS OF YOUR AUDIENCE.** For example: "You might be interested because..." or "It might be important to you because..."

3. **SHARE THE EXPERIENCES, KNOWLEDGE, VALUES, AND IDENTITIES THAT GIVE YOU A UNIQUE PERSPECTIVE ON THE ISSUE.** For example: "I care about this because..." or "It makes a difference to me because..."

1. **WHY YOU?** Your strengths and standpoint play a significant role in your purpose. Remember that publics need a reason to listen to you. Your credibility with them depends on connecting your standpoint to your purpose. Do you have personal *experiences* that give you a special insight or perspective? Do you have relevant *knowledge* that this audience would appreciate? Are you dedicated to *values* that make your words more compelling? Do you have *identities* that make this speech more powerful coming from you? Identify the elements of your standpoint that make your voice meaningful in this speaking situation. What makes you the key person to deliver this message?

2. **WHY THEM?** An audience is more likely to be interested in and affected by your presentation if you can show them why your presentation is important to them. What do they want? What are their needs? What are their challenges? Pay attention to the values, attitudes, and behaviors you uncovered in your audience analysis. If you can see the situation and its exigences from their perspective, you can pinpoint a purpose that will speak to them. What makes this audience the key people to understand and act on this message?

3. **WHY NOW?** What will make your presentation timely? That is, what will make your words more powerful now than they would be at some other time? What will make your presentation more relevant, significant, and

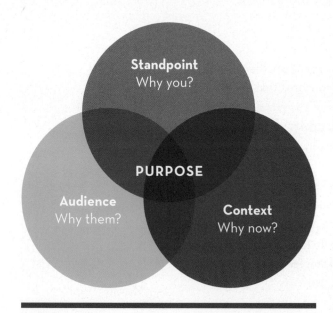

**FIGURE 6.1** You can find your purpose where the exigences of your standpoint, audience, and context intersect.

urgent—at this time of year, at this time in life, at this time in history? The timeliness of your presentation comes from its context: a special occasion, an event in the news, an upcoming deadline, a looming crisis, or an opportunity that might be missed. What makes this the key moment to deliver your message?

You will find your purpose at the intersection of these three questions (see Figure 6.1). Your answer to "Why you?" can help you build credibility and communicate your standpoint to your audience. Your answer to "Why them?" can show you ways to connect with your audience, motivate them, and adapt to their existing attitudes, values, and behaviors. Your answer to "Why now?" can help you choose a topic that is relevant and important in your current context. Having clearly defined answers to these three questions will make preparing your presentation much easier.

### ✓ Critical Thinking Check

1. What is the difference between an exigence and a purpose? How are they related?
2. How does knowing the exigences in your speaking situation help you craft a better presentation?

## Choosing a Topic

**topic**
what your presentation is about

Understanding the exigences in your speaking situation can help you choose more personal, relatable, and timely topics. Your **topic** is what your presentation is about—typically a short phrase like "prosthetic limbs," "government budget deficits," or "campus meal plans." When assigned to speak in a classroom, students sometimes choose generic or overused topics, like marijuana legalization or blood donation. However, these common topics do not always respond to the more pressing exigences of the speaking situation.

If you are going to talk about a popular topic, be sure that your standpoint, audience, or context provides an exigence for addressing that issue. For example, if

# X González's Gun Violence Advocacy

Tragedy propelled X González into the national spotlight. In 2018, their Florida high school was targeted by a man armed with a semiautomatic rifle who killed seventeen students and teachers and injured seventeen more. Two days after the shooting, a member of their school board asked them to speak at a local rally to support firearm safety legislation.[6] González had been studying the influence of special interest groups like the National Rifle Association in their government class, and their speech was full of research that deepened its seriousness and substance.[7] Their pain and anger were so compelling that their speech was rebroadcast nationally. They had no idea their speech would draw the attention it did, describing themself as "an accidental face in this."[8]

Following their speech, fellow student Cameron Kasky invited González to join a student group advocating for better gun control laws. Together, they organized a national demonstration, raising over four million dollars from small donors via GoFundMe, and a couple million more from celebrity megadonors. Less than six weeks after the shooting, they held the March for Our Lives in Washington, DC, attended by hundreds of thousands of people, plus hundreds of thousands more at over eight hundred sibling events. González's speech at the march again drew national attention, particularly for the four-minute period of silence when they stood staring into the crowd, tears rolling down their face.[9]

As a survivor of a school shooting and someone who had been studying and speaking about gun

X González delivered a powerful and emotional speech at the 2018 March for Our Lives Rally in Washington, DC. After two minutes González fell silent, then tears began rolling down their cheeks, their face displayed on large screens before the crowd. Some in the crowd wept with them, some chanted, and some just watched (4:19).

control, González could clearly answer the question, "Why you?" With an audience gathered specifically to protest current gun laws, the answer to "Why them?" was also clear. And the recent shooting at their own school, along with the recurring shootings in schools across America, answered the question, "Why now?" While González's speeches focused on a topic that Americans have debated for decades, the exigence of their speaking situation made clear why their message got so much traction with their public at this moment.

To watch González's speech at the 2018 March for Our Lives rally, do a web search for: Gonzalez powerful March speech full. The video is approximately 7:04 in length.

donated blood saved your sister's life after a motorcycle accident, that connection to your standpoint would give you a powerful exigence for a speech on blood donation. Similarly, if you emphasized the racial inequalities in drug arrests, convictions, and sentencing, you would have a compelling exigence for a speech on marijuana legalization in the context of the Black Lives Matter movement. Regardless of the topic you choose, make sure its exigence is clear—both to you and your audience.

## EXIGENCE AS A SOURCE OF TOPICS

If you are unsure what to speak about for an upcoming presentation, start with the exigences in your speaking situation. Each of the three exigence questions—*why you*, *why them*, and *why now*—can guide you in choosing a topic. The best topics are those that fit your standpoint, your audience, and your context.

**Pathways**

To revisit your strengths inventory, see **Chapter 1, Your Standpoint and Strengths**.

- **STANDPOINT.** Consider your experiences, knowledge, values, and identities—and look for topics that might fit your audience and context. For example, maybe you've had a personal experience with COVID-19 that would help your audience understand what's at stake in efforts to fight the disease. Or maybe your identity as a member of the Wampanoag Tribe gives you a perspective on Indigenous land rights that your audience would not hear from other speakers. Ask yourself: How can my standpoint—my unique intersection of experiences, knowledge, values, and identities—help me connect with this audience in this moment?

**Pathways**

To review the principles of audience analysis, see **Chapter 5, Audiences and Publics**.

- **AUDIENCE**. Your audience's attitudes, values, and behaviors can also be a rich source for speech topics. Do they have values, attitudes, or behaviors that are especially relevant in this speaking situation? For example, maybe they have behaviors—like eating beef—that affect an important social issue—like global climate change. Or maybe they have values—like honesty and truth—that connect with a contemporary problem—like the spread of conspiracy theories and disinformation on social media. Ask yourself: How can my audience's values, attitudes, and behaviors help me address a timely issue or a pressing need?

- **CONTEXT**. The context of your presentation is also essential for understanding your exigence and finding your purpose. Even if a topic fits your audience, it might not be appropriate to your context. For example, a sales pitch for cheaper, faster internet service might be interesting to your audience—but

If you are invited to speak at a special event, the context will usually dictate your topic and create audience expectations. For example, when US Representative Ayanna Pressley and Governor Charlie Baker were asked to speak at the 2020 Martin Luther King Jr. Memorial Breakfast in Boston, they knew that their context and audience would require them to talk about Dr. King and issues of race in America.

it's still not a great topic choice for your eulogy at Cousin Terry's funeral. Ask yourself: Where and when will I be speaking? How long will I have to speak? What virtual or physical space will I be presenting in? Does the event already have a theme or goal, such as a public hearing about a proposed highway project, a "Take Back the Night" rally to raise awareness about sexual assault, or an office party to celebrate a colleague's retirement? As you come up with topic ideas, consider both the social expectations and the practical limitations of your context.

**📋 TRY THIS**

To use the exigences in your speaking situation to discover your topic, try the **Finding Your Topic Worksheet**.

## BRAINSTORMING YOUR TOPIC

In some cases, an ideal topic might leap immediately to mind. Other times, you might come up with several ideas before you find a topic that connects with your audience, fits your context, and makes the most of your own strengths and standpoint. If an ideal topic isn't immediately obvious, brainstorming can help you find one.

**brainstorming**
generating many possible ideas and solutions by suspending judgment

**Brainstorming** is a process for generating ideas and solutions (see Figure 6.2). It can be done alone or in a group. The key to effective brainstorming is capturing every idea, no matter how silly or off-topic it might first appear. Let your imagination run wild, and write down everything that comes to mind, without any judgment or reservations.

Brainstorming can be a fun and inventive way to discover unique topics and approaches for your presentations. It's most effective when you can see all your ideas in one place. A standard sheet of paper can work, but you might want three pieces of paper that you can lay out next to each other on a table. You can also use a whiteboard divided into three areas.

1. **BRAINSTORM STANDPOINT AND STRENGTHS.** On the first sheet of paper or section of the whiteboard, write down any elements from your strengths inventory that connect to your audience and context. Write down as many topics as you can related to your own experiences, knowledge, values, and identities. For example, if you're a first-generation college student, like Pat, you might give a speech on student loan debt. Or if you're genderqueer, like Megan, you might give a speech about the need for more all-gender restrooms on your campus. Stay open, and don't censor yourself. Challenge yourself to come up with at least ten topic ideas based on your standpoint and strengths.

2. **BRAINSTORM AUDIENCE.** On the second sheet of paper or section of the whiteboard, write down values, attitudes, and behaviors from your audience analysis that are relevant to your standpoint and context. For example, if your audience has strong opinions about law enforcement, you could give a speech about police reform. Or if your audience regularly shops online, you could give a speech about working conditions for delivery drivers. Again, come up with at least ten topic ideas that spring to mind when you think about your audience's values, attitudes, and behaviors. For now, focus on quantity over quality, and generate as many new topic ideas as you can.

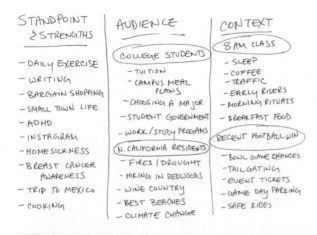

**FIGURE 6.2** Brainstorm potential topics based on your audience, context, and your own standpoint and strengths.

3. **BRAINSTORM CONTEXT.** On the third sheet of paper or section of the whiteboard, write down everything you know about your context. Consider your local context as well as the broader cultural moment. For example, if your campus just changed their parking policy, you could speak about eco-friendly alternatives to driving. Or if a major celebrity recently went into drug rehab, you could speak about the psychology of addiction. Write down any topics, subject areas, or presentation ideas that come to mind. Try not to second-guess your ideas. Just focus on generating at least ten more topic ideas based on your context.

4. **MIX AND MATCH.** Review your three lists and look for any obvious overlap between them. If you have similar or related topics in all three lists, that's a good indication that topic will be a good fit for your speaking situation. Circle that topic and note it as a possible choice for your presentation. Then have a little fun mixing up the topics across your three lists. Randomly pick a topic from the standpoint list, the audience list, and the context list and put them together. How do your topic ideas for standpoint, audience, and context combine, connect, and overlap? Keep randomly combining and finding connections between topics on the three lists until you have four or five strong topic ideas—or an "Aha!" moment when the right topic jumps out at you.

5. **TEST YOUR TOPIC.** Finally, choose a topic you are excited to speak about that fits your standpoint, audience, and context. Test the topic by asking three questions: Can I speak about this topic from my own standpoint or strengths? Can I make this topic interesting or appealing to my audience? Can I link this topic to my context? If you can answer yes to all three questions, you have found an excellent topic.

If you get stuck anywhere in this process, try brainstorming with a partner or group. Work with a friend, family member, colleague, or classmate to come up with ideas. Remember that every topic idea is worth considering, no matter how silly or offbeat it might seem. Even if your first few ideas won't work for your presentation, brainstorming with other people can get

If you get stuck trying to find a good topic, try brainstorming with people who know you or your speaking situation, such as friends or classmates. Sometimes just chatting with another person can help you generate new ideas.

you in the flow, help you think more expansively, and eventually spark the idea for a great presentation topic.

# From Topic to Purpose

Once you know your exigence and topic, you can identify your purpose. Remember that your purpose is the impact you want your presentation to have on your audience. Although you might not explicitly state your purpose during your speech, having a clear understanding of your purpose will help you navigate every choice you make as you develop your presentation. You can start with a general purpose, then narrow it down to a more specific purpose.

## IDENTIFYING YOUR GENERAL PURPOSE

**general purpose**
your overall aim to either inform, persuade, or connect

There are three types of **general purpose**: informing, persuading, and connecting. Consider your standpoint, audience, context, and topic to decide which of these three general purposes best suits your speaking situation.

1. INFORMING. When your general purpose is to inform, your goal is to teach the audience information they do not already know without calling for a significant change in their existing values, attitudes, or behaviors. Informative presentations explain ideas, share discoveries, or demonstrate skills. Class lectures, research presentations, oral reports, workshops, webinars, and tutorial videos are all examples of informative speeches.

2. PERSUADING. When your general purpose is to persuade, your primary goal is convincing an audience to change their existing values, attitudes, or behaviors. Persuasive presentations challenge assumptions, transform beliefs, or motivate actions. Sales pitches, donation requests, motivational speaking, issue advocacy, policy proposals, and political debates are all examples of persuasive speeches.

3. CONNECTING. Although in every speech you should aim to connect with the audience, in some speaking situations connection is your primary goal. Special occasions—like funerals, weddings, and awards ceremonies—call for connecting. Connective presentations use shared values and emotions to connect the speaker with the audience and connect the audience

## Pathways

To learn more about developing speeches with these three types of general purpose, see **Chapter 15, Informing and Educating**, **Chapter 16, Persuading and Motivating**, and **Chapter 17, Connecting and Celebrating**.

members with each other. Eulogies, toasts, acceptance speeches, speeches of introduction, and farewell speeches are all examples of connective speeches.

## PINPOINTING YOUR SPECIFIC PURPOSE

Once you know your topic and general purpose, you are ready to zero in on the specific purpose of your speech. Your **specific purpose** identifies the public, the topic, and the outcome—the who, the what, and the why—of your more general purpose (see Figure 6.3). Who are you informing, persuading, or connecting with? What are you informing, persuading, or connecting with them about? Why are you informing, persuading, or connecting with them about this?

You can write out your specific purpose by adding your public, topic, and outcome to your general purpose. To put it another way: specific purpose = general purpose + public + topic + outcome. For example:

**specific purpose**
a detailed goal including the general purpose, the public, the topic, and the outcome of your presentation

- Specific purpose: to inform [general purpose] college students [public] about the different student loan repayment plans available [topic] so that they can make educated decisions about student loans [outcome].

- Specific purpose: to persuade [general purpose] voters [public] to support increasing income taxes on individuals who make over $400,000 a year [topic] so that they will vote for congressional candidates who support tax increases for high-income earners [outcome].

- Specific purpose: to connect [general purpose] with wedding guests [public] to celebrate the love of Parker & Morgan [topic] so that they will come together as a supportive community for the newlyweds [outcome].

When you take the time to write out your specific purpose, you give your speech a clear goal. Having a detailed picture of your goal—knowing precisely what kind of impact you want your presentation to have—makes it much easier to plan your speech.

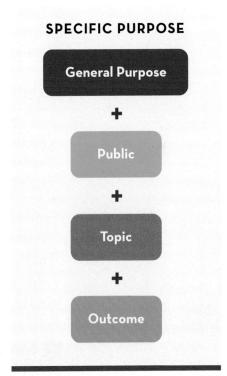

**SPECIFIC PURPOSE**

General Purpose
+
Public
+
Topic
+
Outcome

**FIGURE 6.3** Your specific purpose combines your general purpose, public, topic, and desired outcome.

# EVALUATING YOUR PURPOSE

Like any goal, your specific purpose must be both *meaningful* and *achievable* in order to be effective. A meaningful purpose connects to your own passions, the values of your audience, and the demands of your context. An achievable purpose focuses on an impact that you can create, a change that your audience can make, and an outcome that your context will allow.

Check to make sure your specific purpose is both meaningful and achievable. To be achievable, your purpose must fit within the limits of your speaking situation: the available time and space, your existing credibility with your audience, and their knowledge and beliefs about your topic. But to be meaningful, your purpose must also stretch those limits: filling the time and space, building a stronger relationship with your audience, and increasing their knowledge or changing their beliefs.

## 1 Consider Your Context

Think about the time and space available for your presentation. For your purpose to be achievable, it must fit within those time and space constraints. But to be meaningful, your purpose must also fill the time and space you're given. For example:

- **ACHIEVABLE: FITS AVAILABLE TIME AND SPACE.** If your goal is to inform your town council about the risks of global climate change, that might not be achievable if you have only two minutes to speak. Instead, you might need to focus on just one part of that process—like deforestation—that's particularly relevant to local decisions.

- **MEANINGFUL: FILLS AVAILABLE TIME AND SPACE.** If your goal is to persuade students in your dorm to keep the common areas clean, that alone might not be meaningful enough to sustain an hour-long workshop. You might need to expand your focus to suggest several ways to improve the quality of life in your residence hall.

## 2 Gauge Your Credibility

Reflect on your credibility and relationship with your audience. To be achievable, your purpose must fit the level of credibility and kind of relationship you have with them. But at the same time, your purpose must strengthen your bond with your audience if you want it to be meaningful. For example:

- **ACHIEVABLE: FITS EXISTING CREDIBILITY AND RELATIONSHIP.**
  If your goal is to persuade residents at a nursing home to use condoms to avoid spreading sexually transmitted diseases, that might not be achievable if you haven't already established a personal connection with them. You might need to choose a less intimate public health message—like cancer screening—until you build more trust.

- **MEANINGFUL: ENHANCES CREDIBILITY AND RELATIONSHIP.**
  If your goal is to connect with fellow volunteers by introducing yourself at your organization's annual awards ceremony, that might not be meaningful if they already know you well. You might need to share surprising details or personal stories about your life to pique their interest and build stronger rapport.

**📋 TRY THIS**

To develop, narrow, and evaluate your purpose and create a meaningful and achievable goal for your presentation, use the **Purpose Statement Worksheet**.

## 3 Assess Your Audience's Position

Take your audience's knowledge and beliefs into account. To achieve your purpose, you must connect with their existing ideas about your topic. But you must also increase your audience's knowledge or change their beliefs in order to make a meaningful difference. For example:

- **ACHIEVABLE: FITS EXISTING KNOWLEDGE AND BELIEFS.** If your goal is to persuade your coworkers to get the COVID-19 vaccine, that might not be achievable if they believe that the vaccine will mutate their DNA. You might need to focus on informing them about how the different vaccines work before you can persuade them to get vaccinated.

- **MEANINGFUL: EXPANDS KNOWLEDGE AND BELIEFS.** If your goal is to inform a group of finance majors about compound interest, that might not be meaningful if they've already learned about it in a previous course. You might need to choose a more

Balancing what's achievable and what's meaningful is one of the many challenges of teaching. Here, professor Ricardo Guthrie speaks to students at Palomar College about common cultural artifacts.

# Paxton Smith Finds Purpose in Her Standpoint and Context

On May 30, 2021, Paxton Smith delivered the class valedictorian speech at the Lake Highlands High School graduation ceremony in Dallas, Texas.[10] Although graduation speeches usually have a connective purpose, focusing on shared values, Smith's standpoint and context called her to adopt a persuasive purpose instead. She explained, "Under light of recent events, it feels wrong to talk about anything but what is currently affecting me and millions of other women in this state. Recently the 'Heartbeat Bill' was passed in Texas. Starting in September, there will be a ban on abortions after six weeks of pregnancy, regardless of whether the pregnancy was a result of rape or incest." For Smith, the Texas Heartbeat Bill posed an exigence—a pressing, urgent call to speak—that outweighed the conventional expectations for a graduation speech.

Smith explained that she wanted to address this controversial topic "on a day where you are most inclined to listen to a voice like mine, a woman's voice" because "it's a problem that cannot wait." The urgency of the issue called her to stand up for her own values and challenge the values of her audience members: "I cannot give up this platform to promote complacency and peace when there is a war on my body and a war on my rights, a war on the rights of your mothers, a war on the rights of your sisters, a war on the rights of your daughters." Smith emphasized her standpoint—her voice, her body, her rights—to connect with the rights of all Texas women and their allies.

When asked why she chose to address abortion rights at a graduation ceremony, Smith said that speaking at rallies isn't enough: "If you want any

advanced topic—like calculating net present value—to teach them something new.

Choosing the right purpose is a balancing act. If you don't stretch the limits of your speaking situation at all, your speech won't create a meaningful transformation. But if you reach too far beyond the limits of your speaking situation, your speech won't be able to achieve the transformation you want. Experiment with your specific purpose—changing its focus, elements, and level of detail—to find the sweet spot that is both meaningful and achievable in your speaking situation.

kind of change, you have to reach people who don't care and you need to reach people who flat out disagree."[11] After a classmate posted a one-minute clip of Smith's speech to TikTok, it went viral and was picked up by media across the United States, including every major cable news channel and national newspaper.[12] Numerous state and national figures expressed support and appreciation for her bravery on social media. As activist and legal clerk Erin Brockovich tweeted, "Wherever you stand on the issue you have to admire this young lady standing up for what she believes and believing in the power of her voice."[13]

To watch Smith's valedictorian speech, do a web search for: Paxton Smith Speech Highlands Graduation. The video is approximately 7:52 in length and her speech begins at 4:30.

Paxton Smith gave an unconventional valedictorian address at her high school graduation. Abandoning her original plan to speak on media and content, she felt called to speak on recent restrictions on abortion. She explained that she could not wait, could not stay silent, and needed to use the opportunity she was given on that day to speak about how those restrictions would affect young women like her (7:28).

## ✓ Critical Thinking Check

1. Could you use the same topic with different general purposes? Could you inform, persuade, and connect with the same audience about the same topic? Why or why not?

2. Why might you choose not to share your specific purpose with your audience during your speech? Why is it important to know the specific purpose of your presentation in detail even when you won't be sharing it with your audience?

# Crafting a Thesis Statement

**thesis statement**
a complete, concise, and clear sentence summarizing the main idea of your presentation

While your specific purpose is your guide to preparing your speech, a thesis statement is what you tell your audience about the focus and importance of your presentation. A **thesis statement** summarizes the main idea of your speech. It provides a one-sentence summary of your speech and communicates what your audience will get out of listening to your presentation.

- If your purpose is informing, state (a) what *knowledge* the audience will gain and (b) the *importance* of that information. For example: "I'll explain the differences between mountain bikes and road bikes [knowledge] so you can decide which type of bike is best for you [importance]."

- If your purpose is persuading, state (a) the *change* in attitude, value, or behavior that you recommend and (b) the *reasons* for that change. For example: "I am asking you to join me in voting for Keisha Williams [change] because she has the experience to increase our fund-raising and community outreach [reasons]."

- If your purpose is connecting, state (a) the *occasion* that brings the group together as a public and (b) the *values* represented by that occasion. For example: "Thank you for being here today to celebrate this year's recipients of the Stewardship Award [occasion] for leadership in sustainability and environmental justice [values]."

A good thesis statement tells your audience *what* you will say—the knowledge you will share, the change you will advocate, or the occasion you will honor—and *why* you will say it—the importance of that knowledge, the reasons for that change, or the values that occasion represents. The goal of your thesis statement is to pique your audience's interest and help them remember the key takeaway from your presentation. To increase your audience's interest in and memory of your presentation, make sure your thesis statement is *complete*, *concise*, and *clear*.

## COMPLETE THESIS STATEMENTS

A complete thesis statement explains both what you will say and why you will say it. A thesis statement that doesn't explain the *what*—the knowledge, change, or occasion you are speaking about—can make your presentation confusing and difficult to remember. And a thesis statement that doesn't explain the *why*—the importance, reasons, or values behind your speech—can make your audience less interested and engaged.

**No "why"**  I'm going to teach you how to float on your back in the water.

**No "what"**  I'm going to teach you a simple skill that could save your life.

**Complete**  I'm going to teach you how to float on your back in the water, a simple skill that could save your life.

## CONCISE THESIS STATEMENTS

A concise thesis statement is brief enough to understand and remember. Most speakers get only one chance to make an impact on their audience. Long, complex thesis statements are difficult to grasp and easy to forget. Summarize your main idea in a single sentence, ideally with fewer than twenty-five words.

**Too long**  Loving family, good friends, and other assorted loved ones, on this fourteenth day of March, we are gathered together to celebrate the wedding, the love, the exquisite beauty of these two wonderful young people, Etta and Raj, who are my best friends, the lights of my life, and absolutely perfect for each other.

**Too complex**  We gather today, family, friends, and loved ones, to celebrate. What do we celebrate? The love of the lights of my life, Etta and Raj.

**Concise**  Today, we are gathered to celebrate the love of Etta and Raj, the two lights of my life.

## CLEAR THESIS STATEMENTS

In addition to being complete and concise, a good thesis statement is clear. It leaves your audience with no doubt about what they will get from your presentation. An effective thesis statement can be easily understood by your audience with no other information or explanation. Avoid language that is vague or unfamiliar to your audience, and use terms that are both precise and

**TRY THIS**

To evaluate and refine your thesis statement and make sure it's complete, concise, and clear, use the **Thesis Statement Checklist**.

recognizable. If using an unfamiliar term is unavoidable, introduce it using plain language.

| | |
|---|---|
| **Vague language** | Support the new environmental rules to monitor dangerous chemicals in the water. |
| **Unfamiliar terms** | Submit a public comment on the EPA's UCMR 5 proposal to collect data on perfluoroalkyl and polyfluoroalkyl substance levels in public supply facilities, because even 70 parts per trillion can cause significant health problems. |
| **Clear** | To keep our drinking water safe, tell the Environmental Protection Agency that you support its proposal to track toxic chemicals known as PFAS. |

You might revise your thesis statement several times before settling on the right wording to completely, concisely, and clearly capture the main point of your presentation. But developing a strong thesis statement is worth the effort. Your thesis statement is the single most important sentence in your presentation.

Your thesis statement is usually the only sentence you will state more than once, and it may be the only sentence your audience will remember. You will use your thesis statement in your introduction to build audience interest and promise the payoff of your presentation. Then, you will restate your thesis statement in your conclusion to summarize what you have said and reinforce your main idea. When you've crafted a complete, concise, and clear thesis statement, it will help you achieve your purpose and leave a lasting impression on your audience (see Figure 6.4).

**Exigences**
Why you? Why them? Why now?

**Topic**
What your presentation is about

**General Purpose**
Informing, persuading, or connecting

**Specific Purpose**
General purpose + public + topic + outcome

**Thesis Statement**
What you will say and why you will say it

**FIGURE 6.4** Each step narrows your focus from your exigences to your topic and purpose, leading you toward a complete, clear, and concise thesis statement.

1. Why do you need different types of thesis statements for informing, persuading, and connecting? What elements do those different types of thesis statements have in common?
2. Why is it important for a thesis statement to be complete, concise, and clear? What will happen if your thesis statement is incomplete? What will happen if it's not concise and clear?

# Next Steps

Determining your exigences, topic, general purpose, specific purpose, and thesis statement will give you a road map for preparing the rest of your presentation. To get started, try the Finding Your Topic Worksheet, the Purpose Statement Worksheet, and the Thesis Statement Checklist.

Understanding the exigences in your speaking situation will help you choose a topic that's relevant to your audience, your context, and your own standpoint. Knowing your topic and your general purpose—informing, persuading, or connecting—will help you develop a clear goal for your presentation. Your specific purpose will give you a strategic plan as a speaker: as you prepare your presentation, you will target every choice you make to move your audience toward your purpose. When you know your purpose, you are ready to find the information, reasoning, emotions, and values that will make an impact on your audience.

# Standpoint Reflection

- What experiences, values, and passions do you have that give you a sense of purpose? How might you share that sense of purpose in the speeches that you give?

- How can you use your strengths to connect with your audience? How can you use your strengths to inform them? How might you use your strengths to persuade them?

- What topics would best feature your unique strengths and standpoint? Are there any unusual topics that you have specialized knowledge about or personal experience with? Are there any common topics that would feel completely fresh when presented from your perspective?

- What do you personally feel called to speak about? How might you adapt this personal exigence to fit the exigences of your next speaking situation?

## Key Terms

# Resources for Topic and Purpose

## 📋 "Try This" Exercises

Access the "Try This" exercises as directed by your instructor or online at
digital.wwnorton.com/chapterexercises-conpubspeak

- To use the exigences in your speaking situation to discover your topic, try the **Finding Your Topic Worksheet**.

- To develop, narrow, and evaluate your purpose and create a meaningful and achievable goal for your presentation, use the **Purpose Statement Worksheet**.

- To evaluate and refine your thesis statement and make sure it's complete, concise, and clear, use the **Thesis Statement Checklist**.

---

**Want to practice these skills to prepare for your next speech? Go to INQUIZITIVE to review and apply concepts from this chapter and get personalized feedback along the way.**

YOUTH LEADER AND
IMMIGRATION ACTIVIST  Edna Chavez

# 7 Evidence and Reasoning

Edna Chavez is a youth leader, student, and activist in South Los Angeles. After her father was deported, she began educating people about the experiences of families affected by immigration policy. "I was sixteen years old when I lost my father to immigration," she says. "Because of him, I started creating Know Your Rights workshops, making sure that no family member has to leave their family ever again due to legal status."[1]

She worked with lawyers and experts to provide people with information about immigration policy and testified to the impact such policies had on her and those in similar situations. "I wasn't going to have my father with me anymore," she explains. "This judge looked at me dead in the eye and told me, 'Your father won't be coming back.'"[2]

She speaks out—and helps others speak out—because she believes that we can't reason effectively about issues like immigration without understanding the impact it has on people's lives. "Nobody knows our stories," she says. "Nobody knows the communities we come from."[3]

She argues that decision makers cannot make effective policies unless they understand the experiences of people who are directly affected by those policies: "We know the injustices that affect us and what we want to see for ourselves, our schools, and our communities. We are the ones living it."[4]

Chavez's activism demonstrates that sharing your standpoint can do more than build your credibility—your firsthand knowledge and personal experiences can also provide important evidence to support your cause.

## LEARNING OBJECTIVES

**After completing this chapter, you will be able to**

- Use multiple types of evidence to support your thesis

- Connect your evidence to your thesis with deductive, inductive, and analogical reasoning

- Identify and avoid common errors in reasoning

- Adapt your evidence and reasoning to appeal to your audience

## Pathways

To review the principles for developing effective thesis statements, see **Chapter 6, Topic and Purpose**.

To learn about using common research techniques and tools to gather evidence, see **Chapter 8, Research and Citation.**

As Edna Chavez shows, the evidence you use to make your case matters. An effective public speaker gathers multiple types of evidence to support their thesis, uses that evidence to better understand their topic, ensures their reasoning is sound, and then adapts their evidence and reasoning to their audience. Sharing evidence with your audience is an opportunity to open their eyes to ideas and issues they haven't considered before. Just as you speak from your standpoint—from your unique intersection of experiences, knowledge, values, and identities—your audience members see the world from theirs. By sharing your unique knowledge and experiences and learning from the knowledge and experiences of others, you can help us all see beyond the limitations of our own perspectives, improve each other's reasoning, and reach stronger conclusions together.

# Using Evidence to Support Your Thesis

Gathering multiple types of evidence helps you better understand your topic. Sharing that evidence shows your audience how you reached your conclusions and invites them to draw the same conclusions you have. **Evidence** is the information you use to support your thesis statement. When you offer evidence, you show your audience why they should accept the main idea of your speech. Providing evidence has the power to change your audience's worldview by giving them a window onto your unique way of looking at the world. By showing your audience what you know, believe, and value, you can help them understand an idea or issue in a new way.

**evidence**
information you use to support your thesis statement

**observation**
knowledge formed by seeing, hearing, touching, or otherwise encountering something through the senses

**demonstration**
giving your audience the opportunity to directly observe an event or principle for themselves

Evidence helps your audience see the world in a new way because evidence is based on **observation**: knowledge formed by seeing, hearing, touching, or otherwise encountering something through the senses. You can give your audience a demonstration, allowing them to directly observe an event or principle for themselves. You can share testimony, giving an account of your own observations or observations made by someone else. You can also use statistics, which combine the observations of a large number of events or cases (see Table 7.1, p. 139).

## DEMONSTRATIONS

There's a reason people say, "Seeing is believing." Few things are more convincing than **demonstrations**: letting your audience personally see, hear, touch, or

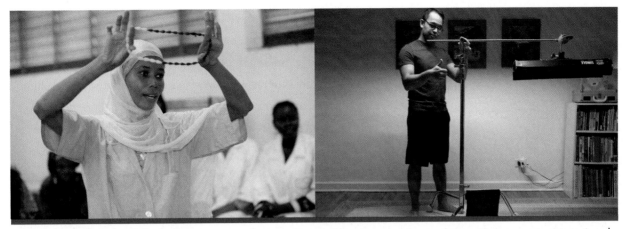

Left: A nurse in West Africa demonstrates how women without access to contraceptives can use menstrual cycle tracking beads to reduce the risk of unwanted pregnancies. Right: Nyv Mercado provides a demonstration of how to stabilize a stand holding a heavy light in a video for his YouTube channel (4:14).

otherwise experience an event or effect. When your audience can experience the evidence for themselves, rather than taking someone else's word for it, the impact will be more powerful and enduring. This is why the death of George Floyd started a national movement: the video evidence allowed anyone to see the horror of police violence against Black Americans—even people with more privileged standpoints who had never witnessed it before.

Displaying photographs or playing audio and video recordings can be effective forms of demonstration. Content creators on YouTube and TikTok sometimes use demonstration evidence, such as creating "how-to" videos that show the audience how to complete a task. And they sometimes offer video clips as evidence of what another creator has said or done. Audiences are increasingly savvy about photo, audio, and video editing, so be sure to preserve the integrity of any media you use as evidence. In some cases, it's better to give your audience an unmediated experience by showing them physical objects or giving them a live demonstration. For example, speakers teaching stress-reduction techniques often walk the audience through a live demonstration to convince them the methods are easy and effective.

**Pathways**

To learn more about using props and audiovisual aids, see **Chapter 13, Presentation Aids and Slides**.

## TESTIMONY

Sometimes giving your audience a direct experience is impractical or even impossible, so speakers often share testimonies of their own experiences and the experiences of others. **Testimony** is an account of an individual's observations,

**testimony**
an account of an individual's observations, knowledge, and experiences

knowledge, and experiences. In a legal setting, testimony means evidence given by someone under oath, such as a witness or a forensic expert describing their own experience or knowledge. But in public speaking, testimony can include quotations and citations from other sources. A speaker may quote a researcher explaining their findings or a person describing an event they experienced personally. Public speakers can also give their own personal testimony when they have relevant expertise or direct experience with the events or issues they are describing. Testimony is the most common kind of evidence used by public speakers and, as Edna Chavez shows, it can be a powerful way to help your audience see the world through someone else's eyes.

## Pathways

To learn more about evaluating and establishing the credibility of your sources, see **Chapter 8, Research and Citation**.

Whether the testimony you offer comes from you or another source, your audience must see the source as credible and trustworthy since they are relying on someone else's knowledge and experience rather than their own. Your audience members' values and attitudes will determine who they see as credible and what criteria they use to make that assessment. You can reinforce the credibility of testimony by sharing similar accounts from multiple sources to establish a consensus. And, as with all evidence, your audience will need to see how the testimony connects to your thesis. For example, you might use testimony to support the thesis "You should adopt a dog because caring for a dog

Left: Paramedic Martin Blunt testifies at the involuntary manslaughter trial of former cardiologist Conrad Murray, the personal physician of Michael Jackson. Right: Graduate student Elena Shrestha presents the results of her research on micro air vehicles. Both are examples of presenting testimonial evidence.

When you are using testimony evidence based on your own personal experiences, you can use four steps to ensure it connects with your audience and supports your purpose:

1. **STATE YOUR CLAIM.** Begin by telling the audience the claim that your personal experience supports. That may be the thesis of your presentation or another claim within your presentation. For example, "Even if you can live in your car, homelessness takes an enormous toll on a person's mental and physical health." Or, "Painting a room yourself is easy and you can get great results if you follow a few simple steps."

2. **ASSERT THE AUTHORITY OF YOUR EXPERIENCE.** Tell your audience that you know because you have witnessed it, lived it, done it, or otherwise experienced it. For example, "I know this all too well because I had to live in my car for a year due to homelessness." Or, "I learned these tricks from a professional housepainter, and I have used them to paint many rooms myself."

3. **PROVIDE DETAILED SENSORY DESCRIPTIONS.** Use one or more of the five senses to provide your audience a rich image of your own experience. For example, "When I was sleeping in my car at night, every two hours the police would shine their spotlights on me and rap on my windows to make me move. Because they would not allow me to sleep, I was constantly tired and weak, was short-tempered and agitated, fell asleep at work, and always felt like my mind was in a fog." Or, "Before I learned how to do it the right way, my painting would dry with thick drops on the walls and you could see lines and seams, but now my paint jobs look smooth and clean."

4. **SHOW THE RELEVANCE OF YOUR OBSERVATIONS TO YOUR CLAIM.** Connect your personal experience back to your stated claim. For example, "That year gave me firsthand experience of just how brutal homelessness can be, even if you have a car to sleep in." Or, "Learning the basic steps of painting took only a few minutes and a little practice, and you can easily learn them, too."

can significantly benefit your physical and psychological health." That testimony might include citing multiple studies showing that dog ownership lowers stress and increases physical activity. But you might also include citations to research about the significant role stress and physical activity play in a person's health.

# STATISTICS

While testimony could include one individual's observation of a single event, a personal life story, or an expert's opinion, statistics report the results of the mathematical analysis of a large number of examples. **Statistics** are the collection, analysis, and interpretation of numerical data. While testimony can tell you what it feels like to be unemployed, statistics can tell you what percentage of people are unemployed within a given population. Often, people trust statistical evidence more than testimonial evidence because it seems more objective—you may have even heard the phrase "numbers don't lie."

Policy arguments often rely heavily on statistics. Here, senators Maria Cantwell, Joseph Lieberman, and Susan Collins use statistics to support legislation that would curb inflation of food and energy prices.

However, the way statistics are calculated and represented can have a big impact on how we interpret them. For example, according to the US Census Bureau, the average (mean) household income in the United States in 2020 was about $97,000.[5] But not so fast—the median household income was around $68,000. And it gets worse—the most commonly reported (mode) household income was $0. So, are most American households making almost six figures, or are most American households making nothing at all?

**statistics**
the collection, analysis, and interpretation of numerical data

**mean**
the average of all the numerical values in a data set

**median**
the numerical value at the midpoint of a data set

- The **mean**, or average, is calculated by adding up all the numbers in a data set and dividing by the number of values in that set. In this case, you would add up the incomes reported by every household and divide by the total number of households. Result: $97,026.

- The **median** is calculated by ordering all the numbers in a data set from lowest to highest and finding the value at the midpoint. In this case, you would line up all the households from lowest income to highest income and locate the income of the household right in the middle, the one with half of all households having lower income and half of all households having higher income: $67,521.

- The **mode** is calculated by finding the number that occurs most often in a data set. In this case, you would comb through the different incomes that all the households reported and find the number that was reported most frequently: $0.

**mode**
the numerical value that occurs most often in a data set

As you can see, numerical data can be misleading. Just a few extremely high numbers in a data set—like a small group of people bringing in millions of dollars a year—can skew the mean average upward. And the most common value in a data set (the mode) is not necessarily the most representative one—although more people reported zero income than any other number, the vast majority of Americans make significantly more than that. Sometimes, numbers do lie. So when you present statistical evidence, be sure you understand how your source gathered and analyzed their data.

📋 **TRY THIS**

To identify what kinds of evidence you need to support your thesis, use the **Evidence Wishlist Worksheet**.

**THESIS:** Employers should provide remote and hybrid work options because they improve recruitment and retention, increase productivity, and create a more equitable and diverse workplace.

| | |
|---|---|
| **Demonstration** | • Walking the audience through an online project management tool that helps remote workers stay connected and on task. |
| | • Giving the audience hands-on experience with videoconferencing software that provides for more inclusive and accessible meetings. |
| **Testimony** | • The personal story of an employee who shifted to remote work and the benefits they experienced. |
| | • A quotation from a professor of business administration who studies remote work and productivity. |
| **Statistics** | • A citation showing the number of job candidates who say that remote or hybrid work options are an important part of deciding where to work. |
| | • Citing a study on the percentage of employees who feel more included and respected when working remotely. |

**TABLE 7.1** You can use various types of evidence to support the same thesis and even combine different types to maximize their impact.

**reasoning**
the process of drawing
conclusions from
evidence

**principle**
a theory, rule, or
definition that applies
to all cases in a given
category

**deductive reasoning**
reasoning from a general
principle to apply it to a
specific case

# Reasoning with Evidence

Evidence alone is rarely enough for a speaker to move an audience or to accomplish their purpose. To make evidence effective, you will need to use reasoning to improve your own understanding of your topic and to help your audience see how the evidence supports your thesis. **Reasoning** is the process of drawing conclusions from evidence. Logical reasoning makes a clear connection between the evidence you provide and the conclusions you draw from that evidence. In some cases, your audience analysis and your own knowledge may indicate that your audience will see the link between your evidence and your thesis without further explanation. But in many cases, it helps to make your reasoning explicit to your audience. There are three main ways to link your evidence to your thesis: reasoning from principles, reasoning from examples, and reasoning from analogies (see Figure 7.1).

## REASONING FROM PRINCIPLES

A **principle** is a theory, rule, or definition that applies to all cases in a given category. Formal definitions set by law or science are two types of principle. For example, "all mammals are warm-blooded" is a principle. **Deductive reasoning** starts from a general principle and applies it to a specific case. Deductive reasoning is most effective when you can show that the case you are describing clearly fits within the limits of the definition or rule you've stated. To reason from a general principle:

1. **STATE THE PRINCIPLE.** Use demonstration, testimony, or statistics to establish a definition, a theory, or a rule. For example: "According to California attorney Diana Adjadj, fraud is when someone intentionally misrepresents a fact, and someone else believes them and is harmed by acting on that belief."[6]

2. **APPLY THE PRINCIPLE.** Explain how the definition, theory, or rule applies to the specific case you are discussing. For example: "The salesperson said the phone was a genuine Samsung product, but they later admitted they knew it was a fake. I bought it thinking it was genuine and ended up buying junk because I believed them."

3. **DRAW THE CONCLUSION.** Make the connection between the principle and the case explicit by using elements of both to state your conclusion. For

example, "Since they told me something they knew was not true and I was harmed by acting on it, what the salesperson did was fraud." In some cases, the conclusion will be your thesis. In others it may be a claim within your presentation that supports your overall thesis.

## REASONING FROM EXAMPLES

An **example** is a specific case that represents its group or type. Speakers often use examples to help an audience understand a concept or use multiple examples to help an audience see what those cases share in common. **Inductive reasoning** starts from a specific case to arrive at a general principle. For inductive reasoning to work, you must be able to show your audience that your example is characteristic of its category, rather than an outlier or an exception. That can be done by showing them a number of similar examples or by providing other evidence that shows the case is not unusual. To reason from a specific example:

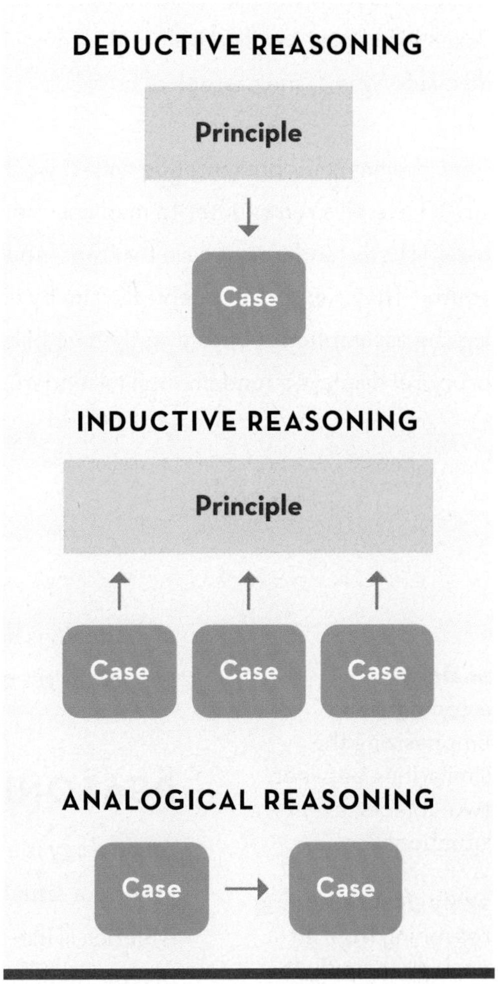

1. **DESCRIBE THE EXAMPLE.** Use demonstration, testimony, or statistics to describe a specific case. For instance: "When Staff Sergeant Wesley Black returned home from Afghanistan with severe stomach pain, the VA hospital initially diagnosed him with irritable bowel syndrome caused by stress. But he later learned that he had Stage 4 lung, liver, and colorectal cancer, leaving him only three to five years to live."[7]

2. **EXTEND THE EXAMPLE.** Show that the example is representative of the category or shares important features with other cases. For example: "According to the nonprofit organization Burn Pits 360, Wesley is one of tens of thousands of veterans with serious health problems caused by the toxic fumes from burn pits and misdiagnosed by the VA."[8]

3. **DRAW THE CONCLUSION.** Connect the example and the similar cases to your claim or thesis. For example, "There is obviously a widespread problem with how

**example**
a specific case that represents its group or type

**inductive reasoning**
reasoning from an example to arrive at a general principle

### DEDUCTIVE REASONING

Principle

↓

Case

### INDUCTIVE REASONING

Principle

↑    ↑    ↑

Case    Case    Case

### ANALOGICAL REASONING

Case → Case

**FIGURE 7.1** Deductive reasoning applies a principle to a case, inductive reasoning uses cases to arrive at a principle, and analogical reasoning compares one case to another.

# Adri Pèrez's Transgender Advocacy

In April 2021, the Texas Senate Committee on State Affairs was deliberating on two bills to restrict the rights of transgender youth. One bill prohibited health-care providers from performing transition-related health care, on penalty of losing their license to practice; the other reclassified administering or consenting to transition-related health care for minors as "child abuse." Transgender Texan Adri Pèrez testified before the committee to advocate against the passage of both bills.[9]

Pèrez begins their presentation with their thesis: "These bills run counter to medical science's established standards of care for transgender youth." They support this central claim by challenging the assumptions underlying the two bills: "This proposal displays a fundamental misunderstanding about the medical treatment for transgender youth." They go on to explain that the current standard of care simply delays the onset of puberty so that transgender youth and their parents can make informed decisions about their medical care.

Challenging the definition of transition-related medical practices as child abuse, Pèrez redefines those interventions as "life-saving care." Pèrez offers their own personal testimony as evidence: "It saved *my* life." After creating an emotional impact with this personal testimony, Pèrez then uses expert testimony to show just how far that impact extends: "When a similar ban on gender-affirming health care was recently debated and unconstitutionally passed in Arkansas, a pediatric doctor reported seeing an increase in visits to the the VA is handling diagnoses, a problem we must resolve to ensure our veterans get the care and support they deserve."

## REASONING FROM ANALOGIES

An **analogy** is a comparison highlighting the similarities between two objects, events, or situations. Any time we say one thing is like another, such as today's America is like the late Roman Empire or driving while high on marijuana is like driving drunk, we are reasoning from analogy. **Analogical reasoning** starts from one specific case and applies that case's qualities to another similar case. Analogical reasoning depends on your ability to show your audience that the two cases

**analogy**
a comparison emphasizing the similarities between two objects, events, or situations

**analogical reasoning**
reasoning from an analogy to apply the qualities of one specific case to another similar case

emergency room by transgender people attempting suicide." Drawing an analogy to a similar ban in another state, Pèrez demonstrates the grave harms that such bills pose for transgender people.

Artfully combining both personal and expert testimony, Pèrez closes with a message of hope addressed to transgender youth: "To the transgender youth across the country who are surely watching this hearing: We see you. You are not alone, and we will never stop fighting for you." By offering evidence grounded in their own personal experience as well as others' medical expertise, Pèrez demonstrates the persuasive power of combining multiple forms of evidence.

You can find a video of Perez's testimony by doing a web search for: El Paso trans advocate testifies. The video is approximately 3:55 in length.

Adri Pèrez addresses the Texas Senate Committee on State Affairs on behalf of themselves and the ACLU of Texas. They opened by explaining that Texas's limits on gender-affirming medical care "run counter to medical science, established standards of care for transgender youth, and the fundamental freedom of parents and families from excessive government intrusion" (0:35).

are sufficiently similar, rather than identifying differences or distinctions between them. To reason from an analogy:

1. **DESCRIBE THE KNOWN CASE**. Use demonstration, testimony, or statistics to highlight the relevant qualities. For example: "Look down at your desk. Now look back at me. Now look at the person next to you. Now look back at me. Are you starting to feel stressed out?"

2. **APPLY THOSE QUALITIES TO ANOTHER CASE**. Be sure to emphasize the similarities between the two cases. For example: "This is just like what happens when you leave multiple windows and tabs open on your

computer screen. There are too many things to look at and your attention bounces around between them."

3. **DRAW THE CONCLUSION**. Emphasize what you want the audience to learn from this comparison. Explain how the similarities between the two cases support your thesis or an important claim within your presentation. For example, "Whenever we clog up our screens with distractions and clutter it increases our stress."

---

✓ **Critical Thinking Check**

1. How would you decide what types of evidence—demonstration, testimony, or statistics—will be most effective to support your thesis? Why might different kinds of thesis statements call for different kinds of evidence?

2. What are the advantages and disadvantages of reasoning from principles? What about reasoning from examples? Reasoning from analogies?

# Logical Errors in Reasoning

Whether deductive, inductive, or analogical, reasoning logically links your evidence to your thesis. But without solid reasoning, those links between your evidence and your thesis can break down—and your audience might notice that your reasoning doesn't add up. Logical errors in reasoning are known as **fallacies**. Understanding these common weaknesses in reasoning can help you avoid them in your own presentations and recognize them in the reasoning of others.

## FALSE AUTHORITY

Citing a source and establishing their authority can help you build credibility and support your thesis—but only if the source's authority is genuine. A source has **false authority** when their credentials are not relevant to the claims they make. People who have genuine authority in one subject or field can be false authorities when they make claims about subjects outside their expertise or experience. For example, celebrities like Nicki Minaj, Joe Rogan, and Matthew McConaughey have offered public health advice during the COVID-19 pandemic. Although they might have considerable expertise to share about the entertainment industry, they are not credible sources of medical information.

**fallacies**
logical errors in reasoning

**false authority**
when a source's credentials are not relevant to their claims

# PERSONAL ATTACKS

While it should be obvious that insults and personal attacks are not sound reasoning, speakers use them with surprising frequency. A **personal attack** attempts to discredit claims, evidence, or reasoning based on irrelevant aspects of a source's personal qualities or background. For example, opponents of female political leaders like Hillary Clinton and Sarah Palin often focus on critiquing their clothing, physical appearance, and romantic relationships rather than engaging with their policies on health-care reform or public funding of religious education.

# UNREPRESENTATIVE EXAMPLES

Examples can illustrate overarching principles, but moving from a specific case to a general conclusion can introduce weaknesses in reasoning. Representative examples share important features with other examples of the same category. For example, a speaker educating an audience about hurricanes might discuss how hurricanes Dorian, Laura, and Michael were devastating because they combined strong winds, heavy rain, and high waves—three things that are characteristic of all hurricanes. **Unrepresentative examples** draw conclusions from a specific case or set of cases that does not adequately characterize the overall group, category, or principle. This error occurs when speakers give an insufficient number of examples or rely on exceptional or unusual cases. For example, motivational speakers often tell rags-to-riches stories to claim that anyone with the right attitude can easily become wealthy. While these stories may be true, they do not represent the experiences of most people born into poverty—only about 4 percent of Americans born into lower-income households become high-income earners as adults.[10]

# OVERGENERALIZED PRINCIPLES

While general principles can apply to individual cases, the move from a general principle to a specific case can also introduce weaknesses in reasoning. **Overgeneralized principles** mistakenly attribute something generally true of a whole to any of its individual parts. Just because a principle applies in many cases does not mean it applies in *all* cases. For example, psychologists generally find that spending time socializing with others is good for people's mental health. This leads many people to believe that everyone needs an active social life to

**personal attack** discrediting claims, evidence, or reasoning based on irrelevant aspects of a source's personal qualities or background

**unrepresentative example** drawing conclusions from a specific case or set of cases that do not adequately characterize the overall group, category, or principle

**overgeneralized principle** mistakenly attributing something generally true of a whole to any of its individual parts

be mentally healthy. But studies also find that some people choose to be alone because they truly enjoy it, and for them solitude actually improves their mental health.[11]

## CONFUSING CORRELATION AND CAUSATION

A **correlation** is a co-relation: an association or relationship between two things. Things are correlated when they usually occur together in a way that seems unlikely to be random chance. **Causation** is a special type of correlation, where one thing leads to another. But just because two things occur together or one occurs after the other does not always mean that one is causing the other—this is **confusing correlation with causation**. For example, children born on the autism spectrum tend to start showing symptoms around twelve to eighteen months of age, about the same time when children receive vaccines for measles, mumps, and rubella. This co-occurrence of events has led the anti-vax movement to conclude that vaccines cause autism, despite overwhelming medical research to the contrary.[12]

## REVERSING EFFECTS

Sometimes a speaker understands a causal relationship accurately, but mistakenly assumes that an effect can be undone simply by removing its cause. This is called **reversing effects**: assuming that removing a cause will erase its effect. When an effect has already taken place, simply eliminating the cause is rarely enough to eliminate the consequences. It may be an essential first step, but often much more must be done. For example, once an area has been contaminated with toxic waste, simply stopping the dumping of additional waste will not make the land or water safe. That's why many communities affected by pollution advocate not only for removal of the cause but also for active cleanup of the waste and restoration of the land and water.

## RISK DISTORTIONS

When people consider the possibility of a negative event, they often misjudge how likely it is to occur. This misjudgment is called a **risk distortion** (see Figure 7.2). Researchers have identified several factors that distort how people perceive risk.[13] We overestimate the likelihood of a negative event when it is

**correlation**
an association or relationship between two things

**causation**
a special type of correlation, where one thing leads to another

**confusing correlation with causation**
assuming that one thing causes another when the two things occur around the same time

**reversing effects**
assuming that an effect can be undone simply by removing its cause

**risk distortion**
misjudging the likelihood of a negative event occurring

unfamiliar or human-created, when it is increasing or has frightening consequences, and when it is under other people's control or affects us personally. On the other hand, we *under*estimate the level of risk when it is familiar or naturally occurring, when the risk is decreasing or has less-alarming consequences, and when the risk is under our control or only affects other people. For example, although you are 73 times more likely to die in a car crash than a plane crash, people often assume that driving is safer than flying because driving feels familiar and under our control.[14]

| We **underestimate** the likelihood of risks that are: | We **overestimate** the likelihood of risks that are: |
|---|---|
| • Decreasing | • Increasing |
| • Familiar | • Novel |
| • Mild | • Grotesque |
| • Natural | • Human-created |
| • Affecting others | • Affecting us |
| • Within our control | • Controlled by others |
| • Equally shared | • Unequally distributed |

**FIGURE 7.2** Risk distortion includes both overestimating and underestimating the probability of an event.

## ✓ Critical Thinking Check

1. Why do using false authorities or personal attacks undermine the credibility of your evidence? How do these fallacies damage your credibility as a speaker?
2. How might unrepresentative examples and overgeneralized principles lead to stereotyping? Are all stereotypes based on errors in reasoning?

# Reasoning with Audiences

Presenting your audience with multiple types of evidence and providing sound reasoning based on that evidence will show them both why you believe your thesis and why they should as well. But audiences do not reason based on logic alone. Often, their reasoning is biased to support beliefs they already hold. **Confirmation bias** is our tendency to interpret new evidence in ways that support our existing beliefs. Confirmation bias leads people to defend their preconceived ideas rather than considering your evidence and reasoning with an open mind. Using reasoning to protect existing beliefs is called **motivated reasoning**.[15]

It pays to understand the motivations behind your audience's reasoning. Ultimately, your audience will be the judge of whether your evidence is compelling

**confirmation bias**
our tendency to interpret new evidence in ways that support our existing beliefs

**motivated reasoning**
using reasoning to protect your existing beliefs

enough to support your thesis. To reason effectively, you need to present your evidence in a way that appeals to your audience. Your evidence must not only be relevant to your thesis; it must also fit with your audience's experiences, self-perceptions, relationships, and values.

## FIT WITH YOUR THESIS

Does your audience understand how your evidence relates to your thesis? Even if you see the connection, that doesn't always mean your audience will. You may need to provide additional information or interpretation so that your reasoning is clear. You don't have to explicitly spell out every step in your reasoning—overexplaining can bore your audience or even insult their intelligence. Just make sure your audience makes the same connections you do. For example, if you argue that a state should legalize recreational marijuana and provide statistics about the state government's budget deficit, your audience may not immediately see the connection. But you could show them how other states that legalized recreational marijuana saw significant boosts in state revenue due to the taxes imposed on marijuana sales.

## FIT WITH AUDIENCE'S EXPERIENCE

Is the evidence you offer supported by the experiences of your audience members? People trust their direct experience. Even for people with extensive scientific training, personal experience drives behavior and belief more than new information, evidence, or research.[16] When you offer your audience a new perspective, demonstrate how their own experiences fit within this new worldview. If your reasoning challenges your audience's personal experience, you can reduce their resistance by referencing sources they trust. For example, if you're presenting on the health risks of smoking, some of your audience members may know someone who smoked regularly and yet was healthy into their nineties. Incorporating evidence that explains how unusual that is could help you account for their experiences in your presentation.

## FIT WITH AUDIENCE'S SELF-PERCEPTION

Does your evidence fit with your audience members' perceptions of themselves? Remember that audience members have attitudes about themselves that filter how they see the world. Does your evidence offer them a positive perception of

# Jamie Margolin's Climate Advocacy

Jamie Margolin is a youth leader, climate activist, and college student. In high school, she founded a climate advocacy group, Zero Hour, and has been speaking across the country ever since. Although her own understanding of climate change is based in science, Margolin knows that using scientific evidence is not likely to further change audiences' opinions or public policy. "The science has already convinced the people that it will," she explains. "People who are going to be convinced by being shown a carbon graphic have already been convinced."[17]

Instead, she focuses on providing evidence that addresses people's motivations and biases around climate change. She recommends "talking about how it's affecting people, talking about stories, talking about how it intersects with other issues people care about."[18] Those issues might include asthma, flooding, crop production, the economy, Indigenous rights, natural beauty, or any other issue affected by climate change. She calls this finding an "in" with the community.

She adapts her evidence and reasoning to fit her speaking situation, whether she is speaking to fellow activists, TEDx audiences, or politicians. At activist summits she emphasizes the diversity and global reach of climate activism, connecting it with movements for Indigenous rights, racial justice, LGBTQ+ rights, and economic justice.[19] When speaking at a TEDx event in South Carolina, she used evidence from the National Resources

At a 2018 rally in Seattle, Washington, Jamie Margolin spoke in support of additional action to prevent climate change. She said, "There's always been a sense that everything beautiful in this world is temporary for my generation."

Defense Council to document the impact of climate change on low-income communities and communities of color.[20] When speaking directly to politicians, she uses evidence like voter testimonies and polling statistics to show that their position on climate change may affect their reelection. She recommends that all public speakers remember "politics is personal."[21] All audiences—even elected officials—respond best to evidence that is personally meaningful to them.

You can find a video of Jamie Margolin's TEDxYouth presentation by doing a web search for: Jamie Margolin TEDxYouth. The video is approximately 9:00 in length.

themselves? If your evidence requires them to view themselves negatively, do you offer them a path to a more positive self-perception? Even if your reasoning is logical and your thesis is well supported by evidence, your audience is likely to reject your reasoning if they cannot reconcile it with their beliefs about themselves. For example, if your evidence indicates that a policy your audience supported in the past is discriminatory, they may feel accused of being racist or sexist. Depicting them as the heroes of the situation and praising their willingness to change policies can reduce the likelihood that they will defend the existing policy to protect their self-perception.

## FIT WITH AUDIENCE'S RELATIONSHIPS

Does your reasoning affirm your audience members' relationships? Audience members are more likely to accept your reasoning when it affirms relationships they consider important—such as family, religion, or political affiliation. On the other hand, reasoning that challenges someone's personal relationships, membership in a valued group, or role in broader society is often met with anger, dismissiveness, and rationalization.[22] If the evidence you provide might threaten their view of the social world, you may need to give audience members a way to reconcile your reasoning with the relationships they value. Or you might convince them that accepting your reasoning produces substantially more positive and promising relationships and social roles. For example, if you ask your audience to reduce their carbon footprint by limiting how often they fly, they might be worried it would keep them from spending time with family. You would need to suggest other kinds of air travel they could cut or other ways to sustain those relationships.

## FIT WITH AUDIENCE'S VALUES

Does the evidence you give resonate with the values of your audience members? Remember that each of us has different value priorities. Your reasoning is most convincing when it aligns with your audience's most important values. If audience members must change one of their values to accept your reasoning, you need to show them how that change serves another value that is even more important to them. For example, if you're arguing to increase social support programs for people experiencing poverty, you may find audience members who highly value self-reliance resistant to your reasoning. You might reach them either by providing evidence that the support programs lead to greater

## Pathways

To learn how you can anticipate the motivations behind your audience's reasoning, see **Chapter 5, Audiences and Publics**.

self-reliance among the people they help or by appealing to a value they consider more important than self-reliance.

As you adapt your reasoning to your audience, you may need to select different types of evidence or modify your arguments. You might choose a different story or tool for a demonstration or use a different source for your testimony. The speech creation process often requires a speaker to cycle back to previous steps as they learn more about their speaking situation. That might even include additional audience analysis, doing new research, or revising your thesis. Remember to let your presentation's purpose be your guide and don't be afraid to step back and rethink your approach when it will help you achieve that purpose.

**📋 TRY THIS**

To anticipate motivated reasoning and connect your arguments to your audience's concerns, see the **Building Bridges Worksheet**.

## ✓ Critical Thinking Check

1. Why do you think people interpret evidence to support their existing attitudes, values, and behaviors? How can understanding confirmation bias and motivated reasoning make you a more effective speaker?
2. What can you do if your evidence or reasoning challenges your audience's experiences, self-perceptions, relationships, or values? How might you change their views using other experiences, self-perceptions, relationships, or values that are important to them?

# Next Steps

Supporting your thesis with evidence and reasoning can broaden your audience's perspective by offering observations and ideas that they may not have encountered before. Because your evidence and reasoning help your audience see the world from your point of view, you can think of them as important tools for sharing your experiences, knowledge, values, and identities. Much more than just justifying your claims, evidence and reasoning provide ways to open other people's eyes, hearts, and minds.

You can use the Evidence Wishlist Worksheet and the Building Bridges Worksheet to help you identify the evidence and reasoning that will best fit your purpose, audience, standpoint, and context. These exercises will help you focus on the evidence and reasoning you need to help your audience understand and accept your thesis. Knowing what kinds of reasoning you will use and what kinds of evidence you need will streamline your research process, making finding sources and gathering information both faster and easier.

# Standpoint Reflection

- How does your standpoint as a speaker shape the evidence you present? How might your standpoint even become evidence for your thesis?

- Which types of evidence do you find the most compelling? Why? Could you use your preferred form of evidence as one of your strengths?

- What are some of the ways you might reason with an audience that has very different experiences and values than your own? How can you honor your own standpoint while also respecting your audience's self-perceptions and values?

- How can sharing your standpoint help you reason more effectively with others? Why might questioning someone's reasoning based on your standpoint be more powerful than expressing disagreement based on facts alone?

## Key Terms

# Resources for Evidence and Reasoning

##  "Try This" Exercises

Access the "Try This" exercises as directed by your instructor or online at
digital.wwnorton.com/chapterexercises-conpubspeak

- To identify what kinds of evidence you need to support your thesis, use the **Evidence Wishlist Worksheet**.

- To anticipate motivated reasoning and connect your arguments to your audience's concerns, see the **Building Bridges Worksheet**.

---

Want to practice these skills to prepare for your next speech?
Go to INQUIZITIVE to review and apply concepts from this chapter and get personalized feedback along the way.

Blair Imani

# 8 Research and Citation

Blair Imani is a social media influencer and public speaker who uses historical research to educate her audience about intersectional identities and social justice. In her Instagram reels, YouTube videos, and in-person speeches, she weaves her own experiences and expertise together with the experiences and expertise of others. In her short "Smarter in Seconds" videos, she includes evidence like clips from other content creators and citations of key experts. Her longer "Get Smarter" video presentations often include quotations from scholars, references to court cases, and interviews with people who have relevant firsthand experience. For example, her YouTube video "Get Smarter: What Is Intersectionality?" references research by Dr. Kimberlé Crenshaw and Dr. Jennifer Nash, connecting their insights to stories that Imani's grandmother told her about working as a Black woman in the 1940s.[1]

Imani's extensive research allows her to address complex and controversial issues, like the intersection between LGBTQ+ identity and religious faith. In her 2019 TED talk, "Queer and Muslim: Nothing to Reconcile," she documents the history of attitudes toward gender and sexuality in the Muslim world.[2] She quotes historians and religious scholars to demonstrate that discrimination against LGBTQ+ people has no basis in Muslim tradition or the Quran. Drawing from expert testimony and historical documents, Imani strengthens both her reasoning and her credibility. While she speaks from her own standpoint, Imani also uses research to reach beyond her personal experience, bringing other historical perspectives and expert voices into her presentations.

## LEARNING OBJECTIVES

**After completing this chapter, you will be able to**

- Develop a research plan to gather evidence for your thesis

- Use research tools including library catalogs, academic databases, news databases, web search engines, and interviews

- Evaluate the reliability of the sources you find

- Craft citations that enhance your credibility as a speaker

Blair Imani demonstrates the true power of research: combining your own voice with the voices of others. Conducting and presenting research shows that you understand both the limits of your own standpoint and the value of others' knowledge and experiences. Through research, you learn from other sources and expand your own perspective. When you bring those insights from other sources into your presentations, you show your audience that you do not speak alone— instead, you offer a whole chorus of voices speaking together.

# The Research Process

By drawing information and insights from other sources, research can both improve your reasoning and enhance your credibility as a speaker. **Research** is the systematic collection and analysis of information. It involves much more than a simple Google search or looking something up on Wikipedia. Being systematic means seeking reliable, accurate, and useful information that you can use as evidence for your thesis. The following tips can help you get started with the process of collecting information.

1. **START EARLY.** Remember that research is only one part of the total time you will need to prepare your presentation. Start your research as soon as you know the specific purpose of your speech to make sure you leave yourself enough time to prepare and practice before your presentation date.

2. **HAVE A PLAN.** In addition to knowing your specific purpose, knowing your thesis statement and the kinds of evidence and reasoning you need to support it can save you time and effort during the research process. Be sure to complete the Evidence Wishlist Worksheet in Chapter 7 so you know what you're looking for. Then you can develop a **research plan**: a map of the evidence you need and where to find it (see Table 8.1).

3. **TAKE NOTES.** Keep a record of all the evidence you find in one place, like a notebook or a file on your computer. Be sure to capture any direct quotations you will be using word for word so you don't have to look them up a second time.

4. **TRACK SOURCES.** In your notes, keep track of the source that each piece of evidence comes from. Writing down source citations as you go will save you time at the end. We'll give you more in-depth details on citing sources later in this chapter.

**research**
the systematic collection and analysis of information

**research plan**
a map of the evidence you need and where to find it

**SPECIFIC PURPOSE:** To persuade students on my campus to volunteer for Habitat for Humanity's Collegiate Challenge.

**THESIS STATEMENT:** Volunteer for Habitat for Humanity's Collegiate Challenge to build lasting spring break memories with your friends and the families you help.

| Principles to support thesis | Evidence for principles | Where to look for evidence |
|---|---|---|
| Definition and rules for the Collegiate Challenge | Expert testimony from Habitat organizers | Habitat's website? Interviews? |
| Concepts and theories about the long-term impacts of affordable housing | Statistics linking affordable housing to health, safety, and economic mobility | Books? Academic articles? News articles? Government agency reports? |

| Examples to support thesis | Evidence for examples | Where to look for evidence |
|---|---|---|
| Examples of college students volunteering with Habitat | Personal testimony from current or previous volunteers | News articles? Interviews? Own experience? |
| Examples of families helped by Habitat's Collegiate Challenge | Photo demonstrations of student volunteers with Habitat families | Habitat's website? Google image search? News articles? Own photo archive? |

| Analogies to support thesis | Evidence for analogies | Where to look for evidence |
|---|---|---|
| Comparison to other memorable spring break trips | Video demonstrations of student volunteers enjoying spring break with friends | Habitat's website? YouTube search? Own video archive? |
| Comparison to other college groups and teams traveling together | Personal testimony from college athletes about bonding on the road | Team website? Campus newspaper? Interviews? Own experience? |

**TABLE 8.1** A research plan combines your specific purpose, thesis statement, and evidence wishlist with ideas for places to look for each piece of evidence.

## Pathways

To learn how to select the best evidence for your speaking situation, see **Chapter 7, Evidence and Reasoning**.

**confirmation bias**
our tendency to interpret new evidence in ways that support our existing beliefs

**anchoring bias**
our tendency to rely too heavily on the first information we encounter

**search terms**
words or phrases you enter into a catalog, database, or search engine to locate sources of information

5. **STAY OPEN**. Research is a process of discovery, and you might change your focus as you learn more. If you discover an interesting example or a surprising statistic, don't hesitate to include it—even if it wasn't part of your original plan. Just like audiences, speakers can fall prey to **confirmation bias**: interpreting new information in ways that support their existing beliefs. Speakers also have to watch out for **anchoring bias**: the tendency to "anchor" their position by relying too heavily on the first information they encounter.[3] You can reduce these biases by actively seeking out information that challenges your current thinking. You can then weigh the evidence on different sides of the issue to reach a more informed conclusion.

# Gathering Information

When you have a research plan in place, you can target your search to find the information you need. **Search terms** are words or phrases you enter into a catalog, database, or search engine to locate sources of information. For example, if you were searching for scholarly articles discussing the limits on political contributions, you might look up the phrase *campaign finance reform* in an academic database. Good search terms are specific enough to exclude irrelevant search results, but not so specific that they exclude important information, sources, or perspectives.

If you are speaking on a topic connected to your standpoint and strengths, you probably already have an idea about the kinds of terms people use when discussing your topic. But remember that people writing from other standpoints or areas of expertise may use different words and expressions. You can modify your search terms or start new searches as you discover new terms. The following strategies can help you get the best results from your search:

- **USE KEYWORDS.** When we ask a person for information, we use full sentences, such as: "What percentage of Americans use the internet every day?" But databases and search engines often respond better to only the keywords: *percentage, Americans, internet,* and *every day.*

- **TRY SYNONYMS.** We often use different words or phrases to communicate the same meaning. For example, *internet* and *web* are often seen as interchangeable, as are *every day* and *daily.* Consider whether another word might return better results.

- **IDENTIFY TERMS OF ART.** A **term of art** is a word or phrase that has a specialized meaning in a particular field or profession. That could be a technical term like *domain name system* or a term that has a specific meaning for a given profession, such as *expert witness* in law. You can spot terms of art by looking for words and phrases that are repeated or unusual. In reference materials, like encyclopedias, wikis, or textbooks, terms of art are often boldface or hyperlinked.

- **SPECIFY KEY PHRASES.** A database may understand a term like *every day* as two words and search for the words independently. Placing the phrase in quotation marks—*"every day"*—tells the search tool to look only for the two words together in that order.

- **ADD CONNECTORS.** Different databases and search engines provide different ways to connect terms together, but most use three functions: *and* (include both terms), *or* (include either term), and *not* (exclude this term). For example, the search *percentage and Americans and internet and daily* finds results containing all the keywords listed. Using *daily or every day* would find results containing either word.

- **INCLUDE TRUNCATORS.** Sometimes a keyword has multiple endings that might all be relevant to your search. You can use a truncator, usually the asterisk (*) symbol, to include all possible endings. For example, *percent**

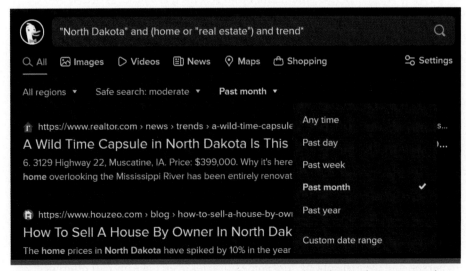

Combining terms, specifying phrases with quotation marks, and using search operators like a truncator (*) can make your searches more effective. You can also use tools like date limiters to ensure your information is recent.

College libraries and public libraries both have reference librarians on staff to assist people with their research.

would include results with the words *percent, percentage, percentile,* and their plurals. But truncating too far can include too many words, such as *perce*\** resulting in *perceive, perceptive,* and dozens of other words unrelated to percentages.

📋 **TRY THIS**

To refine your search terms and produce better results, see the **Search Targeting Worksheet**.

■ **LEARN AS YOU GO.** Remember that research is a process of discovery. The results of your early searches might introduce you to new terms and ideas that you want to look up. For example, if your exploratory search for *disability rights* turned up several results mentioning the Americans with Disabilities Act, you might want to make *Americans with Disabilities Act* your next search. You can narrow, refine, and improve your search terms as you learn more about your topic.

If you need help identifying the right search terms—or you just want to make your research faster, easier, and better quality overall—contact a librarian. Most college and public libraries have professional reference librarians available to help with your research. Almost all libraries offer research assistance in person and over the phone, and some libraries even have on-call reference librarians available via live online chat or email. When you consult a librarian, be sure to share your research plan with them so they know what you're looking for. Librarians have special training in information systems and can help you navigate library catalogs, academic databases, news databases, and web search engines—and even help you identify promising interviewees.

## LIBRARY CATALOGS

A library catalog is a good resource for books, which often provide a deeper and richer explanation of a topic than shorter articles. When you're searching for historical examples or theoretical principles, a library catalog is a great place to start. For example, if you're giving an informative speech about how massive objects warp the fabric of space-time, you might look for guidebooks explaining Einstein's theory of general relativity. Or if you're giving a connective speech honoring the recipient of the Ida B. Wells Award, you might search for biographies describing Wells's achievements. You can begin your library catalog search either on their website or in the library building itself.

1. **SEARCH THE CATALOG.** Every library keeps a searchable record of all the publications they offer, including both print and electronic books. A library's catalog is usually searchable by author, subject, and keyword. Results can also be refined by date, language, format, and other variables.

2. **EXPLORE SUBJECTS.** If you look at the entry for a specific publication, you will find its title, author, publication information, and a list of subjects. You can use the list of subjects to help you find similar entries. In many library catalogs, those subjects are hot-linked so you can click on them to see books and other materials on the same subject.

3. **LOCATE SOURCES.** Each publication will be listed either as available online with a link or available in print with a call number. The call number directs you to a specific shelf where a print copy of the book is kept in the library. Your library will have maps of where different call numbers are located, but if you need help or have questions, just ask a librarian.

4. **SAVE KEY SECTIONS.** Copy important passages from print

**LEARN MORE**

To learn more about using library catalogs, see the **Library Catalogs Video**.

| Title | Ellis Island nation: immigration policy and American identity in the twentieth century |
|---|---|
| Creator | Fleegler, Robert L. > |
| Subject | Immigrants -- United States -- History -- 20th century > |
| | Acculturation -- United States -- History -- 20th century > |
| | Multiculturalism -- United States -- History -- 20th century > |
| | Acculturation > |
| | Emigration and immigration > |
| | Emigration and immigration -- Government policy > |

This library catalog entry shows the book title and author's name, as well as a list of six subjects, each hot-linked to lists of other books on that subject.

sources, either by hand, using a photocopier, or by taking a picture with your smartphone. Passages from electronic publications can often be copied and pasted directly into a text file, but you can use screenshots if the copy/paste function has been disabled. Remember to note where each piece of information comes from so you don't have to retrace your steps.

## ACADEMIC DATABASES

**academic journals**
periodicals that publish research by scholars, scientists, and researchers in a specialized field of study

Academic databases allow you to search for scholarly research published in academic journals. **Academic journals** are periodicals that publish research by scholars, scientists, and researchers in a specialized field of study. They make excellent sources for expert testimony and statistical evidence. For example, if you're giving a persuasive speech about the cancer risks of vaping, you might use academic databases to find statistics about the increasing rates of vaping among young people and quotations from researchers about the carcinogens found in vaping fluid. While academic databases offer complex information, the process of finding scholarly sources is surprisingly simple:

1. **GET ACCESS.** To use an academic database, you will need to log in through a library with a subscription to the database. You can usually log in through your college or public library's website.

2. **CHOOSE A DATABASE.** Academic databases like Academic Search Complete, JSTOR, Project Muse, and Web of Science will search across multiple subjects and fields of study. Many academic disciplines also have field-specific databases for their research, like Communication & Mass Media Complete for communication or PsycINFO for psychology. When you want information from a specific field of study, look on your library's website for a list of academic databases organized by subject, or ask your reference librarian to help you find the right database.

3. **LOCATE ARTICLES.** Most academic databases provide online access to the full text of scholarly journal articles. But some databases only provide abstracts that summarize each article. In that case, you can locate the full article by looking up the journal's name and issue number in a library catalog search.

4. **SAVE KEY ARTICLES.** Most academic databases allow you to download copies of articles and abstracts as PDF files. You can use PDF markup tools

▶ LEARN MORE

To learn more about how to use academic databases, see the **Academic Databases Video Series**.

to highlight important passages or copy/paste those passages directly into a text file. If you are working with the print version of an article, you might choose to photocopy or photograph only the pages that are most relevant to your presentation—along with the title page containing citation information.

## NEWS DATABASES

Libraries can also give you access to news databases, which include both historical and current newspapers, news magazines, and radio and television news transcripts. These news publications often report statistics and quotations of others' testimony and may occasionally provide firsthand accounts of an event.

1. **GET ACCESS**. As with academic databases, to access news databases you will need to log in through a college or public library's website. As always, ask a librarian if you need assistance.

2. **CHOOSE A DATABASE**. Three common news databases provided by libraries are Nexis Uni, NewsBank, and ProQuest News. There are also databases that provide access to reports from specific major newspapers—such as the *Boston Globe, Chicago Tribune, Los Angeles Times*, and *Washington Post*—if you are looking for more targeted or local coverage.

3. **SEARCH BY DATE**. In addition to letting you search by keyword, news databases also often allow you to sort your results by date of publication, which can help you find the most recent information. News databases also allow you to limit your search to a specific range of dates, enabling you to focus on coverage of a specific event or time period.

4. **SAVE KEY REPORTS**. Most news databases allow you to select the news stories you wish to save and then download them in a text file. Using the search function in the text file can make it easy to locate the information you need. You can then use the highlight tools to mark key passages or copy/paste relevant sections into a separate document.

## WEB SEARCH ENGINES

While the academic and news databases provided by libraries tend to focus on more widely respected, mainstream, and professional sources of information, the broader internet offers a much more diverse range of perspectives—and a

**LEARN MORE**

To learn more about using news databases, see the **News Databases Video Series**.

much wider range of quality and accuracy. While web research can be an excellent source of personal testimony and audiovisual evidence, your internet search results will likely include claims made by people without any expertise, experience, or knowledge about your topic.

1. **BEWARE OF FILTER BUBBLES.** Remember, many web search engines—like Google—use your past search history, browsing behavior, and social media activity to filter the information they present to you. You can avoid filter bubbles by using a search engine that does not track your online behavior—like DuckDuckGo or Brave Search.

2. **RECOGNIZE PSEUDO-ACADEMIC SOURCES.** Google has long provided a special search engine for scholarly publications and papers, called Google Scholar. Unfortunately, it now contains many sources that are not of sufficient quality to be included in academic databases: articles from "predatory" academic journals that will publish anything for a fee, as well as writings that have not been published in any journal or book.[4]

3. **SPOT SPOOFED SOURCES.** Well-known people and organizations are often spoofed. **Spoofing** is disguising a website, email, social media post, or other communication to make it look like it comes from someone other than the actual source. Watch out for unusual suffixes to common domain names—like *abcnews.com.co*—or slightly misspelled account names—like @KamalaHaris. Spoofed sites and accounts usually have fewer posts and shorter post histories than legitimate ones.

4. **AVOID ANONYMOUS SOURCES.** In some cases, anonymity may indicate that a source doesn't want their personal credibility tied to the statements they are making. Even if they have nothing to hide, anonymous posts and comments make a source's standpoint and credentials impossible to verify.

**spoofing**
disguising the actual source of a website, email, social media post, or other communication

## INFORMATIONAL INTERVIEWS

Interviews are especially helpful for gathering testimony from people with special expertise or firsthand experience with your topic. For example, if you were preparing a speech on the living conditions in American prisons, you might interview someone who has lived in a prison to hear their stories. You might also interview someone who studies American prisons, who works with a prison reform advocacy group, or who works as a prison guard. Each would provide a different perspective on the topic and different kinds of testimony you could incorporate into your presentation.

1. **CHOOSE AN INTERVIEWEE.** A quick web search can help you find people who have expertise and experience with your topic. For example, a search for *professor who studies prison conditions* turned up references to multiple professors around the country. You can also look for organizations, clubs, or advocacy groups that might have people with the experience you seek. And don't forget your own personal networks as a way to find interviewees. Friends—and friends of friends—are usually more willing to talk with you, but be aware that their social connection to you might make them uncomfortable sharing sensitive information.

2. **REQUEST THE INTERVIEW.** Email is often the best way to request an interview. In your request, briefly introduce yourself to your prospective interviewee, explain the topic and purpose of your interview, and explain why you chose them to interview. Let them know when you hope to complete the interview, and give them different format options for answering your questions—via email, phone, videoconference, or in person. Thank them for considering your request and ask them to recommend an alternative interviewee if they are not available.

3. **CONFIRM THE MEETING.** Send a follow-up email confirming the format and date with your interviewee and provide any needed phone numbers or videoconference links. If you plan to record the interview, be sure the interviewee gives you permission to record when you confirm the interview details.

4. **PREPARE YOUR QUESTIONS.** Plan to begin your interview with a "warm-up" question or two about your interviewee and their interests. For example, "How did you get interested in prisoners' rights?" or "How long have you been working with the Sentencing Project?" This will help them get more comfortable and build some rapport before you dive into your more targeted

**Pathways**

To learn more techniques for effective interviewing, see the informal conversations section of **Chapter 5, Audiences and Publics**.

Informational interviews with people who have personal experience or specialized expertise related to your topic can be an excellent source of testimonial evidence.

questions. When writing your questions, keep them focused on your purpose and topic, as well as the experiences or knowledge of your interviewee. Use your evidence wishlist to help you formulate questions.

5. **RESPECT YOUR INTERVIEWEE.** Be sure to thank your interviewee at the start and end of the interview. Stick to the day, time, duration, and format agreed upon in advance, and choose your attire and setting to communicate respect. Listen actively, and ask follow-up questions when more detail would help you understand your interviewee's perspective.

6. **KEEP A RECORD.** Regardless of whether you are recording, take notes during the interview—it's always possible the recording will fail or be lost. Write down quotations and key details while you listen. If you do record your interview, you can add details and check quotations afterward.

## Pathways

To learn more about how to listen actively, see **Chapter 4, Listening and Responding**.

## ✓ Critical Thinking Check

1. How does taking the time to develop a research plan save you time in the end? How does starting with a research plan help you even if you end up changing direction as you learn more about your topic?

2. How do you know which research tools—library catalogs, academic databases, news databases, web search engines, or interviews—will best help you find the information you're looking for? What are the advantages and disadvantages of each one?

# Evaluating the Reliability of Information

**reliability**
the consistency of information across multiple sources

The quality of information can vary greatly from one source to the next, so it's important to evaluate the reliability of the information you find. **Reliability** is the consistency of information across multiple sources. You can demonstrate reliability by showing consistency between your source and other sources: information is more likely to be accurate when multiple sources can confirm it.

Some sources even build reliability into their publication process. Reputable news outlets have fact-checkers and editors who review submissions before publication. Reputable academic journals and university book publishers use scholarly peer review, where the editor asks two to three experts in that subject to read submissions and assess whether they merit publication. This is why your instructor might ask you to include evidence from scholarly sources. Fact-checkers, peer review, and editorial oversight all help establish consistency and validate a source's reliability.

But you can—and should—do your own fact-checking. Verifying the reliability of the information you find can help you avoid confirmation bias and anchoring bias in your own thinking and recognize any biases that your sources might have. You can test the reliability of information and evaluate its sources using the **SIFT method**: SIFT stands for stop, investigate the source, find better coverage, and trace to original context.[5]

# 1 Stop

When you first encounter information, stop and consider the source. Are you familiar with this source? Does this source use fact-checkers, peer review, or editorial oversight? If the answer to either question is no—or if you are not sure—then the source calls for a higher level of scrutiny. The more important or controversial the information, the more thoroughly you will want to check its reliability. For less important or controversial claims, a briefer check of reliability may be enough.

# 2 Investigate the Source

Do a web search about the source to check for bias. **Bias** is an attitude or motive that creates an unfair or unjustified preference—for example, a news channel might pander to viewers with a particular political leaning or a researcher might accept funding from a corporation. You can look up the source on Wikipedia to see if there is a description of its background and biases. You can also use online tools like Ad Fontes or AllSides to check the reliability and political biases of news outlets and other media sources. In just a couple minutes, you can get a sense of a source's reliability and what agendas or interests they might promote. If you discover any biases that might skew the information your source provides, then it's time to start looking for other sources.

# 3 Find Better Coverage

Now that you know potential biases of the source, you can turn to checking the accuracy of its information. Look for how other sources, especially highly reputable sources, report the same information. By comparing information across multiple sources, you can establish a consensus to verify the accuracy of your

**SIFT method**
a four-step process for testing the reliability of information: stop, investigate the source, find better coverage, and trace to original context

**bias**
an attitude or motive that creates an unfair or unjustified preference

# Spotting Fake News

While some politicians will label any story they don't like as "fake news," the term properly refers to stories and reports that are made up, fabricated, or severely distorted by the reporters or writers. Fake news has been a problem for as long as there have been news sources, and it posed a significant problem during the founding of the United States in the late 1700s.[6] But the 2016 presidential election showed the unique power of the internet for creating and distributing fake news. An extensive study of online behavior conducted by three political scientists found that more than 44 percent of Americans over the age of eighteen visited an article on an untrustworthy website containing fake news in the weeks before the 2016 election—and only 3 percent of people who read fake news checked the facts of those stories.[7]

Perhaps the most infamous creator of fake news in 2016 was Paul Horner, a writer and comedian who had created fake versions of the ABC News, CNN, CBS News, and NBC News websites using the ".com.co" domain suffix. During the 2016 election, the stories Horner made up frequently appeared in Google's top search results and were widely distributed on blogs and social media. Even major political figures and mainstream news outlets redistributed the stories.[8] He made up stories about protestors being paid actors, President Obama banning assault weapons, and Amish Americans promising to vote for Trump.[9] Although notable, Horner was only one of many hucksters spreading fake news during the 2016 election.[10]

After the 2016 election and during the COVID-19 pandemic, many people called for a crackdown on fake news, especially its distribution on social media sites like Facebook and Twitter. While much has been done to limit the distribution of verifiably false information and fake news sites, the best solution is for everyone not to take the news they see at face value, especially on social media.

evidence. Remember to check the potential biases of each new source you find. A collection of unbiased sources all reporting the same information provides a good basis for believing the information is reliable.

**primary source**
a source with firsthand knowledge of the information and interpretations they share

## 4 Trace to Original Context

If you've ever played the "telephone game"—where a chain of people pass a message along from one person to the next—you know how information can get distorted as it moves from one source to another. So, try to locate the primary source of any information that you find. A **primary source** has firsthand knowl-

The InfoWars website and show are classified as fake news sources by experts in media and fact-checking.[11] The site and its creator, Alex Jones, are infamous for making false claims, like calling the Sandy Hook school shooting a hoax. Jones's attorney defended these factually incorrect statements by claiming that Jones is just a "performance artist" who is "playing a character."[12]

If readers had used the SIFT method of checking information, they would have recognized Horner's stories as fabrications. Stopping, investigating the source, finding better coverage, and tracing claims to their original context is the best way to prevent fake news stories from spreading.

edge of the information and interpretations they share. Examples of primary sources include an eyewitness recounting what they saw, a researcher reporting the results of a study they conducted themselves, and a photograph or historical document that provides evidence for your claim. A **secondary source** reports the knowledge, experiences, or statements made by others. Secondary sources include a reporter recounting an event witnessed by others, a journalist describing the results of scientific study, and a scholar quoting a journal article. Whenever you can, follow secondary sources of information back to the primary source. For example, if you read a news report about a scientific study, track

**secondary source**
a source that reports the knowledge, experiences, or statements of others

When someone questions or challenges a claim that you've made, letting them know the source of your information can bolster your credibility:

1. **ACKNOWLEDGE THE DISAGREEMENT.** For example: "It sounds like you're not sold on the idea that..." or "I can see that...is a sticking point for you."

2. **OFFER TO SHARE MORE INFORMATION ABOUT YOUR SOURCE.** For example: "Let me give you a little more background to explain where I'm coming from" or "Let me tell you a little more about where I got my information."

3. **GIVE RELEVANT DETAILS EMPHASIZING THE CREDIBILITY OF YOUR SOURCE.** For example: "There's a book called *Gender and Our Brains* by a neuro-biologist at Aston University. She explains that..." or "I recently saw *Myanmar Diaries*, a documentary that won the Amnesty International Film Award. It showed how..."

down the original research publication. Locating the original source can give you a more complete, accurate, and nuanced understanding of the information you find.

## ✓ Critical Thinking Check

1. Why is it important to test the reliability of the information you discover? How might sharing false or biased information create problems for you as a speaker?

2. Why do you think fake news has become increasingly common? How can you tell when a news story contains misinformation?

# Citing Sources

While the sources you select can improve the reliability of your information, the way you cite your sources can enhance your credibility with your audience. A **citation** is a reference to the source of your evidence. When you cite a source, your credibility depends on you representing that source accurately and fairly. If your audience discovers that you misrepresented the views of a source or misstated the facts, you will lose their trust. Misrepresenting a source can cast doubt

**citation**
a reference to the
source of your evidence

over all the information you presented and damage any connection you built with your audience.

Plagiarism can have even more devastating effects on a speaker's credibility. **Plagiarism** is the act of representing someone else's work as your own, either through direct copying or failing to provide a citation. Speakers who plagiarize deny their own standpoint and present a false standpoint to their audience. It is a theft not just of others' work, but of their voices—and it is a lost opportunity to share your own voice. Plagiarizing destroys your credibility and causes you to miss out on the enormous benefits of source citation for enhancing your contribution and building your identification with your audience. To avoid plagiarism and boost your credibility, include verbal source citations in your presentations and formal source citations in any written materials, such as handouts or slides.

**plagiarism**
representing someone else's work as your own

## VERBAL CITATIONS

Every verbal citation is a strategic opportunity to build credibility: to show your audience that both you and your sources have the relevant experience, knowledge, values, and identities to speak on a particular topic. Unlike formal source citations, which follow precise formats, verbal source citations should always be guided by one question: What do you need to tell your audience to help them see the credibility of your source? The following list contains key elements you might include in a verbal source citation, and how they can help establish the credibility of your source:

- **AUTHOR'S NAME.** This is the most common element to cite. It is most helpful when the person is immediately known by your audience, and when they have a title, degree, position, or personal experience relevant to your purpose. For example: "As Dr. Martin Luther King Jr. once said..." or "President Joe Biden announced..."

- **AUTHOR'S CREDENTIALS.** If you mention the author's name and they are not recognizable to your audience, then you need to provide their credentials to demonstrate their experience and expertise. Their credentials may be a degree, title, or position, but credentials can also come from personal experience, group membership, accomplishments, or an endorsement from someone the audience already knows and respects. For example: "According to Nobel

**TRY THIS**

To craft verbal source citations that enhance your credibility as a speaker, see the **Source Credibility Checklist**.

# Jane McGonigal Shows Gaming Helps You Live Longer

Jane McGonigal is a game designer who wants everyone to play more games. In her 2012 TED talk, she used quality source citations to convince her audience that playing games will help them live longer and happier lives.[13] She uses verbal source citations effectively and efficiently, providing just enough detail to lend credibility to her evidence without sounding awkward or unnecessary:

- "A recent study from Brigham Young University's School of Family Life reported that..."

- "Groundbreaking clinical trials recently conducted at East Carolina University showed that..."

- "Stanford University has been doing research for five years now to document how..."

Notice how each verbal citation provides key details that communicate the credibility of her evidence. In the first, she tells us the specific school of Brigham Young that did the research. In the second, she references "groundbreaking clinical trials." And in the third, she tells us the research has been going on "for five years." In all three cases, she gives us a sense of the timeliness of the information: "a recent study," "recently conducted," and "now." These small details make the citations and the information they support more compelling to her audience.

She even combines one verbal citation with a visual aid that reinforces the citation. Early in her presentation she says, "Hospice workers, the Peace Prize winner Tawakkol Karman..." or "American civil rights activist Fannie Lou Hamer explained..."

- **NAME OF PUBLICATION OR ORGANIZATION.** If the news outlet, academic journal, corporation, university, or government office that shared the information is well known and well respected by your audience, then mentioning it can enhance their perception of the source's credibility. For example: "The *Washington Post* reports that..." or "The NAACP released a statement recommending..."

- **CREDENTIALS OF PUBLICATION OR ORGANIZATION.** If you are relying on a less well-known publication or organization for the credibility

people who take care of us at the end of our lives, recently issued a report on the most frequently expressed regrets people say when they are literally on their death beds." At that moment she shows a screenshot of a headline from a major British newspaper, *The Guardian*, describing that report. She uses this combination only once, in her introduction, when she lays the foundation both for her argument and her own credibility. It would have been distracting to do this for every citation, but she chose a compelling and effective moment early on to add visual emphasis to her source.

To watch her TED talk, do a web search for: TED game extra life McGonigal. The video is approximately 19:30 in length.

Jane McGonigal combines her own personal story with extensive citations to scientific research on happiness, trauma, and gaming. After telling the story of her own traumatic brain injury, she introduces the scientific research on post-traumatic growth and explains how gaming can help make us stronger and happier (10:35).

of your source, include a brief description that demonstrates the source's contribution to your purpose and connection to your audience. For example: "According to Alight, a family of organizations that provides shelter, clean water, and health care to over 3.5 million refugees each year..."

- **DATE OF PUBLICATION.** While not always necessary in verbal citations, mentioning the date can help your audience see that the information is current or relevant to a particular historical moment. For example: "A 2022 study from Oxford University shows..." or "As you can see in this photograph from 1918..."

- **SOURCE'S SOURCE.** A verbal citation can be elevated by including a brief description of how your source reached their conclusions. Firsthand

## Pathways

To review the techniques for building credibility with audiences, see **Chapter 3, Ethics and Credibility**.

observation, key interviews, and archived documents can improve the credibility of news reports. Noteworthy methods, multiyear or cross-cultural data, and teams of experts can make academic studies and government reports more credible. For example: "In a decade-long study of over five thousand people across fourteen countries, an international team of researchers found..."

## FORMAL CITATIONS

While verbal citations show your source's credibility, formal citations provide details that allow others to locate the sources you cite. Formal citations are written records of the sources you reference, usually found at the end of a document in a section entitled "Works Cited" or "Bibliography." While you would never include a formal citation when speaking, most audiences expect formal citations in written material.

| Source | Citation | |
|---|---|---|
| **Book** | APA | Oluo, I. (2019). *So you want to talk about race*. Seal Press. |
| | MLA | Oluo, Ijeoma. *So You Want to Talk about Race*. Seal Press, 2019. |
| **Chapter in an edited book** | APA | Calafell, B. M. (2012). Love, loss, and immigration: Performative reverberations between a great-grandmother and a great-granddaughter. In D. R. DeChaine (Ed.), *Border rhetorics: Citizenship and identity on the US-Mexico frontier* (pp. 151–162). University of Alabama Press. |
| | MLA | Calafell, Bernadette Marie. "Love, Loss, and Immigration: Performative Reverberations between a Great-Grandmother and a Great-Granddaughter." *Border Rhetorics: Citizenship and Identity on the US-Mexico Frontier*, edited by D. Robert DeChaine, University of Alabama Press, 2012, pp. 151–162. |
| **Journal article** | APA | Waymer, D. (2020). Addressing disciplinary whiteness and racial justice advocacy in Communication Education. *Communication Education, 70*(1), 114–116. https://doi.org/10.1080/03634523.2020.1811362. |
| | MLA | Waymer, Damion. "Addressing Disciplinary Whiteness and Racial Justice Advocacy in Communication Education." *Communication Education*, vol. 70, no. 1, 2020, pp. 114–116., https://doi.org/10.1080/03634523.2020.1811362. |
| **Print magazine article** | APA | Carlson, D. L. (2007, May/June). Pledging allegiance: The politics of patriotism in America's schools. *Teacher Magazine, 18*(6), 52–53. |
| | MLA | Carlson, David Lee. "Pledging Allegiance: The Politics of Patriotism in America's Schools." *Teacher Magazine*, 2007, pp. 52–53. |

**TABLE 8.2** This list provides sample APA and MLA citations for the most common types of sources.

| Source | Citation | |
| --- | --- | --- |
| **Online magazine article** | APA | Burleigh, N. (2019, May 1). Mexican border brisis: How volunteers, church groups and NGOs stepped up to help thousands of migrants. *Newsweek*. Retrieved December 13, 2021, from https://www.newsweek.com/2019/05/10 /mexican-border-crisis-volunteers-church-groups-help-thousands-migrants -1409043.html. |
| | MLA | Burleigh, Nina. "Mexican Border Crisis: How Volunteers, Church Groups and NGOs Stepped Up to Help Thousands of Migrants." *Newsweek*, 1 May 2019, https://www.newsweek.com/2019/05/10/mexican-border-crisis-volunteers -church-groups-help-thousands-migrants-1409043.html. Accessed 13 Dec. 2021. |
| **Print newspaper article** | APA | Lang, M. J., Moyer, J. W., & Tiku, N. (2020, March 29). For homeless, a rising risk. *The Washington Post*, pp. C1, C6. |
| | MLA | Lang, Marissa J, et al. "For Homeless, a Rising Risk." *The Washington Post*, 29 Mar. 2020, pp. C1–C6. |
| **Online newspaper article** | APA | Myers, J. (2021, September 27). California's universal voting by mail becomes permanent. *Los Angeles Times*. Retrieved December 13, 2021, from https:// www.latimes.com/california/story/2021-09-27/california-universal-voting-by -mail-becomes-permanent. |
| | MLA | Myers, John. "California's Universal Voting by Mail Becomes Permanent." *Los Angeles Times*, 27 Sept. 2021, https://www.latimes.com/california/story/2021 -09-27/california-universal-voting-by-mail-becomes-permanent. Accessed 13 Dec. 2021. |
| **Website** | APA | Newport, F. (2018, May 22). *In U.S., estimate of LGBT population rises to 4.5%*. Gallup.com. Retrieved December 13, 2021, from https://news.gallup.com/poll /234863/estimate-lgbt-population-rises.aspx. |
| | MLA | Newport, Frank. "In U.S., Estimate of LGBT Population Rises to 4.5%." *Gallup.com*, Gallup, 22 May 2018, https://news.gallup.com/poll/234863 /estimate-lgbt-population-rises.aspx. |
| **Presentation/ lecture** | APA | Akyol, M. (2018, February 8). *Islam and freedom of expression. Rudolph C. Barnes Sr. Symposium*. Columbia, SC. |
| | MLA | Akyol, Mustafa. "Islam and Freedom of Expression." Rudolph C. Barnes Sr. Symposium. 8 Feb. 2018, Columbia, SC. |
| **Online video** | APA | Imani, B. (2019). *Queer & Muslim: Nothing to reconcile | Blair Imani | TEDxBoulder. YouTube*. Retrieved December 13, 2021, from https://www .youtube.com/watch?v=8IhaGUlmO_k. |
| | MLA | Imani, Blair. *Queer & Muslim: Nothing to Reconcile | Blair Imani | TEDxBoulder. YouTube*, 9 July 2019, https://www.youtube.com/watch?v= 8IhaGUlmO_k. Accessed 13 Dec. 2021. |
| **Personal interview** | APA | Ran, K. (2021, October 25). Personal interview. |
| | MLA | Ran, Karan. Personal interview. 25 Oct. 2021. |

## Pathways

To learn how to credit the media you use in your presentation, such as pictures or videos, see **Chapter 13, Presentation Aids and Slides**.

Failing to include formal citations in written material raises questions about your credibility as a speaker. Are the sources you cited made up or misrepresented? Did you plagiarize your sources? Did you just forget to include them? You can maintain your credibility by including formal citations in all written materials, including handouts, outlines, and slides.

Because formal citations serve a different purpose than verbal citations, they also take a different form. There are dozens of different formats for formal citations, but two of the most common are produced by the Modern Language Association and the American Psychological Association. Either format will provide your audience all the information they need to locate your original source. Both have precise guidelines for how you should format different sources (see Table 8.2).

## ✓ Critical Thinking Check

1. How do source citations improve your credibility as a speaker? How might forgetting to cite your sources damage your credibility?
2. What are the differences between verbal source citations and formal written citations? What purpose does each type of citation serve? When would you use a verbal citation? When would you use a formal citation? When do you need both?

## Next Steps

Research is an excellent way to enrich your own understanding with the experience and knowledge of others. It verifies your reasoning by comparing and combining your own observations and conclusions with the observations and conclusions of other sources with other standpoints and strengths. Research and citation can strengthen your voice with a community of other voices.

To learn more about common online research tools, check out the Library Catalogs Video, the Academic Databases Video Series, and the News Databases Video Series. The Search Targeting Worksheet will help you narrow your searches as you use these tools, and the Source Credibility Checklist will ensure you maximize the impact of the research you cite in your presentations. When you've finished your research, you might be surprised to realize that you've already prepared a significant portion of your presentation. You'll have all the basic building blocks of your speech, and you'll be ready to start putting them together. Before you know it, your research will give you everything you need to start organizing and outlining your presentation.

# Standpoint Reflection

- What are some places where you already use information-gathering skills like taking notes and using search terms? How might you translate those existing strengths and skills into researching academic databases and library catalogs?

- How is evaluating the reliability of a source the same as or different than establishing your credibility as a speaker? How does the credibility of your sources affect your own credibility?

- Why does plagiarism have such negative effects on your credibility as a speaker? How does plagiarism affect your ability to speak from your own standpoint?

- How might your standpoint and speaking situation change the information you include in your verbal source citations? Why don't your standpoint and speaking situation change the information included in formal source citations?

## Key Terms

academic journals, p. 162

anchoring bias, p. 158

bias, p. 167

citation, p. 170

confirmation bias, p. 158

plagiarism, p. 171

primary source, p. 168

reliability, p. 166

research, p. 156

research plan, p. 156

search terms, p. 158

secondary source, p. 169

SIFT method, p. 167

spoofing, p. 164

term of art, p. 159

# Resources for Research and Citation

## 📋 "Try This" Exercises

Access the "Try This" exercises as directed by your instructor or online at digital.wwnorton.com/chapterexercises-conpubspeak

- To refine your search terms to produce better results, see the **Search Targeting Worksheet**.

- To craft verbal source citations that enhance your credibility as a speaker, see the **Source Credibility Checklist**.

## 🎞 "Learn More" Tutorials

Access the "Learn More" tutorials as directed by your instructor or online at digital.wwnorton.com/videos-conpubspeak

- To learn more about using library catalogs, see the **Library Catalogs Video**.

- To learn more about how to use academic databases, see the **Academic Databases Video Series**.

- To learn more about using news databases, see the **News Databases Video Series**.

---

Want to practice these skills to prepare for your next speech? Go to **INQUIZITIVE** to review and apply concepts from this chapter and get personalized feedback along the way.

Thandiwe Abdullah

# 9 Organization and Outlining

As a founder of the Black Lives Matter Youth Vanguard, Thandiwe Abdullah says her biggest goal is "to help young people understand that the world we know right now is not something we have to just sit back and accept."[1] She has used her voice to rally for police reform, gun control, and an end to random police searches in schools. On April 20, 2018, she spoke in Santa Monica, California, as part of the National School Walkout protests for the prevention of mass shootings.

In her four-minute presentation, Abdullah uses effective organization to make her speech memorable and keep her audience engaged. She begins by introducing herself and calling on the audience to participate: "Be involved...answer me."[2] She then states her speech's thesis: "It's important when we talk about gun control that we uplift all the Black bodies that continue to be gunned down in streets and targeted in our schools."[3]

She then divides her speech into three main points. First, she shows that many innocent young Black people—like Stephon Clark, Aiyana Jones, Tamir Rice, Trayvon Martin, and Anthony Weber— have been killed by police and parapolice shootings. Second, she describes how police in schools criminalize and target Black students, while failing to make schools safe from gun violence. Third, she emphasizes the importance of young Black voices in the movement against gun violence and police brutality, providing examples of Black youth activism from 1963 to today.

Abdullah concludes by repeating the phrase "When we say we want gun control..." four times to emphasize that gun control advocacy shouldn't become a justification for targeting Black youth. By the end of the speech, you can hear her audience cheering and chanting "Black Lives Matter." It's no wonder that *Time* magazine named her one of the 25 Most Influential Teens of 2018.[4]

## LEARNING OBJECTIVES

**After completing this chapter, you will be able to**

- Identify main points and subpoints that support your thesis

- Choose between multiple techniques for organizing your material

- Guide your audience with clear signposts, introductions, and conclusions

- Craft detailed outlines that help you prepare and deliver your presentations

Thandiwe Abdullah shows how effective organization can help people hear your voice loud and clear. A compelling introduction gets your audience interested and invested in your speech. A clear organizational pattern amplifies each of the main points you're making by grouping similar kinds of evidence and reasoning together. A strong conclusion anchors those points in your audience's memory and reinforces the most important idea, action, or emotion you want them to take away from your presentation. Organizing and outlining your speech is anything but boring: it's the key to getting your point across and keeping your audience engaged.

# Identifying Your Main Points and Subpoints

Organizing your presentation begins with the information you have gathered to support your thesis. This includes both the reasoning—principles, examples, and analogies—and the evidence—demonstrations, testimony, and statistics—you have collected during your research. When you've finished researching your topic, the following steps can help you organize your ideas:

1. **GATHER YOUR EVIDENCE AND REASONING.** Have your research notes handy, along with any other notes you've made brainstorming or preparing your presentation so far.

2. **SORT YOUR EVIDENCE AND REASONING INTO GROUPS.** Look for patterns in the information you've collected. Does this statistic fit with that expert's testimony? Does this photograph demonstrate that principle? Group similar types of information together. For instance, Thandiwe Abdullah presented multiple examples of unjust police shootings together in one group and several examples of Black youth activists in another group.

3. **IDENTIFY YOUR MAIN POINTS.** Your main points come from the groupings of evidence and reasoning you have created. **Main points** are the key ideas that support your thesis statement. For instance, Abdullah grouped examples of Black youth activists together to show that young Black people have made important contributions to the movement against gun violence and police brutality. This main point supported her overall

**main points**
the key ideas that support your thesis statement

thesis that conversations about gun violence must reckon with police brutality against Black Americans.

4. **LIST YOUR SUBPOINTS.** While the groups you create become your main points, the individual pieces of information within those groups become your subpoints. **Subpoints** are the evidence and reasoning that support your main points. To illustrate her main point about the importance of activism led by young people of color, Abdullah gave several examples as subpoints: the 1963 Black Children's March in Birmingham, Alabama; the 1968 East Los Angeles walkouts; and contemporary groups like the Dream Defenders, Students Not Suspects, and the Black Lives Matter Youth Vanguard.

When you've completed a first draft of your main points and subpoints, check to make sure that these key elements of your speech will be easy for your audience to understand and remember. If you have too many main points, if your main points overlap, or if the support for your main points is uneven, your speech becomes much harder for your audience to follow. So, combine and reorganize the sections of your presentation until you have no more than five distinct, balanced main points.

📋 **TRY THIS**

To experiment with different strategies for organizing your supporting information into main points and subpoints, see the **Source Modeling Worksheet**, the **Mind Mapping Activity**, and the **Evidence Shuffling Activity**.

**subpoints**
the evidence and reasoning that support your main points

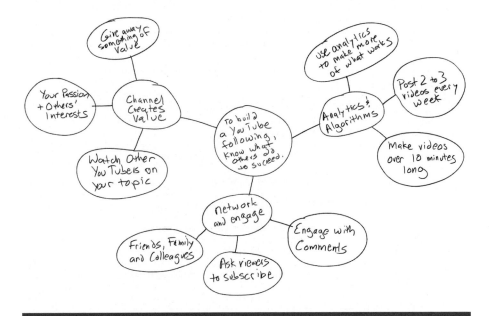

Sorting your evidence and reasoning into groups can help you identify the main points and subpoints that support your thesis.

# NO MORE THAN FIVE MAIN POINTS

You may hear that the magic number for human memory is three, and that three main points is always best. This advice has served speakers well for thousands of years. However, the true ideal number always depends on your topic and speaking situation. Complex or controversial presentations—like a policy speech criticizing the US response to Russia's 2022 invasion of Ukraine—might call for more main points. Simple, unifying presentations—like a toast at your friend's wedding—might call for fewer. The length of your presentation can also be a factor. A two-minute talk may allow time for only two main points, but one that lasts twenty minutes may allow for up to five.

**Miller's law**
in most situations, people can hold at least five items in their short-term memory—sometimes up to nine, with an average number of seven

Research has demonstrated that in most situations, people can hold at least five items in their short-term memory—sometimes up to nine, with an average number of seven. This is known as **Miller's law**: we can only hold "seven plus or minus two" items in our awareness at a given time.[5] For a public speaker, this makes three main points a safe default and an excellent choice, especially for speeches under ten minutes. Following Miller's law, five main points

| | | |
|---|---|---|
| **PURPOSE:** To inform omnivores how to make a plant-based entrée so they can host family dinners with their vegan relatives. | | |
| **THESIS:** Learning to make this roasted vegetable dish can help your vegan relatives feel included during family meals. | | |
| **Too many main points** | I. | Buy vegetables. |
| | II. | Wash and peel them. |
| | III. | Coat with olive oil. |
| | IV. | Place them on a baking tray. |
| | V. | Sprinkle with seasoning. |
| | VI. | Bake for 15–50 minutes. |
| | VII. | Serve with rice or other grains. |
| **Enough main points** | I. | Select vegetables to roast. |
| | II. | Prepare with olive oil and seasoning. |
| | III. | Choose the right baking time. |

**TABLE 9.1** Introducing no more than five main points helps your audience focus on the most important information.

is the upper limit of the safe range for any length of presentation (see Table 9.1).

## DISTINCT MAIN POINTS

Main points are distinct when they do not overlap with each other. One point might lead to or have implications for another, but your main points should remain different enough to avoid creating confusion (see Table 9.2). You know your main points are distinct when you cannot reasonably fit the ideas of one main point under any of your other main points. For example, you could organize a speech on the development of solar power into the past, present, and future of the technology. While these areas might be related, the time periods don't overlap. Similarly, you could organize a speech about COVID vaccines around the three major US manufacturers: Pfizer, Moderna, and Johnson & Johnson. Although the different vaccines may have some similarities, they are topically distinct.

| | | |
|---|---|---|
| **PURPOSE:** To inform remote workers about productivity strategies so they can get more done when working from home. | | |
| **THESIS:** These three strategies can help you stay productive when you're working from home. | | |
| **Overlapping main points** | I. | Get organized. |
| | II. | Set a regular schedule. |
| | III. | Stay on task. |
| **Distinct main points** | I. | Create a distraction-free workspace. |
| | II. | Set a regular schedule. |
| | III. | Reward yourself for completing tasks. |

TABLE 9.2 Dividing your topic into clearly distinct main points makes your speech easier for you to compose and easier for your audience to follow.

## BALANCED MAIN POINTS

Your main points should take up roughly equal time in your presentation. Main points are balanced when they divide your topic into sections with roughly equal substance and length (see Table 9.3). An imbalanced speech can confuse an audience, especially if one of your main points is missing the substance it needs to support your thesis. The balance does not have to be exact, but no main point should be less than half the length of any other. If you find that one of your main points lacks sufficient content to provide balance, you can do more research on that part of your topic or reorganize your main points to create more balance.

| | | |
|---|---|---|
| **PURPOSE:** To connect with friends and family so that we can celebrate Charlie and Sasha's wedding. | | |
| **THESIS:** Thank you for joining me to celebrate the wedding of Charlie and Sasha, a couple whose love and support inspires us all. | | |
| **Uneven main points** | I. | Charlie has always supported me. |
| | | A. Helped me find work when I lost my job. |
| | | B. Came with me to chemotherapy. |
| | II. | Sasha seems supportive, too. |
| **Balanced main points** | I. | Charlie has always supported me. |
| | | A. Helped me find work when I lost my job. |
| | | B. Came with me to chemotherapy. |
| | II. | Sasha has always supported Charlie. |
| | | A. Helped Charlie make it through law school. |
| | | B. Supported Charlie through the death of her father. |

**TABLE 9.3** Offering balanced support for each of your main points ensures that you fully support your thesis.

# Ordering Your Main Points

There are as many ways to organize a speech as there are speakers, audiences, purposes, and contexts. But understanding common organizational patterns can help you arrange your main points in an order that's easy for your audience to follow. Most presentations use one of five general patterns: categorical, spatial, chronological, causal, or motivational. Not all presentation structures fall into one of these five types, but knowing these basic patterns can help get you started when you're organizing a presentation.

When you're asked to speak on the spot without any preparation time, quickly coming up with two or three main points can make your remarks sound polished:

1. **PREVIEW YOUR MAIN POINTS.** For example: "I have two main concerns about this plan: timeline and resources." Or: "When I look at Marcos, I see compassion, generosity, and gratitude."

2. **INTRODUCE YOUR MAIN POINTS WITH A PARALLEL STRUCTURE.** For example: "*First, I'm concerned that we don't have* enough time to conduct two rounds of focus group testing. *Second, I'm concerned we don't have* the resources to recruit participants." Or: "*I see compassion when I see Marcos* reaching out to volunteer with special needs children in our schools. *I see generosity when I see Marcos* organize events like this one that benefit underfunded special education programs. *And I see gratitude when I see Marcos* look around at all the wonderful people who have shown up to support a cause that's so close to his heart."

3. **CLOSE BY INVITING OTHER PEOPLE TO PARTICIPATE.** For example: "I would love to hear some of your ideas for ways we can address these issues." Or: "So let's raise a glass to Marcos, who made all our good work here tonight possible."

## CATEGORICAL PATTERNS

A **categorical pattern** organizes main points into generally recognized types, groups, or sets. For example, when we talk about colleges and universities in the United States, we can divide them into three categories: public institutions, nonprofit private institutions, and for-profit private institutions. Some topics are already divided into categories, such as the four distinct species of giraffes or the five types of chemical reactions. You can also create your own categories to divide up a topic, as long as they offer distinct main points, support your purpose, and don't conflict with your audience's existing knowledge and beliefs:

**categorical pattern**
organizing main points into generally recognized types, groups, or sets

> **Purpose** To inform union organizers about worker resistance strategies so that they can maximize their collective bargaining power.

| | |
|---|---|
| **Thesis** | Understanding the three main types of collective worker resistance can help you advocate for better pay and working conditions. |
| **Main points** | I.  Strikes. |
| | II.  Work slowdowns. |
| | III.  Work to rule. |

# SPATIAL PATTERNS

A **spatial pattern** organizes main points according to location or position in space. That could mean comparing three countries, three cities, or three buildings. For example, a speech could have three main points explaining how changes in higher education are affecting Delaware, Iowa, and Oregon— organized directionally from east to west. You could also think about spatial patterns as narrowing or escalating in scale. A narrowing spatial pattern moves from larger to smaller domains. For example, you might talk about the global, national, and local implications of an economic recession. You can also use an escalating scale, from smaller to larger, such as the city, state, and national levels of your topic:

| | |
|---|---|
| **Purpose** | To inform local voters about voter suppression laws so that they can plan ahead to exercise their right to vote. |
| **Thesis** | Understanding voter suppression laws can help you ensure that your vote gets counted. |
| **Main points** | I.  City ordinances. |
| | II.  State laws. |
| | III.  National laws. |

# CHRONOLOGICAL PATTERNS

**spatial pattern**
organizing main points according to location or position in space

**chronological pattern**
organizing main points into distinct moments in time

A **chronological pattern** organizes main points into distinct moments in time. The most common chronological pattern uses three main points: past, present, and future. But other chronological patterns may better fit different purposes. For example, on the topic of heart transplants, you might start with the first successful heart transplant, then describe turning points in the procedure's development, and finally explain how heart transplants work today. Or you could divide a topic into periods of time, such as classical antiquity, the medieval era, and then the Renaissance. You can also use a chronological pattern to describe a process—like the steps of building a canoe or conducting a scientific experiment. Most stories are told using a chronological organization, and some speeches structure the entire body as one continuous narrative.

## Pathways

To learn more about storytelling and narrative structure, see **Chapter 10, Emotion and Narrative**.

| | |
|---|---|
| **Purpose** | To connect with friends and family members to mourn my uncle's passing and celebrate his life. |
| **Thesis** | It's no surprise to see so many people here to honor Uncle Jesse, a deeply loyal man who always stood up for the people he loved. |
| **Main points** | I. My uncle stood up for my mom when they were young. |
| | II. My uncle stood up for me when I was a kid. |
| | III. My uncle stood up for his mother before she died. |

## CAUSAL PATTERNS

A **causal pattern** organizes main points into causes and effects. To establish a causal relationship, you can move either from effects to causes or from causes to effects. *Cause-to-effect patterns* are most common in persuasive speeches. You can often persuade your audience to take an action by explaining its positive effects. For example, you might persuade a group of college students to pursue summer internships by demonstrating positive outcomes like a stronger résumé, wider professional network, and better job placement. Or you can persuade your audience not to take an action by describing its negative effects. For example, you might persuade dog owners not to overfeed their pets by explaining the negative health consequences:

**causal pattern**
organizing main points into causes and effects

| | |
|---|---|
| **Purpose** | To persuade dog owners not to overfeed their dogs so the animals can live longer, healthier lives. |
| **Thesis** | Overfeeding your dog can cause serious health problems that reduce your pet's life span and quality of life. |
| **Main points** | I. Cause: Many pet owners overfeed their dogs, thinking it's a harmless expression of love. |
| | II. Effects: But overfeeding your dog can cause heart disease, diabetes, and arthritis. |

While explaining the potential effects of a cause is usually persuasive, explaining the causes of an effect can be either persuasive or informative. *Effect-to-cause patterns* begin by describing an outcome, and then identify the factors that contributed to that outcome. For example, you might use this pattern to explain the major causes of global climate change—which might be either informative or persuasive, depending on your speaking situation:

| | |
|---|---|
| **Purpose** | To inform consumers about the causes of climate change so they will understand the environmental impacts of overconsumption. |
| **Thesis** | Understanding how fossil fuel emissions contribute to global climate change can help you make better decisions as a consumer. |
| **Main points** | I. Effect: Climate change is an escalating worldwide problem. |
| | II. Causes: Fossil fuel emissions from manufacturing products, generating electricity, and using transportation all contribute to climate change. |

## MOTIVATIONAL PATTERNS

A **motivational pattern** organizes main points into problems and solutions. A **problem** is either something negative that is happening or something positive that is lacking. You can think of a problem as an unsatisfied need or desire, whether that's for food, safety, good health, a thriving planet, career advancement, or meaningful relationships. After the first main point details the problem or problems, the next main points focus on **solutions**. What can we do about these problems? Solutions are most powerful if they give the audience concrete and effective steps they can take to reduce the problem.

**motivational pattern** organizing main points into problems and solutions

**problem** something negative that is happening or something positive that is lacking

**solution** practical steps an audience can take to reduce or resolve a problem

| | |
|---|---|
| **Purpose** | To persuade my company's managers to stop basing employee performance reviews on customer feedback. |
| **Thesis** | We should start basing performance reviews on feedback from fellow employees and managers because customer feedback is biased and unreliable. |

**Main points**  I. Problems with customer feedback.

　　　　A. Does not represent the average customer experience.

　　　　B. Often displays race, gender, and age biases.

　　II. Solutions for better performance reviews.

　　　　A. Peer evaluations.

　　　　B. Management observations.

## Pathways

To learn more variations on this basic motivational pattern, see **Chapter 16, Persuading and Motivating**.

## ✓ Critical Thinking Check

1. Why is it important to offer your audience no more than five distinct, balanced main points? Can you think of any potential exceptions to this rule?

2. When you're deciding how to order your main points, how do you know what type of organizational pattern to use? What dimensions of your speaking situation would be most important to consider?

# Adding Signposts

Once you have identified your main points and the subpoints that support them, adding signposts can help you signal when you're moving from one point to the next. Just like signs on the road, **signposts** in a speech tell your audience where they are, where they've been, and where they're going. A speech without signposts is like a town without street signs—people are going to get lost. Clear signposts help your audience follow your presentation and remember its content. The three main types of signposts are transitions, internal previews, and internal summaries.

## TRANSITIONS

**Transitions** are bridges that transport your audience from one part of your speech to the next. Like any good bridge, a transition is anchored to both where you are and where you are going, providing a path from here to there. This simple formula can help you build transitions that keep your audience engaged and reinforce the structure of your presentation in their memory:

1. **CLOSING ANCHOR.** Restate the point you are wrapping up: "Now that we understand what created the current anxiety epidemic in students..."

2. **BRIDGE.** Signal a change in topic or focus: "...you might wonder if there's really anything we can do about it."

**signposts**
signals that tell your audience where they are in your speech

**transitions**
bridges that transport your audience from one part of your speech to the next

**internal preview**
a brief list of the subpoints within an upcoming main point

**internal summary**
a brief review of the subpoints within the preceding main point

3. **OPENING ANCHOR.** State your next point: "There are two solutions schools can adopt that are proven to make a dramatic difference."

## INTERNAL PREVIEWS

In presentations longer than just a couple minutes, each main point may be divided into two or more subpoints. When you are introducing a main point that has multiple subpoints, you can help your audience follow along by providing an internal preview. An **internal preview** gives an audience a brief glimpse of the subpoints within the upcoming main point. For example, in the transition example above, the speaker promised that the next main point would contain two solutions. When the speaker begins that new point, they can provide a brief internal preview that lets the audience know what to expect in the next section of the speech:

1. **STATE THE MAIN POINT:** "Two approaches proven to help lower anxiety in students are..."

2. **LIST THE SUBPOINTS:** "...offering anxiety reduction counseling and training teachers in universal design techniques."

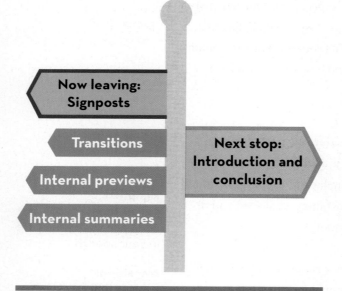

Clear signposts—like transitions, internal previews, and internal summaries—help your audience follow you from one main point to the next.

## INTERNAL SUMMARIES

Like an internal preview, an **internal summary** gives the audience a brief review of the subpoints within the preceding main point. As with internal previews, internal summaries are most helpful when a main point has multiple subpoints you want your audience to remember. For example, after finishing the main point previewed above, the speaker can use an internal summary to reinforce it in the audience's memory:

1. **RESTATE MAIN POINT:** "As you can see, we have strong evidence that schools can make two changes to help students with anxiety..."

**2. LIST THE SUBPOINTS:** "…offering anxiety reduction counseling and training teachers in universal design."

# Developing Introductions and Conclusions

Once you know how you will organize the main points of your presentation, you can create an effective introduction and conclusion. Your **introduction** gets your audience's attention, establishes your connection to your topic, communicates your thesis, and previews your main points. Your **conclusion** indicates that your presentation is ending, reviews your main points, and emphasizes what your audience should take away from your presentation.

Introductions and conclusions are important because they frame your audience's interpretation of your presentation. Just like a camera frame focuses on certain things and leaves others out, your introduction and conclusion show your audience what to focus on and why it is important. Presenting the same information through a different lens changes audience perceptions of that information—this is called the **framing effect**.[6] Your introduction sets the initial frame through which the audience will view the rest of your speech. Your conclusion sets the frame they will use when they look back on your presentation.

In addition to framing your speech, introductions and conclusions play another important role: making your presentation memorable. We tend to remember and place greater importance on information that comes either first or last—this is known as the **primacy effect** and the **recency effect**.[7] The primacy effect makes the first moments of your presentation easy for your audience to remember, while the recency effect makes it easy to remember the final moments of your presentation. Take advantage of this memory trick: emphasize your most important points in your introduction and conclusion, where they will have a lasting impact.

Because of the primacy, recency, and framing effects, scholars and professional speakers often recommend that you spend significant time crafting, revising, and practicing your introductions and conclusions. These are more than just

**introduction**
opening remarks that get the audience's attention, share the speaker's connection to the topic, state the presentation's thesis, and preview its main points

**conclusion**
closing remarks that indicate your presentation is ending, review your main points, and emphasize what you want your audience to take away from your presentation

**framing effect**
presenting the same information through a different lens changes audience perceptions of that information

**primacy effect**
the tendency to remember and place greater importance on information that comes first in a series

**recency effect**
the tendency to remember and place greater importance on information that comes last in a series

7 5 9 2 6 4 9 0 3 8 4 3 5

Briefly scan this string of numbers, and then close your eyes. Which numbers are the easiest to remember?

passing moments in your speech; they will shape how the audience experiences and remembers everything else you say.

## CRAFTING AN EFFECTIVE INTRODUCTION

Every presentation begins somewhere, and a good presentation will have a carefully crafted introduction. This is your moment to get your audience interested in what you have to say. In online communication, introductions often determine whether a viewer will continue listening or close the player. Viewers usually decide in the first fifteen to twenty seconds whether they will skip a video. In person, you have roughly the same amount of time to develop a first impression and pique your audience's interest.

While there are many ways to open your presentation, most effective introductions contain four components: attention material, credibility support, thesis statement, and preview—in that order.

### 1 Attention Material

**attention material**
opening lines used to build your audience's interest and investment in your presentation

The first sentences of your presentation should hook your audience's attention. **Attention material** builds your audience's interest and investment in your presentation. Good attention material is tailored to your audience and their connection to your purpose, context, and standpoint. Your goal is to interest them enough to pay attention. Here are a few common strategies for getting your audience's attention:

- **SURPRISING FACTS.** A surprising fact or statistic can intrigue your audience, pique their curiosity, and make them interested to know more. For example, you might open a speech on drunk driving laws with a statistic about their enforcement: "Did you know that the average drunk driver drives under the influence more than eighty times before their first arrest?"[8]

- **STORIES.** A story can get your audience emotionally invested in both your topic and your unique perspective on it. For example, you might open a speech on gender equality in the US military with the notable story of a woman who served: "In 1781, Deborah Sampson Gannett disguised herself as a man and enlisted to fight in the American Revolutionary War..."[9]

- **QUOTATIONS.** A quotation from a figure your audience admires can build your credibility and identification with your audience. For example, you might begin a speech fund-raising for the NAACP by quoting one of its founding members: "The great civil rights leader W. E. B. Du Bois once wrote, 'The cost of liberty is less than the price of repression.'"[10]

## 2 Credibility Support

Once you've got their attention, let your audience know why they should listen to your unique perspective. Share an aspect of your strengths or standpoint that gives you credibility to speak on this topic. Your connection to the topic may already be built into your attention material—for example, if you start with a surprising fact or a story about yourself. But that's not the only way to share your commitment to your topic with your audience:

- **EXPERIENCE.** You can connect your topic to your standpoint as a speaker by sharing your experiences. For example, after sharing a statistic about drunk driving enforcement, you could talk about how the issue has touched your life: "There's no telling how many times that driver got behind the wheel drunk before the day she plowed her truck into the side of my cousin Anton's car."

- **EXPERTISE.** You can also describe your expertise to demonstrate your credibility on a topic. For example, after telling the story about Deborah Sampson Gannett enlisting as a man, you might share your own credentials: "As a lance corporal in the US Marine Corps, I know what it's like to be a woman who's called to serve her country."

- **PASSION.** Sharing the values that make you passionate about a topic is an excellent way to build goodwill with your audience. For example, after quoting W. E. B. Du Bois, you could explain why you are personally dedicated to supporting the NAACP: "Liberty! That's what it's all about—your liberty, my liberty. No price is too high."

## 3 Thesis Statement

Now that your audience is interested in your topic and your perspective, you want to clearly communicate your thesis. Let your thesis statement flow naturally out of your personal connection to the topic. Your background, experience,

## Pathways

To revisit activities for identifying elements of your background as a speaker that boost your credibility, see **Chapter 1, Your Standpoint and Strengths**, and **Chapter 3, Ethics and Credibility**.

credentials, passion, or standpoint led you to your thesis. You offer your thesis as something you believe, and something you believe has value for your audience. This invests your thesis statement with the emotional power of your standpoint to grip your audience. For example:

- After describing your experience of a drunk driver hitting your cousin, your thesis about drunk driving becomes more powerful: "That is why I am calling on local law enforcement to set up more sobriety checkpoints—so we can stop drunk drivers before they hurt somebody, instead of waiting until they do."

- After sharing your credentials as a Marine, your thesis on promoting gender equality in the US military carries greater authority: "The US military should take active steps to reduce barriers to women's enlistment and advancement, because patriots like me are ready and eager to serve."

- After demonstrating your passion for liberty, your thesis advocating for donations to the NAACP affirms the values that you share with your audience: "So I am asking you to donate to the NAACP, an organization that has been advancing the cause of equal rights and racial justice from Du Bois's time to today."

## 4 Preview

**preview**
an advance statement of your presentation's main points in order

The last part of your introduction should always be a preview of what you will talk about during the rest of your presentation. A presentation's **preview** provides the audience a clear statement of what the main points of the presentation will be, in order. There's no need to go into detail about your subpoints at this stage; just provide the audience a road map of your two to five main points. A numbered list of main points—first, second, third, and so on—is clear and easy to follow, but it sounds more formal and less conversational. Previewing your list with informal sequencers—first, then, next, finally—can sound more approachable. The way you present your preview will depend on your speaking situation and the structure of your speech. For example:

- A speech in a more formal context—like a city council meeting—might introduce a numbered list of main points: "First, I'll discuss the extent of the drunk driving problem in our area. Second, I'll demonstrate that sobriety checkpoints effectively reduce drunk driving accidents. Third, I'll show how the city can fund a greater number of sobriety checkpoints with its existing budget."

Coach Taylor Statham previews his three main points in the introduction to his video tutorial on how to shoot a basketball better (0:17).

- A speech with fewer main points might go into more detail about its subpoints in the preview. For example: "First, I'll suggest some ways to reduce barriers to women's enlistment, like offering more inclusive family leave policies and improving anti-discrimination training for officers. Then, I'll talk about ways to remove barriers to women's advancement through the ranks, like creating mentoring programs and strengthening affirmative action efforts."

- A speech with a clearly recognizable organizational pattern may not need to give numbers or informal sequencers in the preview: "Tonight, I will share past, present, and future milestones in the civil rights movement that NAACP supporters like you make possible."

## CRAFTING AN EFFECTIVE CONCLUSION

With your main body organized and your introduction crafted, you can then create your conclusion. Remember that the conclusion takes advantage of the recency effect: the boost in memory and importance given to the final thing your audience hears. Your conclusion highlights your key ideas and gives your audience a framework for understanding your topic. An effective conclusion has three steps: cueing the ending, reviewing the main points, and providing a takeaway.

# Danielle Young's Body Positivity

Danielle Young creates video presentations for publications like *Essence* and *The Root*, as well as her own YouTube and Instagram channels. Her "Overexplainer" videos for *Essence* break down complex topics related to race, gender, body image, and celebrity culture. These videos are carefully planned and organized to capture audience attention and analyze big ideas in just a few minutes.

Her 2019 video on body positivity is just over three minutes long, but full of both structure and substance.[11] Her opening line immediately grabs your attention: "Body positivity has nothing to do with promoting obesity or an unhealthy lifestyle." After explaining this common misconception about body positivity, she introduces her thesis: "Body positivity is simply the revolutionary notion to embrace and appreciate your body in whatever state it's in right now."

Her first main point focuses on correcting misunderstandings about body positivity, defining it as a social movement that "rids itself of societal ideals that fat, disabled, queer, or any body that deviates from the status quo is bad or undeserving of love and appreciation." She then transitions to her second main point: that body positivity is a form of self-love that helps people pursue their "body goals." She notes that the body positivity movement still promotes mental and physical work to improve your health, even while it encourages you to love your body "in real time." Her third point is that representations of diverse bodies influence our self-perceptions. She uses the public reaction to Nike's size-inclusive mannequins as an

## 1 Cue the Ending

An audience's attention rises and falls during a presentation. Listeners usually perk up when they realize a presentation is ending—even if they have loved every minute of it. To get your audience's attention, signal the conclusion of your speech. There are several strategies you can use to let your audience know you're wrapping up:

- **SWITCH TO PAST TENSE.** Switching to past tense—"I've presented you with a lot of information about..." or "Today, you've learned..."—gives your audience a subtle cue that you are looking back on your speech. For example: "Now you know just how widespread child labor is in the cocoa industry."

example, showing how negative responses to representations of larger bodies damage people's mental and physical health. She asks: "Are we supposed to feel body negativity because we're not some falsified picture of perfection?"

Young's conclusion then briefly recaps her three main points: that size inclusivity and promoting obesity are not one and the same, that body positivity is self-love, and that representation of diverse bodies matters. She then closes with a call for her viewers to "embrace the fact that the world doesn't reflect just one acceptable image; all of our images are acceptable."

Danielle Young organized her 2019 video presentation to create an efficient and effective explanation of body positivity. She closed her presentation with a call to embrace diverse body types, and then capped off the video with a reminder about the series: "Until next time, I'm Danielle Young, and this is 'The Overexplainer'" (3:09).

To watch Young's "Overexplainer" video on body positivity, do a web search for these terms: overexplainer essence body positivity. The video is approximately 3:20 in length.

- **MENTION WHAT'S NEXT.** Previewing the next part of the event—"Before I open the floor to questions..." or "Before I hand the microphone over to our next speaker..."—lets your audience know you're almost done. For example, "Before we move on to the next part of our training, I want to remind you how important it is to wear safety gear when you're working on a construction site."

- **SAY IT DIRECTLY.** When in doubt, simply tell your audience your speech is ending. Phrases like "In closing..." and "In conclusion..." send a clear signal. For example: "I'd like to close by saying again how much winning the Walt Whitman Award means to me."

## 2 Review Your Main Points

Next, briefly summarize the main points of your presentation. But don't just repeat your introduction's preview word for word. Instead, use your concluding review to emphasize the key information and arguments from the body of your speech. Your review doesn't have to be long or detailed, but it should be crafted to show what your presentation has accomplished. Don't just list your main points—explain that you have now demonstrated, validated, or proven them:

- **EMPHASIZE THE EVIDENCE.** For example: "You have seen the numbers showing how many children in West Africa and Brazil are forced to work on cocoa farms, you have witnessed the working conditions those children face, and you have heard stories directly from the children themselves."

- **REVIEW YOUR REASONING.** For example: "Wearing safety gear protects you from dangerous accidents, helps you avoid expensive medical bills, and keeps you working so you can support your family."

- **CONNECT WITH SHARED VALUES.** For example: "I have wanted to be a poet since I was a child, and Walt Whitman has always been an inspiration to me. Having my work recognized by such a distinguished academy of poets is a dream come true."

## 3 Provide a Takeaway

The last part of your conclusion should revisit your thesis, considering everything you have said in your speech. Give your audience a clear, memorable, and brief statement you want them to carry with them. This is the one thing you want your audience to know, think, believe, do, or feel after listening to your presentation. Your takeaway will both restate your thesis and move your audience toward your purpose:

- **INFORMATIVE PURPOSE.** Your takeaway captures the core understanding or knowledge you hope they remember. For example: "So the next time you bite into a piece of chocolate, remember where it came from: corporations that systematically profit off the forced labor of children."

- **PERSUASIVE PURPOSE.** Your takeaway calls your audience to make a decision or take an action. For example: "So please, put on your safety gear—the temporary inconvenience is better than a permanent injury."

In his 2013 TED talk, Ron Finley concludes his speech on guerilla gardening by calling his audience "to become ecolutionaries, renegades, gangsters, gangster gardeners.... If you ain't a gardener, you ain't gangster. Get gangster with your shovel, and let that be your weapon of choice" (9:26).

- **CONNECTIVE PURPOSE.** Your takeaway invites your audience to celebrate together by applauding, toasting, or observing a moment of silence. For example: "I hope you'll join me in a round of applause for all the nominees, who show that the spirit of Walt Whitman still breathes fragrant air into American poetry today."

## ✓ Critical Thinking Check

1. How do you know whether or not you need to include internal previews and internal summaries? When would they be helpful to your audience? When might it be better to leave them out?
2. Why is it important to know how you will organize your main points before you begin developing your introduction and conclusion? What problems might you run into if you tried to write your introduction first?

# Outlining Your Speech

If you have organized the main points of your speech, crafted an introduction, and created a conclusion, then you have already begun creating an outline. An **outline** is a structured summary of the key elements of your presentation—all

**outline**
a structured summary of the key elements of your presentation

your main points and subpoints, as well as your introduction, conclusion, and transitions. Outlining can help you develop and revise the organization of your speech to make it as clear as possible. Using an outline can also make practicing and delivering your presentation much smoother and easier.

## 1 Drafting Your Preparation Outline

**preparation outline**
a detailed, full-sentence outline containing every substantive idea, argument, concept, and fact in your presentation

You'll begin by making a **preparation outline**: a detailed, full-sentence outline containing every substantive idea, argument, concept, and fact in your presentation (see example on the next page). Preparation outlines help you organize your presentation and ensure that your organization is sound. They will show you when you have too many points, when your points overlap, or when one of your points has too much emphasis or not enough detail.

Preparation outlines vary slightly in format. If your speaking situation requires a specific format, always follow the guidelines you've been given. In general, the top-level points of your presentation will be your introduction, each of the two to five points of your main body, and your conclusion. Under each of these will be the different sections and subpoints.

You can think about your main points and subpoints like folders on your computer. You have top-level folders that contain more specific folders, which may contain even more specific folders, and so on, down to the actual content of those folders. You can use Roman numerals (I, II, III . . .), uppercase letters (A, B, C . . .), Arabic numerals (1, 2, 3 . . .), and lowercase letters (a, b, c . . .) to indicate different levels of specificity. Roman numerals represent the most general levels of the presentation, capital letters represent more specificity, Arabic numerals present even greater specificity, and lowercase letters are the most specific:

   I.   Main point (general)

      A.  Subpoint (more specific)

         1.  Information/examples (even more specific)

            a.  Detailed information/example (most specific)

When you finish organizing your main points and subpoints, go back through your preparation outline and write in your transition statements, internal previews, and internal summaries. Add any specific evidence or support at another level of subordinate points. Make sure to include any elements that need to be stated precisely, such as direct quotations, exact numbers and dates, and verbal source citations. If you are citing any sources and will be giving anyone else a copy of your preparation outline, include a list of works cited at the end in a formal citation format such as American Psychological Association (APA) or Modern Language Association (MLA) style.

## Pathways

To review the criteria for effective oral and written citations, see **Chapter 8, Research and Citation**.

### Sample Preparation Outline

**Purpose:** To inform people new to creating online content how to build a following on YouTube.

**Thesis:** To build a following on YouTube, it helps to understand what successful YouTubers do to attract subscribers and grow their channels.

**Organization:** Chronological (step-by-step process).

I. Introduction.
   A. Attention material: Every day, people around the world watch over a billion hours of YouTube videos. Yes, that's billion, with a "B." On average, over five hundred hours of new content are uploaded to YouTube every minute.[12]
   B. Speaker's connection: I've been creating videos for YouTube for about four months. And while my channel is still small, it is growing fast thanks to the research I've done on what it takes to be a successful YouTuber.
   C. Thesis statement: If you want to build a following on YouTube, it helps to understand what successful YouTubers do to attract subscribers and grow their channels.
   D. Preview: Successful YouTubers start by creating a channel with real value. Next, they use networking and engagement to attract their first followers. Then, once their channel grows, they use analytics and algorithms to maximize their impact.

II. Step 1: Create a channel with value.
   A. To start building a following, think of your channel as a contribution to others.
      1. In her book *Stand Out*, Dorie Clark, digital strategy consultant and adjunct professor of business at Duke University, writes that most people build online followings by delivering

something of real value to other people. This works because when people value your content, they will come back for more.

    2. But it also works, Clark says, because of a psychological principle called reciprocity: when you give away something of value to others, they are more likely to want to reciprocate and give you something in return, such as clicking the "subscribe" button.[13]

B. But how do you find something of value to offer your followers? You combine your passion with others' interests.

    1. Robert Glazer, the CEO of a marketing agency and author of multiple best-selling marketing books, suggests you start with something you are passionate about.[14] If you love your topic, your content will be better and it will be easier to keep making content.

    2. Then ask yourself what others who share your interest might want to learn or know. Digital entrepreneur and marketing guru Seth Godin suggests asking what kinds of things people interested in your topic will want to tell other people about.[15] That kind of information not only is valuable, but also will help you grow your audience when they share your videos.

C. You can get an idea of what people value and want to share by watching other successful YouTubers who share your interest.

    1. Whatever your topic area, there are probably others making videos about it too. Study their most popular videos. Read their comment sections. You don't want to copy them, but you can use them as inspiration to help you decide how to get started.

    2. And once you're feeling inspired, start making and posting videos. Get your first couple of videos up on your channel and experiment to see what people like.

Transition: Once you have your topic area and are creating your first videos, you will want to attract your first viewers. And the best ways to do that are to network and engage.

III. Step 2: Network and engage.

A. Professor Clark says most people's first followers are people they already know and who share the same interest.

    1. So, begin by promoting your content in your existing networks. That means sharing it on social media, and asking friends, family, and colleagues to check out your videos and subscribe.

2. Likewise, ask them to use their networks and social media accounts to share your videos and publicize your new channel.

B. You'll also build more followers by directly asking people to click "subscribe" when they watch your videos.

   1. If you watch much YouTube, you've probably seen content creators asking you to click "like" and "subscribe," often at the beginning and end of their videos. That's key to turning people watching a video into people subscribed to your channel.

   2. And if they value what your videos provide, that can be a welcome reminder to the viewer and not just self-promotion. You're helping them get more of what they like!

C. Besides encouraging people to subscribe, ask them to comment.

   1. You can ask them a question or two as prompts for their comments or just ask for their opinions or questions. You can get a lot of great feedback to improve your videos and ideas for future video topics from your viewers.

   2. Make your comment section a conversation between you and your viewers. In a study of scientists trying to build an online following, researchers at the University of California Santa Barbara and the University of Massachusetts found that engaging and interacting with their online audiences determined who succeeded.[16]

Transition: So now you have a channel, you're putting out some videos, and you're attracting a few subscribers. To grow your following, the next step is to use YouTube's analytics and algorithms.

IV. Step 3: Use analytics and algorithms.

A. There's a simple rule for using analytics to shape online content: make more of what your audience wants to watch.

   1. As Bhavik Sarkhedi, a social media consultant, says, analytics are essential to understanding what is working on your channel and what is not.[17]

   2. YouTube's analytics tools can show you which videos are attracting the most attention, how much of each video people watch, and which are contributing the most to building your following.

   3. There are tons of online resources to learn more about using YouTube's analytics. I recommend Cathrin Manning's YouTube channel as a great place to start.

B. Manning also has great information about YouTube's algorithm. The algorithm is the secret formula YouTube uses to decide which videos to suggest to which viewers.
   1. YouTube's algorithm favors videos people like, watch all the way through, and comment on, but it is also more likely to recommend channels that post new videos regularly.
   2. Manning, who built a channel with over 450,000 subscribers, says that to attract a large online following, you will need to consistently produce two to three high-quality videos each week.[18] Creating that many high-quality videos every week can be a lot of work, and it's tough to keep at it when your channel is small.
   3. Manning also says that YouTube is set up to favor longer videos.[19] The algorithm promotes videos longer than ten minutes much more than shorter videos, especially when people are watching most of those videos.
      a. YouTube makes more ad revenue from longer videos because they can place more ads in them.
      b. The algorithm will not recommend a ten-minute video people click away from after thirty seconds, so remember that delivering value to your followers is still your first priority.
      c. If you want to make money from your channel, those longer videos will get you more revenue faster. But if you follow what YouTube's algorithm favors, you are more likely to build a large following fast.
V. Conclusion.
   A. Cue the ending: I could talk all day about building a following on YouTube, but I hope this brief presentation helps get you started.
   B. Review main points: Just remember to create videos with value, engage with your viewers, and use YouTube's algorithm and analytics to help your channel take off.
   C. Takeaway: It can take a year or more of hard work to build a following on YouTube, but people just like you and me are doing it all the time. If you have a message to share, I encourage you to start your own YouTube channel today.

## 2 Revising Your Preparation Outline

In creating your preparation outline, you might need to adjust some elements of your organization to ensure distinctness and balance. You might move different points and subpoints around to provide a smoother flow or a more coherent structure. That is what a preparation outline should do—help you find the best organization for the elements of your presentation.

You can further refine and revise your preparation outline by speaking it out loud. Using your preparation outline, read through your entire presentation in full voice so you can hear any passages that trip up your tongue. If it doesn't flow well, isn't making sense, or just sounds off, stop and rethink your preparation outline. Do you need to add a transition? Introduce your points in a different order? Add more supporting information? If you have formal criteria for how your presentation will be evaluated—such as a time limit or an assigned organizational pattern—consider those criteria when revising your preparation outline.

Keep revising until your preparation outline creates a complete, smooth, logical, and compelling presentation. If you have been asked to speak for eight to ten minutes, time your presentation at this stage to make sure it falls as close to the middle of that range as possible. Your actual live delivery might be slightly slower or faster, so give yourself a margin for error. Staying in your designated time window can be of critical importance in many planned speaking situations, since the time available to other speakers—and even the entire event—can be thrown off if one speaker runs too long or doesn't fill their allotted time.

## 3 Drafting Your Speaking Outline

Once you have created, revised, and practiced your preparation outline, you are ready to craft a speaking outline (see example on the next page). A **speaking outline** is a brief, keyword outline for delivering a presentation. In memorized or manuscript speaking, speakers skip this step and produce a full text copy of the speech to memorize or read. However, since speaking from outlines sounds more natural and conversational, every public speaker should know how to create a speaking outline and use it in a speech.

**speaking outline**
a brief, keyword outline for delivering a presentation

Your preparation outline is the starting point for your speaking outline. Cut down the detail in each point, reducing full sentences to key phrases, words, abbreviations, or other shorthand that will cue your memory when presenting the speech. At minimum, you'll want to include prompts for all the main points of your outline, plus any specific numbers, direct quotations, or citations you need to state precisely.

## Pathways

To learn more about speaking from an outline, from a manuscript, or from memory, see **Chapter 12, Vocal and Physical Delivery**.

Using note cards is an effective way to deliver your speech from a keyword outline.

Most speaking outlines also include prompts for all the subpoints. You might also include a prompt for each major transition between main points. Some speakers include more detail for introductions and conclusions than the main body. How much you trim will depend on the constraints of your speaking context and how much you can practice your presentation.

If you will stand behind a podium to speak, your speaking outline might be two pages long, with the page break strategically placed between two of your main points so you don't lose your place. The font size and spacing may need to be larger so you can quickly scan your outline while it rests on the podium. Arrange your notes so you won't have to pick up or shuffle your papers during your presentation.

If you will be speaking from note cards, use one note card for your introduction, one note card for each of your main points, and one note card for your conclusion. That way you only change cards when transitioning from one main section of the presentation to another. Be sure the print is large enough with enough spacing to reference your notes at a glance while holding them in your hand.

**Sample Speaking Outline**

I. Intro.

- People watch > 1 bil. hrs. each day on YT (w/B!). Add 500 hrs. new content each min.

- I've been creating 4 months; small channel but growing thanks to research.

- If you want to build a YT following, helps to understand what successful YTrs do.

- Successful YTrs = channel w/ real value. Use network & engagement. Use analytics & algorithms.

II. Channel w/ value.

- Think of channel as contribution to others. Dorie Clark, prof. @ Duke U: deliver real value.

- Reciprocity principle.
- Robert Glazer, CEO: start w/ your passion.
- Then ask what others want. Digital entrepr. Seth Godin: content people want to tell others about.
- Learn by watching successful YTrs. In your topic area. Read comments. Get inspired.
- Then start making videos. Experiment.

Trans: Once you have topic & 1st videos, ready to attract first viewers. Network & engage.

III. Network & engage.

- Prof. Clark: 1st followers are ppl. you know. Promote to existing networks & their networks.
- Ask viewers to click "subscribe." You've seen this. If valuable = welcome reminder.
- Ask them to comment. Ask question or 2, or for their opinions or questions.
- Engage w/ comments. Make it a conversation.
- Study of scientists building online following by UCSB & UMass: engage & interact = success.

Trans: Have channel, putting out videos, a few subscribers. To grow, use YT analytics & algorithm.

IV. Analytics & algorithm.

- Create more of what audience wants. Bhavik Sarkhedi, soc media consultant: analytics = understanding.
- YT analytics show attention, % watch, contribution to following.
- Learn analytics from online resources. E.g.: Cathrin Manning.
- Manning also for algorithm. Algo = YT's secret formula for video recommendations.
- Algo favors vids liked & engaged with, but also channels w/ regular posting.
- Manning, 450K subs: 2–3 vids per week. 18 months to 1K subs, but took off w/ consistent posting.
- Manning: Algo also favors longer vids. Over 10 mins. B/c more ad revenue (if people watch).
- Longer vids also = more revenue faster for you.

V. Conclusion.

- Could talk all day about…but brief pres. get you started.

- Remember: videos with value, engage viewers, use YT's algorithm.

- Can take a year or more, but people do it. If you have a message, get started.

## 4 Practicing with Your Speaking Outline

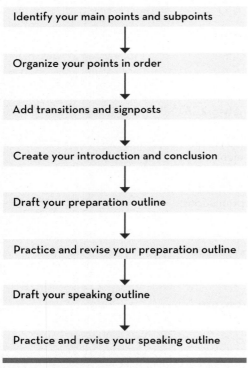

Identify your main points and subpoints

↓

Organize your points in order

↓

Add transitions and signposts

↓

Create your introduction and conclusion

↓

Draft your preparation outline

↓

Practice and revise your preparation outline

↓

Draft your speaking outline

↓

Practice and revise your speaking outline

Organizing and outlining your presentation is a process that involves revision and practice.

Some speakers worry about moving from their detailed preparation outline to their shorthand speaking outline. But the more you practice, the less detail you will need in your notes. By the time you finish developing your preparation outline, you have already begun committing your speech to memory. You will be ready to try improvising the wording and delivery of your presentation.

When you first start practicing with your speaking outline, keep your preparation outline nearby as a reference. If you get stuck on a point while you're practicing, stop and refer to your preparation outline. You may want to change the prompt on your speaking outline to better cue your memory.

Return to your speaking outline, and practice again. Start from the point before the one that gave you trouble. Repeat this process until you can easily deliver your complete presentation from your speaking outline without referencing the preparation outline. Then put away your preparation outline, and shift your practice to focus on improving your delivery.

## ✓ Critical Thinking Check

1. What is the purpose of drafting and revising a preparation outline? Does a preparation outline have value for a speaker even if no one else sees it?

2. What are the advantages and disadvantages of delivering your speech from a speaking outline? What problems might you expect if you tried to deliver your speech from a complete, full-sentence manuscript? What if you tried to deliver your speech with no outline at all?

# Next Steps

Whether you speak from notes, from memory, or from a manuscript, good organization and outlining are essential for shaping your audience's understanding and recollection of your speech. An engaging introduction primes your audience to listen. Clear main points and signposts give them the structure they need to follow along. And a powerful conclusion cements the most important takeaway from your speech in their memory.

To get started organizing your presentation, try the Source Modeling Worksheet, the Mind Mapping Activity, and the Evidence Shuffling Activity. They can help you organize your supporting information into main points and subpoints that back up your thesis. When you're finished organizing your reasoning and evidence, you'll have a complete outline of the structure and substance of your speech. You'll know what you want to say, and you'll be ready to start thinking about how you want to say it.

# Standpoint Reflection

- Some people might think that organization and outlining have less to do with your standpoint than other parts of public speaking. Do you think this is true? Why or why not?

- What are some of the ways that you might spotlight your standpoint in your introduction and conclusion? How might you weave your standpoint into your main points and subpoints?

- Good introductions explain the speaker's connection to the topic of the presentation—but sometimes you are asked to speak on topics that you don't have a strong emotional connection to. What are some other ways you might establish a connection between a topic and your standpoint?

- Some people find that highly detailed speaking outlines increase their confidence in their delivery. Others find that less detailed speaking outlines lead to more spontaneous and conversational delivery. Do you think your own delivery would benefit from a more or less detailed outline?

## Key Terms

# Resources for Organization and Outlining

## ![clipboard icon] "Try This" Exercises

Access the "Try This" exercises as directed by your instructor or online at digital.wwnorton.com/chapterexercises-conpubspeak

- To jumpstart your organizing process when you get stuck, see the **Source Modeling Worksheet**.

- To start from your central idea and work toward your supporting information, see the **Mind Mapping Activity**.

- To start from your supporting information and work toward your main points, see the **Evidence Shuffling Activity**.

**Want to practice these skills to prepare for your next speech? Go to INQUIZITIVE to review and apply concepts from this chapter and get personalized feedback along the way.**

COMEDIAN AND DISABILITY
RIGHTS ADVOCATE        Stella Young

# 10 Emotion and Narrative

As a comedian, teacher, and disability rights activist, Stella Young was a master of emotion. She kept audiences laughing even as she challenged them to rethink their stereotypical expectations about people with disabilities. Her secret? Sharing personal stories about her own encounters with disability stereotypes and showing compassion for the people who hold them.

In her 2014 TED talk, Young tells a story about her experience as a substitute teacher for an eleventh-grade class.[1] Twenty minutes into the class, a student raised his hand and asked when Young was going to begin her motivational speech. When she asked what the student meant, he replied, "When people in wheelchairs come to school, they usually say, like, inspirational stuff?" In that moment, she says, she realized the student had never encountered a disabled person except as an object of inspiration. She explains that it's not his fault—social media feeds us "inspiration porn": images that objectify disabled people to inspire nondisabled people. And disabled people in media are rarely depicted as teachers, doctors, hairdressers, or in any role except as an object of inspiration or pity. She teases her audience: "In fact, I'm sitting on this stage, looking like I do in this wheelchair, and you are probably kind of expecting me to inspire you. Right?"

Rather than responding with shame or guilt, the audience laughs with recognition. They identify with the student in her story—like that student, they have been sold a lie about what it means to be disabled. Critiquing media stereotypes without blaming the people who fall for them, Young teaches her audience a valuable—and enjoyable—lesson about disability representation.

## LEARNING OBJECTIVES

**After completing this chapter, you will be able to**

- Define emotion and explain its importance in public speaking

- Express emotions to evoke audience responses

- Use reasoning to appeal to your audience's emotions

- Craft stories that move audiences to action

**emotion**
an intuitive reaction based on experiences, behavior, values, and attitudes

**emotional contagion**
our tendency to synchronize our emotional experience with the people around us

**behavioral mimicry**
the tendency for people to mimic the emotional expressions of people around them

**affective feedback**
how our own facial, vocal, and postural expressions affect our emotions

Stella Young shows just how important emotions are when you're connecting with your audience, teaching them something new, or asking them to change. **Emotions** are intuitive reactions based on our experiences, behavior, values, and attitudes.[2] We use our emotions to discern whether something is right or wrong, good or bad, important or unimportant. Our emotions move us to care about people, ideas, and values. They drive us to learn, act, and grow. A speech without emotion is like an engine without gas—even if all the parts are in place, it still won't take you anywhere. Sharing your own passions, values, and stories can give you the fuel you need to craft a truly moving presentation.

# Evoking Emotion through Expression

One of the easiest ways to evoke an emotional response in your audience is by expressing that emotion yourself. When we talk with someone happy, it can lift our spirits; when we talk to someone sad, it can bring us down. This process is called **emotional contagion**: our tendency to synchronize our emotional experience with the people around us.[3] Emotional contagion has two steps: **behavioral mimicry** and **affective feedback**.

Emotional contagion occurs when we unconsciously imitate the behavior of the people around us.

1. **BEHAVIORAL MIMICRY.** Most people have the tendency to unconsciously mimic the emotional expressions of the people around them. This includes facial expression, but also vocal expression, posture, and movement.

2. **AFFECTIVE FEEDBACK.** The facial, vocal, and postural expressions we adopt influence our emotional experience. For example, smiling and laughing can make you feel happy; standing up straight and putting your hands on your hips can help you feel proud.

When we unconsciously mimic another person's emotional expression, we start to actually feel the emotion they are expressing ourselves. So as a public speaker, the emotions you express can influence your audience to feel those same emotions. Emotional contagion plays a particularly important role in online public speaking, where viral videos spread from viewer to viewer by evoking a strong emotional response.[4]

You can amplify emotional contagion by asking your audience to actively mimic your behavior. You might ask them to:

- Mirror your posture. For example: "Everybody stand up" or "Let's all take a knee."

- Copy your gestures. For example: "Put your hands in the air" or "Everybody point to the person next to you."

- Repeat your words. For example: "Say it with me: Women's rights are human rights" or "Repeat after me: No blood for oil."

Calling your audience to repeat a series of phrases after you is a technique known as **call-and-response**.[5] You can see the powerful emotional impact of call-and-response when speakers in the Black Lives Matter movement call their audience to "Say his name" or "Say her name" to memorialize the victims of police brutality.

> 📋 **TRY THIS**
>
> To activate emotional contagion in your speech, try the **Call-and-Response Worksheet**.

**Pathways**
To learn more about expressing emotions with your voice, face, posture, and gestures, see **Chapter 12, Vocal and Physical Delivery**.

**call-and-response**
calling your audience to repeat a series of phrases after you

**identification**
communicating shared identities, experiences, and values

**countercontagion**
when people respond with emotions different from the ones you express

While emotional contagion can be incredibly effective, it will only work if your audience imitates the emotions you display. An audience is most likely to reflect your emotional expressions when they identify with you. As a speaker, you can create **identification** with your audience by communicating shared identities, experiences, and values. But if your audience still sees you as different from themselves, expressing strong emotions can create countercontagion instead.

**Countercontagion** is when people respond with emotions different from the ones you express, rather than synchronizing their emotions with yours. If your audience doesn't identify with you, expressing emotion can lead them to respond in unpredictable ways. For example, if a close friend of yours got angry about a parking ticket, you might share their frustration. But if a stranger on the street got angry about a parking ticket, you might be more likely to feel fear or disgust. If a classmate expressed worry about an upcoming exam you're both taking, that might make you worry, too; but if your roommate expressed worry about an exam that you don't have to take, you might feel pity or compassion instead.

## Pathways

To revisit the techniques for creating identification, see **Chapter 3, Ethics and Credibility**.

When your audience doesn't identify with your standpoint or your circumstances, expressing strong emotions is risky—particularly when the emotions you're expressing are negative. If your audience doesn't identify with you, expressing negative emotions—like anger or fear—can lead them to make negative judgments about your credibility as a speaker. So anytime you plan on using emotional expression as a strategy for evoking audience emotion, be sure to establish identification with your audience early in your speech. And anytime your audience analysis reveals significant differences between you and your audience, keep your own emotional expression neutral and use other strategies— like reasoning or narrative—to create the emotional response you want.

## ✓ Critical Thinking Check

1. Why do you think mimicking other people's facial expressions, tone of voice, posture, and gestures leads us to feel the same emotions they do? Why do you think this contagion only works when we identify with the person expressing emotion?

2. Some stereotypes focus on emotional expression—for example, stereotyping Black people as "angry" or women as "too emotional." Do you think countercontagion contributes to these stereotypes? Why or why not?

# Evoking Emotion with Reasoning

While people sometimes think of them as opposites, emotion and reasoning are most effective when they are integrated. Without emotion, reasoning is powerless. If your audience doesn't care, they are unlikely to reason thoughtfully about an issue—or even listen to your evidence in the first place. Even in the most technical or rational discussions, emotions shape our decisions and spur us to take action.[6]

But without reason, emotion can be dangerous. Reasoning gives audiences the tools to think critically about the ideas and events they care about. Reason helps us stay open to other perspectives and check our prejudices and knee-jerk reactions against the best available evidence. Even relatively mundane decisions, like what to eat for breakfast, work best when reasoning helps guide our emotions.

By combining reason and emotion, you can give audiences evidence and arguments that they genuinely care about. In fact, you can use evidence and reasoning to evoke emotions—like anger, fear, compassion, aspiration, and happiness—that move your audience to take action.[7]

## EVOKING ANGER

Countless examples—from Malcolm X's calls for racial justice, to Erin Brockovich's campaign against corporate polluters, to MADD's efforts to reduce drunk driving—show that anger is an important rhetorical tool. **Anger** is the feeling that an unjustified harm has been done to you or someone you care about. While often characterized as a negative emotion, anger can be a normal, healthy, and productive response to an unjust situation. Anger can reveal problems, demand solutions, and motivate people to act.[8] When combined with effective steps for action, evoking anger is one of the most powerful ways speakers persuade their audiences to fight for justice and the common good.[9] To use anger effectively in a speech, you must both demonstrate a harm and recommend a response:

1. **MAKE THE HARM PERSONAL**. Show your audience that harm has been done to them or someone they care about. People experience anger when they themselves are harmed, but also when that harm is directed toward

**Pathways**

To revisit strategies for using reasoning to overcome bias, see **Chapter 7, Evidence and Reasoning**.

**anger**
the feeling that unjustified harm has been done to you or someone you care about

an individual or group that they identify with. For example: "On average, women in the United States are paid only 81 cents for every dollar that men earn. That means your mother, your sister, your girlfriend, your wife, your daughter—and maybe even you yourself—get 19 percent less money for the same work. This isn't just a problem for individual women; this hurts millions of working families."[10]

2. **SHOW THE HARM IS UNDESERVED.** Anger is the feeling that you and the people you care about deserve better—whether that's respect, money, status, freedom, rights, or any other value. You can increase an audience's anger by amplifying the significance of the injustice. For example: "Are women worth 19 percent less? Is work 19 percent less valuable because it was done with a woman's hands? No. Every human being deserves to be fairly compensated for the work they do."

3. **LEGITIMIZE TAKING ACTION.** Emphasize that your audience has the power and right to take action and pursue justice. For example: "We have a right to demand equal pay for ourselves and for the women we work alongside. That is why I am calling on you to ask your employers to sign the Equal Pay Pledge."

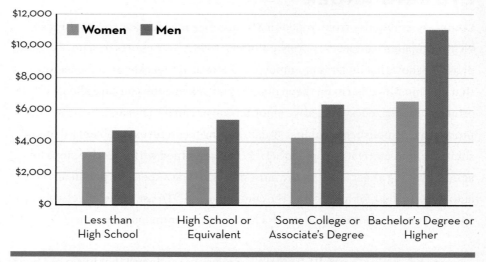

**Adult Workers' Monthly Earnings in 2020**

You can use evidence to demonstrate that a harm is undeserved. For example, this chart shows the income gap between men and women across every education level.[11]

4.  **OFFER A PROPORTIONAL RESPONSE.** Help them see they have a course of action that is proportional to the harm done. A disproportionately small response will not be enough to redress the harm, while a disproportionately large response may cause more harm than good. The audience will need to believe that whatever action you propose fits the severity of the harm. For example: "The Equal Pay Pledge doesn't ask employers for any special treatment. It's just a promise to raise women's wages and salaries to the same level that men receive for performing the same jobs."

5.  **DEMONSTRATE THE ACTION'S EFFICACY.** Show your audience how their action can reduce existing harm, compensate for past harm, or prevent future harm. By recommending an effective response to injustice, you can empower your audience to create positive change. For example: "While the Equal Pay Pledge may not solve the problem overnight, every employer who signs it will make it harder for other companies to continue offering unfair pay. Working women and working families will know where they can expect unequal treatment and where they can expect to get a fair deal."

## EVOKING FEAR

If you've ever seen a public health message warning you not to smoke or a political speech about the problems facing our nation, you understand the value of fear. Although it may not feel pleasant, fear helps us avoid unnecessary risks and protect ourselves from danger. **Fear** is the feeling that some future harm may come to you or someone you care about. To use fear effectively in a speech, you must show your audience that the harm is both significant and likely to happen, and then recommend an action that reduces the likelihood and magnitude of the harm.

**fear**
the feeling that some future harm may come to you or someone you care about

1.  **DEMONSTRATE THE HARM'S MAGNITUDE.** Emphasizing how much will be lost, how damaging it will be, or how difficult it would be to recover are all ways to show audiences the severity of the harm. For example: "Sending just one quick text while you're driving might not seem like a big deal. But getting in a car accident can change your whole life—or even end it."

2.  **DEMONSTRATE THE HARM'S LIKELIHOOD.** Showing your audience that others like them have suffered the same harm, or that people in their position are at greater risk, can evoke fear. A lack of control and a sense of

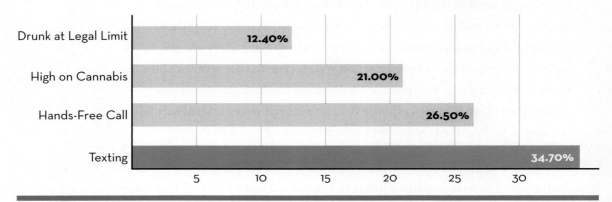

## Impairment of Driver Reaction Time

| | |
|---|---|
| Drunk at Legal Limit | 12.40% |
| High on Cannabis | 21.00% |
| Hands-Free Call | 26.50% |
| Texting | 34.70% |

You can use evidence to emphasize risk. For example, this graph shows that texting slows drivers' reaction times even more than alcohol or marijuana.[12]

uncertainty can also increase the perceived likelihood of the harm. For example: "If you think it can't happen to you, you're wrong. Here in the United States, eleven teenagers die every day as a result of texting while driving. One teenage driver in Kansas died just to text a single letter: 'k.'"[13]

3. **RECOMMEND ACTION TO REDUCE THE RISK.** Give your audience a viable action that can lower the likelihood that a harmful future event will occur. For example: "Texting causes one out of every four car accidents, so you can reduce your risk of a crash just by turning off your notifications before you get behind the wheel."[14]

4. **RECOMMEND ACTION TO REDUCE THE MAGNITUDE.** Show your audience that even if the action doesn't completely eliminate the risk, it will reduce the severity of the damage that occurs. For example: "Even though you can't control what other drivers do, keeping your eyes off your phone and on the road will keep you ready to respond to whatever comes your way."

## EVOKING COMPASSION

If you have ever been invited to donate to a food bank or participate in a walk-athon for cancer research, you know how compassion can move people to help others. **Compassion** is the desire to reduce an undeserved harm suffered by someone else. Appeals to compassion call you to connect with the pain or adversity that others experience and take action to alleviate their suffering.

**compassion**
the desire to reduce an undeserved harm suffered by someone else

1. **EMPHASIZE THE MAGNITUDE OF THE HARM.** As with anger or fear, demonstrating the extent of the harm is critical for evoking compassion. For example: "Russia's recent invasion of Ukraine has killed thousands of Ukrainian citizens, and millions more have fled to seek refuge in other countries."

2. **SHOW THE HARM IS UNDESERVED.** Explain that the people suffering did not cause their own harm. For example: "The Ukrainian people did nothing to provoke this attack—it was a unilateral act of aggression by Russia."

3. **EMPATHIZE WITH OTHERS' SUFFERING.** Help your audience take the perspective of the person or group that has been harmed. For example: "Imagine what it would feel like to wake up to the sound of rockets whistling and bombs exploding into the homes and buildings around you. Imagine seeking shelter in basements and metro stations without food or medical supplies, wondering whether your friends and family are still alive."

**Pathways**

To revisit the concept of perspective taking, see **Chapter 4, Listening and Responding**.

4. **ACKNOWLEDGE THE DIFFERENCE IN STANDPOINT.** Although your audience must be able to empathize with others' suffering to feel compassion, they must also recognize that they cannot fully understand others' experience.[15] For example: "For those of us who are safe here at home, it's hard to fathom what it must be like to have your home, your country, and so many of your friends and neighbors suddenly taken away from you."

5. **RECOMMEND ACTION TO REDUCE THE SUFFERING.** Identify the barriers keeping the other person or group from remedying the harm, and explain how your audience can help. For example: "The Ukrainian people have lost everything—not just their homes and their communities, but the basic resources they need to survive. You can help provide emergency food, water, and medical supplies to Ukrainian refugees by donating to the International Committee of the Red Cross at icrc.org."

Images of Ukrainian refugees crossing into neighboring countries to avoid Russian bombings evoked compassion from people around the world in 2022.

# Stopping the Spread of Viral Hate Speech

Just as online communication has become a powerful tool for spreading ideas and mobilizing people, it has also become a tool for spreading hate. Hate speech uses anger to target groups of people, depicting their identities as dangerous or less than human.[16] The anger created by online hate speech leads to real-world violence and hate crimes against the people it targets.[17]

Why does hate speech go viral on social media? Anger is among the most powerful emotions that drive the reposting and sharing of online content.[18] Appeals to anger—especially those using inflammatory or emotionally charged language—generate likes, shares, and comments.[19] That engagement causes social media platforms' algorithms to promote those angry messages, so even more people see and circulate them. Once that content makes people angry, they become more likely to seek out and share additional information that justifies or inflames their anger.[20] More than other emotions, anger creates motivated reasoning and biased interpretations of new information, making it difficult to challenge messages of hate with reasoning alone.[21]

So how do we stop online hate speech? With equally intense displays of compassion.[22] When

Activists outside of Twitter's Tokyo head office call for the company to combat the rise of hate speech on its platform.

you see someone spreading hate, call it out for what it is. Let your friends and followers know that hate speech causes real harm to people's mental health and physical safety. Emphasize that no one deserves to be insulted, harassed, or threatened based on who they are. Express empathy for individuals and groups targeted by hate speech, while acknowledging that you may not be able to fully understand their experience. Most importantly, tell people what they can do to help the targeted person or group—whether by making a donation, signing a petition, attending a protest, or just sharing a message of support.

# EVOKING ASPIRATION

Aspiration is one of the most common emotional appeals, appearing everywhere from car commercials to Instagram posts to university websites. Aspiration is the inverse of compassion: while compassion is the desire to help others who are less fortunate than you, **aspiration** is the desire to experience the good fortune of others for yourself. Aspiration can take many forms, including ambition, admiration, inspiration, and even envy. At its best, aspiration motivates people to achieve what they value.

Evoking aspiration is one of the most common strategies used by motivational and inspirational speakers. Here, Iyanla Vanzant speaks at the 2014 The Life You Want Weekend in Miami, Florida.

1. **PRESENT AN ASPIRATIONAL FIGURE.** Begin by presenting a person or group that has something that your audience wants. This might include love, freedom, status, money, friendship, health, or any values that are important to your audience. For example: "As one of the cofounders of Twitter, Biz Stone has been recognized as one of *Time* magazine's '100 Most Influential People in the World,' as *Inc.*'s 'Entrepreneur of the Decade,' and even as *GQ*'s 'Nerd of the Year.'"[23]

    **aspiration**
    the desire to experience the good fortune of others for yourself

2. **HELP YOUR AUDIENCE IDENTIFY WITH THE FIGURE.** Emphasize the similarities between the aspirational figure and your audience. The stronger the identification, the more your audience will feel that they can fulfill their desire. Since this person did it, they can too. For example: "While today he's a successful entrepreneur worth over $250 million, he started out unemployed, living in his mom's basement with massive credit card debt."[24]

3. **SHOW HOW THE FIGURE ACHIEVED THEIR GOALS.** Help your audience believe in their ability to accomplish their goals by showing them actions or strategies that others have used to make it happen. The more they believe in the effectiveness of your suggestions, the more likely they are to act on their feeling of aspiration. For example: "He started a blog and used it to interview leaders in the tech field. When he read that Evan Williams, one of the people he interviewed, had his company acquired by Google, Biz reached out and asked for a job—and got it. A couple years later, Biz and Evan left Google to found the start-up that eventually became Twitter."

> **📋 TRY THIS**
>
> To integrate emotional appeals into your reasoning, see the **Emotions and Evidence Checklist.**

4. **RECOMMEND THE SAME STRATEGY TO YOUR AUDIENCE.**
Using the figure as an example, suggest specific steps that your audience can take to get what they want. For example: "Biz Stone shows just how important it is to build relationships with the people you want to work with. If you're just getting started, actively reach out to people in the industry you're interested in. Don't wait for an opportunity—*create* the opportunity that launches your career."

## EVOKING HAPPINESS

Anytime people celebrate an achievement or mark a milestone—like an award, graduation, retirement, wedding, or anniversary—you can see speakers evoking happiness. **Happiness** is satisfaction with yourself and your circumstances.[25] It includes feelings like contentment, joy, pride, and gratitude. While appeals to aspiration show people how they can get what they want, appeals to happiness show your audience that they have already reached their goals and fulfilled their desires. Unlike the other emotions we've discussed, happiness calls for stability and continuity rather than change.

**happiness**
satisfaction with yourself and your circumstances

Rio Rancho student Jordan Montoya delivers the senior speech at her 2016 graduation. Ceremonies and events like graduations and weddings often call for speeches that evoke happiness.

1. **AFFIRM YOUR AUDIENCE'S VALUES.** Remind your audience of their core values and explain why they're important. For example: "As I look out at all the friends and families who are here today to support our graduates, it reminds me just how much our own achievements depend on the people who love us."

2. **DEMONSTRATE HOW THEY HAVE ACHIEVED THOSE VALUES.** Show your audience how their current actions and circumstances fulfill their most important values and desires. For example: "If you need proof that love helps us do great things, just look around you. Look at all the parents and grandparents, the siblings and cousins, the new and old friends who showed up to support you here today."

3. **ENCOURAGE THEM TO MAINTAIN BEHAVIORS THAT UPHOLD THEIR VALUES.** Celebrating your audience's achievements can help them continue their current good habits. The key is to link the happiness they feel with the behavior you want them to maintain. For example: "As you go out into the world, carry that

If your audience's feelings ever get so intense that they become overwhelming or distracting, you can use these strategies to de-escalate their emotional reaction and regain their focus:

1. EXPRESS CALM. Model equanimity by speaking slowly and quietly, presenting a neutral facial expression, and adopting a still, open posture with your palms upward. If necessary, you might even stop speaking and close your eyes for a moment.

2. VERBALLY ACKNOWLEDGE THEIR EMOTIONAL REACTION. For example: "I can see that you're having a strong reaction to this image" or "I know that these statistics can be disturbing."

3. CREATE IDENTIFICATION. Let your audience know that you share their feelings. For example: "I feel exactly the same way" or "When I first heard about this, it really upset me, too."

4. TIE THAT SHARED EMOTION BACK TO THE PURPOSE OF YOUR SPEECH. For example: "That's why I care so much about..." or "This is why it's so important for us to..."

love with you. Keep showing up for each other. Know that you can do anything because this whole stadium full of people has got your back."

## ✓ Critical Thinking Check

1. Is there a difference between manipulating your audience's emotions and evoking their emotions with reasoning? If so, what is it? If not, why not?

2. Do you think appealing to positive emotions—like compassion, aspiration, or happiness—is more ethical than appealing to negative emotions—like anger or fear? Why or why not?

# Evoking Emotion with Stories

Whether you want to evoke happiness, aspiration, compassion, fear, anger, or any other emotion, telling a story is one of the most effective ways to do it. Stories are an important part of how we understand ourselves and the world. Through stories, we can encounter experiences that are usually inaccessible from our own standpoints. Stories let us see life through the eyes of other people who have faced different challenges and taken different actions than we have.

**Pathways**

To learn more about marking happy occasions, see **Chapter 17, Connecting and Celebrating**.

**narrative**
an account of connected events; a story

**exposition**
description of the characters and setting

**crisis**
a significant change in the characters or setting that requires a response

**action**
what the characters in a story do in response to the crisis

**resolution**
where the characters and setting end up as a result of the action

A story, or **narrative**, is an account of connected events. In public speaking, most stories contain the following four elements:[26]

1.  **EXPOSITION.** The **exposition** describes the characters and setting. This often focuses on a main character, who is the central figure of the story. As a public speaker, you may be this central figure, or you may be describing the experiences of another person—but either way, the character and setting you describe should be real, not fictional. For example: "I was a pretty average guy my first couple years of college. I played intramural soccer, I made OK grades in my engineering classes, and I had great friends and a family who loved me back home."

2.  **CRISIS.** The **crisis** is a moment in which the setting or characters undergo some significant change that requires a response. This may include an event, a new character, or an inner realization by the main character. For example: "But then I started losing weight and feeling tired all the time."

3.  **ACTION.** The **action** is what the characters do in response to this crisis. In dramatic or comedic narratives—like the ones you know from novels or movies—this often includes an extended series of interrelated actions. But in public speaking, narratives are much simpler, and may only include a single action. For example: "I went to the doctor, and found out I have Hodgkin's disease: a type of cancer that attacks the body's immune system."

4.  **RESOLUTION.** The **resolution** is where the characters and setting end up as a result of the action. For example: "And I realized that all the things I thought were average—running around on the soccer field, preparing for a

| Exposition | Crisis | Action | Resolution |

In public speaking, narratives contain four key elements: exposition, crisis, action, and resolution.

future career, spending time with the people I loved—were actually pretty special. Facing cancer has taught me how precious life is. Now, I don't take anything for granted."

Together, these four elements—exposition, crisis, action, and resolution—form a narrative that can teach, motivate, and connect with your audience. Whether your entire speech is presented as a story, or a story is just one part of your larger presentation, crafting an emotionally engaging narrative relies on three strategies: identification, imitation, and amplification.

## IDENTIFICATION AND DISIDENTIFICATION

The first key to a powerful story is identification. Remember: identification is communicating shared identities, experiences, and values. So far, we have focused on creating identification between the audience and the speaker. But to tell an effective story, you also need to help your audience connect with the characters, the setting, or the crisis they face.

- **CHARACTERS.** Identification with characters means that the audience members see the characters—especially your main character—as similar to themselves. That may concern elements of their identity, but it may also include their actions and their goals. For example: "My boss started out broke just like a lot of us. He didn't have any special advantages. But he wanted a better life and was determined to make something of himself."

- **SETTING.** Your audience might also identify with the setting, seeing the circumstances of the story as similar to their own situation. For example: "He grew up right here in Detroit, and graduated from high school around the time all the big auto plants started laying people off."

- **CRISIS.** Your audience might identify with the narrative crisis, if they are facing a similar challenge in their own lives. For example: "He knew it wouldn't be easy trying to make his own way. But for blue-collar folks like us, no one else was hiring."

Your goal is to create audience engagement with your story using strong identification—or in some cases, strong disidentification. While identification communicates commonalities, **disidentification** emphasizes differences in

**disidentification**
emphasizing differences in identities, experiences, and values

identities, experiences, and values. For example, you could create disidentification by focusing on aspects of the character, setting, and crisis that set your boss apart from your working-class audience—a penchant for drinking tea in tiny silver cups, an elite prep school background, or a dilemma over whether to accept his uncle's multimillion-dollar offer of start-up capital.

Whether you use identification or disidentification, your audience's relationship to your main character will frame their interpretation of your story. Identification encourages your audience to experience the narrative from the perspective of the character, as though the events of the story were happening to them. Disidentification encourages the audience to reject the character, and root against them as the story unfolds. In both cases, you use your audience's values, attitudes, and behaviors to increase their investment in the action, resolution, and lesson of the story.

## IMITATION AND REJECTION

In creating identification or disidentification, you encourage your audience to evaluate the characters and their actions. You portray the character's actions as good or bad, desirable or undesirable. This motivates the audience to either imitate or reject those actions. By imitating or rejecting the character's actions, the audience applies the lessons of your story to their own lives.

You can encourage either imitation or rejection by framing the character's actions as either positive or negative. You can frame an action as positive or negative based on its intrinsic value, practical outcome, or social judgment:

- **INTRINSIC VALUE.** Is the action right or wrong? Showing that an action fits your audience's values can inspire them to imitate it. For example: "My boss was a humanitarian who focused on hiring employees with felony convictions or a history of drug addiction." But if you indicate that an action goes against your audience's values, they will likely reject it. For example: "My boss was a predator who targeted employees with felony convictions or a history of drug addiction."

- **PRACTICAL OUTCOME.** Is the action beneficial or harmful? Emphasizing the benefits of an action encourages your audience to imitate it. For example:

"Hiring employees who were down on their luck helped them get back on their feet, build community, and reintegrate into society." On the other hand, if you want your audience to reject an action, focus on its harmful effects: "Hiring employees who were down on their luck allowed my boss to pay them the bare minimum and make them work long hours in dangerous conditions."

- **SOCIAL JUDGMENT.** Is the action admirable or shameful? Demonstrating that other people approve or admire the action invites imitation. For example: "My boss has won the National Role Model Award, been featured on *American Morning*, and been honored by the US Institute for Rehabilitation." But showing that other people disapprove of an action cues your audience to avoid it: "My boss has been publicly censured by the local Chamber of Commerce and has had multiple protests outside the factory."

## AMPLIFICATION AND MINIMIZATION

The actions of characters can be framed to make them seem more or less significant. You can make actions appear more significant by emphasizing that they were difficult, risky, or intentional. A risky and difficult action done voluntarily is a greater act—either a greater good or greater bad, depending on its evaluation.

Photographers often play with perspective to make things appear larger or smaller. Public speakers similarly use techniques of amplification and minimization to affect an audience's perception of an event or action.

# Arnold Schwarzenegger's Kristallnacht Story

In the wake of the 2021 US Capitol riots, Arnold Schwarzenegger—action movie star and former governor of California—released a video on his YouTube channel: *Governor Schwarzenegger's Message Following This Week's Attack on the Capitol.*[27] He began by sharing an element of his standpoint and creating identification with his audience: "As an immigrant to this country, I would like to say a few words to my fellow Americans and to our friends around the world about the events of recent days." He goes on to explain that he grew up in Austria and shares his experience growing up in the aftermath of World War II and Kristallnacht, the Night of Broken Glass.

He connects Kristallnacht to the US Capitol attack: "It was a night of rampage against the Jews carried out in 1938 by the Nazi equivalent of the Proud Boys." Immediately, this historical comparison produces an identification between the Nazis and the Proud Boys—leading the audience to disidentify with the Proud Boys and reject their actions.

He continues the comparison: "Wednesday was the Day of Broken Glass right here in the United States. The broken glass was in the windows of the United States Capitol." Here, Schwarzenegger reaffirms his identification with his American viewers, and reaffirms the identification between the Austrian Night of Broken Glass and the American Day of Broken Glass—again calling for the rejection of those actions.

Schwarzenegger then amplifies the magnitude of the harm: "But the mob did not just shatter the windows of the Capitol. They shattered the ideas we took for granted. They did not just break down the doors of the building that housed American democracy. They trampled on the very principles on which our country was founded." By using the

An action that is easy, safe, or unavoidable will be viewed as a lesser act—either less good or less bad.

- ■ **DIFFICULTY.** Is the action difficult or easy? Emphasizing the difficulty of an action makes it seem more important. For example, "I had to overcome my fears to blow the whistle on my boss" sounds more impressive than "All I had to do was make a phone call to blow the whistle on my boss."

Capitol building as a symbol of American values, Schwarzenegger magnifies the harm and intensifies his audience's dis-identification and rejection of the rioters.

He closes the story by describing the consequences of losing those values: "I grew up in the ruins of a country that suffered the loss of its democracy." He relies on his own standpoint as a child who grew up in post–World War II Austria: "Growing up, I was surrounded by broken men drinking away the guilt over their participation in the most evil regime in history." He goes on to explain that his own father, like many men in his community, would often get drunk, hit his children, and scare his mother. By sharing this painful memory, Schwarzenegger uses his own standpoint to paint a vivid picture of the personal costs of losing democratic values.

Simultaneously drawing on his own standpoint and maintaining a strong identification with his American viewers, Schwarzenegger strongly dissuades

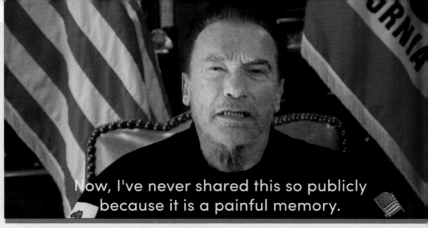

*Now, I've never shared this so publicly because it is a painful memory.*

Former California governor Arnold Schwarzenegger releases a video condemning the January 6, 2021, attack on the US Capitol Building. He compares the attack to the events of Kristallnacht, the Night of Broken Glass (1:26).

them from embracing the identity or the actions of the Capitol rioters. Calling the American public to rededicate themselves to the democratic values of truth and tolerance, Governor Schwarzenegger created an emotionally compelling persuasive narrative that was picked up by nearly every major news source and viewed over six million times on YouTube.

To watch a video of Governor Schwarzenegger's speech, do a web search for: Schwarzenegger message following attack. The video is approximately 7:38 in length.

- ▪ **RISK.** Is the action risky or safe? The greater the risk, the greater the deed. For example, "I risked my livelihood to blow the whistle on my boss" sounds more significant than "When I blew the whistle on my boss, I knew everything would turn out OK."

- ▪ **INTENTION.** Is the action intentional or unintentional? Intentional actions seem more significant than unintentional ones. For example, "I decided to

**📋 TRY THIS**

To structure events into a compelling narrative, see the **Telling Your Story Worksheet**.

blow the whistle on my boss" sounds more heroic than "I accidentally blew the whistle on my boss."

The more you amplify an action, the more you can increase your audience's desire to imitate or reject it. But remember that they must still be able to identify with the person taking the action. If you want your audience to imitate an action, the amplification cannot go so far that they no longer believe the action is within their reach. You can use minimization strategically to make an action seem more accessible. For example, you might frame whistleblowing as easy and safe so your audience will be more likely to attempt it.

You might also use minimization—framing a negative action as an unavoidable accident or an easy mistake to make—to evoke compassion. For example, Stella Young emphasized that her student's stereotypical expectations about people with disabilities were not his fault—instead, they were based on media messages he had received. This allowed her audience to continue identifying with the student, likewise learning a lesson about disability stereotypes without being blamed for them.

## ✓ Critical Thinking Check

1. Why do you think stories are often less complex in public speeches than in novels, television series, and movies? What purpose do the four narrative elements—exposition, crisis, action, and resolution—serve for public speakers?

2. How is establishing your audience's identification with a character similar to establishing their identification with you as a speaker? How is it different? When might you want to create disidentification between your audience and a character in a story? Would you ever want to create disidentification between your audience and yourself?

# Next Steps

Whether you engage your audience's emotions with stories, reasoning, or your own emotional expression, emotional appeals are crucial in any public presentation. In informative speeches, emotion helps you gain and maintain your audience's interest. In persuasive speeches, emotion helps you motivate your audience to change their beliefs and behavior. And in connective speeches, emotion helps you create a stronger bond with your audience.

You can start incorporating emotional appeals into your speeches by using the Call-and-Response Worksheet, the Emotions and Evidence Checklist, and the Telling Your Story Worksheet. These exercises will help you create emotional contagion, demonstrate benefits and harm, and frame effective narratives—putting the key tools for evoking emotions into practice. When you know how to appeal to your audience's emotions, you'll be ready to choose just the right words to inform, persuade, and connect with them.

# Standpoint Reflection

- What are some of the most emotionally powerful speeches you have experienced? What made them so powerful? How might you use those same strategies and techniques in your own speaking?

- How comfortable do you feel expressing strong emotion as a speaker? Would emotional contagion work for you as a strategy for evoking audience emotion, or would reasoning and narrative strategies better fit your strengths?

- Do you have any concerns about using negative emotions—like anger and fear—in your speeches? What kinds of speaking situations would justify appeals to anger or fear? When might appeals to anger or fear be inappropriate?

- What are some of your favorite personal stories to tell? What emotions do they evoke? What do these stories communicate about your standpoint? How might you use those stories as part of your public speaking toolbox?

## Key Terms

# Resources for Emotion and Narrative

 ## "Try This" Exercises

Access the "Try This" exercises as directed by your instructor or online at digital.wwnorton.com/chapterexercises-conpubspeak

- To activate emotional contagion in your speech, try the **Call-and-Response Worksheet**.

- To integrate emotional appeals into your reasoning, see the **Emotions and Evidence Checklist**.

- To structure events into a compelling narrative, see the **Telling Your Story Worksheet**.

Want to practice these skills to prepare for your next speech? Go to INQUIZITIVE to review and apply concepts from this chapter and get personalized feedback along the way.

ENVIRONMENTAL ACTIVIST
AND HIP-HOP ARTIST Xiuhtezcatl Martinez

# 11 Language and Style

As the cofounder of Earth Guardians, Xiuhtezcatl Martinez has helped young people in over sixty countries build environmental movements and pursue social justice.[1] He started locally as a teen speaking out against single-use plastic bags and pesticides in his city's parks.[2] Today, he has become known for his rousing, inspiring, and powerful speeches at climate change conferences, TEDx events, and the United Nations.[3]

One of Martinez's strengths as a speaker is his creative and moving use of language. Repetition and contrast are signature elements of his style. For example, in his speech at the 2016 United Nations Climate Reception, he uses the phrase "I saw..." to start six sentences in a row, listing the environmental and humanitarian crises that motivated him to become an activist.[4] He ties the sequence together by linking the first and final repetition of the phrase to climate change: "I saw ice caps falling into our oceans" and "I saw people suffering from climate change all over the planet."

In his 2014 Bioneers speech, he uses contrast to emphasize the impacts of climate change: "Colorado suffered the greatest fire we have ever seen in our history in the same three months as we've suffered our greatest floods." And he uses repetition to highlight the contrast between the past and present: "We are seeing floods where we never see floods. We are seeing fires and droughts where we never see fires and droughts."[5]

Martinez sees his hip-hop recordings as an extension of his public advocacy and activism. He often raps about climate change and social justice, sometimes even blending hip-hop performances into his presentations.[6] As his track "Boombox Warfare" explains, "more than a method of communication, hip-hop culture is our greatest tool for liberation."[7]

## LEARNING OBJECTIVES

**After completing this chapter, you will be able to**

- Recognize the equal value of different languages, dialects, and speech communities

- Choose language that both expresses your standpoint and connects with your audience

- Adapt to your context and purpose with grand, plain, and middle styles of speaking

- Combine different stylistic elements to develop your personal speaking style

Xiuhtezcatl Martinez shows that our words do more than just reflect the world around us—they have the power to reshape it. His activism demonstrates that language can be poetic in the deepest sense of the word. More than just rhyme or verse, the Greek root *poiesis* means creating or making. Language has the world-making power to change our perceptions, stir our emotions, and motivate us to act. Now is the time to use it.

# Language, Culture, and Standpoint

Using language effectively is all about adaptation—adaptation to different audiences, purposes, contexts, and positions that we occupy in society. **Language** is a shared system of symbols—whether written, spoken, or signed—that a group of people uses to communicate meaning.[8] Meaning-making systems vary widely from one community and culture to the next. Different languages have different rules and norms for vocabulary, grammar, and usage.

- **VOCABULARY.** Symbols have both denotative and connotative meanings.[9] **Denotative meaning** is what a symbol explicitly names or describes—the dictionary definition of the term. **Connotative meaning** is the emotional association a symbol suggests (see Figure 11.1). For example, the word *vintage* literally denotes something from a past era, but it also connotes high quality and nostalgia. Both denotation and connotation are culturally specific. Other languages have words for emotions we don't have in English, like German *schadenfreude*—pleasure derived from another person's misfortune—or Japanese *yūgen*—the melancholic beauty of the universe only partially glimpsed.

- **GRAMMAR.** Grammatical rules explain how to arrange symbols into meaningful relationships. For example, in English, adjectives generally come before the noun they modify, while in Spanish, adjectives usually come after the noun: *"color favorito"* instead of "favorite color." English sentences typically place the subject first, followed by the verb, and then the object: "We like them" rather than "Like we them." But many languages—including Welsh and Filipino—do start with the verb, followed by the subject and object.

- **USAGE.** Usage norms explain how to apply symbols in social situations. For example, even if you know the definition of the English word "ma'am"—a term of respectful address for a woman—you would also need to know when it is

**language**
a shared system of symbols that a group of people uses to communicate meaning

**denotative meaning**
what a symbol explicitly names or describes

**connotative meaning**
the emotional association a symbol suggests

| POSITIVE |
| Youth |
| Teen |
| Adolescent |
| Juvenile |
| NEGATIVE |

**FIGURE 11.1** Words with the same denotative meaning can have a wide range of connotative meanings.

appropriate to use that word. In the southern US, almost anyone who identifies as female can be called ma'am, including young girls. Elsewhere in the US, you might offend an adult woman by calling her "ma'am," because there it implies that she is significantly older than you. And in Great Britain—where "ma'am" is reserved for royalty and ranking officers in the police or military—you might raise some eyebrows by using the word to address an ordinary citizen.

## ADDRESSING SPEECH COMMUNITIES

Languages are complex and diverse, and English is an especially diverse collection of languages. Scholars who study varieties of English find there are over two dozen different versions of the language in the United States alone, and over eighty varieties of English globally.[10] Each has its own distinct rules and norms.

What many people think of as "standard" American English is just one of the language's many forms, which a number of scholars call "white mainstream English."[11] It reflects the particular kind of English commonly used by white Americans with higher education from the northern and western regions of the United States.[12] It dominates English language use in American education and media but is far from the only recognized version of English spoken in the US.

American English varies by region, ethnicity, and culture. Alongside white mainstream English, we have Black English, Cajun English, Pennsylvania Dutch English, Yeshiva English, and several Latinx Englishes that reflect influences from Mexican, Cuban, and Puerto Rican Spanishes. In some cases, American English has been combined with Indigenous languages to create hybrid forms like Gullah and Afro-Seminole Creole. American English also includes a rich spectrum of regional dialects, from Southern Appalachian to High Tider.

Bottom line: there is no one right way to speak English. Instead, our diverse ways of speaking are grounded in different **speech communities**: groups that share common attitudes, values, and behaviors around language use.[13] Speech communities' expectations about language include everything from vocabulary, spelling, and grammar to aspects of delivery like vocal inflection and pronunciation. For example, regional speech communities use different terms to address groups

**speech communities**
groups that share common attitudes, values, and behaviors around language use

## Pathways

To learn more about how aspects of delivery vary across diverse speech communities, see **Chapter 12, Vocal and Physical Delivery**.

of people: "you," "you guys," "youse guys," "you all," "y'all," "all y'all," and even "you'uns." You might participate in multiple speech communities—for example, speaking one language or dialect at home and another at school.

With all this linguistic diversity, how do you know which norms to follow? As a public speaker, you must decide which forms of English—or any other language—best fit your standpoint, audience, context, and purpose. When you and your audience belong to the same speech communities, it's easy to follow the linguistic norms that you share. But when you are addressing audience members who belong to speech communities different from your own, the issue becomes more complex.

## NAVIGATING LINGUISTIC PRIVILEGE AND MARGINALIZATION

Different speech communities have different degrees of power and privilege in society. While language scholars agree that there is no universally correct way of speaking English, white mainstream English has been normalized as the privileged form of language in the US. For example, when your teachers "corrected" your grammar in school, it's unlikely that they suggested changes to better fit the grammatical rules of Black English or the Southern Appalachian dialect. If you speak any language or dialect other than white mainstream English in the US, you have probably faced social and institutional pressure to speak "better" English.

**assimilation**
pressure to conform to the attitudes, values, and behaviors of a privileged group

This pressure to conform to the attitudes, values, and behaviors of a privileged group is called **assimilation**. Linguistic assimilation not only devalues ways of speaking that don't fit the privileged norm, but also devalues people who don't conform. In less than a sentence of speech, listeners draw assumptions about the speaker's background, education, class, ethnicity, race, gender, national origin, and more.[14] When those assumptions carry positive or negative judgments, they reflect how the listener's own speech community privileges or marginalizes different identities.[15]

## Pathways

For more on linguistic privilege and inclusive language, see **Chapter 3, Ethics and Credibility**.

Faced with these pressures to conform, people with marginalized identities often develop fluency in the language norms of privileged speech communities, allowing them to strategically adapt to different audiences. Altering your use of

Notice the languages used around you every day. Which ones are privileged, and which are marginalized? How might the language norms of your community pressure people to assimilate or require people to code-switch?

language to fit the norms of a different speech community is called **code-switching**.[16] Code-switching allows speakers to move between different forms of the same language—for example, between Black English and white mainstream English—or between different languages—for example, between English and Spanish.[17] In many situations—like interactions with employers, health-care professionals, or law enforcement—code-switching can be a survival skill that helps Black, Latinx, and Indigenous Americans reduce the risk of discrimination and violence.[18]

While code-switching can be a vital tool for dealing with discrimination, it can take an enormous toll. Code-switching puts the burden on marginalized speakers to learn the rules of privileged speech communities and constantly monitor their own behavior. Suppressing your identity in this way leads to further marginalization, lower self-esteem, and feeling separated from more supportive or familiar communities.[19] The disconnection from your community can lead to depression, anxiety, chronic exhaustion, and even internalizing negative stereotypes about your own identity.[20] If you find it necessary to code-switch, seek experiences that celebrate your standpoint, connect with communities you find supportive, and give yourself downtime to take a break from code-switching.

**code-switching**
altering your use of language to fit the norms of a different speech community

## CELEBRATING LINGUISTIC DIVERSITY

Rather than placing all the responsibility for adaptation on speakers with less linguistic privilege, everyone can—and should—help foster an environment that welcomes all modes of expression. Suspend judgment and listen actively to

**Pathways**

To revisit strategies for creating inclusive listening environments, see **Chapter 4, Listening and Responding**.

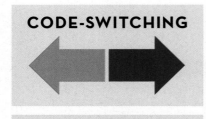

FIGURE 11.2 While code-switching shifts from one language to another, code-meshing blends languages together.

understand speakers from different speech communities. Question your biases and acknowledge how your expectations about language might be specific to particular regions and cultures. Most importantly, appreciate the rich contributions and unique insights that come from different ways of speaking about the world. Do your part to cultivate a context for listening that values every speaker and speech community, speaking from their own standpoints and voices.[21]

When you want to reach out to other speech communities while still expressing your own standpoint, you can combine the language of your own speech communities with the preferred grammar and vocabulary of your audience. **Code-meshing** mixes the norms of multiple speech communities together (see Figure 11.2).[22] This strategy allows you to meet your audience halfway: highlighting the contribution of your distinctive voice, while creating identification with language that your audience recognizes and values. Code-meshing invites your audience to share responsibility for bridging the gap between different speech communities, rather than putting the burden entirely on either you or them.

Code-meshing still requires work from the speaker, who must understand their audience's language norms well enough to build a bridge between multiple speech communities. Misunderstanding or misrepresenting your audience's language norms can alienate them rather than building identification—as many US politicians who speak white mainstream English have found out when trying to speak Spanish or put on a Southern accent.

When code-meshing, be careful to avoid **linguistic appropriation**: taking another culture's language as your own. When using the vocabulary, grammar, or pronunciation of speech communities that you do not belong to, respect their usage rules and give them credit. For example, the term *two-spirit* was coined at the Inter-Tribal Native American/First Nations Gay and Lesbian Conference as an organizing tool for Indigenous people who occupy a distinct gender status and role within their tribe.[23] Using "two-spirit" out of context to describe trans, nonbinary, or queer people from non-Indigenous cultures would show both a misunderstanding of the term and disrespect for the community it comes from.

**code-meshing**
mixing the norms of multiple speech communities together

**linguistic appropriation**
taking another culture's language as your own

# Jamila Lyiscott Uses Three Kinds of English

In 2014, when she was a graduate student studying education, Jamila Lyiscott gave a powerful presentation that highlighted the three kinds of English she learned from the different speech communities she belongs to.[24] She explains: "I speak three tongues. One for each: home, school, and friends." Code-meshing seamlessly between these three types of English, she demonstrates that each has rules or norms that govern its usage, each has a history, and each has power.

She demonstrates how her capacity to flow strategically between different forms of English empowers her speech. She can mix the forms, interject elements from one into the other, and use them not only to adapt but to disrupt and challenge different speaking contexts. She explains, "I have decided to treat all three of my languages as equal." This, she says, is what it means to be articulate.

Four years later, as a professor at the University of Michigan, she spoke about using code-meshing in spaces where people enforce a single notion of "correct" or "proper" English.[25] She says, "The multiple literacies that I bring to the table, my composite linguistic identity, gives me power." But she also recognizes that, too often, the power of multiple literacies is not recognized or valued.

To open her 2014 TED talk, Jamila Lyiscott described a woman sounding "baffled" when observing that Lyiscott is "articulate" (0:15).

She calls on each of us to appreciate the diverse forms of English in different communities—both across the globe and within a single nation, state, or city. She explains, "This is not a promotion of ignorance. It is a linguistic celebration." This linguistic celebration means knowing the power of your own voice, speaking from your intersectional standpoint, and being fully invested in what you say and why you say it. This, she argues, can help us all find more robust and diverse ways of knowing ourselves, each other, and the world.

To watch Lyiscott's TED talk, search the web for: Lyiscott 3 Ways English. The video is approximately 4:29 in length.

## SPEAK OUT

When you are incorporating expressions or idioms from speech communities that you are not a part of, you can use these strategies to avoid linguistic appropriation:

1. **ASK FOR INPUT.** Before using another community's language in a presentation, talk with members of that community to make sure the usage you are planning is respectful. Recognize that individual members do not speak for the whole community.

2. **ACKNOWLEDGE THE STANDPOINT YOU ARE SPEAKING FROM.** For example: "This might sound funny in my Midwestern accent" or "I'm not a queer person myself—just an ally."

3. **GIVE CREDIT TO THE COMMUNITY WHEN YOU INTRODUCE THE PHRASE.** For example: "The fine folks from Texas might call this a case of 'all hat and no cattle'" or "I hope you don't mind if I follow in the fabulous footsteps of the queer ballroom scene and 'spill the tea' with you."

4. **SHOW HUMILITY AND INVITE CORRECTION.** For example: "Now, if I got that wrong, I hope you'll let me know" or "If I start to sound like a fool up here, feel free to start booing."

In addition to using code-meshing to connect with speech communities different from your own, you can use it to showcase multiple intersecting speech communities that make up your standpoint. For example, a speaker from eastern India might combine mainstream Indian English, regional Bengali English, and the Bengali language within a single presentation. A speaker from Louisiana might blend Black English, Cajun English, and white mainstream English. The way you speak—the words, sentence structure, and inflection that you use—can be an excellent way of both celebrating your intersectional standpoint and creating identification across different speech communities.

## ✓ Critical Thinking Check

1. What's the distinction between assimilation and appropriation? What are their different causes and consequences?

2. When considering the ethics of code-switching and code-meshing, does the speaker's standpoint matter? If so, how? If not, why not?

# Style, Purpose, and Context

In addition to using language to express your standpoint and connect with your audience, you can adjust the style of your language to fit your purpose and context. In public speaking, **style** refers to a speaker's use of language to produce a particular effect or sensation. Style focuses not so much on *which* language a speaker uses, but *how* a speaker uses it—the way a speaker selects and arranges symbols to create meaning.

The same facts, ideas, and arguments can be presented in many styles, each producing a different effect. Some speaking situations call for language full of vivid imagery and clever turns of phrase, while others call for much simpler language, focused on accuracy and clarity. Many situations call for language that is neither grand nor plain, but somewhere in the middle. These grand, plain, and middle styles can help you achieve different purposes and adapt to different speaking contexts.[26]

## GRAND STYLE

When you think of speech or writing that is ornate, flowery, or poetic, you are probably thinking of grand style. **Grand style** is language rich with vivid imagery, metaphor, and other figures of speech. Sometimes called tropes or rhetorical devices, **figures of speech** are linguistic patterns that emphasize particular meanings or feelings. An effective figure of speech is like a catchy line in a song; it strikes an emotional chord and sticks with your audience long after they have finished listening. Figures can serve a wide range of functions, like creating emphasis, cuing memory, stirring emotion, changing attitudes, and expressing humor (see Table 11.1).[27] When you're selecting figures to use in your presentations, focus on the effect you want to create.

Grand style is most effective at moments of great importance or great change. It is most commonly seen in political, religious, and ceremonial speaking, but it can be used any time speakers want to inspire their audience to embrace exalted virtues and values. There's a reason that Dr. Martin Luther King Jr.'s "I Have a Dream" is the most notable public speech in American history: his striking metaphors, poetic repetition, and sweeping crescendos rise to meet his momentous occasion and purpose—the 1963 March on Washington calling for racial justice and equal

**style**
a speaker's use of language to produce a particular effect or sensation

**grand style**
language rich with vivid imagery, metaphor, and other figures of speech

**figures of speech**
linguistic patterns that emphasize particular meanings or feelings

### 📋 TRY THIS

To incorporate figures of speech into your presentations, try the **Speech Amplification Worksheet**.

rights. With a grand purpose and context, grand style can be enormously powerful. But use it wisely—grand style can seem overwrought, pompous, or even funny when your topic or speaking situation don't merit such lofty language.

| Figures of sensation | **Function:** Simulating sensory experiences |
|---|---|
| **onomatopoeia** (aa-nuh-maa-tuh-PEE-uh) | **Definition:** referring to something using the sound it makes<br>**Examples:** *rattle, cough, bang, beep, chug, cock-a-doodle-doo* |
| **enargia** (en-AR-gee-uh) | **Definition:** vivid descriptions that appeal to the senses<br>**Example:** *a cool breeze rustled through the golden trees* |
| Figures of repetition | **Function:** Creating emphasis and cuing memory |
| **alliteration** (uh-LIT-er-ay-shun) | **Definition:** repetition of sounds at the beginning of nearby words<br>**Examples:** *last laugh, busy bee, give up the ghost* |
| **rhyme** | **Definition:** repetition of sounds at the end of nearby words or phrases<br>**Example:** *righty tight-y, lefty loose-y* |
| **anaphora** (uh-NAF-or-uh) | **Definition:** repetition of a word or phrase at the beginning of a series of sentences or clauses<br>**Example:** *Let freedom ring from Stone Mountain of Georgia. Let freedom ring from Lookout Mountain of Tennessee. Let freedom ring from every hill and molehill in Mississippi.*[28] |
| **epistrophe** (uh-PIS-truh-fee) | **Definition:** repetition of a word or phrase at the end of a series of sentences or clauses<br>**Examples:** *government of the people, by the people, for the people*[29] |

**TABLE 11.1** When you're incorporating figures of speech into your presentation, consider what functions you want them to perform.

| | |
|---|---|
| **Figures of transformation** | **Function:** Stirring imagination and emotion |
| **synecdoche** (suh-NEK-duh-kee) | **Definition:** referring to a whole with one of its parts<br><br>**Examples:** *boots on the ground, mouths to feed* |
| **metaphor** | **Definition:** describing one thing as another<br><br>**Examples:** *fish out of water, late bloomer, war on drugs* |
| **simile** (SI-muh-lee) | **Definition:** describing one thing as like another<br><br>**Examples:** *rock you like a hurricane, cuts like a knife* |
| **personification** | **Definition:** describing nonhuman creatures or things as human<br><br>**Examples:** *Uncle Sam, Mother Nature, Mr. Fox* |
| **Figures of omission** | **Function:** Saying something indirectly |
| **ellipsis** (uh-LIP-sis) | **Definition:** omitting a word or phrase clearly indicated by the context<br><br>**Examples:** *the b-word, you know who* |
| **paralipsis** (pair-uh-LIP-sis) | **Definition:** drawing attention to something by pretending to omit or disregard it<br><br>**Examples:** *I'm not here to speak about my opponent's drinking problem.*<br><br>*Don't even get me started on gun violence in America.*<br><br>*That's not to mention our honoree's many achievements in the field of medicine.* |
| **systrophe** (SIS-truh-fee) | **Definition:** waiting to name a person or thing until after you've described them or it at length<br><br>**Example:** *Our next speaker needs no introduction. They are one of the most creative young minds on our team, and someone who consistently challenges all of us to think bigger. Let's hear it for Jamie!* |

| | |
|---|---|
| **Figures of reversal** | **Function:** Changing attitudes and perspectives |
| **chiasmus**<br>(kee-AZ-mus) | **Definition:** reversing the order of words in successive phrases<br><br>**Examples**: *When the going gets tough, the tough get going.*<br><br>*Ask not what your country can do for you; ask what you can do for your country.*[30] |
| **antithesis**<br>(an-TITH-uh-sis) | **Definition:** juxtaposing contrasting words and ideas in parallel phrases<br><br>**Examples**: *One small step for man; one giant leap for mankind.*[31]<br><br>*It was the best of times; it was the worst of times.*[32]<br><br>*To err is human; to forgive, divine.*[33] |
| **Figures of absurdity** | **Function:** Expressing sarcasm or humor |
| **irony** | **Definition:** implying the opposite of what you say<br><br>**Example**: *No, I love sitting home by myself while you're all out having fun.* |
| **hyperbole**<br>(hai-PUR-buh-lee) | **Definition:** exaggerating something's importance, size, or degree<br><br>**Examples**: *a bazillion years, a mountain of homework* |
| **litotes**<br>(lai-TOW-teez) | **Definition:** affirms a statement by denying its opposite<br><br>**Examples**: *wasn't half bad, not rocket science* |

**TABLE 11.1** *(continued)*

# PLAIN STYLE

Poetic or flowery language can feel out of place—and even be confusing—when your primary goal is conveying information. That's why many technical, educational, and professional presentations use a plain, no-frills style. **Plain style** uses language that's simple, clear, concise, and direct. That means basic words, short sentences with simple grammatical structures, and clear organizational

**plain style**
language that's simple, clear, concise, and direct

patterns. Unlike figurative language, plain language focuses on accuracy, brevity, and clarity:

- **CHOOSE PRECISE NOUNS AND VERBS.** Rather than using modifiers like adjectives and adverbs, choose nouns and verbs that convey your meaning more exactly. For example, "cottage" is more precise than "house," and "glare" is more precise than "look." Words like these indicate specific qualities without any additional modification. There's no need to say "small cottage" because the word "cottage" already suggests small size. Likewise, there's no need to say "glare angrily," since the verb "glare" already implies anger. Choosing precise words makes your style stronger and clearer. For example, "He bolted up from his recliner" is easier to grasp than "He sat up very quickly from his large plush chair"—even though the two sentences convey the same meaning.

- **ELIMINATE UNNECESSARY WORDS.** In addition to cutting modifiers in favor of more precise language, remove any words, phrases, or sentences that do not add meaning. For example, in the phrase "cruel, merciless, unrelenting wind," the three adjectives mean almost the same thing. Choose the most precise word, and cut the rest. When you're using the plain style, aim for the briefest phrase that accurately conveys your meaning. But remember: brevity is not always a virtue. If fewer words would make a statement inaccurate or unclear, use a longer phrase.

- **USE FAMILIAR TERMS.** Choose words that your audience will recognize. Avoid using **jargon**—specialized vocabulary particular to a profession, group, or area of expertise—that your audience might not understand. For example, a group of medical professionals would know the meaning of the word *ulna*, but with non-specialist audiences you might need to clarify: "the bone along the outside of your forearm, between your elbow and wrist." When using the plain style, resist the temptation to show off your extensive vocabulary. Instead of "equilibrium," just say "balance." Don't use "sagacious" when "wise" will do.

  **jargon**
  specialized vocabulary particular to a profession, group, or area of expertise

- **AVOID AMBIGUOUS LANGUAGE.** You can also help your audience understand you by avoiding words with multiple meanings. For example, the word *biannual* can mean both "twice a year" and "every two years."[34] Say "every two years" if that's what you mean. When you use pronouns—like "he," "she," "they," "it," "this," or "that"—clearly indicate which person, place, or thing you are referring to. For example, consider this sentence: "To keep the squirrel from eating the birdseed, coat it with cayenne pepper." Here, "it"

# Zander Moricz Uses Figures of Speech to Resist Censorship

As the first openly gay class president at his high school, Zander Moricz became well-known for his activism supporting LGBTQ+ rights—especially his opposition to Florida's "Don't Say Gay" law, which prohibits the discussion of sexual orientation and gender identity in public schools.[35] When the time came for him to speak at his graduation ceremony, school administrators told him that if he mentioned his sexuality or his LGBTQ+ activism, they would cut off his microphone and end his speech.[36]

Moricz knew he could not speak honestly from his own standpoint or address the exigences of the moment without addressing his state's ban on discussing gender and sexuality. To navigate this difficult speaking situation, he had to use language creatively—deploying systrophe, metaphor, and ellipsis to talk about LGBTQ+ issues indirectly.

Moricz leads with systrophe, priming his audience to believe he is about to mention his sexual orientation: "I must discuss a very public part of my identity. This characteristic has probably become the first thing you think of when you think of me as a human being."[37] He then pauses, slows his rate of speech, and continues: "I have curly hair." His tone is humorous, and the audience applauds and laughs as he removes his graduation cap and runs his fingers through his curls.

For the next three minutes, he uses his curly hair as a metaphor to talk about the challenges of being gay in Florida. While he omitted any direct mention of his sexuality, the ellipsis was clear from the context: "I used to hate my curls. I spent mornings and nights embarrassed of them, trying desperately to straighten this part of who I am. But the daily damage of trying to 'fix' myself became

could refer to either the squirrel or the birdseed—which one should you coat with cayenne? Choose language with only one possible meaning to avoid confusing your audience.

You may have noticed that many principles of plain style—like avoiding repetition, using accurate terms, and directly stating your meaning—run counter to the figurative language that characterizes grand style. Plain style is most common in informative presentations, but speakers also use it when they are

too much to endure." He uses the story of embracing his "curly hair" as an opportunity to celebrate his teachers, his fellow students, and the community who supported him. He thanks them for helping him when he "didn't have other curly-haired people to talk to."

Moricz then takes on a serious tone, calling for change and expressing anger that he was forced to speak in code about such an important topic: "Do you think I wanted to talk about this? It needs to be about this for the thousands of curly-haired kids who are going to be forced to speak like *this* for their entire lives as students." He points to the suppression of his own identity and message as evidence for the harm that the "Don't Say Gay" bill has already begun to cause.

Moricz's speech received a standing ovation and won wide acclaim in the press and on social media. His artful use of figures made it possible for him to say what he had been forbidden to say—and demonstrated how problematic censorship can be.

Zander Moricz gestures to his family while describing how the love of his community at school gave him the strength to come out to his parents (4:54).

Afterward, he told reporters: "I just had to be clever about it. But I shouldn't have to be, because I don't exist as a euphemism, and I deserve to be celebrated as is."[38]

To view Moricz's complete speech, do a web search for: Zander Moricz grad speech Ballard. The video is approximately 7:00 in length.

persuading about facts—for example, in legal arguments or scientific debates. Plain style is most effective in speaking situations where your audience may struggle to understand you: when you're introducing unfamiliar ideas, explaining complex information, or communicating in a language that either you or your audience members aren't fluent in. Although plain style can help you clarify your meaning, watch out—it can sound boring, impersonal, or even patronizing if it's obvious your audience is having no trouble understanding what you mean.

📋 TRY THIS

To increase the accuracy, brevity, and clarity of your language, try the **Speech Editing Checklist**.

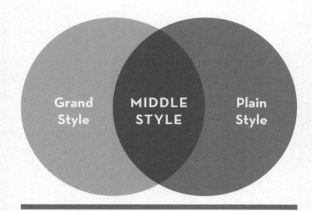

**FIGURE 11.3** Middle style combines elements of both grand and plain styles.

**middle style**
language incorporating elements of both the grand and plain styles

📋 **TRY THIS**

To develop your everyday speech into your own personal style, try the **Signature Style Activity**.

# MIDDLE STYLE

Most contemporary public speaking situations present a Goldilocks scenario: the grand style is too decorative and elegant, the plain style is too drab and dry, but something in the middle is just right. **Middle style** incorporates elements of both the grand and plain styles (see Figure 11.3). You might move between these styles at different moments in a speech—for example, slowing down to introduce a difficult concept with plain style, or ramping up into grand style during a passionate call to action. Or you might blend the grand and plain styles together—for example, describing vivid imagery with short, simple sentences, or crafting poetic turns of phrase with basic vocabulary.

You can use the middle style as a baseline for most of your presentations. To strike the right balance between plain and grand language, start from your own everyday style of speech. How do you speak when talking with your friends, family, and classmates? Some people lean toward plain style, some lean toward grand, but most of us fall somewhere in between. Next, examine your audience, context, and purpose. Does your speaking situation call for you to amplify your personal style to make it grander? Or simplify your style to make it plainer? Remember: middle style is about finding the right balance for your speaking situation, not necessarily the exact midpoint between grand and plain. Turn the dial up or down to find the best mix for your audience, purpose, and context.

✓ ## Critical Thinking Check

1. What are the advantages and disadvantages of the grand style? What are the advantages and disadvantages of the plain style? Does the middle style have any disadvantages? If so, what are they?
2. What kinds of speaking situations call for a grander style? What speaking situations call for a plainer style? What moments within a speech call for grander language? What moments call for plainer language?

# Next Steps

You've learned a wide variety of strategies to help you adapt your message to different audiences, purposes, and contexts. You've seen the spectrum of style from plain to grand—and hopefully embraced the unique combination of speech communities you belong to. Now you're ready to start developing your own personal style as a public speaker. To get started, try the Speech Amplification Worksheet, the Speech Editing Checklist, and the Signature Style Activity.

You've also seen how the words you choose can tailor your message to inform, persuade, and connect with your audience. But meaning isn't only about what you say—it's also about how you say it. In the next chapter, you'll learn techniques of vocal and physical delivery that can help you bring your words to life.

# Standpoint Reflection

- What speech communities do you participate in? Which ones do you identify with most? Which do you feel most comfortable in?

- Do you find yourself code-switching in your daily life? If not, why not? If so, do you feel that code-switching hurts or helps you?

- Does your everyday speaking style lean toward plain or grand language? What are the advantages of that style? How might incorporating elements of the opposite style expand your abilities as a speaker?

- Which figures of speech best fit your own personal speaking style? Do you already use any of these figures in your everyday speech? Are there any other linguistic patterns or turns of phrase that you frequently use?

## Key Terms

# Resources for Language and Style

 **"Try This" Exercises**

Access the "Try This" exercises as directed by your instructor or online at digital.wwnorton.com/chapterexercises-conpubspeak

- To incorporate figures of speech into your presentations, try the **Speech Amplification Worksheet**.

- To increase the accuracy, brevity, and clarity of your language, try the **Speech Editing Checklist**.

- To develop your everyday speech into your own personal speaking style, try the **Signature Style Activity**.

---

**Want to practice these skills to prepare for your next speech? Go to INQUIZITIVE to review and apply concepts from this chapter and get personalized feedback along the way.**

Jordan Raskopoulos

# 12 Vocal and Physical Delivery

In her 2017 TEDx speech on anxiety, Jordan Raskopoulos explains that—ironically—she doesn't get nervous about public speaking.[1] Why? Because she has learned there are simple delivery tricks she can follow. She demonstrates how she can make everyone feel connected by speaking to one person in the front row for a moment and then returning to the full audience. She shows how she can raise her voice, pause, then resume speaking at a softer volume to get her audience's full attention. In fact, she says, knowing these delivery tricks makes public speaking less anxiety-inducing for her than everyday conversations, where there seem to be no clear rules.

But Raskopoulos does more than just describe these tricks—she uses them. She changes the volume, speed, and rhythm of her voice to evoke emotion and connect with her audience. She speeds up when talking about her experience of social anxiety to communicate the feeling of panic. She slows down to express sadness when describing the negative perceptions people have about social anxiety. And she pauses to let her jokes land and give her audience time to laugh.

Raskopoulos also punctuates her talk with movement and gestures that add emphasis and clarity to her message. For example, she points down toward her feet with both hands when talking about her experience onstage, then spreads her arms wide to talk about her audience's experience. She raises one index finger to emphasize "one thing" when she talks about focusing on a single task. Most importantly, she moves around the stage, making eye contact with different parts of her audience, ensuring they all feel seen and addressed.

## LEARNING OBJECTIVES

### After completing this chapter, you will be able to

- Understand and meet the criteria for effective delivery

- Improve your vocal delivery using volume, speed, pitch, rhythm, and articulation

- Enhance your physical delivery with proximity, posture, gesture, facial expression, eye contact, and adornment

- Practice your presentations with strategies that rapidly improve your delivery

Jordan Raskopoulos's speech is a master class in effective delivery. Her carefully orchestrated use of both vocal and physical techniques have all the hallmarks of a great speaker. But unlike most speakers, she reveals that her seemingly effortless delivery is the result of deliberate planning and practice. By learning the tools of vocal and physical delivery, any speaker can develop their own natural speaking style and make their presentations shine.

# Functions of Effective Delivery

Of all the skills they learn, people new to public speaking are often most concerned about delivering their presentations. **Delivery** is the way you communicate the content of your presentation—not what you say, but how you say it. Delivery includes the ways you use your voice, such as volume, pitch, and rhythm. It also includes the ways you use your body, such as gestures, posture, and facial expression.

Effective delivery helps you accomplish your purpose and connect with your audience. For example, when you're telling a story or a joke, the way you deliver it—your tone, expression, and timing—is often the key to getting the response you want. The same is true for any presentation. Your delivery can enhance your presentation in four main ways: it can help you convey information, create interest, communicate credibility, and evoke emotion.

- **CONVEYING INFORMATION.** Clear delivery can help you emphasize important points and reinforce your message. **Clarity** is the experience of understanding something without effort. Clarity means the audience can both perceive your presentation—see, hear, or otherwise sense its important elements—and comprehend it—grasp its key ideas and integrate them into their understanding. While clarity is important in every presentation, presenting unfamiliar or complex information calls for especially clear delivery. For example, if you were introducing your audience to a new process, like changing a tire, you could make your presentation clearer by using gestures to illustrate the different steps as you described them.

- **CREATING INTEREST.** Adding variety to your delivery can help you keep your audience engaged with your presentation.[2] **Variety** is the experience of change, range, or diversity. To produce variety, speakers may speed up or slow down, speak louder or softer, change their posture or gesture, or even shift the

**delivery**
the way you communicate the content of your presentation

**clarity**
the experience of understanding something without effort

**variety**
the experience of change, range, or diversity

clarity, immediacy, and mood of their presentation. Variety is most effective when you change your delivery to indicate and emphasize changes in the content of your presentation. For example, you might say a sentence more loudly to emphasize it; or you might walk to another part of the stage to indicate that you're moving on to another main point.

- **COMMUNICATING CREDIBILITY.** In addition to making your presentations more interesting and easier to understand, effective delivery can enhance your credibility by building trust with your audience. The experience of physical or psychological closeness between a speaker and an audience is called **immediacy.**[3] Usually, immediacy will increase with more smiling, eye contact, open posture, physical proximity, and close-up recordings—but the appropriate level of immediacy varies across cultures and speaking situations. For example, watch people's nonverbal behavior before and after your class period officially begins. Even with the same group of people, you can see more expressions of immediacy in more informal and unstructured interactions.

- **EVOKING EMOTION.** Just as the style and content of your words can evoke your audience's emotions, your vocal patterns, movement, and facial expressions can shape and shift their mood over the course of your presentation. **Mood** is the transitory experience of a feeling or emotion. As you consider how you will deliver your presentation, think about the overall mood you want to set and how that mood will change at different moments in the presentation. For example, a eulogy might begin with more somber facial expressions and tone of voice, but then transition into happier tones and expressions when recounting fond memories or funny stories about the person who passed.

As you can see, each of these four functions gives you criteria for improving your delivery. Your delivery needs clarity to convey information, variety to create interest, immediacy to communicate credibility, and mood to evoke emotion. These criteria—clarity, variety, immediacy, and mood—all share one thing: they are audience experiences. What is clear to one audience may not be clear to another. For example, if you've ever studied a second language, you know that someone speaking at a speed that's clear for fluent speakers may be too fast for new language learners to easily follow. Clarity only exists in the experience of your audience—and the same is true with variety, immediacy, and mood. They are all experiences that occur at the intersection between your delivery and your

**immediacy**
the experience of physical or psychological closeness between a speaker and an audience

**mood**
the transitory experience of a feeling or emotion

audience's interpretation. So, when thinking about how to meet these four criteria, consider how your delivery fits within your overall speaking situation.

## ✓ Critical Thinking Check

1. How can knowing the functions of delivery—conveying information, creating interest, communicating credibility, and evoking emotion—help you become a better speaker? What's the connection between the ways delivery functions and the criteria for doing it effectively?

2. Can you think of any situations where the criteria for effective delivery—clarity, variety, immediacy, and mood—might trade off with one another? How might your speaking situation—your audience, purpose, context, and standpoint—help you decide which delivery criteria are most important?

**vocal delivery**
the way you use your voice to express yourself

**voice**
non-linguistic modifiers that affect the meaning, emotion, and understanding of language use

**volume**
a speaker's level of amplification; how loudly or softly they are speaking

# Delivery with the Voice

Your voice is one of the most important tools you have for conveying information, creating interest, communicating credibility, and expressing emotion. The way you use your voice to express yourself is called **vocal delivery**. While voice is commonly thought of as the creation of sound through the lungs, vocal cords, and mouth, the elements of effective vocal delivery have analogues in sign language, text-to-speech devices, and even live communication via text. So **voice** includes any non-linguistic modifiers that affect the meaning, emotion, and understanding of language use. The volume, rate, pitch, rhythm, and articulation of your voice all influence the effectiveness of your delivery.

## VOLUME

The volume of your voice can both communicate emotion and ensure that your audience receives your message clearly. **Volume** is a speaker's level of amplification—how loudly or softly they are speaking. A speaker may need more volume in a large space, when audience members are farther away, or in a noisy or distracting environment. In sign language, speakers sometimes increase their volume by making their signs larger with more exaggerated movement.

Elements of vocal delivery also appear in sign language—for example, the size and sharpness of a sign can communicate volume.

A soft-spoken style can be effective and distinctive for some speakers—creating greater immediacy and a more peaceful or solemn mood—but only if the audience can still clearly perceive what you are saying. If you find you are speaking too quietly for your audience to easily understand you, first see if you have access to a microphone or other technology to amplify your voice. You can also practice projecting your voice to increase your volume without an amplification system.

**📋 TRY THIS**

To practice increasing your volume, try the **Vocal Projection Activity**.

## RATE

The speed at which you speak can affect the clarity of your presentation. When you speak too quickly, you can lose your audience's attention because it takes too much effort to follow the presentation. **Rate** is how quickly or slowly a speaker is speaking, usually measured in words per minute (wpm). Generally, around 150 wpm is considered a clear and comfortable rate of delivery.[4]

However, many factors in your speaking situation—like the complexity of your topic or the level of distraction in your environment—can cause that number to go down to as low as 75 wpm or up to as high as 200 wpm. Because rate can be subjective and situational, listener feedback is the most reliable way to judge your rate of speech. When practicing your presentation, ask someone to listen and check how fast you are speaking. Don't be surprised if their recommendations seem unusually slow to you. Speakers commonly experience time distortion during their presentations, and think they are speaking much slower than they actually are.

**📋 TRY THIS**

To measure your rate of words per minute, try the **Speed Check Activity**. To get a listener's perspective on your rate of delivery, try the **Speed Feedback Activity**.

## PITCH

When we listen to a singer, we hear them hitting high notes, low notes, and notes that fall somewhere between. **Pitch** describes how high or low a speaker is speaking. Deep voices have a low pitch. Voices we describe as bright or light have a high pitch. For example, actor James Earl Jones is known for his trademark deep voice, while comedian Maria Bamford has made her high-pitched voice part of her signature style.

Research on vocal stereotypes shows that most Americans perceive deeper voices as more competent and more masculine, and interpret high-pitched voices as more likable and more feminine.[5] Consider these stereotypical expectations

**rate**
how quickly or slowly a speaker is speaking, usually measured in words per minute

**pitch**
how high or low a speaker is speaking

## Pathways

To revisit strategies for challenging stereotypes that affect your audience's perception of you, see **Chapter 3, Ethics and Credibility**.

in light of your speaking situation. If your audience, purpose, and context call for a friendly approach, a higher voice can be a strength. Likewise, a deeper voice can be a strength when your speaking situation calls for more authoritative delivery. But if you are concerned that your pitch might send the wrong message, you can challenge these vocal stereotypes directly: for example, "I might sound like Darth Vader, but..." or "Don't let this sweet voice fool you..."

You can also vary your pitch at different points in your presentation to produce different effects. Most speakers do not use just one pitch. They have a range of natural pitch and use a variety of different pitches to communicate different emotions and moods. Higher pitches express excitement, fear, and surprise, while lower pitches express anger, sadness, or calm. Monotone speaking communicates less emotion because it does not vary in pitch.

## 📋 TRY THIS

To find your optimal pitch, try the **Vocal Range Activity**.

Most speakers perform best when they speak at their **optimal pitch**: a comfortable pitch in the middle of their vocal range.[6] Each speaker has their own optimal pitch, which may or may not be the pitch they typically use in everyday conversation. Finding your own optimal pitch will give you greater range for variation, better control over volume, and a stronger voice overall.

## RHYTHM

An indispensable element in music and poetry, rhythm is also a powerful tool for vocal delivery. **Rhythm** is a repeated pattern of sounds. When you repeat key phrases to create emotional effect, you can underscore your words by using the same pattern of volume, speed, and pitch. For example, if you listen to Jahmal Cole repeat "it's not regular" in his speech at the Dr. Martin Luther King Jr. Interfaith Breakfast, you can hear him increase his volume to punctuate the word "regular" each time (see Chapter 5). Or if you listen to Paxton Smith's valedictory speech about abortion restrictions, you can hear her use the same speed and emphasis when she repeats "a war on the rights of your mothers, a war on the rights of your daughters, a war on the rights of your sisters" (see Chapter 6).

**optimal pitch**
a comfortable pitch in the middle of a speaker's vocal range

**rhythm**
a repeated pattern of sounds

**pause**
punctuating the flow and pattern of sound with silence

In addition to repetition, pausing is another important way to create and modify rhythm in your speech. **Pauses** punctuate the flow and pattern of sound with silence. A pause can add emphasis, especially when combined with rhythm and repetition. Consider this effect: "This policy change is *essential* to the future of our company. This. Change. Is. Essential." The pauses—represented by periods—add emphasis without increasing volume. Deliberate pauses can add variety to your rhythm and underscore the special importance of a key moment in your presentation.

Allowing room for silence can help you with verbal fillers, a common problem that speakers face when they're finding their rhythm. **Verbal fillers** are vocalizations that we use to fill gaps in our speech. "Um" and "uh" are common verbal fillers, but people also use words, such as "right," "okay," "like," and "you know." Verbal fillers might feel like they are keeping your rhythm flowing, but they actually make the natural breaks in your speech sound like a stumble or a mistake. If you catch yourself using verbal fillers, let yourself slow down, pause, and maybe even take a deep breath. Instead of filling the silence with meaningless sounds, punctuate your words with a meaningful pause.

## ARTICULATION

Everyone's speech has accents and variations, and most speakers find some sounds easier to make than others. **Articulation** is the ability to make vocal sounds clearly and distinctly. **Pronunciation** is articulating a word in a particular way to conform to the expectations of an audience. In sign language, articulation refers to the ability to make a particular gesture or movement, while pronunciation means performing those signs in the way the audience expects.

Pronunciation in vocalized and signed language is highly situational. Pronouncing a word "correctly" means no more than pronouncing it the way an audience expects you to. Pronunciation can help you achieve both clarity and identification with your audience. If you are concerned about whether you are pronouncing a word in the expected way, you can ask an audience member or search online for a recording of the most commonly used pronunciation.

When a speaker struggles with articulation, it means they find particular speech sounds difficult to make, or they make them in ways not sufficiently distinct from other speech sounds. Misarticulation is common when we speak a second language that contains sounds we didn't learn growing up. For example, English speakers learning Spanish or Italian often find it difficult to roll an "r" to create the "rr" sound. English speakers also struggle with articulation when learning many other languages, just as speakers with other primary languages sometimes

## Pathways

To review repetition as a figure of speech, see **Chapter 11, Language and Style**. For full versions of Jahmal Cole and Paxton Smith's speeches, see the **Appendix: Speeches for Analysis**.

**📋 TRY THIS**

To get a sense of your natural vocal rhythm, try the **Recording Your Rhythm Activity**.

**verbal fillers**
vocalizations that we use to fill gaps in our speech

**articulation**
the ability to make vocal sounds clearly and distinctly

**pronunciation**
articulating a word in a particular way to conform to the expectations of an audience

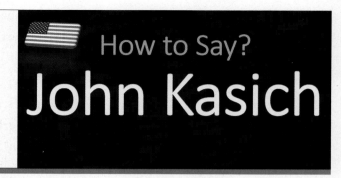

◀)) **UK** /ˈret.ᵊr.ɪk/
How to pronounce **rhetoric** *noun* in British English

◀)) **US** /ˈreṯ.ə.ɪk/
How to pronounce **rhetoric** *noun* in American English

rhetorical

◀)) **US** /rɪˈtɔr·ɪ·kəl, -ˈtɑr-/
How to pronounce **rhetorical** *adjective* in American English

Left: The Cambridge Dictionary provides audio recordings of common UK and US pronunciations for many English words. Right: You can find videos on YouTube of how to pronounce many names, especially names of famous people, such as this video by Julien Miquel on how to pronounce the name of American politician John Kasich.

struggle with certain sounds in English. Disabilities, injuries, illness, and a variety of other causes can also affect articulation.

Remember that your differences—including differences in articulation and pronunciation—are strengths you can use as a speaker. If your articulation or pronunciation might seem unusual to your audience, you can explain its origin or cause and use it to demonstrate your unique standpoint and credibility. You can also use humor to interrupt biases and connect with your audience. Some speakers find it helps to directly address common stereotypes connected to their articulation and pronunciation.

If your differences in articulation or pronunciation make it difficult for your audience to understand you, you can improve your clarity by speaking more slowly and pausing more often. Using images and gestures can also improve clarity by reinforcing or repeating your message in another form. Differences in articulation and pronunciation are an excellent opportunity to highlight your standpoint and engage your audience with multiple modes of delivery.

## Delivery with the Body

**physical delivery**
a speaker's non-linguistic gestures, expressions, movement, and self-presentation

Just as your voice can play a large part in the effectiveness of your delivery, so can the ways you use your body. **Physical delivery** refers to a speaker's non-linguistic gestures, expressions, movement, and self-presentation. Physical delivery can have dramatic impacts on the clarity, variety, immediacy, and mood of a presentation. It can reinforce or even transform the meaning of a speaker's words.

Proximity, posture, gesture, facial expression, eye contact, and adornment are all ways that speakers use their bodies to deliver engaging presentations.

## PROXIMITY

When we feel connected to other people, we sometimes say we feel "close" to them—and when someone seems disengaged, we might say they seem "distant." This is because our experience of immediacy is tied to our perceptions of physical space.[7] The perception of physical distance between a speaker and their audience is called **proximity**. This can be accomplished in person through actual physical distance, or through "close-up" or "wide-shot" framing in visual media. A speaker's proximity to an audience can be divided into public, social, personal, and intimate zones.

**Public Zone** Speaking on a stage or in an auditorium usually positions you at a public distance from your audience. **Public distance** is a perceived distance of greater than twelve feet. Although people often associate public distance with public speaking, public distance is rarely used in speaking situations like meetings and mediated presentations.

As the distance between you and your audience increases, establishing immediacy becomes more challenging. To compensate, a speaker at public distance

**proximity**
the perception of physical distance between a speaker and their audience

**public distance**
a perceived distance of greater than twelve feet, commonly used when speaking in person to large audiences

Close-up and wide-shot framing show that the closer someone seems to us physically, the closer they feel to us emotionally.

needs to use their whole body for expression, with more animated gestures and exaggerated facial expressions. When speaking at public distance, you can narrow the physical gap by moving around to approach different parts of your audience at different points in your presentation.

**Social Zone**  We've all become familiar with the term "social distancing" to describe standing more than six feet away from other people to avoid spreading COVID-19. But nonverbal communication researchers use the term **social distance** to describe a perceived distance anywhere between four and twelve feet—the zone that implies a social rather than personal relationship. Presentations given to small groups, such as business pitches, committee meetings, and classroom speeches, are often given at social distance.

## Pathways

For more about delivering presentations on camera, see **Chapter 14, Online and Mediated Presentations**.

At social distance, your lower legs and feet are usually less visible to your audience. Since the focus will already be on your face and hands, your facial expressions and gestures should be less exaggerated and more conversational. In mediated presentations, social distance is often seen in video of speakers speaking outdoors, video of speakers presenting to an in-person audience, or video of animated speakers who want to highlight their hand gestures. Social distance creates more immediacy than public distance, but you can increase your immediacy even more by moving closer to your audience or camera.

**Personal Zone**  Presentations to small groups or mediated audiences often allow for even more proximity and immediacy. **Personal distance** is a perceived distance between eighteen inches and four feet. This is the equivalent of sitting across the table from someone or engaging them on a videoconferencing platform like Zoom. At personal distance, an audience will primarily see your head and shoulders, spotlighting your facial expression and posture. Personal distance calls for more subtle gestures and facial expressions and a more casual and conversational speaking style.

**social distance**
a perceived distance between four and twelve feet, commonly used when speaking in person to small groups or meetings

**personal distance**
a perceived distance between eighteen inches and four feet, commonly used in online or recorded public speaking

Maintaining personal distance is not always feasible when you're speaking in person, but it's the most common distance used in digital presentations. Positioning your camera at this distance helps your viewers feel like they have a stronger connection to you. In person, that connection is tougher to achieve: with more than a handful of people, it's hard to stay within four feet of every

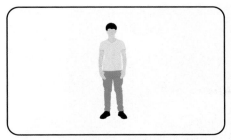

**Public Distance**
**Over 12 feet**

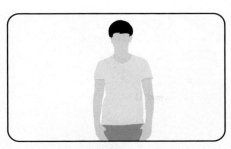

**Social Distance**
**4 to 12 feet**

**Personal Distance**
**4 feet to 18 inches**

**Intimate Distance**
**Under 18 inches**

Your distance from your audience or camera communicates different degrees of immediacy and highlights different features of your physical delivery.

audience member. You can walk out into a larger audience to create more proximity and immediacy—but be careful not to invade anyone's personal space.

**Intimate Zone** If you've ever had someone get too close for comfort while they were speaking to you, then you understand the problem with too much immediacy. **Intimate distance** is a perceived distance of under eighteen inches. This is the distance of a "close-up" camera shot, with only the speaker's face in view. Most Americans reserve this level of proximity for family members, romantic partners, and close friends. In person, intimate distance creates far too much proximity for public speaking because it intrudes on the personal space of your audience members.

But online, vloggers and influencers use intimate distance—zooming in on their faces—in everything from interviews to review videos. At intimate distance, your physical delivery is almost entirely restricted to facial expression and head

**intimate distance**
a perceived distance of under eighteen inches, rarely used in public speaking

An open, upright posture communicates confidence, while a closed, inclined posture can suggest anxiety or defensiveness.

movement. This proximity can work for short reaction shots or deeply emotional topics, but even online, intimate distance can make maintaining professionalism and personal boundaries more challenging.

## POSTURE

**posture**
how someone holds and positions their body

**closed posture**
arms and legs crossed or held close to the body

**open posture**
relaxed arms and feet shoulder-width apart

**inclined posture**
shoulders slouched forward and the head tilted down

**upright posture**
straight spine with the chin up and shoulders slightly back

Whether standing or sitting, we all have different ways we position our bodies at different times. **Posture** is how someone holds and positions their body. A public speaker's posture can affect both the immediacy and mood of their presentation.

Generally, an open, upright posture creates greater immediacy with your audience and sets a more positive mood for your presentation. A **closed posture**—with arms and legs crossed or held close to the body—can communicate distance, discomfort, or even dislike, while an **open posture**—with relaxed arms and feet shoulder-width apart—communicates more immediacy.[8] An **inclined posture**—with shoulders slouched forward and the head tilted down—can express boredom, sadness, or submissiveness, while an **upright posture**—a straight spine with the chin up and shoulders slightly back—communicates confidence, interest, and excitement.

However, depending on your own body, abilities, and persona, your most stable and comfortable speaking posture may not match your audience's expectations about immediacy and mood. In that case, you might choose to draw attention to your posture as a way of introducing a dimension of your standpoint or experience. For example: "After my sports injury last year, chronic pain has made it hard for me to hold any one position for too long." Or: "I have severe vertigo, so I hope you won't mind if I don't stand up." If an open, upright posture is uncomfortable for you, don't worry—you can create immediacy and positivity through other nonverbal cues, such as gesture, facial expression, and eye contact.

## GESTURE

Different speakers have different gestural styles. Some people move around a great deal when they speak, hands flying and body shifting with their words. Other speakers remain relatively still with hands at their side or in their laps. Most of us fall somewhere between. To **gesture** is to move your body—especially your arms, hands, or head—to communicate meaning. Our gestures serve one of six functions: substitution, reinforcement, contradiction, accentuation, regulation, and adaptation.

**Substitution** Some gestures stand alone, conveying a message without words. These **substituting gestures** take the place of verbal communication. A substituting gesture communicates your meaning all by itself, without needing any words to accompany it. For example, instead of saying "yes," you could communicate agreement by nodding your head or giving a thumbs-up. When public speakers stop speaking verbally and use substituting gestures instead, it adds variety to their delivery. This trick is especially useful for getting the attention of a noisy or inattentive audience. But remember: if your audience can't see you clearly—or isn't looking in your direction—they will miss any messages that you only send through gesture.

**Reinforcement** Gestures can also allow speakers to communicate the same message in multiple ways. A **reinforcing gesture** repeats the meaning of your words. For example, you might draw a circle in the air with your index finger while saying

**gesture**
moving your body—especially your arms, hands, or head—to communicate meaning

**substituting gesture**
a gesture that takes the place of verbal communication

**reinforcing gesture**
a gesture that repeats the meaning of your words

The three-finger salute made famous by *The Hunger Games* books has become a symbol of support for democracy in Southeast Asia. Here a monk uses the salute as a substituting gesture at a pro-democracy rally in Bangkok.

Supreme Court Justice Ketanji Brown Jackson uses a reinforcing gesture at her confirmation hearing while speaking about the *particular* factors judges consider when deciding a case.

"circle" or point to yourself while saying "my" or "mine." Reinforcing gestures can add clarity to a presentation by communicating the same message both verbally and nonverbally. Reinforcing gestures are useful anytime you want to make yourself easier to understand, but are especially helpful when you are speaking across a language barrier or when some members of your audience might have difficulty hearing you.

## Contradiction

**contradicting gesture**
a gesture that indicates that we mean the opposite of what we're saying verbally

**accentuating gesture**
a gesture that emphasizes or highlights key words, phrases, or moments in the speech

**Contradiction**  Our words and our gestures don't always send the same signal. A **contradicting gesture** indicates that we mean the opposite of what we're saying with our words. For example, if you say, "It was a really big fish," but make a tiny pinch with your fingers, your gesture communicates that you mean the opposite of what you said. Some gestures, like crossing your fingers, shrugging, winking, or rolling your eyes, use contradiction to indicate irony, humor, or sarcasm. Public speakers usually exaggerate their contradicting gestures to increase the comic effect and ensure that their audience doesn't take their words seriously.

**Accentuation**  Public speakers also use gestures for emphasis. **Accentuating gestures** highlight key words, phrases, or moments in the speech.

National Press Club speaker Marilyn Egerton uses a contradicting gesture to express humor while speaking about the challenges and importance of being a foster parent.

New York City mayor Eric Adams uses an accentuating gesture to emphasize a point.

For example, a speaker might pound their fist on the podium or extend their arms out beside them to bring their audience's attention to an important point. Accentuating gestures don't have a meaning of their own; instead, they support and underscore verbal communication. Accentuating gestures can improve both the clarity and variety of your delivery by drawing your audience's attention to your most important points.

Maryam Rajavi, a leader of Iran's democracy movement, uses a regulating gesture to greet her audience.

### Regulation

Gestures can signal when we are ready to take center stage or turn the floor over to someone else. **Regulating gestures** help us take turns with each other in a conversation. Regulation gives nonverbal cues to indicate that you want to speak, that you have finished speaking, or that someone else may speak. For example, a speaker may hold their open palm out to the audience to solicit comments, or point to an audience member with a raised hand to signal it is their turn to speak. Waving is a common regulating gesture speakers use to indicate the beginning or ending of a presentation.

**regulating gesture**
a gesture that helps us take turns with each other in a conversation

**adapting gesture**
a habitual action a speaker uses to soothe or calm themselves

### Adaptation

Not all gestures are intentional—public speakers often move their bodies in unconscious ways to help make themselves more comfortable. **Adapting gestures** are habitual actions speakers use to soothe or calm themselves. For example, some speakers might tug on their ear, play with their hair, or adjust their clothing. Some might fidget with their hands or bounce from foot to foot. Almost every speaker has adaptive behaviors. If your adapting gestures are distracting your audience, you can use anxiety reduction techniques or additional practice to increase your confidence. You can also turn adaptive gestures into strengths, intentionally integrating them into your presentations as meaningful and distinctive features of your speaking style. For example, if your hands tend to shake when you speak, you could tell your audience to watch your "earthquake meter"—"when my hands start to shake, you know something big is about to happen."

Evangelos Venizelos, former Greek deputy prime minister, uses an adapting gesture during an election rally.

**facial expression**
moving or shaping the
face to communicate
emotion or accomplish
one of the six functions
of gesture

**eye contact**
the experience of being
looked at directly in the
eyes

## Pathways

To review how your
facial expressions
can evoke emotion
in your audience, see
**Chapter 10, Emotion
and Narrative**.

# FACIAL EXPRESSION

Humans have forty-two different facial muscles, which can create a nearly infinite variety of expressions. **Facial expression** refers to moving or shaping the face to communicate emotion or accomplish one of the six functions of gesture. In public speaking, audiences often pay more attention to a speaker's face than any other aspect of their physical delivery. As a speaker moves toward more personal or intimate distance in person or on video, their facial expressions take on more of the work of physical delivery and gesture.

Sometimes speakers convey a fearful or worried expression, making it difficult to emotionally connect with their audience. You can relax your face before a presentation by stretching the facial muscles with exaggerated expressions, and then returning to neutral. Become mindful of the feeling in your face, relax your facial muscles, and adopt a neutral expression. When you begin your presentation from this relaxed baseline, you can then let your expression change to reflect your emotions, interest, and mood.

# EYE CONTACT

Eye contact can be a valuable tool for communicating confidence and immediacy with your audience. In public speaking, **eye contact** is your audience's experience of being looked at directly in the eyes. In person, you can create this experience by actually looking at your audience members' eyes—or, if that is uncomfortable for you, by visually scanning their foreheads. On camera, look directly into your camera's lens—this gives your audience the experience of eye contact, even though you are not looking at them at all.

Making effective eye contact depends on understanding your speaking situation, including your own standpoint, your audience's expectations, your purpose, and your context. While most American audiences expect public speakers to make significant eye contact, eye contact is not essential for effective public speaking. People who are visually impaired can be powerful speakers without any eye contact at all, using other strengths to create immediacy and communicate confidence. For sighted speakers, breaking or reducing eye contact can demonstrate respect for an audience, reduce power distance, and even communicate remorse or sadness. Remember to ask yourself what amount of eye contact is best for your specific speaking situation and standpoint.

The most common impediment to making eye contact is anxiety. If eye contact makes you nervous, start with anxiety reduction strategies. Then work on gradually increasing eye contact during practice. Having someone watch you practice can help you practice your eye contact. If a practice audience is not available, try practicing in the room where you will present, and look directly at the seats where the audience will sit. Practice spreading your eye contact around the room, never staring at any one person, but looking at seats in all four corners and the center of the room.

When working with a camera, it can seem unnatural to look directly into the lens. It may help to imagine the lens as the face of a friendly audience member or a peephole your audience is watching you through. Practice—and reducing any visual distractions around you—will help this feel more natural. On video-conferencing platforms, it may help to choose "Gallery View" or even select "Hide Self View" so that you can keep your eyes on the camera lens instead of your audience or yourself. Remember that on camera your audience probably experiences you at a personal distance, where creating the impression of eye contact is even more important.

## ADORNMENT

Physical delivery is more than just the way you position or move your body—the way you adorn your body also sends a message. **Adornment** is how you present your physical appearance. Your adornment includes clothing, shoes, hairstyle, makeup, jewelry, tattoos, eyewear, and prosthetics—any item, accessory, or process that changes the way you look. You can use adornment to communicate your standpoint, adapt to your context, and identify with your audience.

Your adornment as a public speaker balances your personal self-presentation with the expectations of your audience, context, and purpose. Some public speaking situations call for more formal attire; others call for more casual looks. If you're unsure what is expected, look for pictures or videos of other speakers who have addressed a similar audience in a similar context with a similar purpose to your own. If you are speaking at an event organized by someone else, you can always ask that person what they suggest.

However, you may strategically choose to bend or break social rules for adornment to better communicate your own standpoint, strengths, and relationship to

**Pathways**

To review different techniques for managing public speaking anxiety, see **Chapter 2, Confidence and Anxiety**.

**adornment**
how you present your physical appearance

**Pathways**

To get tips on camera-friendly attire for video presentations, see **Chapter 14, Online and Mediated Presentations**.

After being ejected from parliament for wearing a traditional Māori hei-tiki instead of a Western necktie, New Zealand MP Rawiri Waititi successfully advocated for a more inclusive dress code. Likewise, after the House ban on headwear was amended to allow religious head coverings, Representative Ilhan Omar became the first US congressperson to wear a hijab.

the speaking situation. In some cases, social expectations for self-presentation are based on the normalization of privileged identities. For example, some schools and workplaces may have implicit or explicit rules that ban clothing or hairstyles that communicate your racial, ethnic, gender, or religious identity. If an event organizer, audience member, or institutional policy suggests that some part of your identity expression—like your natural hair, your hijab, your tattoos, or your skirt—is unprofessional or distracting, you can take that opportunity to educate them about your standpoint, using your clothing or hairstyle as a presentation aid.

## ✓ Critical Thinking Check

1. How do your intersecting identities influence audience perceptions of your vocal and physical delivery? For example, how do your race, gender, and socioeconomic status shape the interpretation of your articulation or attire? What other dimensions of your standpoint might shape audiences' judgments about your vocal and physical performance?

2. What types of vocal and physical delivery—for example, pitch control or eye contact—might not be accessible to every speaker? How might speakers with disabilities use other types of vocal and physical delivery to enhance the clarity, variety, immediacy, and mood of their speeches?

When someone questions the way you present yourself, telling them more about your identity can help them better understand your self-expression:

1. **THANK THEM FOR POINTING IT OUT.** For example: "Thanks for noticing my haircut." Or: "It's cool you asked about my graduation stole."

2. **EXPLAIN ITS CONNECTION TO YOUR IDENTITY.** For example: "I'm starting to question my gender identity, and I wanted to see what it would feel like to try out a more masculine cut." Or: "My stole is kente cloth, traditional handweaving from Ghana. Each color has its own special symbolism."

3. **EMPHASIZE ITS PERSONAL MEANING TO YOU.** For example: "I feel more like myself than I have in a long time—it feels really freeing." Or: "Kente cloth is reserved for really important occasions, so I'm proud to be wearing it today."

4. **ASK THEM A QUESTION THAT INVITES IDENTIFICATION.** For example: "Have you ever had that feeling?" Or: "Are you doing anything special for graduation?"

# Planning and Practicing Your Delivery

Now that you know all the elements of effective delivery, you're ready to start putting them together. Above all, remember that delivery is personal and situational. A great speaker sounds like themselves more than they sound like anyone else. That's why the best speakers are so easy to imitate; they have speech patterns and delivery styles that distinguish them from other speakers. So don't aim to be the next Oprah or the next Obama. Aim to be the best *you*—the best you for this audience, context, and purpose.

You can develop a natural, relaxed delivery style by speaking from your strengths and practicing your presentations. Practice can help you reduce your anxiety and emphasize your unique gifts as a speaker. As you gain more experience, your signature speaking style will begin to take shape.

## 1 Prepare to Deliver Your Text

Start by deciding how you will deliver the text of your speech. Will you memorize it, read from a prepared manuscript, work from an outline, or improvise your remarks? Different speaking situations call for different delivery methods, so

**memorized delivery**
reciting a presentation, word for word, from memory

**manuscript delivery**
presenting from a complete, full-sentence copy of a speech

your choice should be based on what best suits your context, purpose, audience, and strengths. Of course, sometimes you may not have a choice—for example, your instructor might require you to speak from an outline or a family member might call on you to make a surprise toast.

▪ **SPEAKING FROM MEMORY. Memorized delivery** is reciting a presentation, word for word, from memory. Live actors use memorized delivery, but it is also common among public speakers who give the same presentation multiple times. Professional public speakers, politicians, and social movement advocates often memorize speeches they will give at multiple events, with only minor changes from event to event. Memorization requires extensive practice to ensure a smooth delivery. This is more achievable in recorded video presentations, where you can memorize shorter sections of a speech and edit them together.

▪ **SPEAKING FROM MANUSCRIPTS.** When a speaker presents from a complete, full-sentence copy of their speech, they are using **manuscript delivery**. In person, a manuscript usually works best when resting on a podium or table in front of you, but if necessary, you can hold it in your hand. In digital presentations, a manuscript can also be displayed on your computer screen or a teleprompter. In either case, position your manuscript to make it as unobtrusive and easy to read as possible. Manuscript delivery works best when precise

2019 Carroll C. Arnold Distinguished Lecture
"Mobility, Containment, and the Racialized Spatio-Temporalities of Survival"
Lisa A. Flores, University of Colorado, Boulder

Speaking from a manuscript is common and widely accepted when presenting academic research or technical information, such as in Dr. Lisa Flores's 2019 keynote lecture at the National Communication Association (24:56).

wording is critical, and when audiences do not expect engaging or interesting delivery. Few speakers can read from a manuscript without sounding stiff and inauthentic, and manuscripts make it difficult to engage your audience with eye contact and gestures.

- **SPEAKING FROM OUTLINES.** Delivering a presentation from an outline is called **extemporaneous delivery**. Whether on note cards, slides, or a tele-prompter, your outline maps out your speech's main points, along with key facts and quotations. Using an outline allows an extemporaneous speaker to speak freely, reading the audience and making adjustments in the moment. Extemporaneous delivery gives you flexibility in delivering your speech, while still allowing you to deliver a structured and substantive presentation.

- **SPEAKING ON THE FLY. Impromptu delivery** is giving a presentation without advance preparation. Impromptu delivery occurs when a speaker needs to respond in the moment to unpredictable questions or events. You might be called to introduce yourself, "say a few words," or answer a question without advance warning or time to prepare. In such situations, speakers must decide on a purpose, thesis, and basic structure for their comments in a

**extemporaneous delivery**
delivering a presentation from an outline

**impromptu delivery**
giving a presentation without advance preparation

Debates require political candidates to speak impromptu, as candidates often do not know what their opponents will say and do not have access to the questions in advance. Here, three candidates for Wisconsin governor face off in a 2022 Republican primary debate: Rebecca Kleefisch, Tim Michels, and Timothy Ramthun.

## Pathways

To review the steps for practicing with an outline and tips for organizing your remarks on the fly, see **Chapter 9, Organization and Outlining**.

matter of seconds. To practice, you can do impromptu drills, where you are given a topic or prompt and speak for a couple minutes after just a few seconds of preparing. Knowing your subject and speaking situation makes speaking on the fly much easier, which is why audiences often see great impromptu speaking as the sign of a true expert.

While each form of delivery has its advantages, audiences usually find extemporaneous or memorized presentations most engaging. Extemporaneous delivery is the easiest for beginners and the most adaptable to different speaking situations. But, as always, your speaking situation should be your guide when choosing your form of delivery.

## 2 Plan Your Vocal and Physical Delivery

Once you've decided how you will deliver the text of your speech, make a plan for the vocal and physical elements of your delivery. How will you ensure that your audience can understand you? What will you do to hold their attention? How will you connect with them and earn their trust? What's the overall mood of your speech?

- **TROUBLESHOOT ISSUES WITH CLARITY.** Check each element of your vocal delivery—volume, rate, pitch, rhythm, and articulation—to determine whether your audience may have difficulty understanding you. If so, make a plan to enhance your clarity by using the projection, speed, range, and rhythm exercises in this chapter or by supplementing your speech with reinforcing gestures and audiovisual aids.

- **MARK UP YOUR TEXT TO ADD VARIETY.** To create variety, mark the passages you want to emphasize in your memorization script, manuscript, or outline. Use brackets to note the specific physical movements or vocal changes you'll make to emphasize those points. For example: [speed up], [pause], [get louder], [point at audience], [shake head], [step out from behind podium], or [remove jacket].

- **GAUGE THE RIGHT LEVEL OF IMMEDIACY.** There are several delivery techniques you can use to create immediacy: positive facial expressions, increased eye contact, closer proximity, open posture, higher pitch, and lower volume. But different purposes, audiences, and contexts call for different kinds of immediacy. For example, positive facial expressions can be

The psychologist Frantz Fanon has a famous line, one Stokely Carmichael and other Student Nonviolent Coordinating Committee members repeated frequently to describe the struggle of Black people against discriminatory social structures and practices: [SLOW] "When **powerless conscience** meets **conscienceless power.**" Martin Luther King Jr. expressed a *nearly identical* sentiment in one of his 1967 speeches, when he describes much of the work of his coalition as the "collision of **immoral power** with **powerless morality.**" In both cases the problem is one of conscience (or morality) on the one hand [LEFT HAND], and **power** on the other [RIGHT HAND]. At heart, [HANDS TOGETHER] **both** Carmichael and King believed that what was necessary was the **reallocation of power.** For immoral power to become more moral was part of King's dream, but the **majority** of his work was focused on the other side of the equation: [SLOW] **to change the distribution of power** so that justice for the Black community might be possible. In other words, King sought to locate and develop power for Black people in America. [PAUSE] King's strategy **was a** strategy of Black power.

Speakers sometimes note important elements of their vocal and physical delivery in their manuscripts, such as this speech manuscript's red text in brackets and use of italics, boldface, and underlining.

inappropriate when discussing disturbing events, closer proximity can feel aggressive if your audience doesn't agree with you, and lower volume can be difficult to hear in a large room. Evaluate your speaking situation to determine what forms of immediacy will build the most trust with your audience.

- **ESTABLISH A BASELINE MOOD.** Step back and consider the overall mood you want to set for your presentation. How do you feel about your topic? How do you want your audience to feel about it? Write a short series of reminders at the top of your memorization script, manuscript, or outline to set a baseline mood at the beginning of your speech. For example: "smile, animated movement, open posture;" "forceful gestures, loud, deep voice;" or "quiet, still, slow."

## 3 Practice, Practice, Practice

Once you have a delivery plan, you're ready to start practicing your speech. Begin by simply reading your manuscript or detailed outline aloud a couple of times, performing the nonverbal behaviors you marked. Then, gradually move away from your manuscript or full-sentence outline as you become more familiar with it—moving toward delivering more of your speech from memory or from a short keyword outline. Even if you plan to deliver your speech from a full manuscript, familiarize yourself with the script so you can read it fluidly and make some eye contact with your audience. We recommend that you practice your speech at least ten times before presentation day. The more often you practice your speech, the better your delivery will be. The following tips can help you maximize the benefits of your practice.

- **DIVIDE UP YOUR PRACTICE PRESENTATIONS OVER MULTIPLE SESSIONS.** Running through your practice sessions all at once is the public speaking equivalent of "cramming" for a test—it increases your performance anxiety and doesn't give you the full processing time you need. Practice two or three times, then wait at least a couple hours and up to a day before your next practice session. Spreading your practice out across multiple sessions will help store the speech in your memory.

- **PRACTICE DELIVERING YOUR SPEECH AS YOU WILL DELIVER IT TO YOUR AUDIENCE.** Practice out loud, with the same volume and gestures you will use during your actual presentation. This associates the content of your presentation with a specific style of delivery, making it more natural for you to deliver the speech effectively. If you feel anxiety interfering with any of your practice sessions, take a short break and use the anxiety reduction and reframing strategies that work best for you.

- **PRACTICE IN AN ENVIRONMENT SIMILAR TO YOUR ACTUAL SPEAKING SITUATION.** If you will speak in front of a live audience, practice in front of a live audience. If you will speak in front of a camera, practice in front of a camera. If you will use technology or presentation aids, practice the presentation with those as well. Practicing in a similar setting with a similar audience will reduce the distractions and surprises you will face during your actual presentation. The more you can replicate the actual context in which you will speak, the more you will benefit from your practice.

- **ASK FOR FEEDBACK.** If you practice in front of an audience, ask them to give you both positive feedback and concrete recommendations for improvement. Roommates, friends, and classmates all make great practice audiences. Your college or university may also have a Speaking Center where you can go to get peer feedback on your speech. If you record your practice sessions, you

## Pathways

To review the guidelines for giving and receiving constructive feedback, see **Chapter 4, Listening and Responding**.

can even give yourself feedback. Video feedback lets you see firsthand where you can improve or modify your delivery—as well as where you shine. If you're giving a mediated presentation, you might even find one of your practice recordings turns out so well that you can use it as the final version.

## ✓ Critical Thinking Check

1. What are the advantages and disadvantages of the different methods—memorized, manuscript, extemporaneous, and impromptu—for delivering text? What types of situations are each of these delivery methods best suited for?
2. What are the benefits of practicing your speech multiple times over a series of separate sessions? Why does it help to recreate the style, context, and audience of your presentation as closely as possible when you practice?

# Next Steps

When you practice a presentation, you're not just improving that one particular speech. You're also building your overall delivery skills and developing your own signature delivery style. The same goes for all of the delivery exercises in this chapter—the Vocal Projection Activity, the Speed Check Activity, the Speed Feedback Activity, the Vocal Range Activity, and the Recording Your Rhythm Activity can all help you improve your delivery and become a better speaker each and every time you use them.

Your voice and body are both indispensable instruments for conveying information, creating interest, communicating credibility, and evoking emotion—but not the only ones. In the next chapter, we'll explore the ways that you can use audiovisual aids to supplement and reinforce your vocal and physical delivery.

# Standpoint Reflection

- What type of speaking—memorized, manuscript, extemporaneous, or impromptu—do you have the most skills and experience with? How might you translate your skills and experience with everyday speaking into delivering your presentations?

- What unique strengths does your standpoint give you when it comes to creating clarity, variety, mood, and immediacy for your audience? What delivery techniques are you especially good at or excited to try? How might those strengths help you cultivate a unique delivery style?

- Of all the different delivery techniques presented in this chapter, which do you find most challenging? What delivery goals would those techniques help you achieve? How might you be able to meet those same delivery goals using different techniques?

- What are your biggest obstacles to practicing your delivery? What steps could you take to make practicing your delivery easier or more convenient for you?

## Key Terms

# Resources for Vocal and Physical Delivery

## "Try This" Exercises

Access the "Try This" exercises as directed by your instructor or online at digital.wwnorton.com/chapterexercises-conpubspeak

- To practice increasing your volume, try the **Vocal Projection Activity**.

- To measure your rate of words per minute, try the **Speed Check Activity**.

- To get listener feedback on your rate of delivery, try the **Speed Feedback Activity**.

- To find your optimal pitch, try the **Vocal Range Activity**.

- To get a sense of your natural vocal rhythm, try the **Recording Your Rhythm Activity**.

---

**Want to practice these skills to prepare for your next speech? Go to INQUIZITIVE to review and apply concepts from this chapter and get personalized feedback along the way.**

John Leguizamo

# 13 Presentation Aids and Slides

John Leguizamo's solo stage show *Latin History for Morons* is a ninety-minute presentation about the history of Latinx people in the Americas.[1] Throughout his performance, Leguizamo uses a large, two-sided chalkboard to write key names, dates, and statistics and to draw charts, maps, and timelines. For example, he draws a timeline on the board to emphasize the three-thousand-year gap in mainstream history textbooks between the Mayan civilization and Latinx culture today. He draws a pie chart of "Latin DNA" to demonstrate the genetic connection between Black, Indigenous, and Latin American people. He draws a map of the Americas and totals up the number of Indigenous people living in each region before and after European colonization to show how the European invasion devastated Indigenous people and cultures.[2]

In addition to visual images, Leguizamo deploys a variety of props to drive his powerful points home. Some props highlight his standpoint as a speaker. For example, to demonstrate how his junior high school history teacher used to police students of color, he attaches a car's rearview mirror to the chalkboard the same way his teacher did. He uses other props to enhance the credibility of his sources. For example, he holds up a physical copy of nearly every book he mentions while discussing the authors' expert testimony and research findings. While Leguizamo introduces his props and drawings with an ease that makes his delivery seem spontaneous, they have clearly been carefully planned and rehearsed.

## LEARNING OBJECTIVES

**After completing this chapter, you will be able to**

- Evaluate and improve your presentation aids with criteria for effective design and delivery

- Support your speaking with physical, visual, and audio content like written text, images, video recordings, and props

- Present your audiovisual aids with slide decks, handouts, posters, and whiteboards

- Handle permissions and credits when incorporating other people's creative work into your presentations

**presentation aids**
physical, visual, and
audio elements that a
speaker adds to their
presentation

John Leguizamo's one-person show features an impressive parade of maps, charts, timelines, and props. Though commonly called visual aids, devices like these are more than just visual: **presentation aids** include any physical, visual, and audio elements that a speaker adds to their presentation. As Leguizamo demonstrates, supplementing your speeches with presentation aids can simultaneously educate, entertain, and influence your audience. Not only do presentation aids provide evidence and reinforce ideas, but they can also share your standpoint, connect with your audience, and express your creativity.

# Using Presentation Aids Effectively

Once you've finished outlining your speech, take some time to consider whether presentation aids might help you deliver your message. When used effectively, presentation aids can enhance a speech in a number of ways. They can help focus your audience's attention on key points and make complex concepts easier to understand. They can add variety and multisensory interest that make your presentation more memorable and engaging. And importantly, well-designed presentation aids can make your speech more accessible for audience members with visual or hearing impairments, dyslexia, autism, attention deficit disorder, and other sensory processing challenges.

But using presentation aids without careful preparation and practice can have the opposite effect. Poorly designed presentation aids can distract or confuse your audience—and exclude audience members with sensory disabilities. Even when your presentation aids are well-crafted, using them without enough time to practice can lead to delivery problems that damage your credibility. Not every speech benefits from physical, audio, or visual aids, so always ask yourself: will using this presentation aid enhance my speech or detract from it? Or, in other words: will using this presentation aid actually aid my presentation? The following criteria can help you evaluate and improve the design and delivery of your presentation aids.

## CRITERIA FOR DESIGNING PRESENTATION AIDS

Whether you are using a prop, distributing a handout, playing a video, or showing slides, you want your presentation aids to both connect with your audience and support the overall purpose of your speech. Three core principles can help you design presentation aids that will reach your audience and achieve your purpose: accessibility, clarity, and appeal.

## Accessibility

Audiences are diverse, and their needs can be difficult to know in advance—even when you've done a thorough audience analysis. So, rather than making disability accommodations an afterthought, consider diverse needs and abilities throughout the design process. This approach—called **universal design**—aims to make presentation aids accessible to as many people as possible. While universal design requires some work, it pays off—not only by making your presentation more accessible for disabled audience members, but also by communicating more effectively with your whole audience.

For example, quality subtitles make video clips more accessible for people who are deaf or hearing impaired, and also increase engagement with viewers in quiet environments or with visual learning styles. Including audio descriptions of visual elements not only improves accessibility for people with impaired vision, but also adds clarity for everyone. Providing text, images, videos, and props large enough to be seen—whether by people with visual impairments, folks sitting at the back of the room, or viewers watching you on a small mobile screen—ensures that your message can reach as many people as possible. Using colors accessible to those with color blindness—like black, white, and yellow—creates visuals with clearer contrast for all viewers. You can also use online color blindness simulators to see how your visual aids look to people with different perceptions of color.

## Clarity

If you've designed your presentation aids with accessibility in mind, it's likely that you've already significantly increased their clarity. But clarity does not only mean designing presentation aids that can be clearly seen or heard; it also means creating presentation aids that are easy to understand and interpret.

## ▶ LEARN MORE

To learn more about creating accessible presentation aids, see the **Implementing Universal Design Video**.

**universal design**
considering diverse needs and abilities throughout the design process

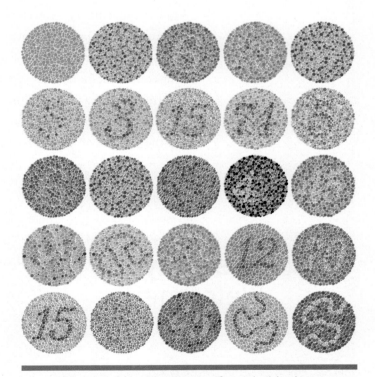

Images like these are used to test for colorblindness. Notice how the low contrast makes many of the images unclear—even if you are not colorblind.

Simple, uncluttered presentations aids with lots of space around and between elements can reduce visual noise and help your audience focus. Eliminate unnecessary words, sounds, and images—anything that doesn't serve a specific purpose is a distraction. Limit the amount of information you display at one time and give your audience enough time to process that information before moving on. Highlight the most important features of your presentation aids with gestures, labels, bolded fonts, or contrasting colors to make key points easier for your audience to grasp.

**Appeal** Your presentation aids are part of the total experience of your presentation. They help communicate the style and mood of your speech. Appeal is a matter of taste, so it's highly situational—a presentation aid that's aesthetically appealing to a preschool class may not be particularly appealing to sales reps for a new skin-care line or a stadium of football fans. Ideally, your audiovisual aids will appeal to your audience, fit your context and purpose, and reflect your own personal style.

While the specific style you choose will depend on your audience, purpose, context, and standpoint, paying attention to continuity, variety, and proportion can help you make any presentation aid look more appealing. Create continuity by using consistent fonts, color schemes, and layouts throughout your presentation aids. Incorporate a variety of textual and graphic elements to add visual interest. Consider the relative size and arrangement of the different elements to make sure they are not off-balance or out of proportion.

These two PowerPoint templates communicate different moods and styles. Each could be appropriate for some speaking situations, but not for others.

# CRITERIA FOR DELIVERING PRESENTATION AIDS

Once you've created accessible, clear, and appealing presentation aids, you will be ready to incorporate them into the delivery of your presentation. Your well-crafted presentation aids will have the most impact when you deliver them with multimodality, immediacy, and focus.

**Multimodality** Presentation aids allow a speaker to communicate a single idea, mood, or concept in multiple ways. **Multimodality** means using more than one mode of communication to accomplish the same goal. Delivering the same message in multiple modes—through spoken words, written text, images, audiovisual recordings, props, and gestures—ensures that your message comes through clearly. Using multiple modes of communication improves accessibility and helps when audience members are distracted, taking notes, or following along with your instructions.

Simply including presentation aids in the first place increases the multimodality of your delivery by incorporating additional physical, audio, and visual elements into your message. To get the full benefit of a multimodal presentation, don't forget to reinforce your presentation aids with spoken language and gestures. For example, when showing a graph to your audience, verbally describe its contents and implications: "As you can see in this graph, over half our support came from downtown businesses." If you are creating a video tutorial, describe what you are doing as specifically as possible at each step: "Go to the upper left of the screen and click on File." Physically or virtually pointing to key elements of your text, images, video, and props as you talk about them can strengthen your message with yet another mode of communication.

**Immediacy** When you're juggling presentation aids, it can be easy to forget about other dimensions of your physical delivery—like eye contact, posture, and facial expressions—that help you build immediacy with your audience. Using slides, whiteboards, and props can tempt speakers to look away from their audience or even turn their backs on them. This breaks your engagement with the audience and reduces their sense of connection with you.

Keep your body and face turned toward the audience unless there is a specific communicative purpose in turning away—like demonstrating a dance move or

**multimodality**
simultaneously using multiple modes of communication to accomplish the same goal

## Pathways

To revisit the principles of effective delivery, see **Chapter 12, Vocal and Physical Delivery**.

revealing a message written on the back of your shirt. Minimize any speaking time spent looking at your own slides, handouts, or props, since that's time you are looking away from your audience or the camera. Because you've designed your presentation aids to attract attention, you may need a little intentional practice to stay engaged with your audience while using them.

**Focus**  Just as your presentation aids can distract you from your audience, they can also distract your audience from you. It's tough trying to talk when your audience is passing around a shiny object, filling out a worksheet, or watching an animation bounce onscreen behind you. Since you still want your audience to focus primarily on you and your message, your presentation aids should only play a supporting role in your presentation.

To maintain your audience's focus, keep presentation aids offstage or offscreen when you are not discussing them. Reduce audio and visual distractions as much as possible, focusing your audience's attention on particular sights or sounds one at a time. Build in extra time to pause and let your audience fully take in the important features of your presentation aids. Think of yourself as a tour guide, walking them through a multisensory experience that you have curated for them. Including audio and visual elements only when they support your purpose—and removing them when they might divide your audience's attention—will let you stay the star of the show.

## ✓ Critical Thinking Check

1. Do you think universal design can be truly universal—that is, fully accessible to all people? Why or why not? What practical implications does your answer have for designing accessible presentation aids?
2. Why do you think presentation aids make it harder to deliver your presentation effectively? Can you think of any ways audiovisual aids might make delivering your presentation easier?

**📋 TRY THIS**

To identify parts of your speech outline that would benefit from presentation aids, try the **Planning Presentation Aids Checklist**.

# Developing the Content of Presentation Aids

Once you understand the basic principles for designing and delivering presentation aids, it's easy to start implementing them. Developing your presentation aids begins with the outline of your speech. What physical, visual, or audio elements

<table>
<tr><td>Eligibility for the US Presidency</td><td>Eligibility for the US Presidency</td></tr>
<tr><td>"No person except a natural born Citizen, or a Citizen of the United States, at the time of the Adoption of this Constitution, shall be eligible to the Office of President; neither shall any person be eligible to that Office who shall not have attained to the Age of thirty five Years, and been fourteen Years a Resident within the United States."<br><br>—United Stated Constitution, Article II, Section 1</td><td>• Natural Born Citizen<br>• At Least 35 Years Old<br>• At Least 14 Years of US Residency</td></tr>
</table>

Even with key phrases bolded, long blocks of text (left) are far more difficult to see and interpret than short, bulleted lists (right).

could you add to make your spoken presentation more accessible, clear, and appealing? How can you reinforce your message with multiple modes of communication, while keeping your audience focused and engaged? There are several types of content that you can use to enrich your presentation, including text, images, audio and video recordings, and props.

## TEXT

Text is great for communicating the structure of a presentation, emphasizing main points, and presenting testimonial evidence. Use keywords and phrases—rather than long blocks of text—to help your audience avoid distraction and stay engaged. Presenting text in numbered or bulleted lists can help your audience follow the outline of your presentation and focus on the most important information.

Another way to condense a large amount of text is to display it in a **table** organized into rows and columns. For example, Table 13.1 organizes several fonts into

**table**
a display of text and numerical information in rows and columns

| Sans serif fonts | Serif fonts | Ornamental fonts |
|---|---|---|
| Arial | Courier New | *Brush Script* |
| Calibri | Garamond | DESDEMONA |
| Helvetica | Times New Roman | Bauhaus |

**TABLE 13.1** Sans serif fonts tend to be more accessible for people with dyslexia, and often make presentation aids easier for all audience members to read.

different categories. You can help your audience interpret tables more easily by providing descriptive captions and circling, bolding, or highlighting the details that are most relevant to your purpose.

While sticking to keywords and phrases improves the focus and clarity of most presentation aids, certain types of evidence may call for longer text blocks. Detailed definitions and extended quotations may require precise wording and need to be presented in their entirety. In these cases, make sure to bold or highlight keywords and phrases within a lengthy block of text to focus your audience's attention.

Don't forget to make your text accessible, clear, and appealing. Text needs to be large enough to be clear to everyone in your audience. Sans serif fonts like Arial, Calibri, and Helvetica are easier to read onscreen than serif fonts like Times New Roman. Fonts without serifs—the little feet or flags attached to the letters—are also more accessible for people with dyslexia.[3] Ornamental fonts are especially hard to read in presentation aids.

Text also benefits from high contrast between light and dark colors. White on any dark color is usually safe, especially dark blue or black. Black on yellow is especially high contrast, but cream colors are usually more visually appealing than brighter yellows.

Multimodal delivery can make your text even clearer and more accessible. Use gestures to draw your audience's eyes to bulleted, listed, and highlighted phrases as you discuss them. Verbally restate and elaborate any keywords or phrases you display visually. But remember: don't put your audience to sleep by reading extended blocks of text aloud from your presentation aids.

## Pathways

To revisit strategies for helping audience members who are emotionally overwhelmed, see **Chapter 10, Emotion and Narrative**.

## IMAGES

You've probably heard the saying "a picture is worth a thousand words"—and it's true that some ideas and experiences are best conveyed visually. Images can simplify complex concepts and make abstract ideas concrete. They can condense large amounts of information into an easy-to-grasp visual format. They can show relationships and clarify details that are difficult to describe verbally. For example, if you want your audience to know what a pangolin looks like, it might be easier to show them a photograph instead of trying to explain it in words (see Figure 13.1).

**FIGURE 13.1** Visual images, like this photograph of a pangolin, can help your audience grasp new ideas and complex details quickly.

Images can also increase your audience's attention and emotional connection to your topic. While this can help get your audience interested in your presentation—look at that cute pangolin!—the emotional impact of images should be used with care. Images of traumatic, horrifying, or grotesque events should be used only when necessary for your purpose and appropriate to your situation. Even then, include a **trigger warning**: let your audience know that the images they are about to see may be disturbing, and give them the opportunity to avert their eyes, leave the room, or skip ahead in a recording. Distressing an audience member guarantees you will lose their attention—and possibly their goodwill.

When using images, do your best to ensure that they're clear and large enough to be seen from multiple vantage points. Stick to high-quality images—blurry or low-resolution graphics may be difficult for your audience to see or interpret. Describe important elements of the image aloud in case some members of your audience cannot see it clearly. To draw attention to a specific part of an image, gesture to it, label it, or circle it in a contrasting color.

Make your images easy to understand by including **image titles** that describe and frame their content, **captions** that explain and highlight their important features, and **legends** that decode any visual symbols you use, like shapes, lines, or colors. Effective titles, captions, and legends are multimodal: they use text to restate and clarify the point that you are making visually (see Selecting the Best Type of Image for Your Purpose, pp. 296–98). Be sure to verify the accuracy of photographs, diagrams, maps, charts, graphs, and timelines just like you would any other piece of evidence.

## VIDEO AND AUDIO CLIPS

Video and audio clips can add variety and provide something close to a firsthand experience or empirical evidence. Like images, they provide clarity and understanding in a way difficult to achieve with words alone. Keep videos as short as

**trigger warning**
a warning that upcoming content may disturb your audience

**image titles**
brief text descriptions that frame an image's content

**captions**
textual explanations that highlight an image's important features

**legends**
text-based keys that decode the visual symbols in an image

## Pathways

To revisit the SIFT method for checking the reliability of information, see **Chapter 8, Research and Citation**.

# Selecting the Best Type of Image for Your Purpose

## PHOTOGRAPHS ADD REALISM

**Photographs** are pictures taken with a camera to capture an accurate representation of people, objects, scenes, and events. For this reason, photographs make excellent evidence, giving your audience the impression that they have observed a phenomenon for themselves. For example, this photograph of a New Jersey home demonstrates the shocking destruction caused by Hurricane Sandy.

## ILLUSTRATIONS CREATE VISUAL APPEAL

**Illustrations** are artistic depictions created through drawing, painting, or graphic design. They can help hook your audience's attention, increase their interest, and anchor ideas in their memory. Because they are artistic and expressive, illustrations can also help you establish a mood for your presentation. For example, this illustration of shipping containers in the shape of a person's head could establish a memorable visual metaphor for rethinking the global supply chain.

## Blended Learning Combines In-Person and Online Instruction

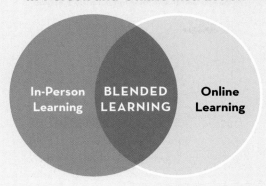

## DIAGRAMS SHOW RELATIONSHIPS AMONG PARTS

**Diagrams** are visual representations of structures or processes. Good diagrams provide labels that highlight each important part and use arrows, shapes, or other symbols to show how the parts fit together. For example, the Venn diagram shown here uses overlapping circles to emphasize the combination of two different instructional strategies.

2020 US Presidential Election Results Show Regional Difference in Political Affiliation

## MAPS SHOW RELATIONSHIPS IN SPACE

**Maps** are representations of the different regions and features in an area. Maps generally depict the relative positions of those regions and features—for example, marking the location of rivers, mountains, roads, buildings, cities, or political borders. But they often include other characteristics of those areas as well. For example, this map shows how different states voted in the 2020 US presidential election.

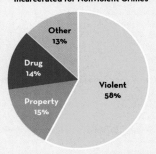

Over 40% of US State Prisoners Are Incarcerated for Nonviolent Crimes

SOURCE: Wendy Sawyer and Peter Wagner, "Mass Incarceration: The Whole Pie 2022," *Prison Policy Initiative*, March 14, 2022.

## PIE CHARTS SHOW PROPORTIONS

**Pie charts** are circular graphs divided into wedges, like slicing a pie. Each wedge represents one part of a whole that makes up the entire pie. Each part or wedge should be of the same general category as the others. For example, this pie chart shows the percentage of state prison inmates incarcerated for different categories of crime. Give your graph a title describing the whole pie, and give each wedge a label with the percentage of the pie it represents.

## BAR GRAPHS SHOW COMPARISONS

**Bar graphs** use either horizontal or vertical bars to show differences in values or amounts. For example, this graph compares the average levels of carbon dioxide emissions produced per person in India, the European Union, China, and the United States. When using bar graphs, make sure that each bar and its value are clearly depicted. Simple, two-dimensional bars make comparing values between bars easier.

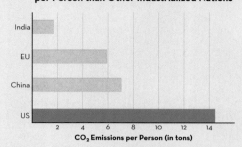

**The US Produces More Carbon Emissions per Person than Other Industrialized Nations**

SOURCE: International Energy Agency, "CO$_2$ Emissions Per Capita in Selected Countries and Regions, 2000–2020," October 28, 2021.

## LINE GRAPHS SHOW TRENDS

**Line graphs** use one or more lines to track changes over time. With two or more lines, viewers can quickly compare two or more trends. For example, this line graph shows that increases in pay have not kept up with increases in productivity. When using line graphs, make sure each line can be seen clearly. If you are tracing multiple trends, use colors and line styles that are different enough for your audience to easily distinguish between them.

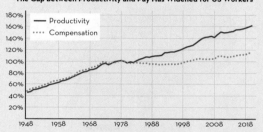

The Gap between Productivity and Pay Has Widened for US Workers

SOURCE: Economic Policy Institute, "The Productivity-Pay Gap," August 2021.

## TIMELINES SHOW SEQUENCES

**Timelines** are graphic representations of events in sequence. For example, this timeline shows major steps in applying to graduate school and when to take them. Timelines are usually horizontal lines with events plotted along them. They are clearest when each event and its date are labeled at a specific point on the line. If your presentation will discuss the events one at a time, it's usually best to reveal the timeline one point at a time, so the audience doesn't look ahead and get distracted.

Plan Ahead When Applying to Graduate School

possible, just long enough to achieve your purpose. Five to ten seconds is often plenty. Once you approach thirty seconds, the audio or video begins to over-shadow your presentation, and you risk losing engagement with your audience.

When using video or audio clips, integrate them into your presentation software or cue them up in advance—don't interrupt your presentation to find, open, or load them. As with images, add multimodality and clarity by describing what was seen in the video and what it means for your presentation. Like images, video and audio clips can be emotionally intense. Introduce video and audio depicting trau-matic, horrifying, or grotesque events with a trigger warning and an option for audience members to skip that part of your presentation.

## Pathways

To learn how to create and edit your own audio and video recordings, see **Chapter 14, Online and Mediated Presentations**.

## PROPS

Props can give your audience an even more direct and immediate experience than photographs or video recordings. A **prop** is a physical object that a speaker shows to the audience to demonstrate or clarify a point. In product review and unboxing videos, the item being reviewed—like a tech gadget or board game—is often used as a prop. In instructional presentations, props might include tools or technology the presenter is showing the audience how to use.

**prop**
a physical object that a speaker shows to the audience to demonstrate or clarify a point

With props, maintaining audience focus is critical. When you are not using or directly referencing the prop, it should be out of the audience's view. You can place it behind a podium, in a box, or off-camera. Only hand a prop to the audi-ence when absolutely necessary. When people hand a prop around, you lose the attention of at least a handful of audience members and encourage them to start side conversations among themselves. You also risk the prop becoming damaged.

Because people and animals are not objects, treat-ing them like props is risky. You cannot be sure how they will behave, and they are more distracting and harder to remove from the audience's view. Other people—especially audience members—may be uncomfortable being objectified as props; always get their permission well before your presentation. Live

Sarah Shah of Board Games in a Minute uses pieces from the board game Shamans as props in her video review of the game (7:08).

# Frans de Waal's Video Evidence

In his 2011 TED talk, primatologist Frans de Waal argued that animals display more empathy and fairness than most people believe.[4] In addition to referencing his own research, de Waal makes extensive use of video as evidence for his claims. He shows videos of primates and elephants cooperating, demonstrating their capacity for empathy, perspective taking, altruism, and fairness. His videos give his audience a direct experience of the moral behavior of animals. The similarities between primate and human behavior make many of the video clips emotionally engaging. The videos also demonstrate how the studies were conducted, and how the researchers reached their conclusions.

Frans de Waal explains how researchers study cooperation in elephants, and then shows a video demonstrating elephant social behavior (5:45).

De Waal displays the videos with no sound, so that he can continue to talk and explain the events while the videos play. He only uses videos when they serve as useful evidence. He introduces each video with the claim that it gives evidence for, explains his reasoning while the video plays, and emphasizes his conclusion at the end of each video. For the audience present in the auditorium, the videos and images he uses are projected large enough to be clearly seen and understood.

When his speech was edited for an online audience, the point of view shifted. The TED recording of his talk shows close-ups of de Waal when there is no action on the screen. When slides are on the screen, wide shots show de Waal on stage with the screen behind him. But for moments when de Waal shows videos, the TED recording switches to a voice-over and shows the videos full screen. These perspective changes create visual interest and ensure that the online audience can clearly see the evidence he is presenting. De Waal's talk is a master class in both presenting evidence and delivering multimedia presentations.

To watch de Waal's speech, do a web search for: de Waal TED talk. The video is approximately 16:52 in length.

animals are not allowed in many speaking contexts, so check with your event organizer or an authority at your venue. If a photograph or video of the person or animal can fulfill your purpose, that is almost always a better choice than using them as a live prop—unless you are a professional animal trainer or stage hypnotist.

## ✓ Critical Thinking Check

1. When you're displaying evidence visually, how do you know which type of image will be most effective? For example, how do you know whether to use a photograph or an illustration? A pie chart or a bar graph? A line graph or a timeline? When might a prop or video be more effective than an image?

2. Why is it important to check the accuracy of images, audio, and video? How can the strategies that you've already learned for verifying textual information help you verify audiovisual evidence? Can you think of any other strategies you might use to assess whether images, audio, and video are reliable?

# Choosing the Channel for Presentation Aids

While some presentation aids—like props—stand alone, most presentation aids contain multiple kinds of content: a mix of text, images, video, and other elements. You can deliver that content through many different channels, including posters, whiteboards, handouts, and slides. Once you know the content you want to share, you can decide which channel will best help you share it.

Comedian Demetri Martin often uses flip charts as part of his stand-up routines. Here he shows a line graph of how he expected a joke to go (the upward-sloping dotted line) and how it actually went (the downward-sloping solid line) (39:12).

## POSTERS AND FLIP CHARTS

Though somewhat old-school in the age of digital presentations, posters and flip charts are still common. They don't require any electricity, expensive software, or buggy hardware. They can make an excellent substitute when slide projection technology is unavailable or unreliable.

But posters and flip charts can create problems with accessibility and clarity. Since they're usually no larger than about two feet by three feet, they can be difficult to see. Audience focus can also be a problem. To help focus audience attention, use a blank cover over a poster or blank pages on a flip chart whenever you are not directly referencing it. If you will need an easel or other stand for your materials, either bring one yourself or check in advance that one will be available.

## WHITEBOARDS AND CHALKBOARDS

Sometimes a speaker wants to spontaneously draw or write during their presentation. Whiteboards and chalkboards are good tools for creating this spontaneity. You can create the same spontaneity with digital whiteboards, both for in-person presentations and online video. Zoom, Microsoft Teams, and Google Meet all have whiteboard functions.

▣ **LEARN MORE**

To learn more about how to use the whiteboard tools on videoconferencing platforms, see the **Using Digital Whiteboards Video**.

Whether analog or digital, whiteboards allow a speaker to visually record audience input and responses. These tools are excellent when speakers want to brainstorm with an audience. They also encourage audience participation. When a speaker writes an audience member's contribution on the board, it provides positive feedback and encourages others to contribute.

Immediacy is the first challenge posed by whiteboards and similar tools. In-person speakers tend to turn their backs and walk away from the audience to write on the board. This also affects accessibility and clarity. If you need to break engagement with your audience to write, use it as a moment to punctuate your presentation with a pause, or to repeat the words you are writing. Do not introduce new ideas with your back turned, as your voice will be less audible and less clear. Remember that any text you write needs to be large and clear enough to read. When you're done discussing an item, remove it from the audience's view by erasing the board or scrolling down to white space.

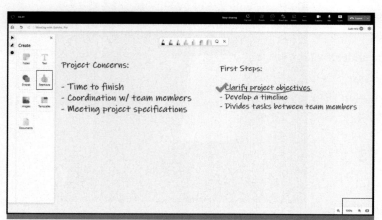

Most online presentation and videoconferencing applications include a digital whiteboard function, such as this one in Microsoft Teams.

## HANDOUTS

Audiences sometimes benefit from being able to take information with them after a presentation. To help audiences retain information or take an action, a speaker can provide a handout. A **handout** is any material a speaker gives an audience for them to keep or use. This might be a voter registration card, a list of additional resources, a worksheet, a copy of the presentation slides, or a card with a website for more information.

Providing handouts can reinforce the information or action steps you want your audience to take away from your presentation.

The biggest challenge with handouts is audience focus. Once you give the audience a handout, their attention will be split between it and your presentation. Whenever possible, wait to distribute your handout until the very end of your presentation, after your conclusion. Presenting the information on a slide, poster, or similar alternative makes it easier to direct your audience's attention.

**handout**
any material a speaker gives an audience for them to keep or use

If you need to provide a worksheet for them to complete during your presentation, put as little information on the worksheet as possible. You don't want them working ahead or reading over the worksheet when they should be listening to you. A blank sheet of paper is ideal. If more is essential, then include only what must be there. Directions, prompts, and details should be provided in your presentation both verbally and visually (on a slide, poster, or whiteboard), and only for each part of the worksheet as they complete it. After your presentation, you may choose to provide them with a complete copy of the worksheet with directions and prompts so they can complete it on their own. If you are using a slide deck, audiences increasingly expect access to a copy of your slides at the end of the presentation.

## SLIDE DECKS

Whether in person or online, slide decks are by far the most common way of presenting visual aids in contemporary public speaking. While PowerPoint is the standard software for creating slide decks, Google Slides, Keynote, and Prezi are also common. Your speaking context is more likely to support PowerPoint than any other presentation software, particularly because a PowerPoint file can work on a Mac or PC, function without an internet connection, be saved to a thumb drive, and even be opened in Google Slides or Keynote. Today, presentation software has become so pervasive and complex that it warrants an extended discussion.

# Using Presentation Slides

When PowerPoint first launched in 1987, it was a basic tool for creating black-and-white text presentations. Today, PowerPoint and other slide deck tools offer robust multimedia platforms that support a wide variety of public speakers. Slide decks are ubiquitous in professional settings of all kinds: they are common in classrooms, scientific and technical presentations, sales pitches, webinars and video presentations, and countless other public speaking situations. Regardless of which software you use, certain guidelines can help your presentations take advantage of these presentation tools and avoid the pitfalls that come with them.

## CHECKING THE AVAILABLE TECHNOLOGY

While all presentation aids add complexity and take time to prepare, slide decks are the most time-intensive, particularly for beginning users. You can save yourself a lot of time and effort by trouble-shooting potential technology issues in advance. Before you start any work on your presentation slides, ask these questions about your speaking context:

- Does it have a projector? If so, does it have a standard 4:3 aspect ratio, or a widescreen 16:9 aspect ratio?

- Is there a screen? If so, is it large enough for the whole audience to see?

- Will some people have an obstructed line of sight?

- Is a computer provided? If so, what kind—Mac or PC? What presentation software is loaded on the computer? Is it connected to the internet? Does it have a USB port for a thumb drive?

- Is a remote or "clicker" available for the presenter? Do you need or want to provide your own?

- If there is no computer or you prefer to use your own, what kind of video and audio connections are available? VGA? HDMI? 3.5 mm audio? Know what your computer supports and what your speaking context supports.

- Will WiFi or an Ethernet connection be available? Is the internet connection high speed and reliable?

- If you are presenting online, what software or platform will you be using—Zoom, Teams, Meet, or something else?

These questions may seem basic, but you might be surprised at how poorly some presenting spaces are equipped. Know the answers before you invest time in creating your presentation aids. If you're not sure, ask your event organizer.

Once you have answers to these questions, you can decide on your presentation software. The default is PowerPoint, so the rest of this chapter will focus on using that platform. Whatever you choose, be sure it will work in your speaking context and that it can be used even if the internet is not working.

## CREATING EFFECTIVE SLIDES

Once you've double-checked the available hardware and chosen your presentation software, you're ready to start creating your slides. Remember that to be effective, your slides should be accessible, clear, and visually appealing. There are three steps to creating slide presentations: choosing a theme, adding your content, and planning transitions and animations.

### 1 Choose a Presentation Theme

The first thing to decide is what theme you will use for your presentation. A **presentation theme** is a set of colors, fonts, and effects used throughout your slides to create a unified look for your whole presentation. Select or create a theme that fits the purpose and context of your presentation and expresses your standpoint and the mood you are trying to set. For example, a college student giving a presentation in an engineering course might look for a theme that appears professional, scientific, and youthful.

PowerPoint and other software provide several suggested themes and design ideas to get you started. You can find

**presentation theme**
a set of colors, fonts, and effects used throughout your slides to provide consistency and set a mood

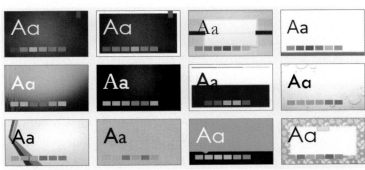

A few of the default themes available in PowerPoint. Notice how different themes communicate different moods and might be appropriate for different kinds of speaking situations.

them in PowerPoint under the "Design" tab. As you review themes, consider how each slide might look for each of the different kinds of content you plan to include. For example, if you know you will be using text, photographs, a bar graph, and a diagram, look for the specific templates in each theme that you would use to display that content. Keep the principles of accessibility, clarity, and visual appeal in mind as you evaluate different themes. When in doubt, simplicity is best. Once you have chosen a theme, you are ready to create your slides.

## 2 Add Your Content

To develop the content of your slides, start with a complete outline of your presentation. Decide what slides you will include and where you will use them. Not every part of your presentation may need a slide. At some points in your presentation, you may want the full attention of your audience. For in-person presentations, add an empty slide with a black background to create the same effect as turning off the projector. In online or recorded presentations, you can toggle between your slides, your camera feed, and picture-in-picture options that show both.

**Pathways**

To revisit the steps for drafting and revising outlines, see **Chapter 9, Organization and Outlining**.

Most slides will include a title or caption along with some additional content, such as text, an image, or a video clip. Unless you are doing a side-by-side comparison, limit yourself to no more than one image per slide. For text-based slides, follow the **5 × 5 rule**: no more than five bullet points on a slide, and no more than five words per bullet point. Only use longer text blocks when introducing evidence—like definitions or quotations—where exact wording is crucial. Whenever possible, avoid any content that requires an internet connection to display. Rather than relying on links that may not work, insert any video or audio files directly into your slide presentation.

**5 × 5 rule**
using no more than five bullet points on a slide, and no more than five words per bullet point

## 3 Plan Slide Transitions and Animations

Slide transitions are visual effects—like zooms, wipes, and dissolves—that play when you move from one slide to the next. Most of these visual effects are extremely distracting, so it's usually best to avoid them—unless you want to create an over-the-top silly mood. More subtle transitions, like fades, can add drama by revealing your next slide more slowly. You can select the "Transitions" tab to preview different transition styles. Before using slide transitions, get a second opinion to make sure they create the effect you want—most presentations are better without them.

**▶ LEARN MORE**

To learn more about how to develop effective slides, see the **Creating Slide Decks Video Series**.

You can also add transitions between elements on a single slide using the "custom animation" function. Custom animation allows different elements—like titles, images, or text bullets—to appear one by one, rather than all at once. This can help your audience focus by keeping elements offscreen until you are ready to discuss them. Simply go to the "Animations" tab in PowerPoint, then select the block of text you want to animate and the animation style you prefer. "Fade" and "Appear" are both good choices. Other animation styles and animation sounds are too distracting for most presentations.

## DELIVERING SLIDE PRESENTATIONS

Slide decks pose unique challenges for maintaining multimodality, focus, and immediacy with your delivery. As a college student, you probably know firsthand how hard it is to pay attention to a speaker reading from their slides in a dimly lit room. You know how difficult it can be to follow along if a speaker blocks your view of the screen or advances the slides too quickly or too slowly. And you've probably seen presenters scramble—or even cancel a presentation—when the computer or projector isn't working. The following strategies can help you avoid these common pitfalls and deliver your slide presentations smoothly.

- **REPHRASE—DON'T READ—YOUR SLIDES.** Delivering a message in multiple modalities can make your speech clearer and more accessible. So make sure to verbally describe any charts, images, or videos and rephrase any text you display out loud. But don't make the mistake of simply reading long blocks of text to your audience word for word. If you've stuck to the 5 × 5 rule, your slides should primarily contain keywords that you can expand and elaborate on as you speak. If your slides do include longer blocks of text—like definitions or quotations—both visually and verbally highlight the most important words and phrases rather than reading the whole thing.

- **MAINTAIN GOOD LIGHTING.** While it may be tempting to dim or turn off the lights so that your audience can see the screen more clearly, low light makes it difficult for them to see you. If they can't see your physical delivery— your facial expressions, eye contact, gestures, and so on—it's hard to keep your audience attentive and engaged. If keeping the lights on truly does make your slides hard to see, distribute them as a handout in addition to projecting them. If you need to, you can lower the lights at key moments—for example, to show an important chart, image, or video. But remember, the longer the lights are down, the more time your audience has to tune out.

- **CONSIDER YOUR PHYSICAL POSITION.** Think about where you will stand at different points in your presentation. Standing behind or beside your computer reduces immediacy by positioning you further from your audience. This encourages the audience to watch your slides far more than they watch you. When available, the best solution is using a remote or "clicker" to control your slides so you can move around, connect with your audience, and gesture to the onscreen content you are discussing. But be cautious about standing directly in front of the screen. Not only can you block audience members' view of your slides, but you may also become the screen, with the slides projected onto your body. Find a position that allows your audience to share focus between you and your slides.

- **PRACTICE SLIDE CUES.** Just as you practice everything else in a presentation, practice using your slides and technology. Mark your presentation notes with an easy-to-see signal—like >> or NEXT SLIDE—to cue yourself when to advance your slides. Practice with your slides exactly as you will use them. Ideally, practice in the room or on the platform where you will present with the same technology you will be using. At minimum, practice with the final version of your slides and the same software you will use when presenting. The more your practice emulates the real speaking environment, the more effective it will be.

- **PLAN FOR TECHNOLOGY FAILURE.** Things break. Internet service goes down. Computers freeze. As fantastic as presentation software can be, it introduces a greater risk of technology failure. Whenever possible, test your slide deck using the technology available in the room or on the platform where you will present. Always have a backup plan. If your projector, computer, software, or camera isn't working, what will you do? If you have built enough multimodality into your presentation, you will still succeed when the technology fails. With all technology, plan for the worst, and hope for the best.

## ✓ Critical Thinking Check

1. Why do you think slide decks are so popular with public speakers today? Can you think of any speaking situations when a slide deck might not be your best choice?

2. Why is it important to check the available technology before you begin preparing your slides? How could you modify your speech if your technology fails unexpectedly?

# Navigating Credits and Permissions

Anytime you include media in your slideshow or other presentation aids, you will want to ensure that you have permission to use them and give credit to their creators. That includes the use of images, audio, and video. Whether you're giving an in-person or online presentation, credits and permissions are expected by audiences and often required by law.

In the United States and throughout most of the world, **copyright** laws give media creators and owners control over media use and distribution. If you find an image, video, or sound recording on the internet, it is probably protected by copyright law—even if there is no "©" (copyright symbol) or statement of copyright. Creators don't need to claim or formally file for a copyright to receive basic legal protection in the United States.

There are two general ways to avoid violating a copyright when using media created by someone else. You can use material in the public domain, or you can use material with the explicit permission of the copyright owner. Securing permission directly from a copyright holder can be time-consuming and expensive—but fortunately, media released under Creative Commons and royalty-free licenses already have permissions agreements in place. You can find public domain, Creative Commons, and royalty-free media through online search databases like Wikimedia Commons or Google's image and video search tools.

## PUBLIC DOMAIN

Materials are considered **public domain** if they are not protected by copyright. Materials in the public domain can be used freely with no additional permission, though audiences will still expect you to provide a citation and give proper credit. Works enter the public domain when:

- The copyright expires—US copyrights last for a bare minimum of seventy years from the date of publication, but much longer in most cases

- The copyright holder explicitly dedicates the work to the public domain

**copyright**
the right to control the use and distribution of creative works

**public domain**
materials not protected by copyright

- An employee or officer of the United States federal government creates them as part of their job

Unless you see a clear statement that a work is in the public domain, you should assume it is protected by copyright—even if it is just an image on Flickr or Instagram, a post on Facebook or Twitter, or a video on TikTok or YouTube. For more details on copyrights, check out the US Copyright Office's website (www.copyright.gov).

## CREATIVE COMMONS LICENSES

▣ LEARN MORE

To learn more about how to find public domain, Creative Commons, and royalty-free media, see the **Finding Copyright-Friendly Media Video**.

While media creators rarely release their work as public domain, many creators release images, videos, and sound recordings under a Creative Commons license. A Creative Commons license allows "a free, simple, and standardized way to grant copyright permissions for creative and academic works; ensure proper attribution; and allow others to copy, distribute, and make use of those works."[5]

A work released under a Creative Commons license is still protected by copyright law, but the owner has granted permission to use it with certain restrictions and expectations. Some licenses allow editing or adaptation of the work; some do not. Some allow works to be used for commercial purposes, and some do not. Most require that you give the original creator of the work credit in some form. To use media released under a Creative Commons license, check the restrictions of the specific license. A list of the different licenses and what they allow can be found on the Creative Commons website (www.creativecommons.org/licenses).

## ROYALTY-FREE LICENSES

Besides material in the public domain and released under Creative Commons licenses, some images, videos, and sound recordings are available under royalty-free licenses. A royalty-free license permits a person to use a copyrighted work without having to pay the owner of the copyright, or in exchange for a one-time payment. If you have video editing software (such as Apple's iMovie) that includes images, music, or video clips, those materials are often provided under a royalty-free license. Graphic design tools like Microsoft Publisher or the online platform Canva similarly include royalty-free licenses to use their images.

| License type | Symbol(s) | Description |
|---|---|---|
| Public domain | (symbol) | Copyright expired or waived by the creator or holder of the rights. Freely available for use by anyone. |
| Creative Commons (CC) | (cc) | Limited use rights granted under a Creative Commons license. You can share and redistribute this material as allowed by the specific license. |
| Attribution (BY) | (i) | You must provide credit to the creator and holder of the rights when you use this material. |
| Share alike (SA) | (symbol) | Anything you create using this material must be freely shared under the same Creative Commons license. |
| No derivatives (ND) | (=) | You cannot make any changes, adaptations, or modifications to the material. |
| Noncommercial Americas/ Europe (NC) | (symbol) / (symbol) | You cannot use the material for any commercial purposes (such as marketing or sales) or in any product for which you will charge. |
| Sample CC license: CC-BY-NC-ND | (cc)(i)(S)(=) BY NC ND | You can reuse and redistribute the materials in any medium if you provide credit to the creator and holder of the rights. But you cannot use the material for any commercial purposes, and you cannot make any changes, adaptations, or modifications to the material. |

Creative Commons licenses provide permissions for some kinds of uses but prohibit others or may require you to freely share anything you create that includes the licensed material. Be sure to read the specific license that governs any Creative Commons materials you use. Details are available on the Creative Commons website: https://creativecommons.org/about/cclicenses/

Restrictions vary from license to license, and the terms are sometimes buried in complicated "terms and conditions" documents. Most licenses forbid using the materials in ways that negatively portray the company, its products, or any identifiable people in the media. The best companies provide a "plain English" version of their license agreement, which explains what you may do with their media.

# CREDITS

## Pathways

To review the elements of written and verbal source citations, see **Chapter 8, Research and Citation**.

Regardless of where you find the materials you use, you will almost always need to include credits for images, audio, and video. Often, credits are required by the license that makes it legal for you to use the material. Providing credits helps avoid misunderstandings where the audience may think you either created or plagiarized the media you are using.

The original source may explain the format you should use for the credit. If not, include the name or title of the material, the name of its creator, the name of the copyright holder (if different), the year of copyright (if provided), and a link to where the material may be found (if retrieved online). Your audience should be able to clearly see or hear your credits, and easily understand what material comes from which source.

On presentation slides, credits can be placed at the bottom of each slide or on a single slide at the very end of your presentation. For video and audio recordings, the credits are most often placed at the end of the recording. In addition to credits within your presentation itself, you may also include credits in the notes, outlines, or handouts that accompany your work.

Credits for images not only ensure proper attribution but also communicate to your audience the source and context for the visual information. For example, this PowerPoint slide includes a public domain image and includes a credit below the image with information about the image source.

## ✓ Critical Thinking Check

1. What's the difference between plagiarism and copyright violation? Can you think of an example of plagiarism that doesn't violate copyright? Can you think of an example of a copyright violation that wouldn't count as plagiarism?

2. What are the benefits of crediting the images, audio, and video you use? What can go wrong if you don't properly credit public domain, Creative Commons, and royalty-free materials?

# Next Steps

Now that you know the principles for designing and delivering everything from props to slideshows, you're ready to start creating presentation aids of your own. To take the next step, grab your speech outline and try the Planning Presentation Aids Checklist. Then check out the Implementing Universal Design Video, Using Digital Whiteboards Video, Creating Slide Decks Video Series, and Finding Copyright-Friendly Media Video. Just follow along, and you'll have accessible, clear, and appealing presentation aids ready to go in no time.

You've learned how to incorporate all kinds of media into your presentations, including images, audio, and video recordings. But what if your entire speech is mediated—like a podcast, recorded video, live webinar, or videoconference? Next up, you'll learn the skills you need to create your own digital presentations from start to finish.

# Standpoint Reflection

- What unique strengths does your standpoint give you when it comes to developing presentation aids? What kinds of presentation aids would feel special coming from you—or could only come from you?

- How might you use the style and design of your presentation aids to express your standpoint? How is this similar to—or different from—other aesthetic considerations, like choosing your attire?

- How can audiovisual evidence—like props, photographs, audio clips, and video recordings—expand the worldview of your audience members? Is witnessing audiovisual evidence the same as or different from having firsthand experience? Why?

- What are some of the most interesting and memorable presentation aids that you've seen presenters use? What made them so interesting and memorable? How might you use those examples to develop strategies for your own presentation aids?

## Key Terms

# Resources for Presentation Aids and Slides

## 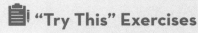 "Try This" Exercises

Access the "Try This" exercises as directed by your instructor or online at digital.wwnorton.com/chapterexercises-conpubspeak

- To identify parts of your speech outline that would benefit from presentation aids, try the **Planning Presentation Aids Checklist**.

## ▶ "Learn More" Tutorials

Access the "Learn More" tutorials as directed by your instructor or online at digital.wwnorton.com/videos-conpubspeak

- To learn more about creating accessible presentation aids, see the **Implementing Universal Design Video**.

- To learn more about how to use the whiteboard tools on videoconferencing platforms, see the **Using Digital Whiteboards Video**.

- To learn more about how to develop effective slides, see the **Creating Slide Decks Video Series**.

- To learn more about how to find public domain, Creative Commons, and royalty-free media, see the **Finding Copyright-Friendly Media Video**.

---

 **Want to practice these skills to prepare for your next speech? Go to INQUIZITIVE to review and apply concepts from this chapter and get personalized feedback along the way.**

PODCASTER AND
COMMUNITY ORGANIZER    Danielle Desir

# 14 Online and Mediated Presentations

Recognizing the need to include more diverse voices on their podcasting platform, Spotify announced a 2018 grant to bring a woman of color to their "Sound Up" podcasting bootcamp. As a blogger planning to start a podcast, Danielle Desir was excited about the opportunity and applied—along with over eighteen thousand other women of color.[1] While waiting for Spotify to announce the winner, Desir began connecting with other applicants on Twitter and found thousands of women of color creating podcasts. While she ultimately didn't receive the grant, she discovered something much more valuable: a community.

She founded WOC Podcasters as a space for women of color to support each other as they develop and launch their podcasts. WOC Podcasters and its online community have provided podcasting resources, skills, and mentorship to over four thousand women of color—and counting.[2] With the support of the community she created, Desir has launched her own popular travel and personal finance podcast, been featured in the *New York Times*, spoken at the Women in Travel Summit, and joined the board of the *Podcast Business Journal*.[3]

Desir recommends that people creating their first online presentation start by knowing that the technology is "a lot easier than you think."[4] She suggests starting without any expectations and experimenting with different formats and technologies.[5] One of her favorite things about being an online speaker, she says, is the ability to "build an intimate connection" with audiences that she wouldn't be able to reach without digital media.[6] As Desir's story shows, digital media can empower public speakers to both share their own message and build more inclusive communities.

## LEARNING OBJECTIVES

### After completing this chapter, you will be able to

- Develop an audience on social media and other digital platforms

- Record and edit audio for mediated presentations

- Record and edit video for mediated presentations

- Prepare, deliver, and engage audiences in live online presentations

More and more, public speakers have been moving online. Over the last two decades, digital tools and platforms have given speakers like Danielle Desir the ability to build communities and connect with audiences that they can't reach in person. As access to those tools and platforms has expanded, the internet has created space for a more diverse range of speakers and audiences than ever before. During the COVID-19 pandemic, the trend toward digital public speaking accelerated, as classrooms, workplaces, and social gatherings moved onto web-based platforms. Today, online public speaking—including audio, video, and live presentation skills—has become an integral part of our civic, professional, and social lives.

## Public Speaking and Media Culture

While the rise of digital public speaking is relatively recent, public speakers have been using media to deliver presentations for over a century. As early as 1898, Emile Berliner produced gramophone records of Chauncey Depew, Dwight Moody, and Robert Ingersoll, "the three best known public speakers in America."[7] In 1933, US president Franklin Delano Roosevelt delivered his first national radio address in a series of "fireside chats." And in 1960, Americans watched the first televised presidential debate between John F. Kennedy and Richard Nixon. **Mediated presentations**—public speeches delivered through audio or visual media—are nothing new.

**mediated presentations**
public speeches delivered through audio or visual media

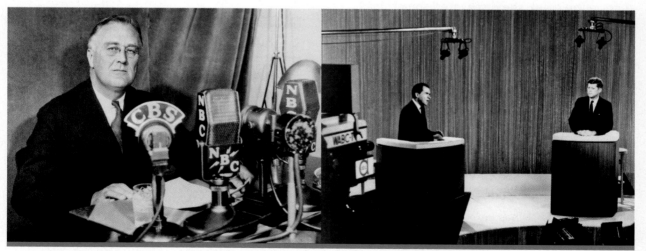

Mediated presentations have been around for as long as recording and broadcast media. Left: Franklin Delano Roosevelt delivers a "fireside chat" via radio in 1934. Right: Richard Nixon and John F. Kennedy debate over live television during the 1960 presidential campaign.

But before the 2000s, most public speakers could only create and share media content if they had access to expensive production equipment and centralized distribution channels like radio and television stations. Because those broadcast media channels only have a limited amount of airtime each day, they can only include a limited number of speakers and topics. Owners, editors, producers, advertisers, and government regulators decide who gets to speak and what they can say. These decision makers—called **media gatekeepers**—select and filter the content on media channels.[8]

By selecting certain topics and speakers and filtering out others, media gate-keepers shape audience perceptions of what's important. This capacity for media coverage to influence an audience's priorities is called **agenda setting**.[9] This is done not only by excluding certain information and points of view, but also by prioritizing some issues and speakers over others—for example, by giving them more airtime or more prominent placement at the beginning of a program.

A surprisingly small number of companies currently serve as the primary broadcast media gatekeepers and agenda setters in the United States. For example, Comcast owns several television networks—including NBC, MSNBC, Syfy, USA, and Telemundo—and film studios—including DreamWorks, Universal, and Focus Features. Paramount Global owns not only Paramount Pictures, but also CBS, CMT, MTV, VH1, BET, Showtime, Nickelodeon, and Comedy Central. After a recent merger between WarnerMedia and Discovery, a single company now owns television networks like CNN, HBO, TLC, HGTV, the Food Network, and the Discovery Channel, as well as film studios like Warner, New Line, and Castle Rock Entertainment. This concentration of media ownership into the hands of fewer and fewer corporations is called **media consolidation**.

Fortunately, public speakers no longer need the backing of these increasingly centralized broadcast corporations to produce and distribute media content. Today, you can create mediated presentations with nothing more than a smart-phone, public WiFi, free software, and online tutorials. And you can share those presentations on free and openly available online platforms. **Platforms** are digital channels or services for distributing media content: for example, Spotify or SoundCloud for audio recordings, YouTube and Vimeo for recorded video, and Instagram Live or Zoom for live online presentations.

**media gatekeepers**
decision makers who select and filter the content on media channels

**agenda setting**
the capacity for media coverage to influence an audience's priorities

**media consolidation**
concentration of media ownership into the hands of fewer and fewer corporations

**platforms**
digital channels for distributing media content

## SPEAK OUT

When you want to get the attention of media gatekeepers—whether online influencers or broadcast journalists—the following strategies can help you build a genuine connection over email or social media:

1. EXPLAIN WHY YOU ARE REACHING OUT NOW. Reference their recent work to make your contact timely. For example: "I just saw your video on..." or "I just read your post about..."

2. EXPLAIN WHY YOU ARE REACHING OUT TO THEM. Tie your issue, cause, or topic to one of their passions or interests. For example: "Since you're someone who cares about..." or "You've always been such a strong supporter of..."

3. EXPLAIN WHAT YOU HAVE TO OFFER. Create identification with them by connecting your purpose and passion to theirs. For example: "I want to help spread the message that..." or "Like you, I'm an advocate for..."

4. CALL THEM TO ACTION. Ask them to take a low-effort step to support you. For example: "Would you be willing to share my..." or "Would you be open to a five-minute interview on..."

Access to media production tools and digital platforms has given a broader range of speakers the ability to connect with a broader range of audiences. Many speakers that have historically been excluded or underrepresented in broadcast media—like people of color, queer people, and people with disabilities—have discovered or created communities online. The internet has also become home to groups interested in a variety of topics and issues that don't get much coverage in broadcast media—from witchcraft videos on TikTok to Discord communities focused on cryptocurrency, the World Wide Web is wide indeed.

Although the number of voices and messages online has multiplied, the internet is not immune to corporate consolidation. For example, Meta Platforms owns Facebook, Instagram, WhatsApp, Messenger, and Oculus, as well as companies working on game development, blockchain, virtual reality, and artificial intelligence. Alphabet Inc. owns all the Google platforms—Google Search, Gmail, Google AdSense, and more—plus YouTube and Fitbit, multiple video game development companies, talent and intellectual property firms, and companies in artificial intelligence, biotechnology, robotics, self-driving cars, home automation, drones, and investing. Given the user data they collect, this consolidation raises perennial concerns about digital privacy and surveillance.

User data has become the basis for new forms of media gatekeeping and agenda setting. Search engines and social media platforms use algorithms that rank content based on user engagement. Engagement metrics—including likes, shares, and comments—determine who and what gets featured in your search results or placed higher in your social media feeds. This has turned audiences themselves into gatekeepers and agenda setters, as their engagement with content tells a platform's algorithm whether to show it to other people—and if so, which ones.[10]

As a result of these user-driven algorithms, social media platforms have also created another group of audience-based gatekeepers: influencers. An **influencer** is a social media creator with a large and highly engaged online following—like Kim Kardashian or Zach King. Because an influencer's followers are more likely to engage with their content, their posts are prioritized by social media platforms. When an influencer shares, links, or retweets a piece of content, the online platform will ensure that a significant number of people see it. Although media gatekeeping operates differently on digital platforms, it still determines which speakers and messages get heard.

**Pathways**

To review how web-based algorithms create echo chambers and filter bubbles, see **Chapter 4, Listening and Responding**.

**influencers**
social media creators with large and highly engaged online followings

# Addressing Audiences Online

Between algorithms that show users more of the same content they've already engaged and influencers who get priority on social media platforms, making your voice heard online can seem like a catch-22: you need to have an audience in order to share your message, but you need to share your message in order to find an audience. While some digital presentations have built-in audiences—like a speech in an online class or a video meeting with coworkers—many digital presentations do not. That makes audience analysis more challenging online than it is in person.

When you're speaking in person, your audience is usually determined for you in advance, giving you a starting point for developing your presentation. First, you gather and analyze information about your audience's attitudes, values, and behaviors; then, you tailor your message accordingly. But digital presentations

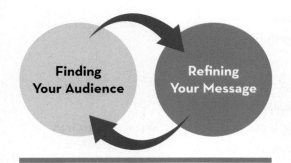

**FIGURE 14.1** Because the audience for digital presentations often isn't given to you in advance, online audience analysis is an ongoing, cyclical process.

often require you to create your own audience. So, which comes first: your audience or your presentation?

The answer is neither—or both. When you're presenting online, audience analysis is a cyclical process of finding your audience and refining your message (see Figure 14.1). Start by looking for existing online groups and networks that you might address. You might find your audience in the social media following you already have, in niche web-based communities, in user data on a digital platform, in the audiences of other online creators, or even in more traditional media audiences.

1.  **TAP INTO YOUR EXISTING COMMUNITIES AND NETWORKS.** If you're already active on social media platforms or other online spaces, develop your digital presentations for these groups first. Not only will they be more likely to listen to what you have to say, but you'll also get valuable feedback and engagement that can help improve your work.

2.  **SEEK OUT NICHE PLATFORMS AND ONLINE COMMUNITIES RELATED TO YOUR TOPIC.** Whether or not you already have an online network of your own, you can connect with existing internet communities that share your passions and purpose. Don't just stick to the big, mainstream sites—look for specialized platforms and interest-based communities. You're more likely to find an engaged audience there who will be interested in what you have to say.

3.  **EXPLORE AUDIENCE ANALYTICS.** Use publicly available data to your advantage by researching what kind of content those existing communities and networks are most likely to engage. This will help you create more targeted presentations that stand a better chance of being seen and heard.

4.  **STUDY YOUR PLATFORM'S ALGORITHM.** Every social media site and search engine has its own way of ranking and displaying content. Research how your platform's algorithm works and what you can do to optimize your presentations for maximum visibility.

5.  **CONNECT WITH INFLUENCERS WHO SHARE YOUR PURPOSE.** Identify influential web creators who care about your topic, then follow and

engage with them on social media. Guest posts, shares, and retweets from influencers are all great ways to get your message in front of a new audience.

6. **DON'T FORGET TRADITIONAL MEDIA GATEKEEPERS.** While social media is a great place to find an audience, don't rule out newspapers, magazines, radio, and television. You can use your social media skills to follow and connect with reporters who cover your topic. You can also respond to journalists' requests for sources using Help a Reporter Out on Twitter—just search for the handle @helpareporter and the hashtags #HAROrequest and #URGHARO.

7. **BE PERSISTENT AND CONSISTENT.** Remember: tailoring your message for an online audience is a process. Don't give up if you don't see hundreds of likes, comments, or followers overnight. Any feedback—even a lack of engagement—gives you useful information about your audience and what they want. The more you put yourself and your message out there, the more likely it is that you'll find an audience.

While addressing an online audience can be daunting, you already have a significant advantage: knowing how to create high-quality public presentations. You understand your own strengths, standpoint, and credibility as a speaker. You're prepared to listen and respond to your audience and adapt to their attitudes, values, and behaviors. You know how to choose a topic and purpose that fit the demands of your speaking situation. You can give convincing evidence, back it up with research, and organize it for maximum impact. You can evoke emotions, tell stories, and use language that connects with your audience. You have practiced your vocal and physical delivery, and you can create interesting and informative presentation aids. You even know how to manage the anxiety that sometimes comes with public speaking. All the public speaking skills you've learned so far—from your first topic ideas to your final delivery—apply equally well to in-person and online presentations.

But digital public speaking also requires some additional skills: recording and editing audio, recording and editing video, and delivering and interacting in live online presentations. Each of these skills builds on the others. Learning how to create audio presentations will help you improve the audio quality of your video recordings and live online presentations. The techniques you learn creating

**Pathways**

To review how to use social media analytics and optimize your content for web-based algorithms, see **Chapter 5, Audiences and Publics** and the sample outline in **Chapter 9, Organization and Outlining**.

recorded video presentations will help you set up and use live videoconferencing platforms. So regardless of which media or platform you will use for your presentations, we encourage you to learn and practice the skills for recorded audio, recorded video, and live video presentations.

# Creating Audio Presentations

Even if you do not plan to deliver and distribute your presentation as an audio-only recording, learning the basics of audio production lays the foundation for creating almost every type of mediated presentation: most live online and recorded video presentations include audio, too. Whether you are creating an audio recording, a video recording, or a live online event, developing audio skills will help you improve your presentation.

While audio skills can enhance almost any media presentation, audio-only recordings have a number of advantages. They are easier to create than media that contain both audio and visual elements, requiring less time and skill than recorded video or live online presentations. They are also easier for some audiences to consume, since people can listen to audio while commuting, doing errands, or working out. This makes audio recordings ideal for longer presentations—for example, popular podcasts typically run from forty-five minutes to an hour per episode.

However, audio-only recordings have disadvantages as well. Because they do not deliver visual information, they do not capture the speaker's gestures, posture, or expressions, and they limit the kinds of presentation aids you can use. They are less accessible for deaf audiences and nonverbal speakers, and their longer format does not always translate well into text transcripts. Audio-only recordings also have limited reach for certain age groups: for example, only about half of people age 12 to 34 and a quarter of people over 55 listen to at least one podcast a month.[11] Interaction and feedback with audiences is also limited to comments or responses after the recording has been distributed, usually in text format. Whether you decide to use audio alone or include both audio and video in your presentation, understanding the basics of sound recording and editing will enhance your listeners' experience.

## RECORDING AUDIO

When you're recording audio, your goal is to capture clear, clean sound. That means you can hear the sounds you want to hear—like your voice or sound effects— but not the ones you don't—like doors closing, phones ringing, or your roommate munching on potato chips. To get the best sound, you need to control noise in your environment and find the best position for your microphone to pick up your voice. Consider whether an outline or a manuscript will give you the smoothest vocal delivery and make multiple recordings so you can edit out any flubs later.

▶ **LEARN MORE**

To learn more about reducing environmental noise, positioning your microphone, and practicing your audio delivery, see the **Recording Audio Presentations Video Series**.

### 1 Choose a Quiet Location

Before recording, choose a place to record that will be free of background noises and have as little echo as possible. A room with a closed door and lots of soft furnishings and fabrics can help reduce echo and noise. Some podcasters even recommend recording audio inside a closet full of clothes when you're not on camera.[12]

### 2 Position Your Microphone

Whether external or integrated into a laptop, tablet, or smartphone, most microphones work best when positioned close enough to pick up your voice but outside the impact of your breath. This helps you avoid the sound of air hitting the microphone when you make *p, b, s, f,* and *th* sounds. You can gauge your breath's impact by holding your hand in front of your mouth and speaking at the same volume you will use when recording. Start at roughly 6 inches away,

Digital media creator Jonny Hatch demonstrates his budget-friendly podcasting setup in a YouTube video (1:21).

Positioning your audio recording device about 6 inches away from your mouth picks up your voice without picking up the sound of your breath.

## Pathways

To review different methods for delivering the text of your speech, see **Chapter 12, Vocal and Physical Delivery**. To learn more about presenting as a team, see **Chapter 18, Group Meetings and Presentations**.

then move your hand a little farther back, if necessary, until you can only lightly feel your breath on your hand. When you find the ideal distance, hold your recording device in your hand or position it on a stable surface directly in front of your face. Do a test recording to troubleshoot any problems before you begin recording your presentation.

### 3 Select Your Delivery Method

Audio-only recordings are one of the few speaking situations where reading from a manuscript won't interfere with your eye contact, gestures, posture, and facial expression—or at least, where that interference won't be visible to your audience. Solo podcasters take advantage of this opportunity to use the more highly polished language that manuscripts allow. However, presenting from a full manuscript can risk sounding stiff. Listeners often complain that unpracticed audio recordings sound like the speaker is "reading at them." Podcasters conducting interviews or presenting as a team often prefer to speak extemporaneously from an outline—or even fully impromptu—to capture the natural flow of conversation.

### 4 Make Multiple Recordings

If you make a mistake or get interrupted, don't worry. You don't have to get everything right on the first take. Just stop, back up to your most recent pause

Reading directly from a manuscript can be effective for recording solo audio presentations because your audience won't see your physical delivery. But extemporaneous or impromptu delivery is best for recording conversations.

between two main points or subpoints, and start delivering your presentation again from there. You can edit multiple takes into a single, seamless audio presentation using editing software like Audacity or Garage Band. If you're recording audio across several separate sessions, make sure to use the same equipment, setup, and location to keep the sound consistent.

## EDITING AUDIO

Once you've captured your audio recordings, you're ready to start editing them together into a finished presentation. Focus on the overall sound quality first, fine-tuning the volume of your recordings and eliminating any noises in the background. When your audio quality is in good shape, you can begin cutting and arranging your sound clips to create an audio file that you can share with others.

### 1 Adjust Volume

Speakers new to audio recording sometimes find that their recordings are too quiet or that the volume is inconsistent between multiple recordings. While this is best handled by practicing your vocal delivery, you may be able to fix minor volume issues with audio editing. Most audio editing software includes an amplification tool to adjust the volume of a recording. When amplifying a recording, be careful to avoid distortion. Too much amplification can sound robotic.

### 2 Remove Background Noise

Most recordings made outside of a professional studio will contain some background noise. Fortunately, most audio editing programs include noise reduction tools. These tools reduce persistent hiss or static sounds in the recording, but they do not eliminate intermittent noises like a door slamming or a dog barking. Some editing software requires you to use a period of silence to set the baseline levels for your recording, so be sure to record twenty to thirty seconds of dead air if you plan to use a noise reduction tool.

### 3 Cut Unwanted Segments

After using your noise reduction tool, remove any remaining unwanted noises and periods of silence from

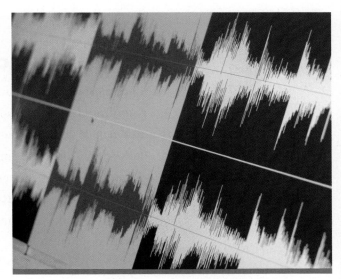

You can use audio editing software to select and delete segments from your voice recording.

## Pathways

To review strategies for improving your vocal delivery—including volume, pitch, rate, and rhythm—see **Chapter 12, Vocal and Physical Delivery**.

### ▶ LEARN MORE

To learn more about how to adjust volume levels, reduce background noise, cut segments, and upload your audio, see the **Editing Audio Presentations Video Series**.

**📋 TRY THIS**

To assess different options for audio editing software, see the **Audio Editing Resource List**.

To assess different options for audio hosting platforms, see the **Audio Hosting Resource List**.

To make sure you've covered all the elements for recording and editing audio, see the **Recording Audio Presentations Checklist**.

## Pathways

To review how to use nonverbal communication to increase immediacy and express emotion, see **Chapter 12, Vocal and Physical Delivery**. To revisit principles for developing accessible, multimodal visual aids, see **Chapter 13, Presentation Aids and Slides.**

your recording using the cut or trim tools in your audio editing software. In addition to the dead air you used to set your baseline audio levels, most recordings have some dead air at the beginning and end that should be cut. You can also cut out flubs, hiccups, or any other problems with your audio. Make cuts only where you can cleanly delete a section without cutting off part of a word or creating any discontinuity.

### 4 Export Your Audio File

In order to upload and share your finished presentation recording, you will need to export it from your editing software in a compatible file type. Most podcasters today recommend exporting and distributing your recordings as MP3 files. If your editing software provides you the option, set your bitrate to a constant 192 kbps for standard voice recordings, or 320 kbps for high-quality music. Avoid "variable bitrate" settings, as they can cause difficulty for some audio players.

### 5 Share Your Audio

There are a wide variety of platforms to distribute recorded audio presentations, including Spotify, Buzzsprout, SoundCloud, and more. Each has different features and costs that change periodically, so explore your options before choosing one. Some limit how many recordings you can upload on a free account, how often you can upload, or how many recordings you can keep. You may also want to pay attention to privacy settings if you want to control the distribution of your recording and limit who can listen. When you have chosen a platform, simply make an account and upload your audio file to start sharing your recording with the people you want to reach.

# Creating Video Presentations

Since most video presentations include sound, the skills you've just learned for recording and editing audio also apply to video production. But video recordings also include visual elements, making them great for highlighting your physical delivery and displaying presentation aids. Video enhances your viewers' emotional engagement and sense of immediacy by showing your facial expressions, gestures, posture, and attire. Because recorded videos can include audio, text, or images, they offer more multimodality and make your presentations more accessible than audio alone.

In addition to being more accessible to audiences with different sensory abilities, recorded video also has much greater reach overall compared to recorded audio.

Roughly half to two-thirds of Americans ages 18 to 29 consume short-form video content on TikTok and Snapchat, and over 95 percent of Americans 18 to 29 and roughly half of Americans over 65 watch videos on YouTube.[13]

Because they require a viewer's undivided attention, recorded video presentations are typically shorter than audio-only recordings that people listen to in the background. Successful videos usually run between two to twelve minutes.[14] Video presentations of two minutes tend to get the highest audience engagement, while twelve minutes tends to be the longest a recorded online video will sustain an audience's attention.[15] But even though videos tend to be shorter than audio presentations, they can be much more demanding to create.

📋 **TRY THIS**

To assess different options for video recording software, see the **Video Recording Resource List**.

## RECORDING VIDEO

When recording a video, you still want to pay attention to the principles for capturing clean audio: recording in a quiet place, positioning your microphone carefully, and making multiple recordings to edit together. But to record high-quality video images, you also need to consider your background, attire, lighting, camera position, and physical delivery.

Selecting a neutral background for your video helps keep the focus on you.

### 1 Create a Neutral Background

When selecting a video background, keep it simple. Often, a blank wall is best. Remove any visual distractions behind you so you are not competing for your audience's attention. If a distraction can't be removed—such as windows or signage—you can use blinds or screening to block the audience's view of it. Or you can reposition your camera to move distractions out of frame.

When wearing eyewear or jewelry, troubleshoot any reflections that might distract your viewers.

### 2 Choose Your Attire

Choose camera-friendly attire appropriate to your speaking situation. You and your clothes should stand out against your background. If your background is

**LEARN MORE**

To learn more about backgrounds, lighting, and camera positioning, see the on **Recording Video Presentations Video Series**.

dark, wear lighter colors; if it's light, wear darker colors. Stripes and other patterns with straight lines can cause problems for some video displays, so generally it's best to avoid wearing them on camera. Reflective jewelry and eyewear can create lighting problems, so do a test recording to troubleshoot any unwanted reflections. You can reduce or eliminate glare by removing reflective items, adjusting the angle of your lighting, or reducing the brightness of any lighting or screens in front of you.

## 3 Use Good Lighting

You don't need fancy or expensive lights to use good lighting principles. Sunny windows, adjustable-arm desk lamps, and even table lamps all make great light sources. The key is to position your light sources—or yourself—so that light illuminates your face with a minimum of shadow. With a single light source, position the light slightly behind the camera lens, above or beside the camera. If a single light source creates shadows on your face, you can add a second light. With two lights, position them to the left and right of the camera, slightly back from the edge of the camera lens. To brighten the background, you can add a third light behind the speaker, pointed away from the camera. However, avoid any light above or behind you that shines toward the camera—it will leave your whole face in shadow and reduce your video quality overall.

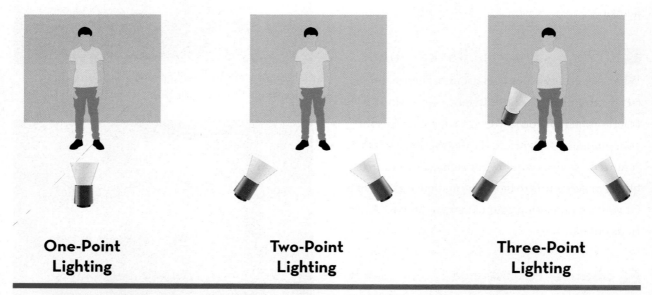

**One-Point Lighting**     **Two-Point Lighting**     **Three-Point Lighting**

One-point lighting illuminates your face directly from the front; two-point lighting illuminates your face at an angle from both sides; and three-point lighting adds another light behind you to illuminate your background.

# All You Need Is a Smartphone

Most people start their YouTube channels with just a smartphone or a webcam. You can even do basic video editing and uploading on most smartphones. Think Media's five-minute video on making videos with your smartphone contains great advice on staging videos.[16] In the video, Heather Torres shows how she started with just a phone and how she prepares for a recording. Sean Cannell joins the video with ideas for YouTubers' first inexpensive upgrades. Their advice is to "start creating content with the phone you already have." If you find that you enjoy making and distributing videos and want to stick with it, you can always add small upgrades later.

First, Torres uses her phone's selfie mode to plan her position and lighting. Holding the phone at arm's length with the selfie video on, she can try out different spots in a room, move objects, close blinds, and move lights around, all the while seeing herself and her background. This gives her a live preview of how her videos will look. Once she finds a position that looks good, she sets her camera up at eye level. Starting out, you can stack the camera on some books or other objects to stabilize it in the right position. If you decide you want to make videos regularly, you can invest in an inexpensive tripod with a phone holder for under $20.

Once the scene and camera are set, Torres makes sure to record using the camera on the back of her phone, not the selfie camera. Torres makes sure her camera is set to its highest-quality setting (1080p or 4k). Finally, she makes a test recording

Heather Torres of Think Media demonstrates how to do a "test shot" to check recording quality, background, and camera position before recording a video (2:42).

to make sure everything looks and sounds good before making her video. She got started using the microphone on her phone, but upgraded to an inexpensive lapel microphone with a long cord when she got serious. A basic lapel microphone for a smartphone can be purchased for around $20.

While there are additional upgrades for more serious YouTubers, Torres emphasizes that preparing quality content matters most. Before she starts, she always plans, researches, and organizes her ideas to ensure she is delivering quality. And when recording, she stops and starts over as many times as it takes to get smooth, effective delivery of her presentation. Even in a basic recording, a great presentation is still a great presentation.

To watch Think Media's complete video, do a web search for: Think Media videos on your phone beginners. The video is approximately 5:31 in length.

Positioning your camera lens at about eye level will produce the best results for most recorded and online presentations.

## 4 Position Your Camera

Position your camera lens at eye level, so your full head and face are entirely in frame with a little empty space above your head. When you will be the only thing onscreen, center yourself in the camera frame. When using slides or images on the screen along with your camera feed, position yourself slightly to the side. Speakers usually appear to the right of the screen, while any text or slides appear to the left. If you are using a camera with an integrated microphone, such as a laptop or smartphone, remember to place the camera close enough to you to produce good audio.

## 5 Record in Sections

Recording video presentations is tougher than recording audio presentations. In addition to smooth vocal delivery, you also have physical delivery to consider—especially eye contact. Because you need to stay focused on the camera rather than your speaking notes, it can help to record your presentation in sections. Review the first main point in your outline, then put your notes down, look into the camera, and deliver that section of your speech. When you're done, pause the recording to review your notes for the next section. In addition to improving your eye contact, recording in sections will help you make cleaner cuts.

## EDITING VIDEO

Just as video recording builds on audio recording, video editing builds on the elements of audio editing—including noise reduction, volume amplification, and cutting and combining segments. But video editing also requires additional skills with visual transitions, presentation aids, file formats, and distribution platforms.

## 1 Cut Unwanted Segments

In many ways, cutting video is similar to the process of cutting audio. Video editing software—like Shotcut and iMovie—contains cut, trim, or blade tools that allow you to remove unwanted segments of your video recordings. However,

### 🎬 LEARN MORE

To learn more about how to cut, add transitions, include presentation aids, and upload your video, see the **Editing Video Presentations Video Series**.

while audio cuts may go completely unnoticed by your audience, video cuts will be noticeable—and potentially distracting. Video cuts work best at transition points between different sections of your presentation.

## 2 Choose Your Transitions

Most online recorded presentations use one of two transitions between video clips: the jump cut and the cross-fade. A **jump cut** is a simple cut with no fading between clips. Jump cuts need to jump either to a completely different scene or to a clip with the exact same background, lighting, and camera position. The other common transition is the **cross-fade** or dissolve, which fades one video clip out while the next fades in. These are more forgiving of minor changes in background, lighting, and camera position, but they are slower and more noticeable transitions than jump cuts. Whichever transition type you choose, you should generally stick to just one type in a recorded presentation.

## 3 Add Presentation Aids

Almost any kind of presentation aid can be added to a recorded video, including text, music, images, slides, graphs and charts, maps, and even props. While props typically appear on camera with the presenter, audio and image files can be imported into video editing software and added to your video recordings. You can display images, slides, or even other videos using picture-in-picture, split screen, or overlay features. Editing software also lets you add **video titles**—onscreen text laid over a video—to identify a speaker, emphasize a point, signal a topic change, or provide subtitles for viewers who have hearing impairments or speak other languages.

## 4 Export Your Video File

To upload your video to a platform like YouTube or Instagram, you will need to export your video file. The most widely compatible file type for videos is MP4. When exporting, set the export to the same resolution as your original recording. If you recorded in HD or 1080p, export as 1080p; if you recorded at 720p, export as 720p. Video processing and exporting can take time, so don't worry if it takes the software a while to produce your finished video.

📋 **TRY THIS**

To assess different options for video editing software, see the **Video Editing Resource List**.

**jump cut**
a simple cut with no fading between video clips

**cross-fade**
a transition where one video clip fades out while another fades in

**video titles**
onscreen text laid over a video

## Pathways

To review the different kinds of presentation aids, see **Chapter 13, Presentation Aids and Slides.**

YouTuber Will Paterson uses split-screen video to demonstrate logo design principles for his subscribers (2:46).

# Jouelzy Uses Video to Educate and Entertain

Jouelzy is a vlogger with over fourteen million views and two hundred thousand subscribers. Her YouTube channel focuses on topics that affect women throughout the African diaspora. Her videos are simultaneously nuanced, insightful, informative, casual, friendly, and humorous. When she began her channel in 2013, her videos were primarily simple talking-head videos shot with the occasional text on screen. Today, her videos are polished multimedia productions that use presentation aids to emphasize key points, enrich viewers' understanding, and reflect her own standpoint.

In 2018 Jouelzy traveled with the Ford Foundation to a Yurok reservation to learn about the relationship between Indigenous people, land rights, and climate change. She shared her experience in a video she called "Storytime: Bishes in the Forest."[17] In under six minutes she used a wide variety of presentation aids to educate her viewers about the impact climate change has on Indigenous people, the role of Indigenous people's science and rituals in sustaining forests, and how it all relates to the experiences of African Americans.

While the majority of Jouelzy's video is her talking to the camera, she adds in video clips, images, sound, and text. In most cases, the video clips are silent. While they play, she explains to viewers in a voice-over what they are seeing, what it means, or how it affected her. The video clips are short, roughly ten seconds or less, keeping the focus of the video on her presentation. At one point she

Jouelzy explains the connection between Indigenous people's land rights, climate change, and the experiences of Black Americans (1:38).

uses a split screen, with video of her speaking into the camera on the left half of the screen and a silent video clip on the right half. This allows her to add a little humor but also emphasizes her point. The split screen is a style she often uses in video interviews on her channel. Watching the video, you might also notice the quick jump cuts to close-up shots for short moments. She never stays in close-up shots long, using them only to emphasize specific items or to make a side comment to her viewers. The result is a video that is a joy to watch and full of substantive thoughts and ideas.

To watch Jouelzy's video, do a web search for: Jouelzy storytime bishes forest. The video is approximately 5:45 in length.

## 5 Share Your Video

YouTube is by far the most common video sharing platform, but other platforms—like TikTok, Instagram, and Facebook—can offer different audiences, formats, and sharing capabilities. Look for the platforms that the people you want to reach are already using and consider each platform's privacy settings and accessibility options. For example, YouTube provides automated captioning for many of the videos people upload at no cost. YouTube also lets you set your video as "private," allowing only you and people you invite to view it. When you're ready to upload your video, remember that large video files can take some time to upload. Make sure your computer is plugged in, and take a break.

### ✓ Critical Thinking Check

1. Which elements of audio recording and editing also apply to video? Which do not? Why not?
2. Why is creating a video presentation more difficult than creating an audio presentation? Can you think of any ways it might be easier?

# Creating Live Online Presentations

Live online presentations take the audio and video skills you've learned and apply them in real time. Prerecorded audio and video are forms of **asynchronous communication**, with a time lapse between the speaker creating the message and the audience receiving it. Live presentations—both online and in person—are forms of **synchronous communication**, where the audience receives a message at the same time the speaker delivers it. Synchronous presentations allow for greater spontaneity, immediacy, and engagement with an audience than asynchronous presentations. Live online presentations offer lots of ways to engage your audience: chat boxes, polls, voice replies, or even live video chat, depending on your platform.

Audience interaction is especially important in live online presentations. When you're competing with environmental distractions in your viewer's home or office, actively engaging your audience can help them stay focused on your presentation. The length of some live presentations can also make it difficult to maintain your audience's focus. For example, webinars and videoconferences are commonly an hour long—with some as short as thirty minutes and some as long

**TRY THIS**

To assess different options for video hosting platforms, see the **Video Hosting Resource List**.

To make sure you've covered all the elements for recording and editing video, see the **Recording Video Presentations Checklist**.

**asynchronous communication**
a time lapse occurs between the speaker creating a message and the audience receiving it

**synchronous communication**
the audience receives a message at the same time the speaker delivers it

**Synchronous Communication**

**Asynchronous Communication**

In synchronous communication, listeners receive and respond to messages at the same time the speaker sends them. In asynchronous communication, listeners receive and respond to the speaker's message later—if at all.

as ninety minutes. Particularly in these extended presentations, audience participation, interactive activities, and discussion questions are crucial—both to keep your audience's attention and to give you a break from speaking.

Because they are delivered in real time, live online presentations are perhaps the most challenging of all mediated presentations. Although they eliminate much of the editing work required for recorded presentations, live presenters have to be sufficiently prepared and practiced to deliver a complete presentation while managing their audiovisual technology on the fly. To your audience, this makes live online presentations feel more like in-person presentations—but from the speaker's perspective, they require considerably more advance preparation.

## PREPARING TO SPEAK LIVE ONLINE

**📋 TRY THIS**

To assess different options for live online presentation platforms, see the **Video Meetings Resource List** and the **Live Streaming Resource List**.

Live online presentations require all the same attention to audio and video quality as recorded audio and video presentations—like reducing background distractions, positioning your microphone and computer, and using good lighting. But there are several additional technological challenges specific to live presentations.

### 1 Understand Your Platform

Live online presentations may occur via a webinar platform like GoToWebinar, a live streaming platform like YouTube Live, or a videoconferencing platform like Zoom. If someone else is organizing your live event, you may have less control over which platform you will be using. So start by knowing which platform you will use and what its capabilities are—both for engaging your audience and using presentation aids.

### 2 Designate a Host

**host**
a person who coordinates a live online event and manages attendees

In a live webinar or meeting, the **host** is the person who coordinates the event and manages attendees. Speakers, event organizers, or both might serve as hosts or co-hosts. Determine in advance who will handle administrative tasks like scheduling the event, starting and ending the event, muting or unmuting attendees, assigning attendees to breakout rooms, and so forth. As a presenter, you may also need host control to show slides, share your screen, or use the virtual whiteboard. Juggling presentation aids, facilitating live chat, and troubleshooting technology issues can be a lot to handle while you're presenting, so teaming up with a co-host can free you up to focus on delivering the substance of your presentation.

## 3 Ensure Privacy and Security

Live video offers opportunities for interaction—but also for disruption. Having disruptive attendees interrupt your presentation can be challenging, even for experienced speakers. Webinar and videoconferencing platforms have a range of features designed to protect your privacy and security:

- **AUDIENCE INVITATIONS.** Some platforms require preregistration or a password to attend, while others provide a link that you can distribute to select invitees.

- **AUDIENCE MANAGEMENT.** On many platforms, the host can control how attendees are admitted, control how and when they communicate, and even lock an event or remove attendees if necessary.

- **RECORDING NOTIFICATIONS.** If you plan to record the presentation and discussion for others to view later, include that information in the invitation or preregistration form, and notify attendees again verbally before you start recording. Many platforms will notify attendees when you start recording or even provide a countdown when recording is about to begin.

## 4 Practice Using the Technology

To ensure a smooth presentation, practice delivering your live online presentation using the same platform and technology you will use when presenting. Test your background, lighting, camera position, and microphone, as well as any presentation aids or

### ▶ LEARN MORE

To learn more about how to manage attendees and ensure privacy and security on videoconferencing platforms, see the **Preparing for Live Online Presentations Video Series**.

You can ensure privacy and security in your video meetings by limiting access only to invited participants.

audience interaction tools you plan to use. If possible, start practicing on the platform several days before your live event to give yourself some time to adapt if any problems emerge during your practice. Practicing your full presentation on the platform once or twice a day in the days leading up to your event will improve your delivery and reduce the risk of technology issues.

## DELIVERING YOUR LIVE ONLINE PRESENTATION

Since delivering a mediated presentation is more challenging in real time, be sure to take advantage of the unique benefits of synchronous delivery. Include opportunities for audience interaction and incorporate elements like live demonstrations and real-time writing or drawing into your presentation aids. Also take care to avoid the pitfalls of synchronous presentations: when speaking, mute your attendees to make sure you're not interrupted, and record your presentation for anyone who was unable to attend live.

### 1 Remember Your Audio

Before you begin speaking, check your settings to enable your microphone and make sure that you are not muted. As the presenter, you can ask attendees to mute their microphones to prevent surprises and interruptions. If you are hosting the event, you can also mute any participants who leave their microphones on by accident. Some platforms have a "mute all" function that you can use right before starting your presentation—just be sure to unmute yourself before you begin speaking.

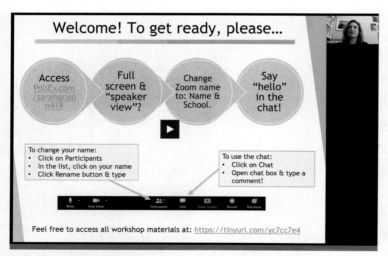

You can use presentation aids, such as a slide, to help you orient an audience to your platform before beginning your online presentation.

### 2 Orient Your Audience to Your Platform

In addition to giving your audience instructions about muting or unmuting their microphones, give them brief instructions on any other actions you want them to take during your live online presentation. You might ask them to keep their cameras on or invite them to turn them off. You might ask them to reduce distractions on their device by turning off notifications and closing other windows and tabs. And you might ask them to submit questions or comments via a chat feature or tap an icon to give instant feedback or signal they want to speak. Don't assume that your audience knows how to use your platform: if you want them to mute themselves, access the chat box, or use any other tech feature, show them how.

## 3 Interact with Your Audience

Live online presentations offer lots of opportunities for audience interaction. On many platforms, you can use the built-in chat box to create engagement during your presentation. Ask quick questions that can be answered in just a word or two by audience members. For example: "I'd like to hear what your biggest challenges are in creating great webinars. Let me know by typing them in the chat box." Then acknowledge their responses as they roll in: "Michaela says 'planning interaction.' Jain mentions issues with transitioning between camera and video—I'm seeing a few people mention that one." Some platforms also offer live polls or instant emoji reactions, like hearts or clapping hands, that can give you instant feedback. If you decide to interact with your audience via live video chat, ask them to raise their hands—or use a built-in "raise hand" feature—to make it easier for you to facilitate discussion. It can be challenging to engage with audience feedback while you're speaking, so plan to pause periodically to ask or answer questions—or find a co-host to answer questions in the chat box as they come up.

## 4 Integrate Presentation Aids

Many live video platforms allow you to incorporate various presentation aids by sharing your screen or a window on your computer. This can allow you to demonstrate something live, such as how to use a piece of software, or to incorporate a series of slides into your presentation. For example, you can open a PowerPoint presentation and then share that window with your viewers. Many platforms also include a virtual whiteboard function. You can write or draw on these whiteboards live during a presentation and

## ▶ LEARN MORE

To learn more about how to interact with your audience and display presentation aids on videoconferencing platforms, see the **Delivering Live Online Presentations Video Series**.

## Pathways

To revisit strategies for facilitating discussion, see **Chapter 4, Listening and Responding**.

Screen sharing allows you to display visual aids during a live online presentation.

viewers will see it in real time. If you plan to use the virtual whiteboard, practice with the one in the platform you will be using, writing and drawing what you expect you might write or draw during the presentation.

### 5 Share a Recording of Your Live Event

After your live online presentation is done, you may want to share a recording of the event. Most webinar, livestream, and videoconferencing platforms have built-in recording functions, and a video will be ready for you shortly after you finish your event. Avoid the temptation to edit the video—let it reflect the spontaneity and dynamism of a live presentation. Then upload your recording to a video platform to share it with both your attendees and anyone who could not attend.

### 📋 TRY THIS

To make sure you've covered all the elements for preparing and delivering livestreams, see the **Live Online Presentations Checklist**.

### ✓ Critical Thinking Check

1. What are the advantages and disadvantages of synchronous presentations? What are the advantages and disadvantages of asynchronous presentations?
2. How are live online presentations similar to in-person presentations? How are they different?

## Next Steps

Seasoned speakers make online and mediated presentations look easy, but they have put in the practice and hard work to make them seem effortless. With similar dedication and practice, you can use mediated presentations to share your standpoint and message with the world.

There are several video tutorials and checklists in the digital resources for this textbook that can help you learn to create great mediated presentations, and countless more tutorials online for any additional software tools or editing techniques you want to learn.

While they take extra effort and skill, online and mediated presentations can help you inform, persuade, and connect with a broader audience. In the following chapters, you'll learn techniques tailored to each of these different purposes. These techniques for informing, persuading, and connecting can help you meet your goals whether you're speaking in person or online.

# Standpoint Reflection

- What types of mediated presentations do you consume most often? What platforms do you use to watch or listen to them? How might you use your knowledge and experience with those media platforms to develop your own mediated presentations?

- What online communities and networks do you participate in? Do you have a connection to any gatekeepers? How might you approach those communities, networks, and gatekeepers to share your mediated presentations and build an audience?

- Do you experience any additional anxiety when it comes to delivering mediated presentations? Why or why not? Which anxiety management strategies might help you build your confidence with mediated presentations?

- Which type of mediated presentation—recorded audio, recorded video, or live online—best fits your own strengths and speaking style? How might you translate your strengths with audio, video, or live online presentations to help you succeed in other public speaking situations?

## Key Terms

agenda setting, p. 319
asynchronous communication, p. 335
cross-fade, p. 333
host, p. 336
influencers, p. 321
jump cut, p. 333

media consolidation, p. 319
media gatekeepers, p. 319
mediated presentations, p. 318
platforms, p. 319
synchronous communication, p. 335
video titles, p. 333

## Resources for Online and Mediated Presentations

### 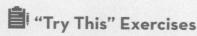 "Try This" Exercises

Access the "Try This" exercises as directed by your instructor or online at digital.wwnorton.com/chapterexercises-conpubspeak

- To assess different options and select the audio recording software that's best for you, see the **Audio Recording Resource List**.

- To assess different options for audio editing software, see the **Audio Editing Resource List**.

- To assess different options for audio hosting platforms, see the **Audio Hosting Resource List**.

- To make sure you've covered all the elements for recording and editing audio, see the **Recording Audio Presentations Checklist**.

- To assess different options for video recording software, see the **Video Recording Resource List**.

- To assess different options for video editing software, see the **Video Editing Resource List**.

- To assess different options for video hosting platforms, see the **Video Hosting Resource List**.

- To make sure you've covered all the elements for recording and editing video, see the **Recording Video Presentations Checklist**.

- To assess different options for video meeting platforms, see the **Video Meetings Resource List**.

- To assess different options for live streaming platforms, see the **Live Streaming Resource List**.

- To make sure you've covered all the elements for preparing and delivering livestreams, see the **Live Online Presentations Checklist**.

## ▶ "Learn More" Tutorials

Access the "Learn More" tutorials as directed by your instructor or online at digital.wwnorton.com/videos-conpubspeak

- To learn more about reducing environmental noise, positioning your microphone, and practicing your audio delivery, see the **Recording Audio Presentations Video Series**.

- To learn more about how to adjust volume levels, eliminate background noise, cut segments, and upload your audio, see the **Editing Audio Presentations Video Series**.

- To learn more about backgrounds, lighting, and camera positioning, see the **Recording Video Presentations Video Series**.

- To learn more about how to cut segments, add transitions, incorporate presentation aids,

and upload your videos, see the **Editing Video Presentations Video Series**.

- To learn more about how to manage attendees and ensure privacy and security on videoconferencing platforms, see the **Preparing for Live Online Presentations Video Series**.

- To learn more about how to interact with your audience and display presentation aids on videoconferencing platforms, see the **Delivering Live Online Presentations Video Series**.

**Want to practice these skills to prepare for your next speech? Go to INQUIZITIVE to review and apply concepts from this chapter and get personalized feedback along the way.**

Hyeonseo Lee

# 15 Informing and Educating

At the age of seventeen, Hyeonseo Lee fled North Korea and spent ten years hiding in China. After finally being granted asylum in South Korea, Lee returned to North Korea to help her mother and brother escape.[1] Since then, she has shared her story in presentations at universities, law schools, and conventions—even the Oslo Freedom Forum and the United Nations.[2] Her TED talk describing her experiences has been viewed nearly twenty million times.[3]

Lee's presentations are packed with information about daily life in North Korea and the perils that people face trying to flee the country. Rather than discussing the problem abstractly, she grounds her talk in her own experiences: seeing neighbors starve to death and witnessing her first public execution at the age of seven. She weaves her personal experience together with details about international border policies to help her audience understand how dangerous it can be for refugees who try to escape North Korea. The stories and photographs she shares provide powerful evidence that increases her audience's awareness of the widespread oppression and deprivation in North Korea.

She supplements her personal narrative with visual aids that help her audience understand how the region's geography and political conditions make escape so difficult. When she tells the story of her own escape from North Korea into China, she shows images of the river where she crossed. She shows pictures of other refugees who were caught—explaining that they likely faced torture, execution, or imprisonment—and uses maps to show the dangerous 2,000-mile route her family took through China and Laos to get to South Korea.

## LEARNING OBJECTIVES

### After completing this chapter, you will be able to

- Assess the level of challenge, controversy, and credibility in your speaking situation

- Link new ideas to your audience's existing knowledge and values

- Make abstract and complex topics easier to understand

- Identify and organize different kinds of informative topics

Hyeonseo Lee's story shows just how transformational informative speeches can be. When you share experiences and knowledge from your own standpoint, you have the opportunity to enrich your audience's understanding of the world. Introducing people to new ideas can expand their perspective, help them make more informed decisions, and even teach them useful skills. Knowing how to present and organize information can help you make a contribution that's both interesting and valuable to your audience.

# Informing in Your Speaking Situation

Speeches that seek to inform or educate an audience are the most common type of presentation in academic, professional, and public settings. Informative presentations happen in businesses, schools, nonprofit organizations, government agencies, military operations, social movements, public campaigns, YouTube videos, and webinars around the world every day. If you are reading this book as part of a college class, you probably spend a large part of your week listening to informative presentations.

When your purpose is informing, your primary goal is providing the audience information or skills that they do not already have. Unlike persuasive speeches, informative speeches do not call for a significant change in their audience's existing values, attitudes, or behaviors. While the information you share may affect your audience's decisions, informative presentations leave any changes in attitudes, values, or behaviors up to the audience.

When you seek to inform, start by analyzing the elements of your speaking situation—your standpoint, audience, context, and purpose—to select and narrow your topic. In particular, consider the three Cs for evaluating informative topics:

## Pathways

To review the three general purposes of public speaking—informing, persuading, and connecting—see **Chapter 6, Topic and Purpose**.

- **CHALLENGE.** What does your audience already know about this topic? How will you challenge them to learn something new without giving them too much to process?

- **CONTROVERSY.** How controversial is this topic for your audience and context? How will you avoid or address potential disagreements to communicate important information?

Informative speeches have a range of specific purposes, audiences, and contexts. For example, researcher Morayo Adebayo (left) presents her findings during an Amnesty International Annual Report in Nigeria. Astronaut Tim Peake (right) answers questions about his mission on the International Space Station.

■ **CREDIBILITY.** How do your strengths—your experiences, knowledge, passions, and identities—connect to this topic? How will you establish that you and your sources are both knowledgeable and trustworthy on this issue?

## BALANCING YOUR SPEECH'S LEVEL OF CHALLENGE

The main goal of an informative presentation is sharing new knowledge with an audience. The level of **challenge** is how much you are trying to extend your audience's existing knowledge or skills. Learning a complex skill or a great deal of information is more challenging than learning a simple skill or a small bit of information. An informative presentation should extend your audience's understanding enough to teach them something new, but not so much that they don't grasp the material.

**challenge**
how much you are trying to extend your audience's existing knowledge or skills

If your audience already knows everything in your presentation, it hardly counts as informative. But any new knowledge you share must also be comprehensible to your audience. For example, you can't teach them calculus if they don't already understand algebra. To inform an audience, you must build from what they already know to teach them something they didn't know before.

## Pathways

To review the process for gathering and analyzing information about your audience, see **Chapter 5, Audiences and Publics**.

Learn what you can about your audience's current level of knowledge on a topic before deciding on the specific focus of your presentation. Offer new information that contributes to the knowledge and skills they already have. Adjust the level and speed of your presentation based on your audience's background, your topic's complexity, and your own strengths as a speaker. Keep the presentation challenging enough that they don't get bored, but not so challenging that they can't follow you. Remember: to teach your audience something new, you've got to meet them where they are. Ask yourself:

- What does my audience already know about this topic?

- What can my unique experiences, knowledge, and strengths as a speaker add to my audience's existing understanding and abilities?

- Is my specific purpose challenging enough to teach my audience something new? Is it too challenging for my audience's current level of knowledge and skill?

- Does my topic fit my context? Is it too challenging to present in the time and space available? Is it challenging enough to fill the available time and space?

## REDUCING YOUR SPEECH'S LEVEL OF CONTROVERSY

**controversy**
a debate or disagreement among different views

While understanding your audience's existing knowledge will help you gauge the appropriate level of challenge, understanding your audience's attitudes, values, and behaviors will help you assess the level of controversy. A **controversy** is a debate or disagreement among different views. Controversy about your topic is a key sign that your speaking situation calls for persuasion rather than informing or educating. If your audience has strongly held opinions, biases, or habits related to your topic, that can make an informative approach inappropriate for your speaking situation.

## Pathways

If your audience, context, or standpoint makes your topic too controversial for an informative speech, see **Chapter 16, Persuading and Motivating**.

For example, presenting new information showing that gun ownership rates are a predictor of homicides could be informative for some audiences, such as scholars of public health. The exact same topic would inevitably become persuasive for another audience, such as a meeting of the National Rifle Association.[4] The question is not whether the topic is inherently informative or persuasive, but whether an informative purpose is a realistic and appropriate approach given your audience, context, and standpoint.

If you must try to inform on a controversial topic—as schoolteachers, newscasters, and mediators are often called to do—give a balanced and accurate account of the controversy and avoid taking a side. To make sure you are accurately representing different points of view, take the perspective of the individuals or groups who hold them: Would they agree with your description of their views? Make sure to research arguments made by people on all sides of the controversy, in their own words, and clearly identify the sources of competing claims.

When you're informing your audience about a contested issue, your goal is to give your audience all the information they need to evaluate different positions and make their own decision. If presenting multiple sides of a controversial issue does not fit with your own standpoint, integrity, and values, then either embrace a persuasive approach to your topic or choose a less controversial topic better suited to an informative approach.

Before preparing an informative speech, consider how controversial your topic will be in your speaking situation. Ask yourself:

- Does my audience already have attitudes, values, or behaviors related to my topic? What are they?

- Do my audience's attitudes, values, and behaviors support or oppose the specific purpose of my speech? Will I be presenting any information that might call their attitudes, values, or behaviors into question?

- Are my audience's attitudes, values, and behaviors around this topic similar to my own? If not, can I remain neutral and present all sides of the argument? Do I feel ethically bound to take a particular position on this issue?

- Is my context requiring me to inform on a controversial topic? Could I give a persuasive speech on this topic instead? Could I give an informative speech about a different topic?

## Pathways

To revisit strategies for perspective taking, see **Chapter 4, Listening and Responding**.

## RAISING YOUR SPEECH'S LEVEL OF CREDIBILITY

Informative presentations can sometimes feel generic, as if any speaker could be conveying this information. Show your audience why this information is more credible and meaningful coming from you. Remember: **credibility** is your

**credibility**
your audience's trust that you have the relevant experience, knowledge, values, and identities to speak on a particular topic

audience's trust that you have the relevant experience, knowledge, values, and identities to speak on a particular topic. Choose an informative purpose that takes advantage of your own standpoint and strengths. You can build your credibility as an informative speaker by sharing your unique experience and passion for your topic.

## Pathways

To review strategies for increasing your audience's trust in you and your sources, see **Chapter 3, Ethics and Credibility**, and **Chapter 8, Research and Citation**.

To establish credibility in an informative presentation, your audience must see you as a knowledgeable and trustworthy source of information. Presenting quality information from sources your audience respects will increase their perception of your knowledge. For example, if you're presenting a speech on the Hubble telescope to an amateur astronomy club, you might cite the famous astrophysicist Neil deGrasse Tyson. If you're discussing your state's marijuana laws with local lawyers, you might cite the state attorney general. Your ability to demonstrate knowledge will increase dramatically with good research and verbal source citations.

Admit when you do not know something or when your information may be unreliable. A great deal of human knowledge is a good estimate, but not a settled fact. For example, if you're presenting the preliminary results of a pilot study, you'll want to note the limitations of its data and research method: "The study I'm describing only had fifteen participants, so it's unclear whether these results will hold up in a broader population. But the results from this small sample have the potential to change some of our basic theories about the ways cancer spreads." Build trust by pinpointing exactly how your information may be flawed, then explain the benefits that still make the information worth considering.

If you have any bias or conflict of interest, share it with your audience. For example, if you're making online video tutorials about using a product, you should disclose any sales commissions or sponsorships you receive for promoting it: "This product review has been sponsored by Apple. Working with Apple lets me try out new products before they're released, so I can get you all the details you need before you head to the store." Rather than detracting from your credibility, acknowledging your biases shows your audience that you care about transparency and gives you an opportunity to reframe those biases as insider knowledge.

When you're planning an informative speech, assess how your specific purpose, audience, context, and standpoint affect your credibility. Ask yourself:

- Have my specific purpose and topic already been determined for me? If so, how can I connect them to my strengths and standpoint as a speaker? If not, what specific purposes and topics will best showcase my unique experiences, knowledge, passions, and identities?

- Where do I need to supplement my own knowledge and experience with research and citations from other sources? Which sources will my audience find most credible?

- What limitations or biases in my perspective might affect my ability to present information accurately and fairly? How can I acknowledge my limitations and biases in a way that will enhance my credibility rather than detract from it?

**TRY THIS**

To select a topic for your informative speech that gives you high credibility, low controversy, and the right level of challenge, try the **Three Cs Checklist**.

## ✓ Critical Thinking Check

1. What is the problem with presenting information that doesn't challenge your audience enough? What's the problem with challenging your audience too much?

2. Why are highly controversial topics better suited to persuasive presentations than informative ones? What makes it difficult to inform an audience about a controversial issue?

3. How does acknowledging your limitations and biases enhance your credibility? Can you think of any situations where it might damage your credibility?

# Choosing Strategies for Informing and Educating

When you've chosen a topic that gives you minimal controversy, high credibility, and just the right amount of challenge for your speaking situation, you're ready to select the informative strategies that will best help you fulfill the purpose of your presentation. In some informative situations, you might deploy every tool available. In others, you might focus primarily on one technique. These strategies—emphasizing meaning, connecting to your audience's existing knowledge, clarifying ambiguity, visualizing complexity, and balancing

# Jim Al-Khalili Explains Quantum Biology

Jim Al-Khalili is one of the UK's most famous and respected scientists. A professor of physics, he has hosted multiple science programs on television and radio and frequently gives public presentations about science. His 2018 presentation at the Wired UK Live conference showcased his skill at communicating complex scientific theories to a public audience.[5] In just twenty minutes, he took on the enormous task of showing how an emerging field called quantum biology can explain what distinguishes living matter from inanimate matter. That is, what life is and how it can exist. Throughout his presentation he challenges his audience to expand their knowledge of both physics and biology. He compares what they already know (like how a tennis ball moves) with what he is trying to teach (how atoms move). He uses metaphors,

analogies, and stories to help them rise to the challenge. And he reminds the audience throughout the presentation about the practical value and meaning of what they are learning.

He also is careful to avoid controversy as he introduces these new ideas. Because his audience is made up of people with an interest in science and technology but who may not be scientists or experts, some of his presentation may be less controversial than if he was speaking to fellow experts in physics who hold different views. But he also acknowledges areas of disagreement and uncertainty as he presents research and theories. He uses phrases like "we think," "we don't know," "not sure," and "speculative" to highlight aspects of his presentation that might be more controversial

abstraction and specificity—can all help your audience grasp new knowledge and understanding.

## EMPHASIZE MEANING

Sometimes an audience may lack interest in your information or fail to see its relevance for them personally. For example, if your specific purpose is informing your audience about the wetlands in your state, they may wonder why the wetlands are worth learning about. Emphasizing the meaning and relevance of your topic in the introduction and conclusion of your speech will increase your audience's interest in and memory of your presentation.

within a scientific community, even if not controversial to his audience.

And his credibility is well established throughout his speech. His title slide contains his name along with his credentials: "Professor of Physics at the University of Surrey; President of the British Science Association." Throughout the presentation he references not only his own research and publications, but those of other scientists as well. He particularly emphasizes names that are more likely to be familiar to his audience, like physicists Stephen Hawking and Erwin Schrödinger, but doesn't flood the audience with names or details that are not meaningful. His recognition of controversy further bolsters his credibility by even acknowledging

Jim Al-Khalili considers whether quantum mechanics can explain the difference between animate and inanimate matter at the 2018 Wired Live conference in London (10:41).

that some of the theories sound "wacky" or "out there." By doing so he helps reduce any skepticism his audience might develop from becoming doubtful about his own credibility. Overall, he shows us why he is such a prominent scientist and public figure and in such demand as a public speaker.

To watch Al-Khalili's full speech, do a web search for: Wired UK Al-Khalili Question of Life. The video is approximately 22:05 in length.

Use your introduction and conclusion to connect your topic to attitudes, values, and behaviors that are important to your audience. You can tell a story about someone your audience will identify with. You can use vivid descriptions to demonstrate the value and importance of information. You can emphasize your topic's relevance by linking it to values your audience already deems important.

1. **START WITH CONNECTION.** Open your informative speech by linking your topic to your audience's existing attitudes, values, and behaviors. For example, you might begin your introduction with some surprising information: "Did you know that a single natural feature in our state protects us from floods, improves our water quality, and prevents the erosion of our

## Pathways

To review strategies for effective introductions and conclusions, see **Chapter 9, Organization and Outlining**.

soil? In fact, the security and well-being of nearly every living thing in our state depends on this one part of our environment, but most people don't give it a second thought. It may surprise you to learn that this miracle of nature is our state's wetlands." The objective of this attention material is to personalize something they don't think about—the wetlands—by showing its importance for values they do care about—security and well-being.

2. **CLOSE WITH PERSONAL IMPACT.** End your informative speech by reinforcing how the information you've shared personally affects your audience. For example: "Now that you know the important role that wetlands play in our state, you'll be able to see their impact every day. When you look at the natural beauty around you, you'll know the wetlands are protecting our soil. When it rains, you'll know they are helping protect us from floods. And every time you pour a glass of water, you'll know that the wetlands protect the quality of the water you and your family drink."

## CONNECT TO EXISTING KNOWLEDGE

Topics that are completely unknown to your audience can be difficult for them to grasp and hard for you to communicate. For example, how would you explain cellular respiration to someone unfamiliar with biology or nutrition? How would you explain the Sikh rite of *amrit sanskar* ("nectar ceremony") to someone unfamiliar with the religion? When you're discussing an item, idea, or issue that your audience has never encountered before, it can help to link that new topic to something they already understand.

1. **START WITH A FAMILIAR TOPIC.** Choose a topic that your audience already understands to compare and contrast with the new idea you want to introduce. For example: "We're all familiar with the tires on cars. They are thick rubber, full of air, and always at risk of being punctured."

2. **NOTE THE SIMILARITIES.** Show what your new topic has in common with the topic the audience already knows. For example: "Self-sealing tires are also made of thick rubber and full of air. Just like your regular tires, they can be punctured."

3. **EXPLAIN THE DIFFERENCES.** Indicate what makes the new topic you are introducing different from the topic the audience already knows. For example: "But self-sealing tires have a coating of goo on the inside of the

tire. If something punctures the tire—like a nail—the goo flows into that puncture and seals it up."[6]

4. **DESCRIBE THE NEW TOPIC.** Now you're ready to elaborate your topic on its own terms. For example: "That's what makes the self-sealing tire new and exciting. With self-sealing tires, you can keep driving for days after a puncture, and get the tire repaired when it's convenient for you."

## CLARIFY AMBIGUITY

Sometimes the meaning of a new term, concept, or idea is vague or confusing. Your audience may have heard the term used before but not understand its precise definition. For example, they might recognize the phrase "eminent domain" from news reports about a highway being planned in your town but not know the legal principle behind it. They may have picked up a general idea of the concept from context clues—it seems like "eminent domain" must have something to do with land use—but they might not fully understand how to apply it. You can clarify the meaning of unfamiliar terms by using exemplars, examples, and exclusions.

1. **START WITH A MODEL.** Offer an exemplar of the thing you are trying to clarify. An **exemplar** is a recognizable model or a typical example that demonstrates all the qualities of whatever you want to clarify. For example, to introduce young children to the concept of triangles, you might start by showing them an equilateral triangle, where all three sides of the triangle are the same length and their angles are the same 60 degrees.

2. **PROVIDE A DEFINITION.** Define the thing, concept, or category you are trying to communicate. Refer back to the exemplar to illustrate each part of your definition. For example, you might define a triangle as "a shape with three straight lines connected at three angles," pointing to your picture of an equilateral triangle to illustrate the definition.

3. **GIVE MORE EXAMPLES.** Follow your definition with additional examples that fit into this concept or category. Use different examples to illustrate the full range of cases that fit the definition you just shared. For example, you might show pictures of several triangles with lines of different lengths and angles of different degrees.

4. **MARK THE LIMITS.** Illustrate the boundaries of the definition by show-ing your audience some exclusions. **Exclusions** are cases that fall outside the

**exemplar**
a recognizable model or a typical example

**exclusion**
a case that falls outside the limits of the definition

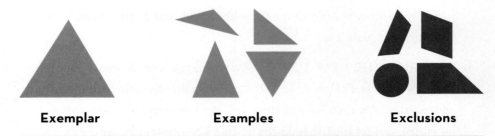

| Exemplar | Examples | Exclusions |
| --- | --- | --- |

The exemplar shows a model triangle, the examples illustrate the range of shapes that count as triangles, and the exclusions show shapes that don't qualify as triangles.

limits of the definition. They show your audience cases that fail to meet all the criteria for your definition, even though they may share some similarities with your other examples. For example, you might display shapes that look similar to triangles—like a trapezoid or three disconnected lines—and explain why they do not fit the definition of a triangle.

## VISUALIZE COMPLEXITY

While visual representations help with simple shapes like triangles, they help even more with topics that are more complex. The more complex your topic, the more you can use visual images to your advantage. Any topic—from concrete objects to abstract concepts—can benefit from visual representation: from how a computer works, to the flow of money in the economy, to relationships between characters in a novel.

Visual representation is one of the most common teaching techniques—seen everywhere from hands-on workshops to online video tutorials. If you've ever had a teacher walk you through the parts of a whole, piece by piece, on a chalkboard, whiteboard, or slides, this is the technique they were using. To get the best results, introduce aspects one at a time, starting with the first, most fundamental, or most recognizable element. Don't overload your audience—wait to show them the whole until after you have introduced each part.

1. **PREVIEW THE ELEMENTS**. Start by listing the different parts you will discuss. For example, if you were giving a presentation on how a central air-conditioning system works, you might begin by dividing it into distinct

elements: "A central air conditioner has two main parts: an indoor unit and an outdoor unit."

2. **INTRODUCE THE FIRST ELEMENT.** Both describe it verbally and display it visually. That visual display could be a photograph, a diagram, some text, or any other clear way to represent that part (see Figure 15.1). For example, you might start with the indoor unit: "The indoor unit is called an evaporator. It looks like a large rectangle with air ducts running in and out of it. This indoor unit pulls warm air from inside your home, blows it over a set of cold coils, and then pushes that cooled air back into your living space."

3. **INCLUDE TRANSITIONS.** Connect one part to the next.
   **Rhetorical questions**—questions that you ask and answer yourself—often make effective transitions in informative speeches. For example: "But how do those coils stay cold? That's where the outdoor unit comes in."

**rhetorical questions**
questions that you ask
and answer yourself

4. **INTRODUCE THE NEXT ELEMENT.** Again, combine your verbal description with a visual display. If your topic has multiple parts, repeat this process with the next part, and the next, and so forth, connecting each part to the others. For example, you can show your audience how the outdoor unit connects to the indoor unit: "The outdoor unit, sometimes called a compressor, looks like a large metal box, usually with a fan on top and fins or grates around the sides. The outdoor unit cools refrigerant and pumps it to the evaporator coils inside."

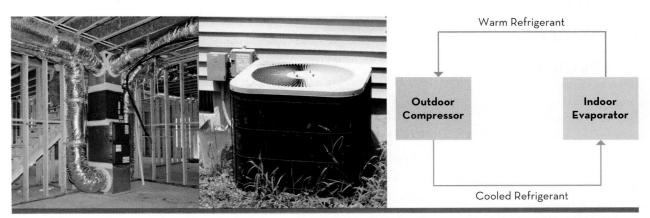

**FIGURE 15.1** Left: The indoor evaporator of a central air conditioner. Center: The outdoor compressor of an air conditioner. Right: A diagram of how the two parts work together.

To identify the informative strategies that are most important in your speaking situation, try the **Informative Troubleshooting Checklist**.

5. **DESCRIBE THE WHOLE**. After all the parts have been introduced and linked to each other, show how they all connect together to form a single system. For example: "These two parts work together to keep your home cool. The outdoor unit cools the refrigerant and sends it inside to the evaporator. The indoor unit uses the cold refrigerant to cool the air. As the air inside cools down, the refrigerant warms up. Then, the evaporator pumps the warm refrigerant back outside to the compressor. It goes around like this until your home reaches the desired temperature."

## BALANCE ABSTRACTION AND SPECIFICITY

Any topic can be described in more abstract or more specific ways. Your home could be a city, or an address, or precise GPS coordinates. A recipe could call for "a handful" or "a quarter cup" or "37 grams." The level of abstraction or specificity you need depends on your situation. More technical purposes and more expert audiences might call for more specificity. But for a non-technical purpose and a non-specialist audience, more abstraction might be appropriate. Consider the right balance for your situation.

ABSTRACT

Nature

Forests

Trees

Maples

SPECIFIC

Language that is too abstract may make it difficult for your audience to grasp your meaning; language that is too specific may contain irrelevant details that distract your audience from your point.

- **AVOID VAGUE LANGUAGE.** Being too abstract risks ambiguity and misunderstanding. If someone giving you directions said, "Take some of that stuff there, and put it with the other stuff," then you'd likely be confused about what you are supposed to do. If the information is relevant, be specific with dates, locations, directions, and descriptions. "Kind of tall" is a wide range. Do you mean six feet? Seven feet? You don't have to give a number, but offer enough specificity to make the statement meaningful. "Tall like a basketball player" or "a couple inches taller than me" might be specific enough to communicate your meaning. In other cases, exact details may be important. For example, describing the height of a WNBA draft pick might call for more precision: "six foot seven."

- **ELIMINATE UNNECESSARY DETAIL.** Being too specific can create confusion if you include details that are not relevant to your purpose or not useful to your audience. Your audience will try to retain that detail and look for a way to connect it with the rest of the presentation. If the detail never comes up again, it can leave the audience wondering if they missed something. When a speaker consistently provides too much detail, it can create information overload, presenting the audience with more than they can process. Think of a person who recites the number pi—3.1415 . . . —out to the fortieth digit or further. Even NASA scientists only use pi out to the sixteenth digit for their highest accuracy calculations.[7] Specifying more detail beyond that is just showing off. Always put your audience and their understanding first.

## Pathways

To revisit other techniques for using plain style in informative speeches, see **Chapter 11, Language and Style**.

### ✓ Critical Thinking Check

1. Which of these five informative strategies—emphasizing meaning, connecting to existing knowledge, clarifying ambiguity, visualizing complexity, and balancing abstraction and specificity—can help you gain and maintain your audience's interest? Which can help them understand new ideas? Which can help them remember information?

2. Why is it important to link the information you share to your audience's existing knowledge and values? What happens when a speaker fails to create those links?

# Framing and Organizing Informative Topics

While the number of informative topics is practically infinite, most fit into one of five categories: events, people, objects, processes, and concepts. Sometimes the way you approach a topic changes its category. For example, how would you categorize a speech about a dog?

- If you're describing the time you met an Instagram-famous dog—like Tuna from @tunameltsmyheart—that would be an event.

- If you're talking about your own pet's personality, upbringing, or daily life, then you'd be speaking about the dog like a person.

- If you're detailing the characteristics of a breed of dogs, like poodles, then you would be talking about dogs like objects.

- If you're teaching your audience the proper way to groom a dog, that would be a process.

- If you're explaining what makes some canines count as dogs and not others, you would be discussing a concept.

## Pathways

To revisit the basic types of organizational patterns, see **Chapter 9, Organization and Outlining**.

These different categories frame your topic in very different ways. Look back at your specific purpose and thesis statement to see which of these five topic categories best fits your presentation. Each topic category—events, people, objects, processes, or concepts—lends itself to particular organizational patterns and techniques.

## EVENTS

**event**
an occasion or an occurrence

When your focus is on what happened, what happens, or what will happen, then you are probably treating your topic as an event. An **event** is an occasion or an occurrence. Some events are immediately meaningful to an audience, such as an upcoming festival for people who plan to attend. When your event is not immediately meaningful to your audience, show them how learning about the event connects to their values, goals, and identity.

You can make events more interesting and memorable for your audience by adding details or stories that bring the event to life. Show them the feeling and personality of the event, the primary characters in the event, and examples of interesting minor characters. By sharing details that help your audience identify with the characters and setting, you can increase their investment in the information you want them to learn about an event.

Chronological organization is a common way to organize a presentation about an event, but not the only way. Almost any organizational pattern could be used for events. A presentation about the impacts of a hurricane could be organized spatially around the area within a half mile of the coast, from a half mile to two miles from the coast, and from two miles to five miles from the coast. A presentation about a hurricane might be organized categorically around the different categories of hurricanes. Or it could even use an effect-to-cause pattern, starting with the rise in hurricane activity as the effect and then explaining the different causes for that increase. Speeches about events can be organized in multiple ways. For example:

United Nations Under-Secretary-General Catherine Pollard gives a live video briefing on sessions of the 2021 Seoul Peacekeeping Ministerial.

| | |
|---|---|
| **Purpose** | To inform activists about how women in the US gained the right to vote so they can use those strategies today. |
| **Thesis** | People working for social change today can learn important strategies from the ways women in the United States fought for the right to vote. |
| **Organization** | Chronological. |
| **Main points** | I. The struggles of early women's suffrage activists (pre-1900). |
| | II. New coalitions and state-level victories (1900–1915). |
| | III. The campaign to pass the Nineteenth Amendment (1915–1920). |
| | IV. What activists today can learn from women's suffrage. |

## Pathways

To revisit strategies for telling stories and creating identification with characters, see **Chapter 10, Emotion and Narrative**.

| | |
|---|---|
| **Purpose** | To inform Texans about what caused the 2021 power outages so they make more informed decisions when voting. |
| **Thesis** | The widespread power outages across Texas in 2021 were caused by a combination of weaknesses in the electrical grid and laws governing utilities. |
| **Organization** | Effect (I) and causes (II, III). |
| **Main points** | I. The impact of the 2021 Texas power outages. |
| | II. Weakness in the Texas electrical grid that caused the power outages. |
| | III. How Texas laws contributed to the power outages. |

# PEOPLE

Your topic may be an individual person or a group of people. **People** are human beings, with all of the capacities, rights, and endowments that humanity confers. Your topic may describe real people or fictional characters. Your topic might even be a personified figure—like an animal or a machine—that the speaker discusses as if it were human. When discussing people, you can increase audience interest in your topic by:

**people**
human beings, with all of the capacities, rights, and endowments that humanity confers

- Showing your audience what they can learn from the person or people

- Creating identification between the audience and the person or people

- Demonstrating how the person or people connect to the audience's values, goals, and identities

When discussing an individual person, give the audience a sense of the person's attitudes, values, and behaviors, especially when they connect to your purpose. This can be done through short stories about their actions, descriptions from others who are close to the person, and quotations directly from the person. When discussing a group of people, you can still use these approaches—either by describing the group as a whole or by using an individual in the group as an example. Just remember to add enough detail and complexity to avoid totalizing or essentializing the group and its members.

## Pathways

To revisit the concepts of totalizing and essentializing, see **Chapter 3, Ethics and Credibility**.

As with events, presentations about people are often organized chronologically. But sometimes, this structure creates imbalance in a presentation. Chronological organization can also make it difficult to present distinct main points when someone has notable actions or qualities that continue over time, such as a business leader and philanthropist. Consider the specific purpose and thesis of your presentation, and choose an organizational pattern that accomplishes your purpose. For example:

| | |
|---|---|
| **Purpose** | To inform aspiring actors about Laverne Cox's career and activism so they can use their acting for public advocacy. |
| **Thesis** | Aspiring actors can learn a lot about how to succeed and make a difference from actress Laverne Cox's life, career, and public activism. |
| **Organization** | Chronological. |
| **Main points** | I.  Her life as a transgender woman from the South. |
| | II.  How she became an award-winning actress. |
| | III.  How she has used her platform to advocate for transgender rights. |

| | |
|---|---|
| **Purpose** | To inform international football fans about what makes Liverpool FC a great football club so they can better appreciate the team. |
| **Thesis** | Extraordinary players, coaches, and fans make Liverpool FC one of the best football clubs in the world. |

**Organization**  Categorical.

**Main points**  I.  Liverpool FC's roster includes some of the world's best players.

II.  Liverpool FC's coaches develop great strategies and bring the best out of the players.

III.  The fans of Liverpool FC not only support the team but embrace the diverse international nature of football.

## OBJECTS

If you are discussing your topic as something you see, touch, taste, hear, or otherwise sense, you are likely discussing it as an object. An **object** is a material thing that can be sensed and acted on. If you are describing your topic as something you act on or use, that frames it as an object.

A tour guide points out the important features of an object—the Wall of Tears—to tourists on Ecuador's Isabela Island.

Anything that has a visible or tangible form can be treated as an object. A machine can be an object. So can a building or any other place. This also includes fictional objects, such as Hogwarts Castle in the Harry Potter books or the Razorback spacecraft on *The Expanse*. Sometimes animal and human bodies are discussed as objects—for example, when studying anatomy or discussing medical conditions. But avoid treating people themselves as objects—just like **personification** humanizes nonhuman creatures or things, **objectification** dehumanizes people.

As with all topics, you'll want to make the object meaningful to your audience in the first moments of your presentation—if it isn't meaningful to them already. When the object is unfamiliar to your audience, connect it to something they know. Props, images, videos, and detailed descriptions can help your audience visualize complex objects. Remember to introduce one part of the object at a time, connecting each part to the ones that came before. For example:

**object**
a material thing that can be sensed and acted on

**personification**
describing nonhuman creatures or things as human

**objectification**
treating or discussing people like objects

|  |  |
|---|---|
| **Purpose** | To inform biology students about the nature and function of the human heart so they are better prepared for their MCAT exams. |
| **Thesis** | The human heart is a complex and vital organ made of many parts. |
| **Organization** | Spatial. |
| **Main points** | I.  The atriums of the heart receive blood and move it to the ventricles. |
|  | II.  The ventricles pump blood to the body. |
|  | III.  Arteries run across the surface of the heart and provide oxygen to its muscles. |
|  | IV.  Nerves running throughout the heart control the entire operation. |

|  |  |
|---|---|
| **Purpose** | To inform people with hearing impairments about the new Earlens hearing aid technology so they can decide if it is a good option for them. |
| **Thesis** | Earlens is a new hearing aid that uses an entirely different way of helping with hearing impairments, offering important improvements but with considerable costs. |
| **Organization** | Categorical. |
| **Main points** | I.  Differences between the Earlens technology and other hearing aids. |
|  | II.  Benefits of the Earlens technology. |
|  | III.  Drawbacks and costs of an Earlens hearing aid. |

## PROCESSES

**process**
a series of actions or steps that leads to some result or outcome

Training, tutorial, and "how-to" presentations all typically describe processes. A **process** is a series of actions or steps that leads to some result or outcome. Baking a cake is a process. Manufacturing computer chips is a process. Giving CPR is a process. Showing an audience how to complete a process is one of the most common types of informative speech.

When you are using a demonstration to teach a process, these strategies can help your audience retain the information:

1. **EXPLAIN WHAT THEY WILL LEARN.** For example: "Today, I'm going to teach you how to..." Or: "In this video, I'll show you..."

2. **WALK THROUGH EACH STEP ONE BY ONE.** For example: "First, you start with..." Or: "Finally, you're ready to..."

3. **USE PRESENTATION AIDS.** Illustrate each step in the process with visual demonstrations—for example, props, photographs, diagrams, video, or whiteboard drawings.

4. **DELIVER WITH GESTURES.** Physically interact with your presentation aids. For example, you might point to relevant details on a photograph or video. You might draw diagrams on a whiteboard or chalkboard. Or you might handle a prop to demonstrate how it works.

Process presentations usually have a chronological structure, where the main points each represent one major step or stage of the process. But sometimes the actual process is only one main point of the presentation, and the other main points provide other information. For example, a baking how-to sometimes starts with an enticing description of the item being baked, then covers all the ingredients needed, and then gives the baking directions only in the third main point. Exactly how you organize your process presentation will depend on your speaking situation.

With process presentations, be sure to clarify ambiguity, visualize complexity, and balance the abstract and specific—even for relatively simple processes. When teaching new bakers to make bread, you may need to clarify ambiguity about types of flour or yeast. You might need to visualize complexity by demonstrating how to knead the dough to the proper consistency. And you might need to be very specific about measuring the ingredients. That level of specificity might be less appropriate, however, if you were giving tours of a bakery to visitors who are not there to learn how to bake bread themselves. As always, your speaking situation should be your guide. For example:

# Angela Walters Teaches a Process

Angela Walters is the host of the Midnight Quilt Show, a Youtube video series that she records at night after her kids are in bed. In each 10–12-minute video demonstration, she shows viewers how to sew a quilt pattern from start to finish.

Her "Weave It Be" Lattice Quilt video introduces an easy pattern pitched for beginners: "If you've never made a quilt before, or you just need to make one quick, then tonight's quilt is for you."[8] She knows that her audience includes a lot of beginners because she's been paying attention to their feedback: "I've been reading the comments, and I know some of you out there have never made a quilt." To create identification, she shares how she became interested in quilting for the first time: "That's how I got started—my husband's grandpa taught me how to quilt."

After a short introduction inviting beginners to join in, she walks through each of the steps one by one. In the first step, she shows viewers all the material needed to make the quilt. Next, she demonstrates how to measure and cut the fabric strips. Then, she demonstrates how to sew the fabric strips together into quilt blocks. Along the way, she explains some common beginner mistakes.

After explaining each step on camera, she cuts away to time-lapsed video of her completing that step. These cutaways give close-up shots of her props—like her fabric, cutting mat, and sewing machine—so viewers can see the details of how

| | |
|---|---|
| **Purpose** | To inform college graduates about the process for receiving public service loan forgiveness so they can make informed repayment choices. |
| **Thesis** | Many college graduates can receive public service loan forgiveness if they ensure their loans qualify, certify their employment, and properly apply for loan forgiveness. |
| **Organization** | Chronological (step by step). |
| **Main points** | I. Ensuring your loans qualify for public service loan forgiveness before starting repayment. |
| | II. Certifying your public service employment every year and tracking progress. |

she works with her tools and materials. In addition to using props on camera, she also uses downloadable handouts as presentation aids: "If you're loving this quilt pattern, you can find all the information about it as well as the quilting diagrams I put together for you in the description box below." While she announces this verbally, she also uses video titles to highlight these extra resources. A purple box pops up onscreen that reads: "Find the link to Angela's free quilting diagrams in the description box below."

Walters closes the video with a series of shots featuring the finished quilt, and an invitation to engage: "Make sure you comment on here and let

Angela Walters demonstrates how to sew in straight lines to enhance the basket-weave pattern on a quilt (10:10).

me know what your favorite part of this quilt is." With a clear understanding of her audience, easy step-by-step instructions, and great visual aids, this video tutorial has been watched over 615,000 times.

To watch this video demonstration, search the web for: Lattice Midnight Quilt. The video is approximately 12:58 in length.

III. Applying for loan forgiveness once you are eligible and appealing if denied.

| | |
|---|---|
| **Purpose** | To teach beginning woodworkers to make a simple workbench so they can make one for their own workshops. |
| **Thesis** | A workbench is an easy first project you can assemble with just two basic parts. |
| **Organization** | Chronological. |
| **Main points** | I. Tools and materials required. |
| | II. Creating the base. |
| | III. Creating a top to fit the base. |

# CONCEPTS

Concepts are by far the most intangible of all the types of informative topics. A **concept** is an abstract idea—a value, an attitude, a belief, or a theory. Concepts include religious and spiritual beliefs, philosophical and scientific theories, economic principles, theories of the mind, theories of communication, and much more. Because they are so abstract, most concepts benefit from being divided into more specific parts.

A UK Army officer uses the whiteboard and handouts to visually represent abstract concepts for new recruits.

When informing about a concept, you may need to deploy every strategy you have for informing. Your audience may need you to make the concept meaningful to them. They may need you to connect it to the known. They may need you to clarify the ambiguous. You will likely need to balance the abstract and the specific. Your audience may need you to help them visualize complexity.

When you're introducing a concept, visualizing complexity may be the most important of all these strategies. When a concept is both complex and abstract, visual representation will help. That may be a chart, diagram, or table of the major elements, but even just a list with numbers or bullets can help. Think about when you have learned about an abstract and complex concept. What helped you or made it more difficult for you to understand? Clear organization can help make a complex concept easier to grasp:

|  |  |
|---|---|
| **Purpose** | To explain to investors what a cryptocurrency is so they can make better investment decisions. |
| **Thesis** | Modern cryptocurrencies offer a decentralized form of money that is publicly verified and can be made secure. |
| **Organization** | Categorical. |
| **Main points** | I. How government-backed, centralized currencies differ from cryptocurrencies. |
|  | II. How the blockchain publicly verifies ownership of a cryptocurrency. |
|  | III. What protects your ownership of a cryptocurrency. |

**concept**
an abstract idea—a value, an attitude, a belief, or a theory

**Purpose** To inform members of the moot court team about the right to privacy in the US Constitution so they are prepared for an upcoming competition.

**Thesis** The right to privacy is an important principle in the US Constitution with an uncertain future.

**Organization** Chronological.

**Main points**

I. How US courts found the right to privacy in the Constitution, even though it isn't explicitly mentioned.

II. How the right to privacy led to courts recognizing other rights, like educational rights, reproductive rights, and marriage rights.

III. Concerns that the current Supreme Court may reduce or eliminate the right to privacy and related rights.

📋 **TRY THIS**

To identify the best organizational pattern and topic type for your informative presentation, try the **Framing Informative Topics Checklist**.

## ✓ Critical Thinking Check

1. Can you think of any other examples of topics that could be framed in multiple ways? For example, as either an object or a concept? As either an event or a process? As either an event or a person?

2. How would you organize a speech about an event differently from a speech about a concept? How would you structure a speech about a process differently from a speech about an object? How would you outline a speech about an object differently from a speech about a person?

# Next Steps

Try out the Three Cs Checklist, the Informative Troubleshooting Checklist, and the Framing Informative Topics Checklist to identify the best informative strategies for your speaking situation. These exercises will help you build your credibility as an informative speaker, challenge your audience to expand their knowledge and skills, and sidestep controversies that might distract them from learning.

But what if a controversy is too big—or too important—to ignore? What if your topic, audience, context, or standpoint calls you to take a position rather than impartially reporting the evidence for each side of an argument? Or what if that evidence itself is a matter of debate? In that case, you might need to rethink your purpose and focus on persuading your audience instead.

# Standpoint Reflection

- What interests and passions do you have that might make a good topic for an informative speech? What do you do in your free time? What are your favorite books, blogs, movies, and TV shows about? What content do you follow on social media?

- What experiences have you had that got you interested in or passionate about those topics? How might you share those experiences to give you extra credibility in an informative speech?

- What unique knowledge or perspective does that experience give you for understanding those topics? Do you think about those topics differently than someone who hasn't had that experience?

- You've experienced thousands of hours of informative presentations over the course of your education. Who are some of the best teachers you've had? What are some of the best informative presentations you've seen? What made them so good? How might you use these strategies in your own informative speaking?

---

## Key Terms

challenge, p. 347

concept, p. 368

controversy, p. 348

credibility, p. 349

event, p. 360

exclusion, p. 355

exemplar, p. 355

object, p. 363

objectification, p. 363

people, p. 361

personification, p. 363

process, p. 364

rhetorical questions, p. 357

# Resources for Informing and Educating

 **"Try This" Exercises**

Access the "Try This" exercises as directed by your instructor or online at digital.wwnorton.com/chapterexercises-conpubspeak

- To select a topic for your informative speech that gives you high credibility, low controversy, and the right level of challenge, try the **Three Cs Checklist**.

- To identify the informative strategies that are most important in your speaking situation, try the **Informative Troubleshooting Checklist**.

- To identify the best organizational pattern and topic type for your informative presentation, try the **Framing Informative Topics Checklist**.

---

**Want to practice these skills to prepare for your next speech? Go to INQUIZITIVE to review and apply concepts from this chapter and get personalized feedback along the way.**

ENVIRONMENTAL ACTIVISTS
AND YOUTH ORGANIZERS

Melati and Isabel Wijsen

# 16 Persuading and Motivating

Sisters Melati and Isabel Wijsen run a global network of young activists, but their work began with a local problem: every year tons of plastic garbage washes up on the beaches around their island home of Bali.[1] To tackle the problem, they created a campaign to convince the governor of Bali to ban single-use plastic bags.

The Wijsen sisters started by giving speeches at schools, markets, and festivals across the island. They organized beach cleanups, distributed reusable bags, and ran a petition drive. In the process, they learned that creating change requires persistence, patience, and a network of supporters. Their first successes came when local city governments and businesses stopped using plastic bags.

As they kept giving speeches, their network grew. They were invited to present at TED conferences, the United Nations, and the World Economic Forum, further expanding their influence.[2] They made videos and posts for social media to reach even more people and increase support for their cause.[3] After six years of consistent work, the two sisters reached their goal: Bali finally banned single-use plastic bags and straws in 2019.

Today, the Wijsen sisters are helping other young activists develop their skills and find the support they need. They've created an online international youth network, Youthtopia, to provide free training and mentoring for young people working to make a difference.[4] Youthtopia brings together up-and-coming changemakers from around the world, providing training on key skills for starting and maintaining social movements, including public speaking, viral videos, and persuasive strategies.

## LEARNING OBJECTIVES

**After completing this chapter, you will be able to**

- Define persuasion and explain why it requires controversy

- Assess the level of controversy in your speaking situation

- Identify the best persuasive strategies for changing attitudes, values, behaviors, and policies

- Organize persuasive presentations about facts, values, actions, and policies

As Isabel and Melati Wijsen show, persuasion can be an incremental process. Changing a public policy rarely happens in a single speech or video presentation—it requires an ongoing persuasive campaign to change the attitudes, values, and behaviors of multiple communities and decision-makers. Persuading your audience to change their minds or their habits can take both time and skill. Although your audience may initially be divided—from your purpose and from each other—learning persuasive strategies can help you build common ground that unites them in support for your cause.

# Finding the Level of Controversy

Anytime you encourage your audience to take action or reconsider their beliefs, you are engaging in persuasion. **Persuasion** is changing someone's attitudes, values, or behaviors. Because persuasion is all about change, it requires an element of **controversy**: a debate or disagreement between your audience's existing position and the one you want them to adopt. If your audience is already completely on board with the attitudes, values, or behaviors you recommend, you are not persuading them. Why? Because you are not asking them to change.

At the same time, pushing your audience to change too much too fast can backfire. Because they will evaluate your message based on their current attitudes, values, and behaviors, your audience may refuse to listen to you at all if you ask them to step too far outside their current worldview.[5] For example, pressuring a longtime hunter to go vegan may be too much to ask—you might have more luck convincing them to cut back on beef for health reasons.

Understanding your audience's existing attitudes, values, and behaviors can help you select a persuasive goal that is both meaningful and achievable. To find the right balance, pinpoint the precise source of your disagreement. Consider why your audience disagrees with the attitudes, values, or actions you are promoting. Do they disagree with your presentation's thesis statement? Do they disagree with specific claims supporting your thesis? By understanding what kind of disagreement exists, you can choose the techniques most likely to persuade your audience.

Controversy can occur at four levels: the level of fact, the level of value, the level of personal action, and the level of policy.[6] Usually, you will need to establish

**persuasion**
changing someone's attitudes, values, or behaviors

**controversy**
a debate or disagreement among different views

## Pathways

To revisit strategies for analyzing your audience's attitudes, values, and behaviors, see **Chapter 5, Audiences and Publics**. To review principles for selecting a meaningful and achievable purpose, see **Chapter 6, Topic and Purpose**.

agreement at the lower levels before addressing disagreement at a higher level (see Figure 16.1). Before you can persuade your audience to change their values about an issue, they will need to agree on the facts. Before you can persuade them to change their personal actions or institutional policies, you will need to find common ground at the level of both facts and values. Start your persuasive efforts by focusing on the most basic level of disagreement and work upward, gradually leading your audience from their current attitudes, values, and behaviors toward your persuasive goal.

| Policy |
| Action |
| Value |
| Fact |

**FIGURE 16.1** Agreements about policies are built on agreements about actions, agreements about actions are built on agreements about values, and agreements about values are built on agreements about facts.

> 📋 **TRY THIS**
>
> To gauge the level of controversy in your speaking situation, try the **Ladder of Persuasion Checklist**.

## DISAGREEMENTS OF FACT

A **disagreement of fact** occurs when people disagree about evidence gained through observation, scientific method, or historical analysis. Disagreements of fact occur around questions of truth or falsehood. Trials often involve disagreements of fact, where the two sides debate whether the defendant committed an act. Debates about scientific theories are likewise disagreements of fact, where different experts offer different interpretations of research findings.

Anytime you disagree about whether something is real, true, or accurate (Did American astronauts actually land on the moon in 1969? Did the universe really begin with the Big Bang?), you disagree about facts. Arguments about cause and effect—such as what causes global climate change—are disagreements of fact. Arguments about whether something fits a definition—such as whether an economic downturn qualifies as a recession—are also disagreements of fact. While facts often imply a value judgment or even demand an action, some persuasive speeches focus solely on the disagreement of fact itself, without mentioning the value or policy implications of those facts.

**disagreement of fact**
a disagreement about evidence gained through observation, scientific method, or historical analysis

## DISAGREEMENTS OF VALUE

A **disagreement of value** occurs when you disagree about whether something is good or bad, important or unimportant. Disagreements of value can be about the value of anything, including behaviors, attitudes, objects, theories, and even

**disagreement of value**
a disagreement about whether something is good or bad, important or unimportant

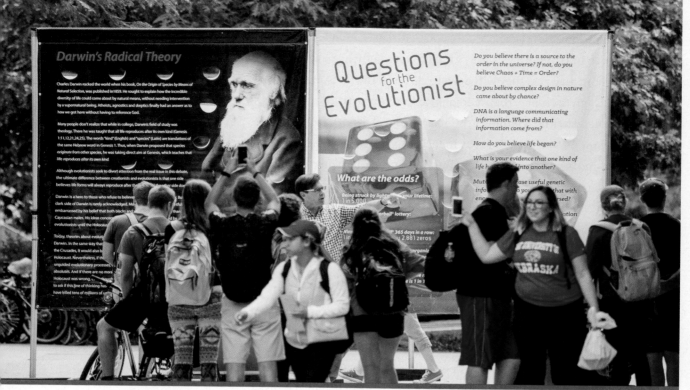

Debates over scientific theories, such as the theory of evolution, represent disagreements of fact.

values themselves. For example, a disagreement of value occurs when lawyers debate the severity of someone's actions. Questions about the ethics of political candidates also occur at the level of value.

To engage in a disagreement of value, you and your audience must first agree to the facts relevant to the disagreement. If your audience disagrees with you about the facts, you will need to resolve that disagreement before you can engage with a disagreement of value. This is why many value questions in trials are only debated after the jury has decided the facts of a case. Sometimes, what looks like a disagreement of value is actually a disagreement of fact. For example, your audience might agree that a significant rise in sea levels would be a big problem—even if they disagree about whether it is actually happening.

**disagreement of personal action**
a disagreement about what members of the audience should do or how they should behave

## DISAGREEMENTS OF PERSONAL ACTION

A **disagreement of personal action** occurs when you disagree about what members of the audience should do or how they should behave. Disagreements about personal action can include whether they should recycle, donate blood, adopt a pet, work out, volunteer time, donate money, buy a product, join a group, attend a protest, and much more. Most people encounter public messages about personal action more than any other kind of persuasion.

Disagreements about personal action are sometimes rooted in disagreements of fact or value. For example, a disagreement about whether materials put into recycling bins end up in landfills is a disagreement of fact. A disagreement about whether the benefits of recycling are enough to justify the inconvenience is a disagreement of value. If your audience doesn't agree that recycling has benefits—or that those benefits are important—it will be difficult to motivate them to recycle. A disagreement about facts or values may be what's keeping your audience from taking action.

But disagreements about personal action can occur even when the audience agrees about the facts and the values—they might share your beliefs, but still not adjust their behavior. In those cases, the most likely causes are either not enough internal motivation or too many external obstacles. If an audience member thinks they can't do something, they probably won't try. You can help them by boosting their confidence in their abilities and removing any barriers to taking action. Often, advertising follows this model: "so cheap, fast, and easy, anyone can do it!"

## DISAGREEMENTS OF POLICY

A **disagreement of policy** occurs when you disagree about what policies an organization or institution should adopt. That could be a law or government regulation. It could be a company's hiring policies or a product return policy. It could be a university's policy on attendance. It could even be a club's policy on membership fees. Just as with personal action, the audience will need to agree about the facts and values before you can persuade them to make a policy change. Persuading an audience to make a policy change usually also requires some personal action to enact that policy.

When speaking directly to people who can enact a policy, their personal values and motivations may matter as much—or even more—than whether that policy

**disagreement of policy**
a disagreement about what policies an organization or institution should adopt

Debates over abortion laws are an example of a disagreement of policy that is often complicated by underlying disagreements about facts and values.

**TRY THIS**

To learn strategies for using your audience's existing attitudes, values, and behaviors to persuade them to change their minds, try the **Overturning Beliefs Worksheet**.

benefits the larger organization or community they represent. Politicians are more likely to enact policies that will help their chances of reelection, and managers are more likely to enact policies that will help them get promotions, raises, and other rewards. At the same time, you will need to persuade them that the policy fits with their vision for the government, business, or other organization. When speaking to people who can only indirectly influence a policy change, you will need to both convince them to support the policy and motivate them to take action that will make a difference. Persuasion about policy change is the most complex of all the forms, requiring agreement about facts, values, and personal motivation, as well as support for the specific policy change you are seeking.

## ✓ Critical Thinking Check

1. What ethical challenges might you encounter when asking your audience to change their attitudes, values, and behaviors? Can you think of any situations when failing to call for change might be ethically problematic?

2. Can you think of any disagreements about policy that are rooted in disagreements about personal actions, values, or facts? Is it necessary to address underlying disagreements about facts, values, or personal actions in order to resolve a disagreement about policy? Why or why not?

3. Why might a disagreement about facts lead to a disagreement about values? Why might a disagreement about values lead to a disagreement about personal actions or institutional policies? Could a disagreement about facts lead to a disagreement about personal actions or institutional policies, even if people share the same values?

# Malala Yousafzai's Call to Educate Girls

Many people in the United States take it for granted that every child, including girls, should have access to education. But under some political regimes, educating girls is so controversial that people are killed for advocating it. From the age of eleven, Malala Yousafzai has been speaking out for the rights of young girls to access education in her home country of Pakistan and around the world.

The Taliban in her country had barred most girls from schooling and destroyed schools for girls. Malala often received death threats for speaking out publicly on the issue; many of these threats were published in Pakistani newspapers. When Malala was fifteen years old, Taliban leaders met and decided that she must be killed for speaking out against them.[7] Taliban troops found her and shot her in the head. She survived the attack, and after multiple surgeries, she redoubled her advocacy for every girl's right to an education.

Two years after the shooting, Yousafzai became the youngest person ever to receive a Nobel Peace Prize. In her acceptance speech, she advocated for all "66 million girls who are deprived of education."[8] She donated the prize money to a foundation that bears her name, committing to building more schools for children in places like Pakistan and ensuring that girls around the world have access to quality education. She noted how "education went from being a right to being a crime" in Pakistan when intolerant religious views took over the country.

Malala Yousafzai talks about the "thirst for education" that she and her female friends shared before the Taliban shut down schools for girls (8:25).

At heart, Yousafzai's goal is simple—and uncontroversial for many people both within Pakistan and around the world. As she said, she simply "wants to see every child getting a quality education." While her purpose may be uncontroversial for many—including her audience at the Nobel Peace Prize ceremony—that same purpose was highly controversial for supporters of the Taliban regime. Yousafzai's activism demonstrates that no cause or topic is inherently controversial or uncontroversial: the level of controversy comes from the attitudes, values, behaviors, and policies of your audience.

To watch Yousafzai's complete Nobel Peace Prize speech, do a web search for: Malala Yousafzai Peace Prize Lecture 2014. The video is approximately 28:29 in length.

# Persuading about Facts

Because so many of our values and behaviors depend on what we think is true, persuading an audience to change their view of a fact can lead to a radical transformation. For example, in the 1990s, convincing people that secondhand smoke causes cancer created a dramatic change in Americans' values, personal actions, and public policy around smoking.

The next time you disagree about a question of fact with someone, think about the different evidence that your audience might rely on to support differing views. To persuade an audience about a controversial fact, follow these five steps: state the audience's existing belief, acknowledge its plausibility, demonstrate its inadequacy, state the belief you want them to adopt, and then illustrate its explanatory power.[9]

## 1 State Existing Belief

When addressing a disagreement of fact within your speech, begin by stating what the audience already believes to be true. If the belief is trivial to the audience or they are already uncertain about it, you can use a phrase like "Many people believe..." or "You might think..." These phrases signal to your listeners that you disagree and will argue a different view. For beliefs that are more firmly held or deeply important to your audience, you may not want to indicate your disagreement until later in the argument. In that case, ascribe the belief to a source other than your audience or yourself. For a commonly misunderstood scientific fact, you can present it as a popular view: "You have probably seen the many reports that drinking red wine improves a person's health. These reports suggest that a little alcohol now and then might help you live longer."

## 2 Acknowledge Plausibility

**plausibility**
the appearance of being true or credible, even if incorrect

Next, show why it is reasonable for the audience to hold their existing belief. **Plausibility** is the appearance of being true or credible, even if incorrect. By describing their mistaken belief as plausible, you help preserve identification and goodwill between you and the audience. You need this identification and goodwill before you can move to the next step, where you will explain why their belief is incorrect. You don't want them to feel like you are belittling them or dismissing their views without consideration. With the red wine example, you could explain the evidence for the health benefits: "The Mayo Clinic notes that studies have found a substance called resveratrol in red wine has heart benefits."[10]

## 3 Demonstrate Inadequacy

Once you've set up the existing belief, you then turn to evidence that it is insufficient, incomplete, or incorrect. Explain why the evidence for plausibility is flawed and provide additional evidence to the contrary: "The evidence for the benefits of red wine sounds strong, but the Mayo Clinic goes on to say that resveratrol can be found in other foods." You could then follow this with additional evidence that contradicts the existing belief: "The largest and most comprehensive study to date, using twenty-six years of data from 195 countries, showed that, on average, people who drink die younger than people who do not."[11] This combination—showing flaws in the existing evidence and providing additional contradictory evidence—is a powerful way to unsettle an audience's firmly held belief.

## 4 State New Belief

Once you've created uncertainty in the audience's beliefs, they may be more receptive to considering another fact, theory, or belief. Simply state the new belief as a fact. You want to be clear, plain, and unambiguous in this statement of fact. For example: "The truth is that drinking alcohol shortens your life span." If you expect significant resistance from the audience, use a strong source citation to support your fact: "That comprehensive study and others like it are why the World Health Organization, the Centers for Disease Control and Prevention (CDC), the UK's National Health Service, and many other agencies now say that there is no safe level of alcohol consumption. Any amount of alcohol consumption increases your risk of dying earlier, and the more someone drinks, the greater their risks."[12]

## 5 Demonstrate Explanatory Power

Having weakened the existing belief and provided an alternative, you now need to strengthen the evidence for the alternative by showing its explanatory power. Quality source citations supporting the belief you advocate will add credibility, but the final step requires showing the audience how the new belief better explains or accounts for the audience's own experience. With alcohol consumption reducing life expectancy, you might say, "If you've ever woken up feeling sick after a night of drinking, listen to what your body is telling you: alcohol is bad for your health."[13]

## Pathways

To review methods for establishing and preserving identification with your audience, see **Chapter 3, Ethics and Credibility**.

# Persuading about Values

Once you and your audience agree on the facts, you might expect their values to automatically shift to fit those new facts. But because we all hold multiple values and prioritize those values in different ways, even people who believe the same facts often come to different conclusions about what is important or good. In these cases, speakers need to persuade their audiences that the issue affects one of their high-priority values.

To persuade about values, you can use a four-step process: identify a high-priority value for your audience, amplify the importance of that value, establish criteria for that value, and apply those criteria to the issue in question. This four-step process takes the values that are most important to your audience and uses them to help your audience evaluate an issue in a new way.

This process can be a powerful way to change someone's priorities, and even alter their view of themselves and the world.

## 1 Introduce the Value

Start by introducing a value that your audience already holds in high priority. The higher the value in the audience's value priorities, the more powerful the persuasive effect will be. Ideally, this value will also be a high priority for you. That will help build identification and allow you to speak authentically from your standpoint.

In her video presentation on toxic productivity, Dr. Julie Smith argues that you're placing too much value on productivity when it interferes with your physical or mental health (1:00).

Introduce that value to the audience in a way that will resonate with them. For example, if you were speaking to a group of college students looking forward to their lives after college, you might focus on the value of success: "You have so many accomplishments ahead of you, so many triumphs and achievements, and life goals that you will meet." Describe the value in a way that helps your audience feel understood, that lets them know that you want for them what they want for themselves.

## 2 Amplify the Value

Once you've introduced this high-priority value, build up the importance of that value for your audience. You can do this by connecting this high-priority value to their other values. For example, after introducing the value of success, you could link it to other values your audience considers important:

> Your accomplishments will make it possible for you to find work that is fulfilling and rewarding. They will bring you the freedom to pursue passions that you've always dreamed of. They will help you build friendship, belonging, and social connection. And they will help you bring more beauty, peace, and love into the world. Whatever your life goals, they are waiting for you to go out and achieve them.

As you can see, figures of speech—like repetition, climax, and comparison—can amplify the importance of the initial value you mentioned by placing it in an escalating series of increasingly important values. The more you amplify that value, the more the audience will be committed to achieving or preserving it, even at the expense of other values.

**Pathways**

To review figures of speech, see **Chapter 11, Language and Style**. To learn more about using climax and comparison to amplify values, see **Chapter 17, Connecting and Celebrating**.

## 3 Set Value Criteria

Now that you've identified and amplified the value, establish criteria for that value. **Criteria** are standards for evaluation—standards for judging whether something fits your values. Criteria give your audience a way to assess whether the issue you are discussing fits their values. Describe your criteria so that you can easily use them to support the value argument you are making. For example, after introducing and amplifying the value of success, you might want to use that value to argue for something that affects your audience members' health. To do so, you would first need to establish caring for one's health as one of the key criteria for success:

**criteria**
standards for judging whether something fits your values

> Accomplishing your life goals will depend on having the energy, focus, resilience, and good health to pursue them. If someone doesn't take care of themselves and their health, achieving every one of their life goals will become harder. No matter what your current level of health or ability, doing what you can to protect and improve your health is fundamental for your future success.

## Pathways

To revisit the principles of deductive reasoning, see **Chapter 7, Evidence and Reasoning**.

At this point, we have introduced success as a high-priority value, and defined success as meeting your life goals. We amplified the importance of success by connecting it to values like family, work, fulfillment, freedom, passion, dreams, beauty, peace, and love. And now, we have established taking care of yourself and your health as core criteria for determining whether something will help you achieve those life goals. Clearly establishing these criteria will help your audience with deductive reasoning: applying a general principle—one of their values—to a specific case—your topic.

## 4 Apply the Criteria to Your Topic

Now we are ready to tackle the controversial issue. You've introduced a value your audience believes in, you've magnified its importance, and you've given them standards for judging whether they're living up to those values. Now, take those criteria and apply them to the issue or topic you want to persuade your audience about. If you want them to value something more, show how that thing meets the criteria you established. If you want them to value something less, show them how it fails to meet those criteria. For example:

> This is the true cost of consuming alcohol. As the World Health Organization, the CDC, and the UK's National Health Service have all stated, the negative impacts on your health start with just one drink and get worse with each additional drink. Every drink you take means less heath, less vitality, less energy, less focus, and less resilience. Less ability to do fulfilling work. Less ability to build a happy family. Less freedom to pursue your passions. Every drink you take takes you further away from your biggest goals in life.

## ✓ Critical Thinking Check

1. What is the difference between informing and persuading about facts? How are the strategies for persuading about facts different from the strategies for informing? How do you know whether to use informative or persuasive strategies when discussing facts?
2. When you're persuading about values, why is it necessary to link your topic to one of your audience's highest-priority values? What might go wrong if you connected your topic to a value that's not very important to your audience?

# Persuading about Personal Actions

Even if you persuade your audience to reevaluate an issue, that change in their values may not immediately affect their actions. Almost all of us sometimes stick with behaviors that are out of line with our values—even our most important values. So don't expect an audience to change the way they act just because you have convinced them that something is better or worse than they thought. Changing their actions will require you to go even further.

If your audience already agrees about the facts and values relevant to your topic, but they are not yet changing their behavior, then it's time to focus on persuading about personal actions. That could mean asking them to take a one-time action, like attending an event. Or it could mean asking them to change a behavior they engage in many times each day, like their eating habits. Once they agree with you about the value of an action or habit, you can motivate them to put those beliefs into practice.

When your audience resists an action that they recognize as good, it's usually because the perceived difficulty or costs of the action outweigh its value. You can motivate your audience to take an action either by emphasizing its importance or by minimizing its obstacles. A process called Monroe's Motivated Sequence can do both. Named for its creator, Alan Monroe at Purdue University, **Monroe's Motivated Sequence** is a five-step method to motivate an audience and reduce barriers to action.[14] Its five steps are attention, need, satisfaction, visualization, and action.

**Monroe's Motivated Sequence**
a five-step method to motivate an audience and reduce barriers to action, including attention, need, satisfaction, visualization, and action

## 1 Attention

First, draw your audience's attention to your topic or central issue. At this stage, you want their attention focused on the general topic rather than the specific action or behavior you want them to adopt. Remember that your audience's values and emotions have significant impact on their behavior, so engage their emotions and values right away in your attention material. For example:

> What if I told you there was one simple thing you could do to improve your energy, focus, and resilience? One simple thing that would extend your life span, improve your health, and even help you lose weight? One

thing that would improve your ability to pursue your passions, find fulfilling work, and build a happy family?

## 2 Need

Next, help your audience feel that they have an unmet need or strong desire. That may be a need to reduce something negative or a need to increase something positive. Researchers find that people are more motivated by avoiding loss than achieving gains—this is called **loss aversion**.[15] But the best way to establish need is using both strategies together. Tell your audience what they will gain if they take the action you recommend, and what they will lose if they don't. No two audiences are the same, so use your audience analysis to identify the gains and losses that will matter most to your audience. For example:

> The truth is, most of us engage in a behavior that shortens our life span, harms our health, impairs our thinking, and can damage our relationships. This activity is so common and widely accepted that most people never stop to think about how much it is costing them and how much they could gain if they stopped. I'm talking about drinking alcohol.

## 3 Satisfaction

Now that you've created a feeling of need, offer your audience a way to satisfy that need. Tell them what action they can take to avoid the loss or secure the gains they want. The action should be concrete, clear, and easy for them to take. You want them to feel empowered and capable of taking this action. Leave no ambiguity and keep the action within the scope of their control. For example, in our presentation about the costs of drinking alcohol, the action can be simple:

> If you don't drink, don't start. If you already drink, stop if you can. Get help if you find that you cannot control your drinking. And if you are not able or ready to stop drinking, at least minimize the amount you consume as much as possible. Every drink you don't take brings you closer to achieving your life goals.

To make this action easier for your audience to take, remove or reduce any barriers standing in their way. One common barrier is a lack of knowledge. Many personal advocacy presentations fail because they convince the audience they should

**loss aversion**
the tendency for people to be more motivated by avoiding loss than achieving gains

## Pathways

To revisit how to conduct audience analysis, see **Chapter 5, Audiences and Publics**.

take the action, but don't give the audience the information they need to take it. For example, you might convince an audience they should get help if they cannot control their drinking. But if they don't know where to go for help, they may continue to drink.

Another common barrier to personal action is inconvenience. Littering, recycling, and voting are all behaviors significantly affected by their level of convenience. With drinking, you may need to provide convenient alternatives, like suggesting they order a non-alcoholic beverage the next time they're out with friends.

Persuading young adults to register and vote— such as at this "Rock the Vote" event—requires speakers to demonstrate that voting can satisfy a need important to people in their late teens and early twenties.

You may also need to address other audience needs and desires that conflict with the action you want them to take. For example, if your audience already drinks, it's likely because they believe drinking helps meet an important need. The most common reasons people drink alcohol are to socialize and to escape unpleasant feelings.[16] You can reduce these barriers to action by:

- **SHOWING HOW THE ACTION YOU ADVOCATE BETTER MEETS THEIR NEEDS:** "Drinking to deal with emotions just numbs the pain, while quitting lets you start processing those emotions in a healthier way."

- **SHOWING HOW FAILURE TO TAKE ACTION THREATENS THEIR NEEDS:** "Some people drink to bond with their friends, but too often, when someone has had a drink or two, they say or do something thoughtless that can ruin a friendship."

- **SHOWING ALTERNATIVE WAYS TO MEET THEIR NEEDS:** "If you're struggling with negative feelings, you can use techniques like meditation and deep breathing, or you can seek out a therapist to help you."

- **SHOWING THAT THOSE CONFLICTING NEEDS ARE LOWER PRIORITY THAN THE NEEDS MET BY THE ACTION:** "Is drinking to fit in worth all the risks to your health, your future accomplishments, and your life goals?"

**Pathways**

To review figures of speech that can help you evoke sensation and emotion, see **Chapter 11, Language and Style**.

## 4 Visualization

Now that you've established a need, provided an action that can satisfy that need, and reduced barriers to taking that action, your next step is to create a strong emotional commitment to the results. To do that, help your audience imagine what it will be like when they have satisfied that need and fulfilled their highest-priority values.

Visualization relies on helping your audience imagine themselves having taken the action and satisfied their desire. Build your audience's vision of their future selves: They have taken the action you recommended. That action satisfied their feeling of need. The action helped them get or keep things that they want. It helped them avoid or get rid of things that they don't want. Then, compare this envisioned future to either their present self or the negative future self that awaits if they do not take the action you recommend.

Use vivid sensory description, repetition, metaphor, and other figures of speech to elicit strong feelings. You want your audience to picture and feel the results of taking the action, to make the results real in their minds. This may be more or less specific depending on your audience, the values you are focusing on, and the action you propose. Even a relatively broad description can still create vivid and emotional visualization. For example:

> We all have dreams. We have goals in life, things we want to accomplish. Whatever those are, imagine that you have achieved them—everything you are hoping for and looking forward to. The kind of life you are looking forward to living. See your family around you, your partner or spouse, the love you share. Imagine yourself in your ideal work, doing something you've always wanted to do, feeling fulfilled and rewarded. Picture yourself pursuing your passions; feel the excitement and joy in your body. Know that you have friendships, belonging, and social connection where you are welcomed and accepted. That kind of a future is possible for you, as it is for each of us. There may be work ahead, struggles, challenges, and even setbacks, but you can accomplish all of this and reach your life goals if you make the right choices.

## 5 Action

The final part of the sequence is a call to action. Reinforce the specific action you want your audience to take.

- **REPEAT OR PARAPHRASE YOUR ACTION RECOMMENDATION.** Again, the action you call for should be concrete and clear. For example: "Remember: If you don't drink, don't start. If you already drink, stop if you can. Get help if you find that you cannot control your drinking. And if you are not able or ready to stop drinking, at least minimize the amount you consume as much as possible."

YouTuber Heather Ramirez demonstrates how to create animated "subscribe" buttons that call viewers to take immediate action (0:06).

- **ASK THEM TO COMMIT TO TAKING THE ACTION.** Encourage them to make a decision right now. For example: "So right now, make a promise to yourself. Make a promise to your dreams and aspirations. Make a promise to your future, to your future family, to your future passions, to your future self. Promise that you will not let alcohol put that future at risk. Make that promise to yourself now."

- **GIVE THEM AN IMMEDIATE ACTION TO TAKE.** Give them first steps that are easy for them to take as soon as your presentation ends. For example: "Start planning what you will change to keep that promise. If you need help to stop drinking, call the national substance abuse helpline at 800-662-HELP. If you can stop drinking on your own, be prepared for situations that might challenge your promise to yourself. What will you do when offered a drink? What will you do with friends, colleagues, or family who drink? Decide now what you will do and say to keep that promise. Make a plan to protect yourself and your future."

# Persuading about Policies

Sometimes you may want to go beyond convincing people to change their personal actions and instead persuade people to change a law, rule, or other policy. Almost every organization has policies, from national governments down to local clubs. To change those policies, you have to figure out which individuals or groups you need to persuade. A **change agent** is a person or group of people with the direct power and authority to change a policy.

In governments, laws are usually set by legislators, like representatives or council members, while rules are set by the directors of agencies like the Environmental Protection Agency or the Internal Revenue Service. Sometimes, judges

**change agent**
a person or group of people with the direct power and authority to change a policy

**📋 TRY THIS**

To identify the right audience for your policy speech, try the **Identifying Change Agents Worksheet**.

Change agents on the New York City council debate their immigration relief and enforcement policies.

can also create or eliminate government policies through an opinion of the court, especially the state or federal Supreme Court. Sometimes citizens can change laws directly through ballot initiatives. In businesses and nonprofit organizations, policies may be set by a board of directors, or by an executive, manager, owner, or president of the organization. Similarly, clubs and civic organizations often give their leaders control over some policies and give the full membership the right to vote on others.

## Pathways

To review information-gathering strategies that can help you find the change agent for your topic, see **Chapter 8, Research and Citation**.

When researching your topic, try to identify the change agent. Who has true decision-making authority over the policy you want changed? Persuading the change agent is the most direct form of policy advocacy. If you cannot speak directly to them, then you may need to motivate another audience to take personal action to influence the change agent. For example, many public presentations about government policies seek to persuade voters to write or call the political leaders who have decision-making authority. A persuasive case for policy action requires four parts: significant harms, causes, plan, and solution.

## 1 Significant Harms

**Significant harms** are the reasons that a policy needs to be changed or implemented. They are the problems or imperfections we need a policy change to fix. They can be something bad the policy change would avoid or something good we will miss out on without the policy change. The significance of a harm can be quantitative, qualitative, or both.

**significant harms**
reasons that a policy needs to be changed or implemented

**quantitative significance**
the scope, frequency, or degree of a problem

**qualitative significance**
the priority and severity of a problem

**Quantitative significance** demonstrates the scope, frequency, or degree of a problem. You can emphasize a problem's scope by showing how broadly the problem extends, such as how many people are affected. You can emphasize a problem's frequency by showing how often the problem occurs. Or you can emphasize quantitative significance by showing the degree it increases a risk.

**Qualitative significance** demonstrates the priority and severity of a problem. You can emphasize a problem's priority by linking it to high-priority values your audience already holds. You can also emphasize a problem's severity by showing how deeply it violates those values. Vivid descriptions and emotional language related to the audience's values will also increase qualitative significance. The more significant the problem, the more likely your audience is to implement a policy change.

When communicating significance to your audience, you will often blend the quantitative and qualitative elements together. For example, if you were trying to persuade the US Department of Agriculture (USDA) to change its official recommendations on alcohol consumption, you could talk about how widespread alcohol consumption is in the US and its negative impacts:

> We now know that there is no safe level of alcohol consumption. Yet, just over half of US adults drink alcohol on a regular basis.[17] And those drinks mean they die earlier and live in poorer health than if they did not drink. Alcohol consumption is one of the highest risk factors for disability and premature death.[18] And in the Americas, alcohol consumption causes or contributes to nearly 400,000 deaths each year.[19]

## 2 Causes

After you've convinced the audience there's a significant harm, you may need to help them understand why it continues. If the present situation is so bad, why haven't we already changed it? Identifying the causes of the problem explains why the significant harm persists and shows that it will not be resolved without changing the policy.

Causes generally come in two kinds: structural and attitudinal. **Structural causes** include laws, policies, rules, systems, physical barriers, natural elements, or organizational structures that prevent change and allow the harm to continue. **Attitudinal causes** include attitudes, beliefs, emotions, values, social norms, or cultural elements that prevent change and allow the harm to continue. Often, a harm will have both structural and attitudinal causes. For example, racial and gender discrimination in a workplace may have both structural and attitudinal dimensions. By pinpointing the cause, you show your audience exactly what needs to change in order to fix the problem. For example:

> Many Americans drink because they believe moderate alcohol consumption is healthy. That belief comes, in part, from the USDA's statement that one to two drinks a day is safe.[20] That message is widely repeated by the media and often used to justify drinking.

## Pathways

To revisit strategies for establishing qualitative and quantitative significance with emotional appeals, see **Chapter 10, Emotion and Narrative**.

**structural causes**
laws, policies, rules, systems, physical barriers, natural elements, or organizational structures that prevent change and allow a harm to continue

**attitudinal causes**
attitudes, beliefs, emotions, values, social norms, or cultural elements that prevent change and allow a harm to continue

# Tarana Burke's "Me Too" Movement

The Me Too movement was founded in 2006 by activist Tarana Burke and launched onto the national stage again nearly a decade later.[21] After multiple women reported that they had been sexually assaulted or harassed by film producer Harvey Weinstein, actress Alyssa Milano asked others to help demonstrate the significance of the problem for women everywhere.[22] Milano tweeted: "If all women who have been sexually harassed or assaulted wrote 'Me too' as a status, we might give people a sense of the magnitude of the problem." The #MeToo hashtag exploded on social media, and the larger Me Too movement to increase awareness about sexual violence generated thousands of articles, over a thousand new web pages, and more than thirty-two million tweets—testimony for the significant harms that sexual harassment and assault cause for millions of people worldwide.[23]

Following this wave of personal testimonies, Tarana Burke presented a TED talk entitled "Me Too Is a Movement, Not a Moment."[24] She emphasized both the quantitative and qualitative significance of the problem. She said that Me Too "is a movement about the one in four girls and the one in six boys who are sexually assaulted every year and carry those wounds into adulthood." She added startling and gut-wrenching statistics about the sexual assault and harassment of Indigenous

## 3 Plan

Now that you've established the significant harms of the current policy and explained why those problems persist, you are ready to detail your proposed policy change. Clearly and concretely describe who should implement what policy. Identify the policy change agent by their role in the organization, and state specifically what policy change you are asking them to make. The "who" in your plan must be a true change agent. They need the power and authority to make the change in order for your plan to be effective. For example:

> The USDA should change its dietary guidelines to recommend no alcohol consumption, rather than one to two drinks a day. The USDA and US Department of Health should publicize the new recommendation and the science that supports it. That publicity should especially focus on reaching people in their early twenties.

women, trans women, people with disabilities, Black women, and low-wage workers. After powerfully articulating the scope and frequency of the problem, Burke also emphasized its severity by describing the long-term effects of sexual violence: "The violence is also the trauma that we hold after the act. Remember, trauma halts possibility. It serves to impede, stagnate, confuse, and kill. So our work rethinks how we deal with trauma." Ending with a message of hope, possibility, and belief in a better future, she urged her listeners to keep fighting to change public policy: "I can't stop, and I'm asking you not to stop either. We owe future generations a world free of sexual violence. I believe we can build that world." Tarana Burke explains that public policy isn't always something you can change all by yourself—sometimes

Tarana Burke describes how the Me Too movement is changing conversations about sexual assault and harassment in the workplace (5:26).

you need to start a movement of multiple voices saying, "Me Too."

To watch Burke's complete presentation, do a web search for: Burke Me Too movement TED. The video is approximately 16:16 in length.

For some policies, you may also want to detail how the policy would be funded and enforced. Proposals for universal health care in the United States often raise questions about funding. Arguments for limiting access to handguns are often met with questions of enforcement. In these cases, your policy change statement should include details that address these questions. These are not necessary for every policy change, but it helps to anticipate any questions about funding and enforcement that your audience might have. For example:

The changes to the guidelines and their publicity will create only a minor cost, easily covered by the existing communication budgets of the USDA and US Department of Health. Colleges, universities, youth groups, media outlets, and nonprofits can help spread the message and ensure it reaches young people. Of course, each person will still be free to make their own choice about drinking—this isn't a ban or restriction on alcohol. They

When the change agents you want to persuade might feel partially responsible for a problematic policy, you can use these strategies to minimize their defensive reactions:

1. **DEPERSONALIZE THE CAUSE.** Frame policies—not people—as the cause of the harm. For example, say: "This rule discriminates against..." instead of "This company discriminates against..." Or, say: "This protocol places an unfair burden on..." instead of "This committee places an unfair burden on..."

2. **DISTINGUISH OUTCOMES FROM INTENT.** Emphasize that the people involved in creating or enforcing the policy did not mean to cause any harm. For example: "When we implemented this rule, we didn't realize that..." Or: "Of course, when this protocol was developed, the goal wasn't to..."

3. **PRAISE POSITIVE VALUES.** Show that the harmful policy doesn't fit the change agent's values. For example: "Equality has always been an important part of our company's mission." Or: "This committee has actively worked to make its decisions as fair as possible."

4. **CALL FOR CHANGE.** Explain how the change that you're recommending will realign the policy with the change agent's values. For example: "By eliminating this rule, we can reaffirm our commitment to..." Or: "By revising this protocol, you can make it easier for everyone to..."

would simply have more accurate information and recommendations to inform their choices.

## 4 Solution

The final part of a complete policy argument is demonstrating that the solution will work. To demonstrate that your plan will solve the problem, provide evidence that implementing your plan can overcome the problem's existing causes and reduce its significant harms. Show how your plan solves the problem.

Providing a solution does not always mean that a problem goes away entirely. Simply reducing the significance of the harms may justify your policy change. But just as the harms have to be significant enough to justify changing the policy, the solution must alleviate enough of the harms to make the policy change worthwhile. Your solution has to justify the degree of change you're asking for in your plan. If your plan calls for a big change, it should provide a bigger and better solution. If you're only asking for a minor amendment to a policy, even a small advantage might make the change worthwhile. For example:

> The new guidelines won't change everyone's behavior and they won't prevent every death and disability caused by alcohol consumption. But they will make a positive difference. Research by a team of experts at the University of Vermont has shown that when people hear about USDA recommendations, many change their behavior.[25] And since the early twenties is when most Americans establish their drinking behavior, if we focus on people that age, we have a real chance to make a positive difference.

## ✓ Critical Thinking Check

1. What are the differences between persuading about personal actions and persuading about institutional policies? Why might persuading someone to change an institutional policy also require you to persuade them to take personal action?
2. When you're persuading about policies, why is it important to demonstrate both the qualitative and quantitative significance of a harm? What would happen if you established the priority and severity of the harm without showing its scope or frequency? What if you described its scope and frequency without explaining its priority or severity?

# Next Steps

Now you know each step on the ladder of persuasion. You understand how to analyze the level of controversy in your speaking situation, and you have all the tools you need to persuade an audience about facts, values, actions, and policies. To start preparing your next persuasive presentation, try the Ladder of Persuasion Checklist, the Overturning Beliefs Worksheet, and the Identifying Change Agents Worksheet.

Persuasion is inherently challenging—it challenges audiences to change their attitudes, values, and behaviors, and it challenges speakers to engage controversial issues with people who disagree. But what if you want to affirm and celebrate your audience's attitudes, values, and behaviors, rather than changing them? What if your goal is to create a connection rather than engage a controversy? The next chapter will show you how.

# Standpoint Reflection

- Have you ever experienced a persuasive message that you found too controversial? How did you react? Have you ever experienced a persuasive message that you found completely uncontroversial? What was your reaction?

- Think back to the last time that someone persuaded you to change your attitudes, values, or behavior. How did they do it? What strategies convinced you to make the change?

- Do you have any ethical concerns about asking others to change their attitudes, values, or behavior? How can you use persuasion in ways that support your own standpoint and values?

- Which persuasive strategies fit best with your own standpoint and strengths? Do you recognize any strategies in this chapter that you already use? What new strategies are you excited to try?

---

## Key Terms

attitudinal causes, p. 391

change agent, p. 389

controversy, p. 374

criteria, p. 383

disagreement of fact, p. 375

disagreement of personal action, p. 376

disagreement of policy, p. 377

disagreement of value, p. 375

loss aversion, p. 386

Monroe's Motivated Sequence, p. 385

persuasion, p. 374

plausibility, p. 380

qualitative significance, p. 390

quantitative significance, p. 390

significant harms, p. 390

structural causes, p. 391

# Resources for Persuading and Motivating

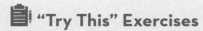 **"Try This" Exercises**

Access the "Try This" exercises as directed by your instructor or online at digital.wwnorton.com/chapterexercises-conpubspeak

- To gauge the level of controversy in your speaking situation, try the **Ladder of Persuasion Checklist**.

- To learn strategies for using your audience's existing attitudes, values, and behaviors to persuade them to change their minds, try the **Overturning Beliefs Worksheet**.

- To identify the right audience for your policy speech, try the **Identifying Change Agents Worksheet**.

 Want to practice these skills to prepare for your next speech? Go to **INQUIZITIVE** to review and apply concepts from this chapter and get personalized feedback along the way.

POET AND
ACTIVIST  Amanda Gorman

# 17 Connecting and Celebrating

Momentous events often call for grand speeches with carefully crafted language that inspires people and brings them together. Amanda Gorman, the first US National Youth Poet Laureate, is a master of these unifying speeches. She explains that poetry is a powerful form of public speech because it "has always been the language of bridges."[1]

Gorman's poems celebrate common values associated with American identity, like freedom, courage, justice, diversity, community, and resilience. For example, her 2021 presidential inauguration poem—"The Hill We Climb"—called for national harmony after a divisive election that led to an attack on the US Capitol.[2] At the end of her speech, she repeats the phrase "We will rise" to start four consecutive lines, calling the West, Northeast, Midwest, and South to rise together in unity.

Her poem at the 2021 Super Bowl—"Chorus of the Captains"—likewise focused on national healing.[3] The video tribute celebrates three people the National Football League named honorary captains for the game: a Marine veteran, an ICU nurse, and an educator chosen for their contributions as frontline workers during the COVID-19 pandemic. She praised these honorary captains for their "courage and compassion" and called her audience to follow their example. She used those common values—and collective pronouns like "we," "ours," and "us"—to create identification between herself, her honorees, and her audience. In doing so, Gorman helps us all "envision a way in which our country can still come together."[4]

## LEARNING OBJECTIVES

**After completing this chapter, you will be able to**

- Use sayings, quotations, and stories to celebrate your audience's values

- Understand and apply the five basic elements of connective presentations

- Adapt the core strategies of connective presentations for different occasions

- Use connective speaking to bond your audience together as a community

Our lives are marked by special occasions. We celebrate together, we mourn together, we meet new people, and we connect to one another. Often in these moments, we are called to make a speech—to introduce someone, to give or receive an award, to make a toast, or to remember those who have passed on. As Amanda Gorman shows, these special occasion speeches have the power to unite communities in moments of both joy and sorrow.

# Building a Connective Presentation

Speeches on special occasions make connecting a central part of their purpose. The speaker connects themselves to their audience, connects their audience members to each other, and connects both themselves and their audience to the subject of their speech. Your **subject** is the person, group, place, or event that your connective speech celebrates. The subject of a connective speech is often an individual—such as an award recipient or a person whose passing is being mourned—or a group of people—such as a couple at a wedding or a team in an organization. Connective speeches may also commemorate important events— like Juneteenth—or places—like the 9/11 Memorial.

**subject**
the person, group, place, or event that a connective speech celebrates

Speeches that seek to connect and celebrate go beyond informing audiences about a subject. Even though you will share details and stories about your subject, your goal is to link them to the values that you and your audience share. Unlike persuasive speeches, connective speeches affirm their audience's values rather than trying to change them. Shared values bring your audience together as members of a community, family, organization, or other group.

Connective speeches celebrate their subjects in order to bond a community together. While every connective presentation will be unique and tailored to its public speaking situation, most will need to contain five core elements to unify their audience (see Figure 17.1).[5]

## ▣ Introduction: Praise Your Audience's Values

The secret to a great speech of connection or celebration is focusing on your audience's sense of collective identity. Even when your speech appears to be celebrating an individual—like in an award speech or eulogy—your true goal is praising your audience and their shared values. For example, if you gave a speech honoring a soldier for their courage, you'd be praising more than just that one person: you'd be exalting the virtues of a wider community of military personnel and patriotic citizens who aspire to bravery.

Look for an overarching ideal that glorifies not only your subject, but also your audience and yourself. Consider the positive values that your subject demonstrates and identify which of those values are important to your audience members. Be sure the values you focus on suit your broader context and reason for speaking. Most importantly, choose values that you share with your audience. By connecting your subject's and audience's values to your own standpoint, you'll enhance your credibility.

Choose wisely: the rest of your presentation will depend on the power of these values to connect your subject, your audience, and your own strengths and standpoint as a speaker. To introduce these key values, open your speech with a saying, quotation, or story:

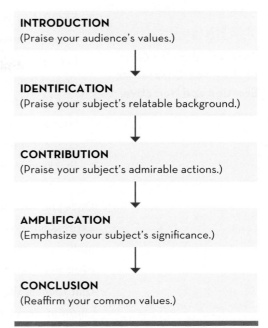

**INTRODUCTION**
(Praise your audience's values.)

**IDENTIFICATION**
(Praise your subject's relatable background.)

**CONTRIBUTION**
(Praise your subject's admirable actions.)

**AMPLIFICATION**
(Emphasize your subject's significance.)

**CONCLUSION**
(Reaffirm your common values.)

**FIGURE 17.1** Connective speeches use five key elements to celebrate their subject and unify their audience.

- **SAYINGS.** *A common saying can hook your audience with immediate recognition.* **Sayings** are short, pithy statements sharing folk wisdom or advice—like "great minds think alike" or "nothing ventured, nothing gained." The saying you choose should be one your audience will easily agree with and connect to their own high-priority values. You might even use a common saying developed by the group themselves: their motto, their mission statement, or a line from their anthem. For example, an American audience might respond to a reference to "the land of the free and the home of the brave."

  **sayings**
  short, pithy statements sharing folk wisdom or advice

- **QUOTATIONS.** You can also make an instant identification with your audience by opening with a quotation from a figure they admire. The quotation you choose should resonate with your audience's values and come from a person they identify with. You might quote a respected member of your audience, a founder of their organization, a leader in their community—or even the subject of your speech. For example, you might begin a connective speech to an interfaith organization by quoting a well-known religious leader: "The Dalai Lama once said, 'My religion is very simple. My religion is kindness.'"

**Pathways**

To review the elements of story, see **Chapter 10, Emotion and Narrative**.

- **STORIES.** When using a story, it should be short and simple: short enough to fit into your introduction, and simple enough to clearly express the value you want to emphasize. You could recount a memorable event in the group or organization's history, an anecdote about someone the audience admires, a well-known parable or fable, or any other story that illustrates values that are important to your audience. Sharing a personal story can be an especially meaningful way to connect your audience's values to your standpoint as a speaker—especially if that story explains your relationship to the subject of your speech.

Once you have shared your saying, quotation, or story, explain the value that it expresses, and connect that value to the subject of your presentation. Tell your audience what this value and this subject mean to you. Ideally, a speech of connection or celebration comes from someone with a personal reason for giving that speech. What aspect of your standpoint—experience, interest, passion, emotion, or relationship—is calling you to speak? Explain why the subject of the speech and the values they exemplify are meaningful to you as a speaker.

When you put these pieces together, you will have a strong introduction for a speech of connection and celebration:

1. **ATTENTION MATERIAL.** Connect to your audience's values with a saying, quotation, or story. For example: "Here at Chico State, our motto is 'Today decides tomorrow.' We know that our education today prepares us for all of our tomorrows."

2. **CREDIBILITY SUPPORT.** Connect those values to your own standpoint. For example: "For me, higher education is a goal that I once thought was out of reach. I never thought I would be at a ceremony like this today, looking forward to the tomorrow it promises."

3. **THESIS STATEMENT.** Connect your standpoint and values to your subject. For example: "That's why I am honored to introduce Tami Garza as our speaker today. Ms. Garza's tireless efforts have made higher education more accessible to countless students across our great state."

## 2 Identification: Praise Your Subject's Relatable Background

Next, provide some background about the subject of your speech. Your main goal in this section is to build identification between your subject and the public you are addressing. Consider what connects your audience together as a public in this speaking situation. Then use that shared identity as the basis for connecting them to your subject. This might include telling stories about your subject's upbringing, family background, education, place of origin, or past experiences. You might even discuss hardships they overcame that your audience also experienced, or behaviors your subject shares with the audience.

## Pathways

To review the principles of identification and contribution, see **Chapter 3, Ethics and Credibility**.

In this section, focus on details that help the audience see your subject as a member of their group—or at least as similar to themselves. This not only emphasizes your audience's connection with your subject, but also intensifies the connection the audience members share with each other. Focusing on relatable details both builds group identity and reduces any initial distance or unfamiliarity your audience might have with your subject. For example:

> Twenty years ago, Ms. Garza was right where you are today: getting ready to walk across this very stage to receive her bachelor's degree in education. Like me—and like so many of us—she was the first member of her family to receive a college degree. She depended on our school's financial aid and academic support programs to achieve her dream of graduating.

## 3 Contribution: Praise Your Subject's Admirable Actions

Now that you've created identification between your audience and your subject, demonstrate your subject's contribution by describing admirable acts. If your subject is a person, focus on praiseworthy actions that they themselves have taken. If your subject is an event—like the first American Constitutional Convention or your baby's first steps—or a place—like the Vietnam War Memorial or your high school gymnasium—focus on praiseworthy actions that your subject inspired, made possible, or commemorated. Either way, emphasize the specific accomplishments, achievements, and behaviors that illustrate your subject's connection to the values you praised in the beginning of your speech. Focus on events that elevate your subject, raising them up to be admired by the audience.

These events should not only reflect the audience's values, but also connect with the audience's ideal self. While the previous section showed how the subject is similar to the audience, this section shows that the subject is the kind of person the audience strives to be. Describe their actions as specifically and concretely as possible. Don't just tell your audience that your subject's actions are admirable—show them. For example:

> After graduation, Ms. Garza worked in our state's Department of Education, where she championed initiatives like the single application system, making it possible to apply to all our state schools with a single form and fee. She worked with legislators and the governor to keep college costs down and increase access for students living in remote areas. She created the College Pathways Foundation, which has been helping first-generation students get into college and find the support they need to succeed for over ten years.

## 4 Amplification: Emphasize Your Subject's Significance

Once you've described the relatable background and impressive actions of your subject, it's time to show your audience just how significant your subject's contribution is. Of course, it helps if you personally admire your subject—that way, you can connect them to your own interests, values, and passions. When your

We sometimes make connective speeches to mark a holiday or anniversary. Here, activist, author, and lawyer Dr. Shola Mos-Shogbamimu speaks at a 2018 event celebrating International Women's Day and the centennial anniversary of women gaining the right to vote in the United Kingdom.

subject's contributions are meaningful to you, it's easier to communicate their significance to your audience.

Remember that your audience will judge the significance of your subject's contribution in relation to their own values—especially the values most relevant to your speaking situation. The context and purpose of your presentation may make some of your audience's values and some of your subject's actions more important to highlight. You can amplify the significance of your subject's contributions by using comparison and climax.

## Comparison

You can emphasize the significance of your subject's contributions by comparing them to other people or groups that your audience admires. By putting your subject's contributions alongside the contributions of other noteworthy figures, you lift your subject up to their level. Choose your point of comparison carefully: choose figures who are impressive enough that they elevate your subject's status, but not so impressive that they make your subject look small by comparison. For example:

> Sixty years ago, Dorothy Donahoe's advocacy led to the creation of our state university and community college systems to guarantee the people of California broader access to higher education. Today, Tami Garza continues her mission, working to ensure that every student in California has the chance to pursue a college degree.

## Climax

You can also amplify your subject's significance with a climax that builds from good, to great, to greatest acts. A **climax** arranges a series of words or phrases in order of increasing importance. Start with one significant admirable act, then introduce a second more significant act, and then a third act that's even more significant. Combining that strategy with a repeated structure can help build the emotional impact of the climax. For example:

**climax**
arranging a series of words or phrases in order of increasing importance

> Ms. Garza not only made it easier to apply to college, but made those applications more affordable. She not only reduced the cost of college, but expanded access to students throughout our state. She not only served our state proudly in the Department of Education, but created a foundation that has helped tens of thousands of students every year realize their dream of becoming a college graduate.

## 5 Conclusion: Reaffirm Your Common Values

**callback**
revisiting your opening lines in your final words

Conclude your speech by reaffirming the common values that connect you, your audience, and your subject. First, cue the ending of your speech by revisiting your opening lines—this is known as a **callback**. Whatever saying, quotation, or story you used initially to introduce the audience's values, return to it now. Then, review your subject's relatable background and admirable acts, explicitly connecting them to the values you praised in your introduction. Finally, invite your audience to join you in celebrating your subject—giving a round of applause, raising a glass, or observing a moment of silence. For example:

1. **CUE THE ENDING.** Make a callback to the opening saying, quotation, or story. For example: "Yes, Ms. Garza knows that today decides tomorrow."

2. **REVIEW.** Connect the callback to your subject's background, acts, and contributions: "Twenty years ago she stood here, just as we do now, and dreamed of her tomorrows. In pursuing her dreams, she made today possible for many of us. She gave us the power to make better and brighter tomorrows for ourselves, our families, and our communities."

3. **TAKEAWAY.** Invite your audience to celebrate together: "Please join me in a round of applause to welcome Ms. Garza to the stage!"

## THE BASIC STRUCTURE OF CONNECTIVE SPEECHES

## Pathways

To review strategies for identifying main points and crafting effective introductions and conclusions, see **Chapter 9, Organization and Outlining**.

These five elements form the core structure of a speech of connection or celebration. This model works for the vast majority of connective speeches, whether they be speeches of introduction, award speeches, eulogies, or toasts. In longer connective speeches, you might extend the body into additional main points; in shorter speeches, you may combine some elements together. Remember to let your speaking situation be your guide. This five-part structure is a time-tested approach—but if your audience, your purpose, your context, or your own standpoint calls for a different structure or strategies, don't hesitate to adapt this basic outline to your speaking situation.

I. Introduction: Praise audience values.

    A. Attention material: Affirm audience values with a saying, quotation, or story.

B.  Credibility support: Connect audience values to your standpoint.

C.  Thesis statement: Connect audience values to your subject.

II.  Identification: Describe relatable aspects of your subject's background that connect to audience experience.

III.  Contribution: Describe admirable actions to illustrate the subject's commitment to audience values.

IV.  Amplification: Emphasize the significance of the subject's contributions to the audience and their values.

V.  Conclusion: Reaffirm common values.

A.  Cue the ending: Call back to the introductory saying, quotation, or story to emphasize your subject's value.

B.  Review main points: Link the value from your callback to the subject's relatable background, admirable actions, and significant contributions.

C.  Takeaway: Invite the audience to celebrate together by toasting, applauding, or observing a moment of silence.

## ✓ Critical Thinking Check

1.  Why is it important to praise your audience's values in a connective speech? What's the problem with focusing solely on celebrating your subject, without any attention to your audience's values?

2.  What function do each of the five basic elements serve in a connective speech? How do each of these five elements help you unify your audience?

# Occasions for Connecting and Celebrating

While the basic structure of connective speeches can help you develop all sorts of connective speeches, it's important to adapt this basic structure for the specific type of occasion you're celebrating. In public speaking, an **occasion** is a specialized context that defines your purpose. In other words, an occasion is an event that gives you a specific reason for speaking. Occasions for connecting and

**occasion**
a specialized context that defines your purpose

celebrating include speeches of introduction, award speeches, toasts, and eulogies. Each of these occasions comes with its own challenges and opportunities—which call for different strategies.

## SPEECHES OF INTRODUCTION

**speeches of introduction** presentations that connect an audience to someone they do not yet know or enhance an existing connection with someone they do know

**Speeches of introduction** either connect an audience to someone they do not yet know or enhance an existing connection with someone they do know. Sometimes you may be introducing yourself to a group unfamiliar with you. Other times, you may be introducing someone else—perhaps as a guest or speaker.

### Introducing Yourself

Speeches of self-introduction are the most common yet most overlooked kind of connective presentation. When we meet a new group of people, we are often asked to introduce ourselves. For example, you might give a quick self-introduction at the beginning of a job interview, on the first day of a new class, or the first time you attend a meeting of a club or organization. Whether you will formally present to the group or introduce yourself more informally, the elements and structure of a self-introduction are the same.

The challenge of self-introductions is describing and amplifying your own credibility without coming across as bragging or valorizing yourself. The trick is to talk about yourself while focusing on the virtues of your audience. Open with what you hope to learn from them, what you admire about them, or why you are excited to meet them. Describe what you hope to contribute to the admirable acts of the group you are meeting.

Your goal is to create identification based on your shared values and commitments. Sometimes, this means positioning yourself as a member or aspiring member of the group. In other cases, it means positioning yourself as a supporter or ally of the group's admirable contributions. Amplify their work and commitment to those values, and emphasize your commitment to contributing to or supporting those values. Close with an expression of gratitude for meeting this group and recommitment to the values you praised in the opening.

I.  Values: "Thank you all for this opportunity to meet you. Your commitment to socially responsible innovation has inspired me, and I have admired your amazing work for some time."

📋 **TRY THIS**

To master the type of connective speech that you will give most often, try the **Self-Introduction Worksheet.**

II. Background: "My name is Pat Gehrke, and I'm a professor of communication. For the past twenty-five years, my work has focused on communication ethics and the relationship between public communication and emerging technologies."

III. Actions: "I am thrilled to have the chance to work with you on transformative projects like your rural broadband expansion initiative and your digital citizens project."

US Navy Second Class Petty Officer Gabriela Sealy introduces herself at the Military Ambassador Reception in San Antonio, Texas.

IV. Significance: "I hope my expertise and experience in communication education, technology, and public engagement can add to projects like these, where you have used new technologies and public education to strengthen local democracy and improve the lives of thousands of people."

V. Values: "I am looking forward to working with you, learning from you, and being a part of promoting socially responsible innovation."

**Introducing Others**  You will have more freedom to sing the praises of your subject when you're introducing someone other than yourself. But speeches introducing others still need to flatter your audience and connect their values to your subject. Unlike introducing yourself—where you are the subject of your speech—introducing others requires you to connect your subject to your standpoint more explicitly.

Remember the three key questions for determining your exigence: Why you, why them, and why now? Explain why you are introducing this person to your audience on this occasion. As always, begin by praising the audience's values, especially as they relate to the person you are introducing and the reason you are introducing them. Explain why you are the right person to make the introduction. Even if the speech has been assigned to you, find a way to connect your subject to your own experiences, values, passions, or identity. Next, boost your subject's credibility with identification and contribution. Describe the aspects of their background that are most relatable to your audience and relevant to your context. As you describe and amplify that person's admirable acts, focus on your audience's values.

**Pathways**

To revisit the three questions for determining your speech's exigence, see **Chapter 6, Topic and Purpose**.

Outgoing White House Press Secretary Jen Psaki introduces incoming Press Secretary Karine Jean-Pierre—the first Black and openly LGBTQ+ person to hold the office.

Don't forget to personalize your remarks: include stories about the person, kind words others have said about them, or your own personal reflections or admiration for them. Give the introduction a personal feeling that introduces them as an individual, and not just a résumé or Wikipedia entry. Many speeches of introduction have been ruined by the speaker rattling off a list of achievements, awards, or accomplishments, without creating any identification between the speaker and the audience. This might impress your audience, but it is unlikely to make them feel connected to you, your subject, or each other.

I. Values: "When I first met our keynote speaker at a sales conference three years ago, I had no idea that I was talking to one of the world's top marketing experts. I was young and cocky, and I had a lot to say. Rowan listened to me, made me feel like a peer, and never let on that they had literally written the book on personalized marketing."

II. Background: "You probably know Rowan Kim as the author of the best seller *You Have to Listen First*. But they weren't always a famous marketing guru. They started small just like a lot of us, selling paper for a midsized company in Pennsylvania. There, they learned to create loyal clients and durable business relationships."

III. Actions: "Rowan realized that listening to their clients was what made them so successful. So they opened their own consulting firm to teach marketing teams how to sell more by talking less. In under three years, Rowan built a team of thirty consultants that's become one of the country's most sought-after personalized marketing firms."

IV. Significance: "It's rare that a field as old and large as marketing encounters a revolution. And it's even rarer to find a trailblazer who can teach others the secret of their success. But that's just what Rowan has done. Not only have they built their own business empire, but they have also taught us how to increase our business by creating lasting client relationships."

V. Values: "That's the power of listening. When you learn to listen like Rowan does, every encounter is an opportunity to build a relationship—even if you're talking to some cocky youngster who's just starting out. Maybe it's humility. Maybe it's strategy. But either way, we're honored and privileged to be listening to Rowan Kim today."

## AWARD SPEECHES

**Award speeches** include any remarks recognizing the achievements of an individual or group. Many awards are given during a ceremony or special event, where someone delivers a speech presenting the award to the recipient, and then the recipient of the award delivers an acceptance speech. Award speeches sometimes celebrate multiple recipients—for example, a graduation speech collectively honors all the students being awarded a diploma.

Awards are also presented informally in workplace meetings, academic organizations, and sports competitions. Sometimes, people will even spontaneously deliver or call for impromptu speeches when celebrating a victory or accomplishment. These can also be treated as award speeches. Whether formal or informal, rehearsed or unplanned, the same five elements of connective presentations apply to all award presentations—but with some important differences depending on whether you are giving or receiving the accolades.

### Presenting Awards

When presenting an award to someone else, your introduction should praise audience values related to the specific award being given. Awards are often created to express the values of a community—like the American Civil Liberties Union's Bill of Rights Awards—to reflect the values of an important figure—like the Elizabeth Blackwell Medal—or to encourage the development of certain values—like the Nobel Peace Prize or an Employee of the Month award. Even awards designed purely to recognize an achievement—like the Pulitzer Prize for Investigative Reporting or the Norton Speaker's Prize for outstanding public speaking students—celebrate the value of a particular field or endeavor.

When preparing to present an award, take some time to research its history, its mission or purpose, and what the award means to the group that gives it. If the award is named after someone—such as the Heisman Trophy in college football—it may help to know something of that person's background, acts, or values that are admired by your audience. Describing the meaning of the award both builds up the values of your audience and lays the groundwork for celebrating the recipient.

**award speeches**
remarks recognizing the achievements of an individual or group

📋 **TRY THIS**

To practice delivering connective speeches on the fly, try the **Impromptu Celebrations Activity**.

## Pathways

To revisit strategies for impromptu delivery, see **Chapter 12, Vocal and Physical Delivery**.

NASA Administrator Charles Bolden presents a special achievement award to mathematician and physicist Katherine Johnson, who calculated trajectories for John Glenn's first orbital flight in 1962.

## Pathways

To review the principles of audience analysis, see **Chapter 5, Audiences and Publics**.

When you're presenting background information about an award recipient, be aware that your audience may already know the highlights. Use your audience analysis to gauge what they already know and find new or surprising details to help increase their identification with your subject. When describing and amplifying the award recipient's contributions, emphasize those that reflect the values of the audience and the meaning or purpose of the award. Be as specific as possible when discussing the recipient's acts, providing personal praise for their contributions.

In your conclusion, explicitly connect the recipient's admirable acts to the audience's values and the meaning of the award. If you will be physically handing them the award, wait until the very end of your speech. In some circumstances, it can help to plan how and where you will hand the award to them, especially if the event is being photographed or recorded.

I.   Values: "The National Communication Association's Lambda Pi Eta Honor Society takes its name from three Greek letters. Each letter represents one of Aristotle's three pillars of persuasion: *lambda* for *logos*, or logic; *pi* for *pathos*, or emotion; and *eta* for *ethos*, credibility and ethics. Tonight, it is my honor to induct a new group of outstanding communication majors with all the intelligence, heart, and character that Lambda Pi Eta stands for."

II.  Background: "These students represent the best and the brightest from all across the country. This year's inductees come from fifteen different states, including several from our home state of Kansas."

III. Actions: "These amazing students have led book drives, youth mentoring programs, and green initiatives in our community. They've served our campus as honor council members, admissions ambassadors, and student government officers. They've all consistently made the dean's list, and some of our students have even presented original research at the Central States Communication Association's annual conference."

IV. Significance: "Not only do these students bring their many talents into the classroom and onto our campus, but they're also bringing their gifts out into the world."

V. Values: "Lambda. Pi. Eta. Intelligence, heart, character. These timeless principles are reflected in the academic and humanitarian achievements of every one of our new members. Let's give them all a well-deserved round of applause!"

**TRY THIS**

To submit one of your best speeches from this class for the Norton Speaking Prize, see the **Norton Speaking Prize Submission Guidelines**.

**Accepting Awards** Award recipients are sometimes told in advance that they will be asked to speak, and other times are asked to speak without warning. Sometimes the nominees for an award don't know who will receive it until the ceremony, in which case each nominee needs to be prepared. Even when the organizer tells the award recipient they will not need to speak, it's a good idea to have at least a few words prepared. Particularly in less formal settings or with less experienced presenters, plans can change spontaneously depending on the timing of the event and the mood of the audience.

If you've ever watched an awards show, you may have noticed that the best acceptance speeches do not focus on the speaker. Instead, the recipient uses their acceptance speech to praise others. The true subject of a successful acceptance speech is the audience and the community the award represents. Recipients praise the audience and the people who contributed to their accomplishments. They also express gratitude for the award, for the values and community it represents, and for the support that made their success possible.

As with giving an award, the values most relevant to your speaking situation might be found in the history and purpose of the award itself. Or, if your standpoint differs significantly from past award recipients, there might be a special significance to you receiving this award. Either way, consider your audience. How have you been inspired or supported by this community? How have their founders shaped your work and that of others? Your speech will have meaning for your audience if you praise their values in a way that is both personal to you and specific to them. When your acceptance speech is personal and specific, your praise, admiration, and gratitude will create a stronger sense of connection.

# Bong Joon-ho's Oscar Acceptance Speech

When Bong Joon-ho won the Academy Award for Best Director in 2020, he faced the challenge of creating identification with attendees and at-home viewers of the awards ceremony. As a South Korean filmmaker, he was addressing an audience that was primarily American and Western European. Over half of Oscar viewers are from the United States, with only about 1 percent tuning in from South Korea.[6] Although Bong had directed popular American films before, he was unknown to most US filmgoers—especially compared to some of the other nominees, like Quentin Tarantino and Martin Scorsese. Bong built identification by connecting himself with the other nominees and celebrating their shared values and achievements.

Speaking in a mix of South Korean and English, he opened with a quotation: "When I was young and studying cinema, there was a saying that I carved deep into my heart, 'The most personal is the most creative.'"[7] He then revealed that the saying was a quotation from "our great Martin Scorsese," earning Scorsese an immediate standing ovation from the attendees. Bong thanked Tarantino for promoting his films and helping him to find an audience in the United States, adding, "Quentin, I love you." After adding his admiration for the other two nominees—Sam Mendes and Todd Phillips—Bong joked that he wanted to split the Oscar statue into five pieces and share it with all of them. By lifting

During his Oscars acceptance speech Bong Joon-ho discusses the impact fellow nominee Martin Scorsese had on him as a film student (1:55).

others up rather than focusing on himself, Bong captured the hearts of viewers and the media. As one reporter put it, "Bong acknowledged his peers and idols in the audience, firmly establishing himself as part of a grand moviemaking tradition, country of origin be damned."[8]

To watch Bong Joon-ho's full speech, do a web search for: Bong Joon-Ho wins Best Director. The video is approximately 4:28 in length. Bong's speech begins at 1:35 and runs approximately 2:50 in length.

I. Values: "I'll never forget what Coach said to us when we lost our first game of the season: 'Learn to love the loss.' Loving the loss taught me to love the game, win or lose. It taught me to grow from my mistakes and stand by my team no matter what."

II. Background: "When I was recruited to play for Memphis, I was honored but also intimidated. Ever since Win Wilfong and Forest Arnold in the 1950s, Tigers basketball has been home to great players who are also good people. I knew Memphis would be a place where I could learn and grow, where I would work with players and coaches who love the game with all its highs and lows."

III. Actions: "I remember my first week, Jamirah and Lanyce working with me on side shuffle drills and building up my confidence. Every game I've been surrounded by players who always have my back and love being on the court just as much as I do. Even when things weren't going our way, I'd see Jada, Hannah, Serena, Tanyuel, and everybody, just living and breathing the game."

IV. Significance: "I'm humbled to receive our team's Most Valuable Player award because I know our performance on the court comes from what every player gives every game: Emani with the wild steals, Lanetta grabbing the rebounds, and Madison sinking those fadeaway three-pointers. And of course, there's Coach: always pushing us, guiding us, and loving the game just as much as we do."

V. Values: "So I've learned to love the loss. I've learned to love the win. But mostly, I've learned to love this team. I feel your love on the court every single day. Thank you."

## TOASTS

A **toast** is a short tribute to someone or something that traditionally ends with a celebratory drink. Speakers give toasts at parties, dinners, and receptions of all kinds. Toasts also happen in contexts where the audience is not drinking, but still wishes to recognize a person, event, or accomplishment together. In these cases, the drink is often replaced with a round of applause, but the structure and purpose of the toast remain the same.

Toasts are brief, usually less than a minute. Even formal, ceremonial toasts are best kept to no more than three minutes. They should contain only positive,

**toast**
a short tribute to someone or something that traditionally ends with a celebratory drink

Toasts are commonly given by the honor attendants at a wedding—such as a best man, maid of honor, or nonbinary best friend.

heartfelt sentiments that honor the audience and subject of your speech. Embarrassing stories, crass jokes, or sexual innuendos that humiliate or shame your subject or your audience will almost always fail. Even a humorous toast must be a genuine celebration that includes everyone. Remember: your job is to reinforce identification and build community between yourself, your subject, and your audience.

Toasts are especially common at weddings. While norms for wedding toasts vary from culture to culture, they often include elements of introduction. Some guests might not know one of the people getting married, and some might not know you. Wedding toasts require you to introduce each person getting married, explain your connection to the couple, and connect both of them to an audience that may have never gathered together before.

Start with the partner you know best, providing background, describing admirable qualities, and amplifying their significance. Then turn to the other partner and do likewise. Conclude by praising the couple together and invite your audience to join you in wishing them a bright future.

I. Values: "Thank you all for being here today to celebrate the fearless hearts of my best friend, Maria, and her wonderful new husband, Kai. They are living proof that love conquers all."

II. First subject.

   A. Background: "Maria has been a force of nature for as long as I can remember. She was always the first one to climb a tree or pop a wheelie on her bike. Once, Mr. and Mrs. Rivera even had to stop us from jumping off the roof in our Wonder Woman capes."

   B. Actions: "Today, Maria is a real-life wonder woman, working as a medic for Doctors Without Borders. She has gone into countries torn apart by war and natural disasters, risking her life to save the lives of others."

## SPEAK OUT

When you are unable to attend an event in person—or when you are attending an event with a videographer—you can use these steps to deliver a quick but compelling video tribute:

1. GREET YOUR AUDIENCE. For example: "Hey, sports fans!" or "Hello, Portland!" If the subject or subjects of your speech will be in your audience, address your greeting directly to them. For example: "Hi, Jackie and Etta!" or "Hello, class of 2023!"

2. INDICATE WHERE YOU ARE SPEAKING FROM. If you are being recorded live at an event, praise the occasion. For example: "I'm here at your wonderful wedding, and..." If you were unable to attend the event, offer your regrets. For example: "I'm sorry I couldn't be there today, but I didn't want to miss this chance to say that..."

3. CELEBRATE YOUR SUBJECT WITH VALUES THAT ARE IMPORTANT TO YOU AND YOUR AUDIENCE. For example: "I can see the love shining in your eyes every time you look at each other." Or: "This is one of the brightest and most promising groups of students I have ever had the pleasure to teach."

4. CLOSE WITH A SIMPLE SEND-OFF THAT EXPRESSES EMOTION. For example: "Wishing you both many happy years together!" Or: "I am so proud of you all. Congratulations!"

 

III. Second subject.

    A. Background: "I never thought she'd meet her match. But when she told me that Kai took her bungee jumping on their first date, I knew Maria had finally found someone with the same unshakable spirit that she has."

    B. Actions: "Kai has been an unfailing advocate for the third-grade students that he teaches. He leads after-school programs for low-income students, and he even started an anti-bullying campaign for kids with special needs."

IV. Significance: "Maria and Kai are both forces of nature in their own right. But together, they are unstoppable. They not only inspire each other to dream bigger, but inspire us all to follow our biggest and boldest dreams."

V. Values: "Love really does conquer all. So let's raise our glasses to Maria and Kai, as they go out to conquer the world together."

# Oprah Winfrey's Celebration of Rosa Parks

When civil rights hero Rosa Parks died in 2005, political activists, religious leaders, and other dignitaries gathered with Parks's family and friends at the Metropolitan AME Church in Washington, DC, to mourn her passing and celebrate her many contributions to the US civil rights movement—including her landmark 1955 refusal to give up her seat to a white man on an Alabama bus, a courageous act of resistance that inspired the Montgomery Bus Boycott. Media icon Oprah Winfrey delivered a speech of celebration that was notable for the ways it created a personal, emotional connection between Parks's legacy and Winfrey's own standpoint as a speaker.[9]

Winfrey opens with a personal story from her childhood, recalling the time her father first told her the story of Rosa Parks: "In my child's mind, I thought, 'She must be *really* big.' I thought she must be at least a hundred feet tall. I imagined her being stalwart and strong and carrying a shield to hold back the white folks." She then compares this legendary image to her experience meeting Rosa Parks as an adult: "Here was this petite, almost delicate lady who was the personification of grace and goodness."

Winfrey uses this contrast between Parks's small size and enormous bravery to illustrate the value of her contribution: "After our first meeting, I realized that God uses good people to do great things." Through this comparison, Winfrey simultaneously amplifies the value of Parks's contribution and creates audience identification with

## EULOGIES

**eulogy**
a speech of praise given after someone's death

How we respond to the passing of a loved one is deeply personal. It differs widely not only across cultures, but even across families and social groups. The word **eulogy** literally means "good words," and usually refers to a speech of praise given after someone's death. Eulogies are most commonly given either at a funeral service or at a reception before or after the service. Not all religions include eulogies as part of a funeral, and the norms for eulogies differ across the cultures and religions that do include them. Sometimes, eulogies are given at public ceremonies or memorials to praise a deceased individual or group who received significant recognition and admiration from a larger community.

her—great things are possible for any good person, however small they might seem. Then, Winfrey further amplifies Parks's contribution with a climax:

> I thank you again, Sister Rosa, for not only confronting the one white man whose seat you took, not only confronting the bus driver, not only for confronting the law, but for confronting history, a history that for 400 years said that you were not even worthy of a glance, certainly no consideration. I thank you for not moving.

Winfrey closes with a callback that repeats the civil rights protest slogan, "We shall not be moved." But in her final line, Winfrey personalizes

In her 2005 eulogy for Rosa Parks, Oprah Winfrey describes her experience meeting the civil rights leader for the first time (1:40:33).

that slogan: "I shall not be moved." By personally connecting and dedicating herself to continuing Rosa Parks's legacy, Winfrey invites her audience to do the same.

To watch Winfrey's complete eulogy, do a web search for: CSPAN Rosa Parks Memorial Service. The video is approximately 2:56:28 in length. Winfrey's speech begins at 1:38:45 and runs approximately 4:15 in length.

Eulogies are even given as commemorative speeches marking the anniversary of someone's passing, particularly for celebrated public figures.

Eulogies are not for the deceased. They are for the living who gather to mourn a loss, celebrate someone's life, connect with one another, and begin to heal their grief. Your first concern when preparing a eulogy should be for those most deeply affected by the loss, which may include yourself. If you expect that you will be unable to speak or that speaking will be too painful for you, talk with the organizer of the ceremony and those close to you about having someone else speak on your behalf. You may need time to process the loss before you can speak about it.

If you will give a eulogy, talk with the funeral organizers and those who have been most affected by the loss about their feelings, hopes, and expectations for the ceremony. As the meaning "good words" implies, this is a time to speak of the positive qualities of the deceased and provide words of love and healing. If your own relationship to the deceased or the audience does not offer you a way to authentically focus on good words, either simply decline the invitation to speak, or ask the funeral organizer and those closest to the deceased to see if someone else could speak in your place.

Natalie Hixon gives a eulogy for her brother Chris Hixon, who died in the Parkland school shooting, during a rededication ceremony at the National Fallen Educators Memorial.

You can use the basic elements of connective speeches to celebrate the life of someone who has passed. Open by praising a core value of the audience you believe was personified by the deceased. If audience members may not know who you are, explain your relationship to the deceased and express gratitude for that relationship. When describing admirable acts or qualities of the deceased, use true stories or anecdotes to evidence those qualities. Ideally, choose stories that include other members of the audience and evoke positive emotions for them, like appreciation, happiness, affection, pride, and belonging.

When amplifying the value of those acts or qualities, keep it personal and specific to both the deceased and your audience. National events, broad social issues, and other less personal topics should be included in a eulogy only when they were of special importance to the deceased and are meaningful to your audience. Connect the mourners together with inclusive "we" and "us" language that encourages everyone to remember the deceased and acknowledge their loss.

I.   Values: "'How can there be a story that has no end?' That's a line from one of Grandma Margie's favorite lullabies, 'The Riddle Song.'"[10]

II.  Background: "When someone's story ends, it's easy to feel like their time with us was too short. I didn't get to spend much time with my grandma when I was little because we lived several states away. But one summer when I was seven or eight, I got to go visit her while my parents were on vacation."

III. Actions: "As a little kid in an unfamiliar place, I had a hard time getting to sleep. Grandma sat down with me by the bed, stroking my hair and singing that lullaby to me for hours until I fell asleep."

IV. Significance: "All my life, anytime I've had trouble sleeping, I just close my eyes and remember her singing me that song. Memories of deep love like that stay with us forever."

V. Values: "It's like the song says: 'The story of I love you, it has no end.'" So I invite you all to take some time now and remember a special moment that you shared with Margie Franklin, a memory that you'll always hold in your heart."

**TRY THIS**

To modify the basic structure of connective speeches to fit different contexts and purposes, try the **Occasion Adaptation Checklist**.

## ✓ Critical Thinking Check

1. What special challenges do you face in self-introductions and award acceptances where you are the subject of your own speech? What strategies can you use to overcome those challenges?

2. How is a connective speech celebrating a couple different from a speech celebrating an individual? How is celebrating an individual or couple different from celebrating a group? What would you do differently when praising one, two, or multiple subjects?

# Next Steps

Now that you know the basic structure of connective speeches and how to adapt it for different occasions, you're ready to begin preparing and practicing your next celebratory speech. To get started, try the Self-Introduction Worksheet, the Impromptu Celebrations Activity, and the Occasion Adaptation Checklist. They'll help you modify your speeches to fit a variety of contexts and purposes, so you can bring people together in any situation.

But your audience isn't the only group you can bring together with public speaking. Speakers often make presentations in groups and teams—from classrooms and workplaces to podcasts and live video meetings. The next chapter will show you how to take advantage of group synergies—and manage group conflict—to make the most of your team presentations.

# Standpoint Reflection

- Why is it important to connect your own standpoint to the subject of your speech? What would happen if you gave a speech of connection and celebration that did not connect to your own standpoint?

- How is establishing the audience's identification with your subject the same as or different from establishing identification between your audience and yourself? How is establishing your subject's contribution to the audience the same as or different from establishing your own contribution?

- How comfortable are you with occasions—like self-introductions and award acceptances—that call for you to celebrate yourself? What strategies might help you sing your own praises without alienating your audience?

- What are some of the best and worst toasts, eulogies, introductions, and award speeches you have experienced—whether in person, in the news, or on film? What can you learn from their successes and mistakes?

## Key Terms

# Resources for Connecting and Celebrating

## 📋 "Try This" Exercises

Access the "Try This" exercises as directed by your instructor or online at
digital.wwnorton.com/chapterexercises-conpubspeak

- To master the type of connective speech that you will give most often, try the **Self-Introduction Worksheet**.

- To practice delivering connective speeches on the fly, try the **Impromptu Celebrations Activity**.

- To submit one of your best speeches from this class for the Norton Speaking Prize, see the **Norton Speaking Prize Submission Guidelines**.

- To modify the basic structure of connective speeches to fit different contexts and purposes, try the **Occasion Adaptation Checklist**.

---

**Want to practice these skills to prepare for your next speech? Go to INQUIZITIVE to review and apply concepts from this chapter and get personalized feedback along the way.**

IMMIGRATION ACTIVISTS
AND ORGANIZERS

Lights for Liberty

# 18 Group Meetings and Presentations

On July 12, 2019, Lights for Liberty held vigils in over seven hundred cities to protest US immigration and detention policies.[1] Each event featured speakers from a diverse range of standpoints and drew hundreds—sometimes thousands—of attendees.[2] Lights for Liberty started by recruiting activists from around the country, offering them press releases, graphics, posters, and promotional videos to facilitate events in their towns.[3]

The local organizers then formed their own small groups to plan events. In Atlanta, Georgia, the New Sanctuary Movement joined with local faith organizations, activists, immigration lawyers, and politicians to create a presentation that included more than a dozen speakers.[4] By the day of the event, over six hundred people had committed to attend, and the speakers were practiced and ready. The organizers set up a podium with a microphone and seating for those who needed it. They printed handouts that included the list of speakers, where to go for immigration assistance, and how to contact elected representatives.[5]

One of the event organizers served as the emcee, making introductory remarks, handling transitions between speakers, and emphasizing their shared mission. When it began to rain, the emcee and others held up umbrellas and signs to shield speakers from the downpour. Despite the rain, hundreds cheered and chanted as the speakers expressed their opposition to US immigration policy.

While they protested in Atlanta, thousands more were protesting across the country. Each Lights for Liberty rally was the result of hard work by small teams of organizers and speakers who shared a common purpose.

## LEARNING OBJECTIVES

**After completing this chapter, you will be able to**

- Identify and perform group leadership skills

- Prepare and deliver group presentations

- Facilitate and reach effective decisions in group meetings

- Mediate group conflict with listening and boundary setting

Although we commonly think of public speaking as something an individual does alone, teams of people are often involved in the preparation and delivery of public presentations. Groups present together in school, at work, and at public events, with each member contributing their unique standpoint and strengths to the project. As the Lights for Liberty protests show, uniting to serve a common purpose not only makes your message more powerful, but also gives you the support you need to make a difference. There's no need to dread group presentations—when you know how to share leadership, make decisions, and resolve conflict as a team, your voices become stronger together.

# Sharing Group Leadership

## Pathways

To revisit your strengths inventory and share it with your teammates, see **Chapter 1, Your Standpoint and Strengths**.

Working in a group has significant advantages over working alone. Group presentations let you both play to your own strengths and benefit from the strengths of your collaborators. You can divide work among your group members to highlight each person's talents and reduce the load on everybody. Because working in groups gives you input from multiple people with different standpoints, it often leads to richer ideas and more creative solutions that make your message more powerful.

Each group member's unique standpoint and strengths will help them shine in particular roles. For example, if you have a group member who's been personally affected by your topic, they might share their experience as testimonial evidence.

If you have a group member with a background in graphic design, they might focus on developing your slide deck. When you're divvying up tasks, consider the unique experiences, knowledge, passions, and values of each of your group members.

Any role—from making decisions to supporting others—can be an opportunity to demonstrate leadership. **Leadership** is the ability to contribute to a group and guide them toward their shared goal. Leadership comes from an individual's credibility within a group. Remember that credibility comes from a balance of identification and contribution. Genuine

Successful groups share leadership, with each member contributing their own unique strengths and skills.

leadership comes from group members seeing you as part of the team and offering a valuable contribution.

Leadership is not the same as formal authority. **Formal authority** is having a recognized position in an organization, like manager or president. Formal authority can grant power—like assigning tasks or deciding rewards and punishments—but it cannot grant you the credibility necessary for genuine leadership. If you've ever had a boss who didn't know what they were doing, you already understand the difference between credible leadership and formal authority.

A healthy group may or may not have someone in a position of formal authority, but it must contain multiple leaders helping to advance the group's goals. For example, in a group presentation for a class, someone might step up to organize meetings, another person might facilitate group discussion, and someone else might step in to mediate disagreements. To be successful, group members need both task leadership skills that help get the job done and social leadership skills that help the group feel like a cohesive team.[6]

## TASK LEADERSHIP SKILLS

To develop a presentation together, groups need members focused on planning, gathering information, and making decisions. **Task leadership** is helping group members take action to prepare and practice their presentation. Task leadership skills include organizing, contributing, and clarifying. All three types of task leadership are important for a group to function well. Which of these task leadership roles are the best match for your strengths?

- ■ **ORGANIZING.** Anytime you're planning a group presentation, you need someone to schedule meetings, set agendas, arrange for rooms or videoconference links, and make sure the group finishes its tasks on time. **Organizers** coordinate group tasks and activities. They handle the details of when, how, and where a group will collaborate and help group members combine their individual work on the presentation into a unified whole. When you're planning a group presentation, designating one or two members as your group's organizers can help everyone get things done with fewer headaches.

**leadership**
the ability to contribute to a group and guide them toward their shared goal

**formal authority**
holding a recognized position in an organization

**task leadership**
helping group members take action to prepare and practice their presentation

**organizers**
group members who coordinate group tasks and activities

## Pathways

To revisit the balance of identification and contribution that creates credibility, see **Chapter 3, Ethics and Credibility**.

**contributors**
group members who provide information, generate solutions, and take action on group tasks

**clarifiers**
group members who summarize contributions, refine ideas, and identify action steps

**social leadership**
creating and maintaining positive relationships between group members

**encouragers**
group members who ensure that all members of a group feel valued by recognizing people's contributions, raising people's spirits, and affirming the collective work of the group

■ **CONTRIBUTING.** In group presentations, every member should be a contributor. **Contributors** provide information, generate solutions, and take action on group tasks. Early on, discuss what each group member will contribute to the presentation based on their own unique strengths and skills. For example, a history major might provide background on an issue, a math major might ensure that you're representing statistical evidence accurately, and a theater major might coach the group on their delivery. Highlighting the special talents and perspectives of each group member will help your presentation stand out.

■ **CLARIFYING.** Without a clear understanding of each member's contributions, groups sometimes miss great ideas, postpone decisions, or fail to understand a challenge facing the group. **Clarifiers** summarize contributions, refine ideas, and identify action steps. To clarify another group member's point, you might rephrase, elaborate, or provide illustrations that help everyone better understand new information or next steps. Sometimes a group will nominate one member to take notes at a meeting, both to keep a record of everyone's contributions and make sure you're all on the same page at the end.

## SOCIAL LEADERSHIP SKILLS

In addition to task-related skills that focus on getting things done, team members also need social leadership skills that help their group feel connected and keep group members on good terms. **Social leadership** is creating and maintaining positive relationships between group members. Social leadership skills include encouraging, facilitating, and mediating interaction among your group members. Since every group experiences occasional social tension and stress, each of these skills is essential for a productive group. Which of these social leadership skills best fit your own strengths?

■ **ENCOURAGING.** Everyone needs a pep talk now and then. **Encouragers** ensure that all members of a group feel valued by recognizing their contributions, raising their spirits, and affirming their collective work as a group. To encourage your group, praise their skills and accomplishments—"Nice job with that introduction!"—and help them see their individual tasks and shared goals as achievable—"We've got a tight deadline, but we can do this." In a group presentation, you can encourage your team members anytime they

start or complete a task—but it's especially important to use this skill when you see a group member
struggling.

- **FACILITATING.** While some group members find
  it easy to offer their ideas and opinions, others may
  be more reticent. **Facilitators** promote group discussion and seek input from all members. Facilitators lead group brainstorming activities and guide
  collective decision-making processes. They notice
  when other group members are not speaking up
  and invite them to join in. Facilitators might even
  play devil's advocate, asking people to share
  unvoiced concerns and contrary opinions. While

A facilitator leads her group through a brainstorming process.

every member of your group can help facilitate discussion, choosing a designated facilitator can make your group meetings more inclusive and
productive.

- **MEDIATING.** While bringing together the unique strengths and standpoints
  of your group members can help you create a stronger presentation, your
  differences in perspective will inevitably lead to disagreements. **Mediators**
  resolve disagreements and conflicts to ensure that their group members feel
  like a team. The secret to mediating group conflict successfully is being able
  to recognize the difference between productive and disruptive conflict. Later
  in this chapter, we'll explain the difference between healthy disagreements
  and disruptive behaviors and give you strategies for navigating both. Engaging
  ideas and opinions different from your own may not always be easy, but it is
  the only way you can learn from other people.

**facilitators**
group members who
promote discussion
and seek input from all
members

**mediators**
group members who
resolve disagreements
and conflicts to ensure
that group members feel
like a team

## ✓ Critical Thinking Check

1. Why is it important to consider the unique standpoint and strengths
   of each of your group members before starting to plan a group
   presentation?
2. What's the difference between leadership and formal authority? Why do
   group members need to share leadership for a project to be successful?
3. Why do groups need both task and social leadership? What could go
   wrong in a group project without task leadership? What could go wrong
   without social leadership?

# Contributing to Group Presentations

There are many ways to combine the strengths and skills of different speakers into a unified group presentation. A group presentation can be structured as a single speech divided among team members, as a series of individual speeches on a shared topic, or as a discussion among speakers with different experience and expertise. If your format is not set by your instructor or event organizer, you can select the one that best fits your group's strengths and speaking situation:

- **TEAM PRESENTATIONS.** A single speech prepared and delivered by a group is called a **team presentation**. In team presentations, each group member takes responsibility for different parts of the preparation and delivery. Sometimes, each member of the group delivers the part of the presentation that they prepared; in other cases, one or two group members might present a speech prepared by a larger team. Team presentations are most effective when the group shares a common purpose and thesis—for example, when pitching a business strategy to a client or providing an analysis of options to a decision-maker. This format allows each member to work on the tasks that are most aligned with their own strengths. Presenting in teams requires significant collaboration and coordination at every stage of speech preparation and practice.

- **SYMPOSIUMS.** Sometimes, group members will share a common theme, but each will present their own separate, prepared presentations—like the speakers at the Lights for Liberty rally. A collection of speakers presenting individual speeches on a single topic or theme is called a **symposium**. This format allows every speaker to work individually and present from their own knowledge, experience, and standpoint. While team presentations require all members to share a purpose and thesis, symposium speakers often have their own specific purpose and thesis—and may even contradict or contest each other's claims. A symposium requires an organizer who can ensure that all the presentations are on topic and relevant to the audience.

- **PANEL DISCUSSIONS.** Some group presentations use a discussion format. A **panel discussion** is a moderated conversation between a group of speakers— whether in person or online. Panel discussions may include brief opening remarks from each speaker, but the majority of the time the panelists will be responding to questions from the moderator, the audience, and each other. As in a symposium, speakers in a panel discussion each have their own positions

**team presentation**
a single speech prepared and delivered by a group

**symposium**
a collection of speakers presenting individual speeches on a single topic or theme

**panel discussion**
a moderated conversation between a group of speakers

and may not share the same views. Panel discussions are excellent for providing diverse perspectives on a controversy or a range of experts on a complex issue. A good panel discussion relies on the careful selection of panelists for their expertise and willingness to engage in open dialogue. It requires a moderator who can adapt on the fly, draw out contributions from more reticent panelists, and rein in speakers who try to dominate the conversation.

The Congress for the New Urbanism holds a panel discussion on "Combating the Suburbanization of Poverty" in Seattle.

Of these three group speaking formats, team presentations are by far the most common in university courses—and the most challenging overall. Because team presentations require group members to work together to prepare, practice, and deliver a speech that accomplishes their shared purpose, they require more collaboration from each member. To create a team presentation, your group will need to work together to analyze your speaking situation, assign presentation tasks, organize your presentation, prepare your presentation, and practice your delivery.

## 1 Analyzing Your Speaking Situation

Since team presentations rely upon sharing the same purpose and having one consistent message, your group will need to begin by examining your speaking situation—just as you would for any speech. After establishing your group's norms for planning and decision-making, discuss how each of you views your purpose, your audience, your speaking context, and your individual strengths and standpoints. Conduct your audience analysis and strengths inventories together before settling on your group's common purpose. Much like the purpose of any speech, your **common purpose** is the impact you want your group presentation to have on the audience you address.

## 2 Assigning Presentation Tasks

Once you've analyzed your speaking situation, your group can then assign presentation tasks to each member. If you have not already shared your individual strengths inventories with each other, now is a good time to do so. From those, you can create a group strengths inventory, highlighting areas where the

**Pathways**

To revisit strategies for Q&A discussion, see **Chapter 4, Listening and Responding**.

**common purpose**
the impact you want your group presentation to have on the audience you address

**Pathways**

To review the process for developing your team presentation's purpose and thesis, see **Chapter 6, Topic and Purpose**.

📋 **TRY THIS**

To lead a discussion on the unique experiences, knowledge, values, and identities that each of your group members brings to the table, try the **Group Strengths Inventory Worksheet**.

standpoints, knowledge, experiences, and skills of each group member can best contribute to the group's shared purpose. Some members may have stronger research skills than others, some may have better organizational skills, and some may be better at creating presentation aids and media.

Likewise, different delivery styles and personas might fit different parts of your presentation. Speakers who are great at building audience interest, connecting, and establishing credibility might be especially strong delivering introductions and conclusions. Speakers who are masters at communicating detailed or technical information might be ideal for a specific section in the body of a presentation.

Workflow and timeline may also affect the division of tasks. If one team member cannot do as much work early in the process but will have more time later on, they might choose to work on your team's introduction, conclusion, or presentation aids, since those are developed after the main body of the presentation is complete. Create a project plan and timeline for each task and make sure every member knows the deadlines for their individual contributions. Plan ahead to leave ample time for group feedback and revisions.

### 3 Organizing the Presentation

Team presentations require coordinating the organization of the speech with the tasks and strengths of the team members. This may mean choosing an organizational pattern or even a number of main points that suit both the number of team members and their strengths. With three to six team members, you can often divide the organizational pattern so that one presents both the introduction and conclusion, while the others each present one main point of the body.

## Pathways

To review different organizational patterns, see **Chapter 9, Organization and Outlining**.

The introduction and conclusion speaker can focus on developing outstanding delivery, building interest, establishing credibility, reinforcing memory, and creating a memorable closing takeaway. While they might have less of a research burden, they carry the largest burden for the artistry and framing of the presentation. Having one speaker handle both the introduction and conclusion also provides a sense of wholeness to a team presentation. Then, each speaker responsible for a main point can focus on their own area of knowledge and research. If each speaker must present a main point, then usually one speaker handles the introduction and first main point, a different speaker handles the conclusion and last main point, and the remaining speakers each handle one of the interior main points.

Whatever organization you use for the presentation, only change speakers during major transitions in your speech—not in the middle of a main point. Each speaker can then conclude their portion of the presentation with an internal summary and a transition to the next main point that introduces the next speaker. For example:

> So now that we've seen the unmet need in the market and the customers actively looking for a new product, I'm going to turn things over to Sarah. She'll show you how, by simply modifying your marketing, you can meet those customers' needs with products you are already making.

Anytime you shift between speakers, a transition and introduction like this will pique the audience's interest and keep them engaged.

## 4 Preparing the Presentation

With presentation tasks assigned, the team can get to the business of preparing the presentation. At this stage, the group members may be working individually, in pairs, or as a full group. Everyone should know their task and the deadline for sharing their work with the group. If you have divided your team presentation into sections, each group member should know how much presentation time they have for their portion of the speech.

Since consistency and commitment to one shared purpose are key to team presentations, group members should share updates and ideas with the other members, even when working individually. A communication tool like Slack, Discord, or even a group text chain can facilitate quick and organized communication among team members. A file-sharing service like Dropbox or Google Drive can help team members organize and share research, work in progress, and completed work.

Plan meetings to share progress, discuss obstacles, and ensure consistency across the presentation. If multiple people are developing visual aids, you will want them to all follow the same style, including color scheme, fonts, sizing, and transitions. If you will be citing the same research, group members should coordinate how best to do that. The more everyone knows about what everyone else is doing, the more likely you will produce something that feels like one continuous and coordinated presentation.

# QPay's Team Shares the Spotlight

One of the most common types of team presentations is the business pitch. Marketing teams sometimes pitch strategies to clients, and business teams often pitch together to investors. By having team members pitch together, each can speak to their own strengths and knowledge and no one person has to represent every aspect of the business. The team that founded Australia's QPay app used precisely this strategy on the TV show *Shark Tank* to land a major investment and expand their company.[7]

The three presenters, each a member of the QPay team, took a portion of the presentation as their own. Moe Satti spoke first, handling the introduction and a brief first main point. He opened with "We're QPay, and we're here to change banking for millennials." He then stated their group purpose: the investment they were seeking. He finished up his part of the team presentation with a main point about the problems with the existing banking industry. Zakaria Bouguettaya, the second member of the team, then described the second main point: how QPay planned to revolutionize the banking industry and address unmet needs in their market. Then the third team member, Andrew Clapham, provided the third main point. He detailed the company's success and accomplishments so far, demonstrating its solid foundation and growth. Clapham then

## 5 Practicing the Presentation

Ideally, a group should have at least two team practice meetings. If you're lucky, your professor, manager, or event organizer will set aside practice time for you—but in many cases, groups may need to arrange their own time to practice. Before these meetings, each member should practice their portion of the presentation multiple times and be ready to deliver it within their scheduled time slot. Then, at each of the group practice meetings, the entire group should practice the full presentation at least twice.

## ▣ LEARN MORE

To learn more about how to present together as a group in an online format, see the **Online Group Presentation Video Series**.

Those rehearsals should include any presentation aids, software, tools, or technology that will be used in the actual presentation. If your group will be presenting in person, practice in the room where you will give the presentation. If that isn't possible, try to find a similar room or emulate that room in whatever space you have. If your group will be presenting online, hold your group practice sessions on the same online platform you will use to deliver your actual presentation.

delivered the conclusion, connecting back to Satti's initial point about the problems with the current banking industry.

Andrew Clapham, co-founder of QPay, explains how their business will transform the banking industry and provide young people better financial services (2:33).

The team accomplished all of this, with three speakers, in just two minutes. It was clearly a well-planned and practiced presentation. Yet, there was one significant oversight: the speakers never introduced themselves or their roles, only the company they represent. The first question they received when they finished was: "Who are you?" The second was: "So who's the boss?" Even with that omission, their impressive pitch and ability to answer investors' questions with compelling details led to two of the investors vying for a stake in the company.

To watch QPay's complete team presentation, do a web search for: Shark Tank Australia QPay Highest Earning Business. The video is approximately 12:32 in length.

In your first rehearsal, work out the details of coordination and troubleshoot any inconsistencies or issues in the presentation that need to be resolved. In that meeting, you will decide where each person will sit while others are speaking, how you will coordinate transitions between speakers, how to hand off any technology, and how to manage presentation aids.

If you are using presentation software like PowerPoint, your presentation will be smoother and more effective if all the speakers' slides are combined into one visually consistent slide deck. At the transition point between speakers, insert either a blank black slide or a title slide for the next speaker's section.

If you coordinate and practice together, you can have a team member who isn't speaking advance the slides for the one who is. A preparation outline with slide transitions clearly marked allows someone not speaking to follow along and advance slides with no cue or action from the speaker. Ideally, the person advancing the slides is not the person speaking next.

## Pathways

To review the principles for practicing your delivery and working with presentation technology, see **Chapter 12, Vocal and Physical Delivery**, **Chapter 13, Presentation Aids and Slides**, and **Chapter 14, Online and Mediated Presentations.**

**Pathways**

To review strategies for giving constructive peer feedback, see **Chapter 4, Listening and Responding**.

In live online group presentations, know how to set each group member as a host, administrator, or moderator so they can handle presentation aids when others are speaking. You may want one member to be responsible for most moderator duties, but someone else should handle those duties when that person is speaking.

After your first practice meeting, group members should give each other individual feedback for improvement and address any coordination issues between different parts of the presentation. Then use your second practice meeting to reinforce your memory and smooth out delivery for all the team members.

## ✓ Critical Thinking Check

1. Why do you think team presentations are the most common type of group presentation used in college courses? What advantages might there be to structuring your group presentation as a symposium or panel discussion instead?
2. How is developing a team presentation similar to developing an individual speech? How is it different?

# Organizing Group Meetings

When developing team presentations, groups often need to meet to make decisions, collaborate on tasks, and discuss challenges. Planning group meetings with your collective goals in mind will make them more enjoyable and more productive.

Group meetings should only occur when there is a clear social or task benefit to meeting. Meeting "just for the sake of meeting" interrupts the individual work of team members and communicates disrespect for others' time. If communication or decision-making can occur equally well without a meeting—for example, via email—then use those other means instead.

There may be group goals—such as social cohesion—that warrant a meeting, even though they are not directly related to a task. If you organize a meeting for purely social reasons, be explicit and clear about the purpose. Recognize that some members of your group may need convincing that meeting for social reasons is appropriate and valuable. When you plan a group meeting for social reasons, make sure that you are fulfilling the collective social goals of the group, rather than your own personal preferences.

When your group does need to meet, you'll get the most out of it if there is a clear plan for the meeting. Unplanned meetings often meander through topics, fail to reach decisions, and leave attendees confused about why they are meeting and how they should prepare. To plan a meeting, start with its role in your overall project plan. Then set clear goals for the meeting, create an agenda, and coordinate the details.

Teams organize meetings to discuss collective decisions and collaborate on group tasks.

## 1 Develop a Project Plan

Your first meeting with your group should lay out a plan for how you will complete your project together. A **project plan** is a document that maps out the steps and tasks required to complete your project. It should contain a timeline from your starting point to the completion of your group project. Break down the project into its major steps (see Table 18.1).

**project plan**
a document that maps out the steps and tasks required to complete your project

As you develop your project plan, you will find moments in your timeline when people will work individually and moments when they will need to collaborate or meet. Mark those meetings on your timeline as well. Set deadlines for each task on your timeline, divide the tasks between group members based on their strengths, and reserve future dates and times for any meetings needed to complete the project. All your future meetings will now have a scheduled day, time, and purpose.

## 2 Set Meeting Goals

Each meeting should have at least one specific goal. If you have created a project plan, then the initial goals of planned meetings will already be in that plan. However, as you work on your project, your group may discover additional challenges or opportunities that justify adding another goal to a planned meeting, or even adding another meeting to your plan.

Whoever is serving as the organizer for a meeting should reach out to all the other group members in advance, to share any goals already set for the meeting

| Dates | Main step | Group member(s) |
|---|---|---|
| April 3 | **MEETING:** Complete speaking situation analysis and decide common purpose. Each group member selects a specific research area and role in the presentation. Make project plan. | All |
| April 8 | Each group member shares their research on our topic and ideas for main points with the full group via email. | All |
| April 9 | **MEETING:** Group creates a rough presentation outline. | All |
| April 14 | Members creating main points of the body send first-draft outlines to full group via email. | Tonia, Lauri, Patrice |
| April 15 | Member creating slides sends a mockup of the slide format and templates to the group via email. | Theo |
| April 17 | **MEETING:** Each group member provides feedback on first-draft outlines and slide mockups. Discuss any needed revisions. | All |
| April 19 | Group member creating introduction and conclusion sends first draft to group for feedback via email. | Kim |
| April 20 | Members creating main points revise outlines and send them via email to the rest of the group. | Tonia, Lauri, Patrice |
| April 21 | **MEETING:** Review first-draft introduction and conclusion. Discuss any needed revisions. | All |
| April 23 | Drafts of all slides for the presentation sent to the group via email. | Theo |
| April 24 | Introduction and conclusion finalized and sent to the group via email. | Kim |
| April 25 | **MEETING:** Review drafts of slides. Discuss any needed revisions. Review the complete presentation for consistency. | All |
| April 27 | Slide deck finalized and sent to the group via email. | Theo |
| April 28–29 | Group members practice individually. | All |
| April 30 | **MEETING:** First round of group presentation practice | All |
| May 1 | **MEETING:** Second round of group presentation practice | All |
| May 2 | **FINAL PRESENTATION** | All |

**TABLE 18.1** Planning out the major steps in your project in advance can help ensure that you have enough time to coordinate your team's efforts and accomplish your shared goals.

📋 TRY THIS

For a step-by-step guide to creating your project plan, try the **Group Project Planning Worksheet**.

and ask if the team members want to add any additional meeting goals. Goals for a meeting might include reaching a group decision, finding a solution to a problem, sharing and discussing important information, and any other action needed to move the group forward on their project. If you do not have a goal for the meeting that supports the group project, then a meeting is probably not necessary.

## 3 Create a Meeting Agenda

Once you know the goals for the meeting, the next step is to create a meeting agenda. An **agenda** is a list of topics or tasks for a meeting, in the order they will be addressed. Your meeting agenda might contain items related to a particular step in your project timeline, and it might also include unexpected issues or challenges that have come up during your work on the project. An effective agenda communicates the specific goal or outcome needed for each agenda item. For example, rather than "discuss our slides," a better agenda item would be "make a plan for creating uniform and effective presentation slides."

**agenda**
a list of topics or tasks for a meeting, in the order they will be addressed

When putting items in order, first check whether any agenda items depend on having other issues settled or tasks completed. If so, you may need to reorganize the agenda or add items to ensure meeting goals are met. Otherwise, place the most important items first on the agenda to ensure they are given the most time and attention. At the end of every agenda, plan to summarize what the group accomplished that day and discuss the group's next steps forward.

Once your agenda is set, consider the time each agenda item will require, the total time you will need for the meeting, and the time you have scheduled. Set a time limit for each item to ensure you accomplish all your goals for the meeting. Agenda items usually take longer than expected, so allow for extra time. Once the agenda is complete, distribute it to all the group members—and any other meeting attendees—at least a couple days before the meeting. Here's a sample agenda for your first group meeting to get you started:

1. **BRIEF INTRODUCTIONS.** We each introduce ourselves to the group. (5 minutes)

2. **GROUP STRENGTHS INVENTORY.** Complete the Group Strengths Inventory Worksheet together. (15 minutes)

3. **GROUP DECISION-MAKING METHOD**. Discuss how the group will reach decisions and agree on the method we will use for this project. (5 minutes)

4. **SPEAKING SITUATION ANALYSIS**. Analyze our speaking situation together by reviewing the speech assignment and other elements of the situation. Create a list of the fixed factors in our situation and what we know about them. (15 minutes)

5. **COMMON PURPOSE**. Each group member suggests at least one potential shared purpose for our group presentation. Together, we discuss each idea's pros and cons, evaluate how well it fits our speaking situation, and decide on our presentation's topic and purpose. (20 minutes)

6. **PROJECT PLAN**. Break the presentation preparation down into major steps, schedule them on a timeline, and divide tasks between group members. Everyone receives a copy of this information. (20 minutes)

7. **NEXT STEPS**. Check that everyone understands our common purpose, knows their next task, and commits to a deadline. Set a date, time, and place for our next meeting. (5 minutes)

## 4 Coordinate Meeting Details

In addition to setting an agenda, someone will need to coordinate the details of the meeting: where and when people will meet. Sometimes this is done before the agenda is set, but as items are added to the agenda, the time you need may change.

Set the venue for your meeting before setting the day and time. The venue can affect group members' availability. If meeting online, you must decide on an agreeable platform; if in-person, find an agreeable location. When everyone knows where they will meet, they can better estimate their availability and travel time.

Online scheduling tools like Doodle are a great way to coordinate possible meeting times, but this can also be done via group text or email. Be sure to allow ample time for replies and coordination. Once the venue, day, and time are set, clearly communicate them to all group members and any other attendees.

▶ **LEARN MORE**

To learn more about how to use videoconferencing tools to conduct a group meeting, see the **Online Group Meetings Video Series**.

# Meeting Online, In Person, or Both?

Online meetings have significant advantages over in-person meetings, but also some shortcomings. Online meetings can be attended from any place with a decent internet connection and appropriate device. Platforms like Zoom, Teams, and Meet work on almost any smartphone and most computers. They allow greater flexibility in scheduling and reduce the transportation costs and time required by meetings. They also allow sharing of files, links, images, and screens to facilitate collaboration.

Some people are more comfortable and willing to contribute via video chat than in person. During the COVID-19 pandemic, many people who are introverted, socially anxious, on the autism spectrum, or suffering from post-traumatic stress found they thrived in online meetings compared with in-person meetings. But not everyone has access to reliable internet or an appropriate device. For those group members, video meetings may create an unreasonable burden. Video meetings also make open discussion and free-flowing communication more difficult for some people. In video meetings, people use more structured ways to take turns speaking and indicate their desire to speak. That can be a significant advantage for people who find more subtle or informal turn-taking difficult, but a disadvantage for others.

To best encourage everyone's participation, ask whether online or in-person meetings are more accessible for your group members. If your group members have different needs or preferences, try a hybrid format: let some group members gather in person, and set up a laptop or other device so the rest of your group can join the meeting via videoconference.

When your group members have different needs and preferences, a hybrid between in-person and online meetings can be a good solution.

# Making Group Decisions

When you're planning a presentation as a group, there are a lot of collective decisions to make, from how you will organize your presentation to how you will divide up tasks. To make good decisions, groups need to navigate the different ideas and perspectives of their members. On one hand, you need to welcome as many ideas as possible so that you have a more complete picture of the issue and your options. On the other hand, you need to weigh those options carefully to arrive at the best solution for your group.

**groupthink**
making decisions based on maintaining group harmony rather than critically evaluating ideas

**Groupthink** occurs when you make decisions based on maintaining group harmony, rather than critically evaluating ideas. When group members feel pressure to conform to the group—due to a desire to fit in or to avoid conflict—they might go along with the majority opinion even though they have doubts.

Groupthink leads to less than optimal decisions. Groups who feel pressure to agree may jump to conclusions, failing to consider evidence or recognize problems. Groupthink can also mask conflict and division: group members who disagree may feel silenced by the group.

Highly cohesive groups are more likely to fall prey to groupthink in order to maintain harmony. Groupthink is also more common in groups that are isolated from outside perspectives because members are not exposed to other points of view. Formal authorities or unofficial leaders of a group can make groupthink worse if they discourage discussion or downplay disagreements.

## FACILITATING GROUP DISCUSSION

You can help avoid groupthink by encouraging your group members to question their assumptions, seek outside information, and express dissenting opinions. To ensure that you include every group member's views, build these best practices for open communication into your decision-making process:

**TRY THIS**

For a guide to facilitating productive group discussions, try the **Group Decision-Making Activity**.

1. **SHARE INFORMATION.** Before you start generating solutions, make sure your group has all the information they need. Invite all group members to share their experience and knowledge about the issue. In some cases, you may realize you need to do additional research before you can make

an informed decision. Ask your group: "Is there anything else we need to know?"

2.  **BRAINSTORM IDEAS.** Challenge your team to come up with as many possible solutions as they can. This brainstorming stage should be a free-for-all where all ideas are welcome. Invite wild, silly, and counter-intuitive suggestions—you never know what might spark a great insight. Suspend all judgment until you have a long list of possibilities. Ask your group: "Does anybody have any other ideas?"

3.  **ESTABLISH DECISION CRITERIA.** Before your group starts evaluating different ideas, discuss what factors matter most for making your decision. For example, groups commonly weigh the time, cost, resources, and effort that different solutions require. You might also identify other important criteria based on the specific purpose and values of your group. Ask your group: "Are there any other factors we should consider?"

4.  **EVALUATE OPTIONS.** Use the criteria you've identified to weigh the advantages and disadvantages of each solution. If you see your group members rush to agree on one idea without considering its potential downsides, play devil's advocate. Ask your group: "What are the pros and cons of each choice?"

5.  **CALL FOR A DECISION.** Be sure to give your group sufficient time to discuss and consider each option. If the issue you're discussing is time-sensitive, let your group know how long they have to decide. If the issue isn't urgent, don't pressure them to make a choice right away. Ask your group: "Are we ready to make a decision?"

Call for a vote when all your group members have had a chance to thoroughly consider all their options.

## REACHING GROUP DECISIONS

When you're ready to make a group decision, there are four main methods you can use: simple majority vote, super majority vote, consensus decision, and single-party decision (see Figure 18.1). Different groups and tasks benefit from different decision-making methods. Decide your method for making decisions in

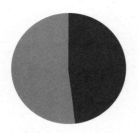

**Simple Majority**

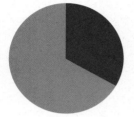

**Super Majority**

**Consensus Decision**

**Single-Party Decision**

FIGURE 18.1 Different decision-making methods require different levels of group agreement.

advance, and make sure everyone in your group is comfortable with it. Each way of making decisions has its own risks and advantages.

- **SIMPLE MAJORITY VOTE.** A **simple majority vote** means that a decision is reached when more than half of the voting members agree. Using a simple majority runs significant risks: marginalizing minority opinions and reducing the richness and creativity of group ideas. Simple majority is not functional when people affected by a decision feel shut out and ignored by the majority.

- **SUPER MAJORITY VOTE.** To alleviate the problems of simple majorities, some groups rely on a higher level of agreement. A **super majority vote** means that a decision will only be reached with a proportion of votes significantly higher than half, such as two-thirds or three-quarters. A super majority can still risk marginalizing minority voices and disenfranchising group members—but since it requires a larger number of members to agree, minority voices need fewer allies to affect a decision. Since a super majority requires more agreement than a simple majority, it also can sometimes require more discussion and time to reach a decision.

- **CONSENSUS DECISION.** To ensure all voices are heard, and to give every member the chance to influence key decisions, some groups use consensus. **Consensus** requires the agreement of all the voting members to reach a decision. Consensus requires groups work through disagreements and come to agreement, rather than voting to move forward past a disagreement. It makes it more likely that every group member feels empowered, included, and invested in group decisions. That also makes it more likely that each member of the group will complete their tasks and contribute to the group's goals. At the same time, a single uncooperative group member can use consensus to obstruct a group's progress. Consensus can sometimes cause groups to move slowly, requiring more time and discussion to reach decisions.

- **SINGLE-PARTY DECISION.** In some groups, speed and authority are considered more important than agreement or inclusion. A **single-party decision** method means that either an individual or a small collective of people makes the decisions. Other group members can make arguments or appeals to the single party, but they have no say in the final decision. This allows for quick action when a discussion to reach agreement is not feasible. It also allows the responsibility for decisions to rest on someone who either holds formal authority or has expertise that makes them the only qualified person to decide. Single-party decisions risk leaving many people feeling unheard, causing them to stop contributing to the group. To be effective, single-party decision-making requires decision-makers to include all voices in the process, show respect and appreciation for everyone's contributions, and maintain the respect of group members. A single-party decision-maker will need exceptional credibility to make informed decisions and motivate individual members to pursue the group's goals.

When deciding which method your group should use, consider your group members' strengths and standpoints. Discuss what your values are individually and as a group. And look at your group's project to see what decision method best suits your goals. You may find one method is most suited for most group decisions, but for others you might use different methods. For example, a group may want consensus for their purpose and thesis, but allow the design of PowerPoint slides to be decided by the visual artist in their group. The important thing is ensuring that everyone understands how your group will reach decisions, and agrees that method will promote your group's goals.

# Mediating Group Conflict

Making decisions with multiple people—who each have their own perspectives and priorities—can create the potential for disagreement. In many cases, these differences of opinion can be productive: they interrupt groupthink, improve group decisions, and help group members better understand other points of view. But when one of your group members starts disrupting the group's progress, it can bring your project to a standstill. Knowing how to recognize and respond to disruptive behavior can help you keep moving forward—even in the most challenging groups.

## RECOGNIZING GROUP DISRUPTIONS

Unlike productive conflict, disruptive behavior threatens a group's social cohesion and its ability to accomplish its shared purpose. **Group disruptions** are actions that claim personal power within a group at the expense of the group's collective goals. When someone persistently disrupts a group, it diminishes the

**simple majority vote**
a decision is reached when more than half of the voting members agree

**super majority vote**
a decision is reached only with a designated proportion of votes significantly higher than half, such as two-thirds or three-quarters

**consensus**
requiring the agreement of all the voting members to reach a decision

**single-party decision**
either an individual or a small collective of people makes decisions for the group

**group disruptions**
actions that claim personal power within a group at the expense of the group's collective goals

group's ability to work effectively as a team. Knowing how to recognize disruptive behavior—like attention seeking, blocking, freeloading, and attacking—is the first step to getting your group back on track.

- **ATTENTION SEEKING.** Whether we call them class clowns, show-offs, or drama llamas, sometimes a group member consistently makes themselves the center of attention. **Attention seeking** is disrupting group tasks by pursuing disproportionate personal attention. A group member might make distracting jokes, demonstrate irrelevant expertise, talk far more than other group members, or use group task time to discuss personal issues. When a team member frequently demands personal attention, they assert power by insisting that the group focus its time on themselves rather than group tasks.

- **BLOCKING.** Sometimes a group grinds to a halt because one member is stubborn, unyielding, and uncooperative. **Blocking** is standing in the way of group progress when you don't agree with group decisions. Sometimes group members may have legitimate concerns that are important enough to stop the group's work—but in those cases, it's crucial to cooperate or compromise with others to find a way forward that everyone can agree with. When a team member blocks group progress, they assert power by holding a task hostage until the group changes course.

- **FREELOADING.** Sometimes a group member doesn't actively block the group's progress, but simply doesn't participate. **Freeloading** is refusing to contribute to group tasks while receiving group credit or rewards. If you've ever had a classmate do the bare minimum on a group project—or not show up at all—you know how frustrating freeloading can be. Failing to attend group meetings, participate in group discussions, or complete individual portions of a group task are all classic signs of freeloading. Group members who don't respond to messages or complete their work on time force others to pick up the slack and jeopardize the whole group's ability to meet their goals. When a team member freeloads, they assert power by reaping the benefits of the group's work without doing their fair share.

- **ATTACKING.** The most damaging and difficult disruption to deal with in groups is behavior that belittles other group members, attacks them personally, or ridicules their contributions. **Attacking** includes intimidating,

**attention seeking**
disrupting group tasks by pursuing disproportionate personal attention

**blocking**
standing in the way of group progress when you don't agree with group decisions

**freeloading**
refusing to contribute to group tasks while receiving group credit or rewards

**attacking**
intimidating, bullying, or insulting fellow group members

When one of your group members is disrupting group progress, you can use these strategies to express empathy and mediate the conflict:

1. **AVOID BLAME.** When you express your concerns, focus on the behavior rather than the person. For example, say: "I've noticed a few missed deadlines lately" instead of "You dropped the ball." Or say: "It seems like this discussion is getting a little heated" instead of "You're out of line."

2. **ASK FOR MORE INFORMATION.** Aim to understand the context behind their disruptive behavior. For example: "Is everything OK?" Or: "Can you tell us a bit more about why you're upset?"

3. **LISTEN ACTIVELY.** Paraphrase their response to show that you've heard them. For example: "It sounds like you've got a lot on your plate right now." Or: "It sounds like you feel that the group doesn't value your opinion."

4. **OFFER SUPPORT.** Ask how the group can help. For example: "Is there anything we can do to make it easier for you to get your work in?" Or: "How can we do a better job of recognizing everyone's ideas moving forward?"

bullying, and insulting fellow group members. If you witness attacking behavior in a group, deal with it immediately. When one group member starts attacking others, it destroys the social cohesion of the group and makes it difficult for anyone to stay productive. Sometimes, aggressive behavior comes from insecurity. It can also be a symptom of a more serious mental health issue. When a team member attacks others, they assert power by creating fear and self-doubt in their teammates.

## RESPONDING TO GROUP DISRUPTIONS

Many of the leadership skills you've already learned provide ways to handle group disruptions. For example, your organizing skills can help steer distracted group members back on task. Your facilitating skills can make sure that everyone has a chance to weigh in on group decisions. Most importantly, encouraging group members who are struggling can help you better understand what kind of support they need. Although dealing with group disruptions can be uncomfortable, the process for responding to disruptive behavior is surprisingly simple:

- **EXPRESS EMPATHY.** In many cases, it can help to discuss a group member's disruptive behavior with them privately. If you feel comfortable sharing your concerns with the person one-on-one, you will likely get a less defensive reaction. Start from the assumption that this is a good person engaging in these behaviors because they feel insecure, threatened, unheard, or excluded. Ask them how they feel about their role in the group and its tasks. Mention that you've noticed that they seem upset or distant in the group meetings and ask if they are alright. You might be surprised at how they experience the group and its tasks differently from their standpoint. You might also learn that they are struggling with issues unrelated to the group, in which case you can help them find support.

## Pathways

To revisit strategies for listening and setting boundaries, see **Chapter 4, Listening and Responding**.

- **SET BOUNDARIES.** If someone's behavior is severely disruptive, it may be best to stop the group meeting and address it immediately. When a group member's behavior crosses the line, you may need to communicate boundaries. Calmly express your concern about their statements or actions, using "I" and not "you" statements. Then follow it up with a clarifying question. For example: "I feel like you're saying my ideas aren't worth contributing. Is that what you meant?" Or: "What I'm hearing you say is that you won't move forward with us on this project if we don't do what you want. Is that accurate?" After listening to their response, build common ground and invite them to make a productive contribution. For example: "I hear your concerns, and I agree that it's important to test these ideas to see if they will work. Could you suggest some ways to do that?"

- **CONSIDER REMOVAL.** If a group member persistently disrupts group progress despite your attempts to empathize or set boundaries, they cannot be ignored without risking the goals and cohesion of your team. A person who won't stop distracting group attention, blocking group goals, freeloading group rewards, or attacking group members should be removed from the team, either by group consensus or by appealing to a formal authority who can remove them. In a class, that may be your instructor, department chair, or a student ombuds office. At work, it may be a supervisor or human resources officer. When filing a complaint, be specific. Take detailed notes about the disruptive behavior and present them with the complaint. If a group member is threatening your mental health or physical safety and cannot be removed from the group, seriously consider leaving the group yourself. No one has the right to treat you with disrespect.

1. What is the difference between productive disagreements and disruptive behavior? What do all the different types of group disruption—attention seeking, blocking, freeloading, and attacking—have in common?

2. How do you know which response to use when a group member is being disruptive? When is it best to express empathy in a private conversation? When is it most effective to set boundaries in a discussion with the whole group? When is it appropriate to appeal to an outside authority to remove a disruptive group member?

# Next Steps

We hope this book leaves you with this message: that you and your voice deserve respect. We hope this book has given you a newfound respect for your unique strengths and standpoint as a speaker. And we hope that this book has inspired renewed respect for the voices and perspectives of people who have standpoints different from your own.

As always, there are exercises to help you apply the lessons in this chapter: the Group Strengths Inventory Worksheet, the Group Project Planning Worksheet, and the Group Decision-Making Activity. These exercises are designed to make teamwork easier and help you more fully appreciate what each of your teammates has to offer. In addition, the Online Group Presentations Video Series and Online Group Meetings Video Series offer tutorials on how to use common online platforms and tools to enhance your group's effectiveness. Remember: your voices are stronger together.

# Standpoint Reflection

- What are some of the roles that you most commonly play in groups? Are these the roles that best reflect your personal strengths? Are there any other roles that might also play to your strengths?

- Have you ever found yourself playing a disruptive role in groups? How did the dynamics of the group contribute to positioning you in that role? What insights does that experience give you for handling group conflict?

- What is your preferred method of group decision-making? What are its advantages? Are there any situations when you might choose a different method for making group decisions?

- What are some of the best and worst experiences you have had working in teams? What has helped your teams succeed in the past? What would you want to avoid in future team work?

## Key Terms

# Resources for Group Meetings and Presentations

## 📋 "Try This" Exercises

Access the "Try This" exercises as directed by your instructor or online at digital.wwnorton.com/chapterexercises-conpubspeak

- To lead a discussion on the unique experiences, knowledge, values, and identities that each of your group members brings to the table, try the **Group Strengths Inventory Worksheet**.

- For a step-by-step guide to creating your project plan, try the **Group Project Planning Worksheet**.

- For a guide to facilitating productive group discussions, try the **Group Decision-Making Activity**.

## 📹 "Learn More" Tutorials

Access the "Learn More" tutorials as directed by your instructor or online at digital.wwnorton.com/videos-conpubspeak

- To learn more about how to present together as a group in an online format, see the **Online Group Presentation Video Series**.

- To learn more about how to use videoconferencing tools to conduct a group meeting, see the **Online Group Meetings Video Series**.

---

**Want to practice these skills to prepare for your next speech? Go to INQUIZITIVE to review and apply concepts from this chapter and get personalized feedback along the way.**

# Speeches for Analysis

## Greta Thunberg

Greta Thunberg (she/her) is a Swedish environmental activist and the founder of the global School Strike for Climate movement. She delivered this address at the United Nations Climate Action Summit when asked, "What's your message to world leaders today?" To read more about this speech, see pages 12–13.

This is all wrong. I shouldn't be up here. I should be back in school on the other side of the ocean. Yet you all come to us young people for hope. How dare you!

You have stolen my dreams and my childhood with your empty words. And yet I'm one of the lucky ones. People are suffering. People are dying. Entire ecosystems are collapsing. We are in the beginning of a mass extinction, and all you can talk about is money and fairy tales of eternal economic growth. How dare you!

For more than thirty years, the science has been crystal clear. How dare you continue to look away and come here saying that you're doing enough, when the politics and solutions needed are still nowhere in sight.

You say you hear us and that you understand the urgency. But no matter how sad and angry I am, I do not want to believe that. Because if you really understood the situation and still kept on failing to act, then you would be evil. And that I refuse to believe.

The popular idea of cutting our emissions in half in ten years only gives us a 50 percent chance of staying below 1.5 degrees [Celsius], and the risk of setting off irreversible chain reactions beyond human control.

Fifty percent may be acceptable to you. But those numbers do not include tipping points, most feedback loops, additional warming hidden by toxic air pollution or the aspects of equity and climate justice. They also rely on my generation sucking hundreds of billions of tons of your $CO_2$ out of the air with technologies that barely exist.

So a 50 percent risk is simply not acceptable to us—we who have to live with the consequences.

To have a 67 percent chance of staying below a 1.5 degrees global temperature rise—the best odds given by the IPCC [Intergovernmental Panel on Climate Change]—the world had 420 gigatons of $CO_2$ left to emit back on January 1st, 2018. Today that figure is already down to less than 350 gigatons.

How dare you pretend that this can be solved with just "business as usual" and some technical solutions? With today's emissions levels, that remaining $CO_2$ budget will be entirely gone within less than eight and a half years.

There will not be any solutions or plans presented in line with these figures here today, because these numbers are too uncomfortable. And you are still not mature enough to tell it like it is.

You are failing us. But the young people are starting to understand your betrayal. The eyes of all future generations are upon you. And if you choose to fail us, I say: We will never forgive you.

We will not let you get away with this. Right here, right now is where we draw the line. The world is waking up. And change is coming, whether you like it or not. Thank you.

# Jahmal Cole

Jahmal Cole (he/him) is a community organizer and founder of My Block, My Hood, My City, a youth mentorship and outreach program in Chicago. He delivered this keynote speech when he received the City of Chicago's Champion of Freedom Award at the Dr. Martin Luther King Jr. Day Interfaith Breakfast. To read more about this speech, see page 83.

"So last night I couldn't sleep, and you know it wasn't because we don't have heat. We just heat the house with the oven. Not having heat on my block, that's regular stuff. I still couldn't sleep last night.

And it wasn't because I heard gunshots. I hear gunshots all the time. I tell myself they firecrackers, I go back to sleep. Hearing gunshots on my block, that's regular stuff.

I still couldn't sleep last night.

It wasn't even because I saw helicopters. I mean helicopters fly above my house all the time. They fly in threes. When they go up and down, they float like dragonflies. Rattle the house.

It still wasn't why I couldn't sleep.

I couldn't sleep 'cause the lights from the helicopters were shining through my window at 3:00 a.m. They had the whole block lit up. You could see every bullet casing on the ground at 3:00 a.m., and I couldn't sleep because of it.

I live in a house with my aunt and her husband. Both of them are drug addicts. Nobody says that where I'm from, that's regular stuff. The last time I seen my aunt, she came into the house. She had a black T-shirt on with a Batman logo on her chest. Actually, half of her ear was missing. She got into a fight with a drug addict outside and she laid on the kitchen floor bleeding. It's the last time I seen her, a couple of weeks back.

My house is ran by my older cousins, both of them in gangs. They sell drugs, but that's regular stuff. We don't say we in gangs where I'm from. We say, 'This is my set, these are my friends. I'm a product of my environment. I'm a victim of my circumstances. I'm in the trenches,' it's regular stuff.

I don't care what none of y'all say though. I love my cousins. LOVE my older cousins, and I love 'em 'cause they tell me I'm smart! They say I'ma be the next Nino Brown and my teachers don't say I'm smart. My cousins, they say I'm smart 'cause I'm the lookout. I know every car that's supposed to be on my block. Nine of 'em. I know it's a Chevy with a black 10, baby blue Cadillac, van with the curtains in it, the man with the motorcycle, the royal blue Acura, there's a Toyota Camry with a City College bumper sticker, there's a lady with a Cherokee, there's a all-black Charger with silver rims and there's a brown Honda minivan. Any car pulls up that not one of those nines I say, 'Look out! There's danger.' They say I'm smart 'cause I'm the lookout on the block.

I order my breakfast every morning at the corner store. I order it through 3-inch bulletproof glass windows that has mugshots of black faces on it. The windows are so thick I gotta yell my order. I said, 'Hey man, I want the Doritos. No, I don't want the spicy Nacho. I want the Cool Ranch, the blue bag, the blue bag, the blue bag!' And the guy goes to get it, drops my Doritos in a bulletproof glass jar and he slides it out to me like I'm an inmate in solitary confinement. I'm in the real world though. ShotSpotter sit on top of holes listening to gunshots, blue lights are flashing, boarded-up businesses for blocks? Man, if society was a person, I wouldn't think society trusted me, so I steal anyway.

I'm looking forward to going to school today, I guess, because I'm a part of the afterschool program. It's ran by this guy named Jahmal Cole. Jahmal is always telling us that he can't afford to take us to China, so he takes us to Chinatown. He can't afford to take us to Poland, so he takes us to Jefferson Park. He can't afford to take us to India, so he takes us to Divine Avenue. Jahmal is always saying, like, we can travel the world without leaving Chicago. And just last week, Jahmal took us downtown and we went to a museum. But the coolest part wasn't the museum, no. The coolest part was I never seen anybody wait for a taxi before. And Jahmal let us all get out, wait for a taxi, and we got to ride a few blocks. I thought that was pretty dope.

Hey, I was telling Jahmal, I don't like to go see my dad. He just got out of jail, he on house arrest. Every time I see him, he's sending me on errands. But I noticed when my mom posted a picture of her new boyfriend on Facebook, my dad liked that picture. But when my mom posted a picture on Facebook of me having a 3.5 GPA, my dad never liked that picture. That bothered me."

Hey look, my name is Jahmal Cole. I thought it was important to start off and tell that story because the more we're separated as a city, the less empathy we have for each other.

And man, when most people hear about something negative happen in another Chicago community, especially where people are a lot different from them, it might as well happen in another country. Well, when you visit different communities and you interact with the residents, it could change all that.

I grew up in a household where all three of my older cousins and brothers, one doing eighty years in Statesville, forty years, twenty years, same house, man.

And I'll write my brothers, I write my cousins. I always write them by hand, so they know I still love them, you know what I mean? And I ask them, how is it in the Statesville? My older cousin told me, he said, Jamal, you know what? On my block, you know, 'cause in jails it's blocks, A block, B block, C block, he said on my block I'm not in here with no, I'm not in jail with any pedophiles. There's no rapist where I'm at. I'm in here with guys that have sold a little drugs, racketeering, armed robbery, you know, regular stuff. He really said regular sh—, you know what I mean? But man, it got me thinking. It's not regular for German shepherds to be sniffing kids on 79th Street. It's not regular for helicopters to be landing on top of people's houses at night. It's not regular to have to order your breakfast through bulletproof glass windows every day.

If you all just ate your quiche through a bulletproof glass window right now, you'll be traumatized.

It's not regular to walk inside of a Walgreens and all the cough syrup be locked up. It's not regular for all the billboards in my community to promote cheap divorces and six-thousand-dollar tax advances.

All right? It's not regular, man. It's not regular for there to be fifteen currency exchanges and no banks. How am I supposed to save?

It's not regular for there to be a liquor store on every other corner. I might as well get drunk!

It's not regular for there to be a holding cell in the basement of a funeral home.

It's not regular for there to be two paddy wagons parked outside the front of my high school. That's not regular.

It's not regular for 80 percent of the kids in my program to know somebody that's been murdered, but only 10 percent of the kids in my program know somebody that's been to college.

That stuff is not regular. And they say, like, it's regular, they say that I work with at-risk youth. Man, the integrity of this city is at risk. If we're not supporting programs like My Block, My Hood, My City.

So I want to thank Mayor Emanuel for the Champion of Freedom Award. I want to thank you all for coming. I want to thank my board, but ain't no freedom on 79th and Cottage, man. It's just the Happy's Liquors. Ain't no freedom on Roosevelt and Pulaski. It's just the Mitchell PCS and the bulletproof glass. Freedom without equity ain't freedom. That's just the struggle.

Oppression is super real, y'all. It's a structural part of this country in its history, it was created intentionally. And nowadays it's cloaked up in trumped-up laws and false media and we have a hard time recognizing how injustice is being sustained.

It's not regular to see the cheap divorce signs, man. It's not regular.

So, I want to thank you guys for coming out and then I want to charge you with supporting organizations like My Block, My Hood, My City. You can do that easily. You can text message *Explore* to 55222 and you can sponsor one of our kids to go through our program for a year. Again, that's *Explore* at 55222 because it's cool to say, "Oh great speech, great speech." I need support! This ain't, this ain't, it's hard to take all these kids around the city. So I charge you guys. If you really want to make a difference, text message *Explore* to 55222 and see how you can get involved.

Dr. Martin Luther King said, "In a real sense all life is interrelated." He says, "All men are caught in an inescapable network of mutuality, bound by a single garment of destiny." He says, "What affects one person directly affects all of us indirectly." He said, "I can't be what I ought to be until you are what you ought to be, and you can't be what you ought to be until I am what I ought to be." That's the interrelated structure of reality.

In this interconnected Chicago that I envision, all seventy-seven community areas need to contribute to the music in the city, right. The residents of Humboldt Park, they gonna to play the timpani, the residents of the Gold Coast, they gonna to play the cymbals. The residents of Woodlawn will play the xylophones and you know Chatham, you gon' play the bass drums. We got the most Bucket Boys in the city, right? It just makes sense. Hey, the point is all seventy-seven community areas contributes to the music of the city. And if one community is struggling and can't play their part, the entire piece is gonna suffer and we're all gonna be concerned. Thank you, guys.

# Paxton Smith

Paxton Smith (she/her) is a recent high school valedictorian who received national acclaim for her graduation speech on abortion rights. She delivered this speech to her graduating class at Lake Highlands High School in Dallas, Texas, in response to the passage of the Texas "Heartbeat Bill," which prohibits abortion after six weeks of pregnancy. To read more about this speech, see pages 124–25.

I'm not usually very good at expressing my gratitude for the people that I care about. But I would like to say "thank you" to Coach. I think he's had a bigger role in my life than he realizes. [deep breath]

OK.

As we leave high school, we need to make our voices heard. Today, I was going to talk about TV and media and content, because it's something that's very important to me. However, under light of recent events, it feels wrong to talk about anything but what is currently affecting me and millions of other women in the state.

Recently, the Heartbeat Bill was passed in Texas. Starting in September, there will be a ban on abortions after six weeks of pregnancy, regardless of whether the pregnancy was a result of rape or incest.

Six weeks. That's all women get. And so, before they realize—most of them don't realize that they're pregnant by six weeks—so before they have a chance to decide if they are emotionally, physically, and financially stable enough to carry out a full-term pregnancy, before they have the chance to decide if they can take on the responsibility of bringing another human being into the world, that decision is made for them by a stranger.

A decision that will affect the rest of their lives is made by a stranger.

I have dreams and hopes and ambitions. Every girl graduating today does. And we have spent our entire lives working towards our future. And without our input and without our consent, our control over that future has been stripped away from us.

I am terrified that if my contraceptives fail, I am terrified that if I am raped, then my hopes and aspirations and dreams and efforts for my future will no longer matter. I hope that you can feel how gut-wrenching that is. I hope you can feel how dehumanizing it is, to have the autonomy over your own body taken away from you.

And I'm talking about this today—on a day as important as this, on a day honoring twelve years of hard academic work, on a day where we are all gathered together, on a day where you are most inclined to listen to a voice like mine, a woman's voice—to tell you that this is a problem, and it's a problem that cannot wait.

And I cannot give up this platform to promote complacency and peace, when there is a war on my body and a war on my rights. A war on the rights of your mothers [cheers], a war on the rights of your sisters, a war on the rights of your daughters.

We cannot stay silent. Thank you.

# Adri Pèrez

Adri Pèrez (they/them) is a policy and advocacy strategist for the American Civil Liberties Union of Texas. They addressed the Texas Senate Committee on State Affairs to testify against Senate Bills 1646 and 1311, which restrict transgender children's participation in sports and access to gender-affirming medical care. To read more about this speech, see pages 142–43.

ADRI: Hi. Good afternoon, Chairman Hughes and honorable members of the committee. My name is Adri Pèrez. I am a transgender Texan and a policy advocacy strategist with the ACLU of Texas. I will be testifying today on behalf of myself and the ACLU of Texas in opposition to SB-1646 and SB-1311. Across the country a number, a record number, of bills targeting transition-related health care have been introduced by several Republican lawmakers. These bills run counter to medical science, established standards of care for transgender youth, and the fundamental freedom of parents and families from excessive government intrusion. SB-1646 and SB-1311 are a senseless, dangerous, and unnecessary attempt by lawmakers to bully transgender children. This proposal displays a fundamental misunderstanding about the medical treatment for transgender youth. Being transgender is not something that can, or should, be changed by external forces. Current care simply delays puberty and allows a young person and their family to make informed medical decisions about their care. All of the medical interventions for transgender youth and adults such as myself are rooted in medical practices that have been used with non-transgender youth and adults for years. This bill would take away choices, irreversibly force youth through endogenous puberty, and undermine the prevailing recommendations of every major medical association. Legislators need to trust transgender youth, their doctors, and the people who love and support them, to make the best decisions for themselves and their lives. When the Texas legislature considers discriminatory bills such as these, that seek to deny transgender people's existences, it causes immense psychological harm and emotional distress to kids across the state. Gender-affirming care is lifesaving care. It saved my life. Passing this legislation sends a message that trans kids and people are not welcome in this state, and it is that message that causes an increase in rates of depression and suicidality. When a similar ban on gender-affirming health care was recently debated and unconstitutionally passed in Arkansas, pediatric doctor[s] reported seeing an increase in visits to the emergency room by transgender young people attempting suicide. This is the reality of the harm these bills cause. Chairman, may I please finish my statements?

CHAIRMAN HUGHES: If you can, you can kind of bring it to a close, we're, you notice I'm doing this with everybody, no matter what side they're on, so, so, wrap it up for us, please.

ADRI: Moreover, all of this is happening at a time when our state should be focused on ensuring an equitable recovery from multiple overlapping crises. The failure of the state's power grid, an estimated two hundred Texans dead from a winter storm, a global pandemic, and hundreds of thousands of Texans facing unemployment, eviction, and economic despair. All Texans, including those of us who are transgender, deserve better. To the transgender youth across the country who are surely watching this hearing, we see you, you are not alone, and we will never stop fighting for you. Thank you, Chairman Hughes and Senator Powell, for being here.

CHAIRMAN HUGHES: Thank you for your testimony. Any questions? Thanks for being here.

# Blair Imani

Blair Imani (she/her) is an award-winning public educator, historian, and influencer known for her "Get Smarter" video series on YouTube and her "Smarter in Seconds" videos on Instagram. In this video presentation, Imani responds to a question from a viewer asking her to explain the concept of intersectionality. To read more about this speech, see page 155.

Hey, Smarties! My name is Blair Imani. I'm an author, educator, and historian. Today, we're going to get smarter! We have a question from a Smartie named Debbie. Debbie asks: "Blair, I've tried my best, I've done my research, but I'm still not grasping intersectionality; can you help?" I sure can, Debbie. Today, let's get smarter about intersectionality.

So, what are we getting smarter about? Intersectionality! Intersectionality describes our overlapping identities and the ways that those overlapping identities connect to systems of oppression. Keep in mind it's not just being oppressed, sometimes it's being privileged, and we'll break it down further. Basically, it's our identities and how those overlapping identities relate to systems of oppression. Not just one, not just the other, all together at the same time. And we get that from Dr. Kimberlé Crenshaw, who we'll learn about here in a minute.

For example, I am Black, bisexual, Muslim, a woman, et cetera. "Et cetera" is not an identity, it means "everything else," and it's abbreviated as "etc." Anyway, it's not just these identities but also how they relate to systems of oppression. I'm harmed by anti-Blackness and I benefit from colorism. I'm harmed by biphobia, I'm harmed by Islamophobia, sexism, etc. Understanding these things together is what makes intersectionality an analytical framework or way of understanding the world around us. It helps us inform our approaches to activism, our approaches to feminism, but how did we get here in the first place where we have this framework?

In 1989, Dr. Kimberlé Crenshaw coined the term *intersectionality* in her legal essay "Demarginalizing the Intersection of Race and Sex." In this essay, she broke down, from her framework as a Black legal scholar, feminist, and educator, that Black women were being erased from discourse around racism and feminism. Why? Because anti-racism discourse was exclusively looking at race, and feminism discourse was exclusively looking at gender. So Black women, like myself, were being removed from that and Dr. Kimberlé Crenshaw's work is absolutely foundational, but the idea and need and theory of intersectionality predates her coinage of the term and she acknowledges this herself. We'll get a little history lesson about that in just a bit. But Dr. Crenshaw is a key figure to learn about. She founded the African American Policy Forum; she founded the Center for Intersectionality and Social Policy Studies; she's absolutely amazing and continues to do the work. In fact, she gives us the #SayHerName, which is a movement to recognize victims of police violence who are Black women.

Dr. Jennifer C. Nash is an amazing scholar who has informed a lot of my understanding around intersectionality. In *Reimagining Black Feminism After Intersectionality*, which came out in 2019, she highlights how intersectionality itself is not a tactic for fighting oppression, but it is a lens through which we can look to create those tactics.

As you know, from the intro of this video, I'm a historian, so we're going to sneak in a history lesson. Let's look at Black women here in the United States, who informed the basis of Dr. Crenshaw's legal essay, and let's go back to the 1940s with Rosie the Riveter. I did an excellent, if I don't say so myself, cosplay of Rosie the Riveter and I used it as an opportunity to break down the need for a historically intersectional approach to looking at history, especially when it comes to Black women in the context of labor in the United States.

So, when it comes to Rosie the Riveter, it was used strategically as a campaign to get women to join the war effort, and it was representative of a time when women were being applauded for joining the workforce. But Black women had always been part of the workforce in the United States. Chattel slavery in the United States, which was the form of slavery suffered by enslaved Africans here in the US for most of our country's history, that was passed down matriarchally.

That meant that an enslaved woman's child was themselves enslaved. And being born into slavery and having no agency or autonomy about directing your life was a defining feature of what it meant to be Black in the US, so joining the workforce was not optional, and it wasn't even celebrated the way that it was when white women were joining the workforce in droves during the 1940s.

Take, for example, my grandmother Eloise, an amazing Black woman; she grew up in Mississippi and, through the Great Migration, which I discuss in my book *Making Our Way Home: The Great Migration and the Black American Dream*, she moved to Los Angeles as a child. And Los Angeles was an industrial center during the 1940s. She started working on the assembly lines at Lockheed, later called Lockheed Martin, an aircraft manufacturer, to be part of that "Arsenal of Democracy" that FDR called America's assembly lines. But, because of the wage gap—not just the gender wage gap, but the racial wage gap and the gender-racial wage gap—she was making less than white men, white women, and Black men, which meant that she and many other people in her community had to work on weekends as well—as domestic workers or as hairdressers—to try and even approach what their counterparts, whether that was along race or gender lines, were able to bring in as income.

Black women have had to work harder than their white counterparts, than their male counterparts, to get the same amount. And without intersectionality, we're not even acknowledging this vast community and part of history or present struggles. Intersectionality is majorly important. Some people think, "Oh, well, I'm just not going to concern myself." But if you're not concerning yourself with intersectionality, then you're going to end up doing what Dr. Kimberlé Crenshaw discussed in her legal essay. Talking about sexism, with just looking at gender, talking about anti-racism, just looking at race, but systems of oppression are intersectional whether or not our movements for liberation are. So, we may as well consider people existing at multiple identities, in multiple contexts, at the same time, because we're not going to get free one at a time. History can show us that, the present can show us that. We must be intersectional in our approaches to doing the work, because the movements against us sure as hell are.

So, Smarties, that brings us to the end of our lesson on intersectionality. Did you learn anything new? I certainly hope that you did! Do you have anything to contribute? Please chime in in the comments below. And if you want to be like Debbie and submit one of your questions on "Get Smarter with Blair Imani" just go to blairimani.com/questions, and I'll do my best to help us all get smarter!

# Malala Yousafzai

Malala Yousafzai (she/her) is an internationally renowned advocate for gender equality in education—both in her native Pakistan and around the world. She delivered this acceptance speech when she became the youngest person to receive the Nobel Peace Prize. To read more about this speech, see page 379.

---

*Bismillah hir rahman ir rahim.* In the name of God, the most merciful, the most beneficent.

Your Majesties, Your Royal Highnesses, distinguished members of the Norwegian Nobel Committee:

Dear sisters and brothers, today is a day of great happiness for me. I am humbled that the Nobel Committee has selected me for this precious award.

Thank you to everyone for your continued support and love. Thank you for the letters and cards that I still receive from all around the world. Your kind and encouraging words strengthens and inspires me.

I would like to thank my parents for their unconditional love. Thank you to my father for not clipping my wings and for letting me fly. Thank you to my mother for inspiring me to be patient and to always speak the truth—which we strongly believe is the true message of Islam. And also thank you to all my wonderful teachers, who inspired me to believe in myself and be brave.

I am proud, well, in fact, I am very proud, to be the first Pashtun, the first Pakistani, and the youngest person to receive this award. Along with that, along with that, I am pretty certain that I am also the first recipient of the Nobel Peace Prize who still fights with her younger brothers. I want there to be peace everywhere, but my brothers and I are still working on that.

I am also honored to receive this award together with Kailash Satyarthi, who has been a champion for children's rights for a long time. Twice as long, in fact, than I have been alive. I am proud that we can work together, we can work together and show the world that an Indian and a Pakistani, they can work together and achieve their goals of children's rights.

Dear brothers and sisters, I was named after the inspirational Malalai of Maiwand, who is the Pashtun Joan of Arc. The word *Malala* means grief-stricken, "sad," but in order to lend some happiness to it, my grandfather would always call me Malala—"the happiest girl in the world"— and today I am very happy that we are together fighting for an important cause.

This award is not just for me. It is for those forgotten children who want education. It is for those frightened children who want peace. It is for those voiceless children who want change.

I am here to stand up for their rights, to raise their voice…it is not time to pity them. It is not time to pity them. It is time to take action, so it becomes the last time, the last time, so it becomes the last time that we see a child deprived of education.

I have found that people describe me in many different ways.

Some people call me the girl who was shot by the Taliban.

And some, the girl who fought for her rights.

Some people call me a "Nobel laureate" now.

However, my brothers still call me that annoying bossy sister. As far as I know, I am just a committed and even stubborn person who wants to see every child getting quality education, who wants to see women having equal rights, and who wants peace in every corner of the world.

Education is one of the blessings of life—and one of its necessities. That has been my experience during the seventeen years of my life. In my paradise home, Swat, I always loved learning and discovering new things. I remember when my friends and I would decorate our hands with henna on special occasions. And instead of drawing flowers and patterns, we would paint our hands with mathematical formulas and equations.

We had a thirst for education, we had a thirst for education because our future was right there in that classroom. We would sit and learn and read together. We loved to wear neat and tidy school uniforms and we would sit there with big dreams in our eyes. We wanted to make our parents proud and prove that we could also excel in our studies and achieve those goals, which some people think only boys can.

But things did not remain the same. When I was in Swat, which was a place of tourism and beauty, suddenly changed into a place of terrorism. I was just ten that more than four hundred schools were destroyed. Women were flogged. People were killed. And our beautiful dreams turned into nightmares.

Education went from being a right to being a crime.

Girls were stopped from going to school.

When my world suddenly changed, my priorities changed too.

I had two options. One was to remain silent and wait to be killed. And the second was to speak up and then be killed.

I chose the second one. I decided to speak up.

We could not just stand by and see those injustices of the terrorists denying our rights, ruthlessly killing people and misusing the name of Islam. We decided to raise our voice and tell them: Have you not learnt, have you not learnt that in the Holy Quran Allah says: "If you kill one person it is as if you kill the whole humanity"?

Do you not know that Mohammad, peace be upon him, the prophet of mercy, he says, "Do not harm yourself or others."

And do you not know that the very first word of the Holy Quran is the word *Iqra*, which means "read"?

The terrorists tried to stop us and attacked me and my friends who are here today, on our school bus in 2012, but neither their ideas nor their bullets could win.

We survived. And since that day, our voices have grown louder and louder.

I tell my story, not because it is unique, but because it is not.

It is the story of many girls.

Today, I tell their stories too. I have brought with me some of my sisters from Pakistan, from Nigeria and from Syria, who share this story. My brave sisters Shazia and Kainat who were also shot that day on our school bus. But they have not stopped learning. And my brave sister Kainat Soomro who went through severe abuse and extreme violence, even her brother was killed, but she did not succumb.

Also my sisters here, whom I have met during my Malala Fund campaign. My sixteen-year-old courageous sister Muzoon from Syria, who now lives in Jordan as refugee and goes from tent to tent encouraging girls and boys to learn. And my sister Amina, from the north of Nigeria, where Boko Haram threatens, and stops girls and even kidnaps girls, just for wanting to go to school.

Though I appear as one girl, though I appear as one girl, one person, who is five foot two inches tall, if you include my high heels (it means I am five foot only), I am not a lone voice, I am not a lone voice, I am many.

I am Malala. But I am also Shazia.

I am Kainat.

I am Kainat Soomro.

I am Muzoon.

I am Amina.

I am those 66 million girls* who are deprived of education. And today I am not raising my voice, it is the voice of those 66 million girls.

We see many people becoming refugees in Syria, Gaza, and Iraq. In Afghanistan, we see families being killed in suicide attacks and bomb blasts.

Many children in Africa do not have access to education because of poverty. And as I said, we still see, we still see girls who have no freedom to go to school in the north of Nigeria.

Many children in countries like Pakistan and India, as Kailash Satyarthi mentioned, many children, especially in India and Pakistan, are deprived of their right to education because of social taboos, or they have been forced into child marriage or into child labor.

One of my very good school friends, the same age as me, who had always been a bold and confident girl, dreamed of becoming a doctor. But her dream remained a dream. At the age of twelve, she was forced to get married. And then soon she had a son, she had a child when she herself was still a child—only fourteen. I know that she could have been a very good doctor.

But she couldn't, because she was a girl.

Her story is why I dedicate the Nobel Peace Prize money to Malala Fund, to help give girls quality education, everywhere, anywhere in the world and to raise their voices. The first place this funding will go to is where my heart is, to build schools in Pakistan—especially in my home of Swat and Shangla.

In my own village, there is still no secondary school for girls. And it is my wish and my commitment, and now my challenge, to build one so that my friends and my sisters can go there to school and get quality education and to get this opportunity to fulfil their dreams.

This is where I will begin, but it is not where I will stop. I will continue this fight until I see every child, every child in school.

Dear brothers and sisters, great people, who brought change, like Martin Luther King and Nelson Mandela, Mother Teresa and Aung San Suu Kyi, once stood here on this stage. I hope the steps that Kailash Satyarthi and I have taken so far and will take on this journey will also bring change—lasting change.

My great hope is that this will be the last time, this will be the last time we must fight for education. Let's solve this once and for all.

———————

* Note: UNESCO now estimates more than 130 million girls around the world are out of school.

We have already taken many steps. Now it is time to take a leap.

It is not time to tell the world leaders to realize how important education is—they already know it—their own children are in good schools. Now it is time to call them to take action for the rest of the world's children.

We ask the world leaders to unite and make education their top priority.

Fifteen years ago, the world leaders decided on a set of global goals, the Millennium Development Goals. In the years that have followed, we have seen some progress. The number of children out of school has been halved, as Kailash Satyarthi said. However, the world focused only on primary education, and progress did not reach everyone.

In year 2015, representatives from all around the world will meet in the United Nations to set the next set of goals, the Sustainable Development Goals. This will set the world's ambition for the next generations.

The world can no longer accept, the world can no longer accept that basic education is enough. Why do leaders accept that for children in developing countries, only basic literacy is sufficient, when their own children do homework in algebra, mathematics, science, and physics?

Leaders must seize this opportunity to guarantee a free, quality primary and secondary education for every child.

Some will say this is impractical, or too expensive, or too hard. Or maybe even impossible. But it is time the world thinks bigger.

Dear sisters and brothers, the so-called world of adults may understand it, but we children don't. Why is it that countries which we call "strong" are so powerful in creating wars but are so weak in bringing peace? Why is it that giving guns is so easy but giving books is so hard? Why is it, why is it that making tanks is so easy, but building schools is so hard?

We are living in the modern age, and we believe that nothing is impossible. We have reached the moon forty-five years ago and maybe will soon land on Mars. Then, in this twenty-first century, we must be able to give every child quality education.

Dear sisters and brothers, dear fellow children, we must work . . . not wait. Not just the politicians and the world leaders, we all need to contribute. Me. You. We. It is our duty.

Let us become the first generation to decide to be the last, let us become the first generation that decides to be the last that sees empty classrooms, lost childhoods, and wasted potentials.

Let this be the last time that a girl or a boy spends their childhood in a factory.

Let this be the last time that a girl is forced into early child marriage.

Let this be the last time that a child loses life in war.

Let this be the last time that we see a child out of school.

Let this end with us.

Let's begin this ending together, today, right here, right now. Let's begin this ending now. Thank you so much.

# Glossary/Index

Note: This glossary/index defines key terms and concepts and directs you to pages in the book where you can find specific information on these and other topics. The words set in SMALL CAPITAL LETTERS are themselves defined in the glossary/index. Page references followed by an italicized "*f*" refer to figures; page references followed by an italicized "*t*" refer to tables. Boldface page references indicate locations of boldface key terms.

**agenda, 439-40** A list of topics or tasks for a meeting, in the order they will be addressed.

**agenda setting, 319** The capacity for media coverage to influence an AUDIENCE's priorities.

algorithms, online platforms and, 321, 322

Al-Khalili, Jim, 352–53

**alliteration, 248** Repetition of sounds at the beginning of nearby words.

ambiguity, clarifying, 355–56

amplification
    connective presentations and, 401*f*, 404–5
    speeches of introduction, 409–11
    use of stories and, 231–34

**analogical reasoning, 142-44** REASONING from an ANALOGY to apply the qualities of one specific case to another similar case.
    research plan and, 157

**analogy, 142** A comparison emphasizing the similarities between two OBJECTS, EVENTS, or situations.
    reasoning from, 142–44

**anaphora, 248** Repetition of a word or phrase at the beginning of a series of sentences or clauses.

**anchoring bias, 158** Our tendency to rely too heavily on the first information we encounter.

anchors, transitions and, 191–92

ancient Greeks, 4, 42

ancient Romans, 4

Anderson, Gillian, 7

**anger, 219-21** The feeling that unjustified harm has been done to you or someone you care about.

animations, in slide decks, 306–7

**antithesis, 250** Juxtaposing contrasting words and ideas in parallel phrases.

**anxiety,** 12, **25** A negative label for intense physiological and psychological stimulation. *See also* excitement
    adapting gestures and, 273
    affective strategies for, 29–30
    behavioral strategies for, 32–35

clinical anxiety disorder, 28, 29*f*
    cognitive strategies for, 31–32
    deep breathing techniques, 30, 30*f*
    dimensions of, 27–28, 29*f*
    environmental stress reduction, 32, 34
    eye contact and, 274–75
    inner critic, 31
    Inverted-U Model, 24, 24*f*, 25
    mindfulness techniques for, 29
    muscle relaxation techniques for, 30
    personal model of resilience, 35–36
    physical movement techniques for, 30–31
    positive self-talk and, 31–32
    positive visualization, 32
    preparation and practice, 34–35
    reclaiming as a strength, 24–27
    support, seeking sources of, 34

APA (American Psychological Association) style guide, 174–76

apologies, 53–54

appeal, of presentation aids, 290

articles
    academic databases, 162–63
    news databases, 163
    source citations, style for, 174–75

**articulation, 265-66** The ability to make vocal sounds clearly and distinctly.

**aspiration, 225-26** The desire to experience the good fortune of others for yourself.

**assimilation, 242-43** Pressure to conform to the ATTITUDES, VALUES, and BEHAVIORS of a PRIVILEGED group.

**asynchronous communication, 335,** 336*f* A time lapse occurs between the speaker creating a message and the AUDIENCE receiving it. *See also* synchronous communication

**attacking, 446-47** Intimidating, bullying, or insulting fellow group members.

attention
    connective presentations and, 402

Baker, Charlie, 117
Bamford, Maria, 263

**bar graphs, 298** Graphs that use either horizontal or vertical bars to show differences in numerical values or amounts.

**behavioral anxiety, 27–28,** 29*f* Outward expressions of ANXIETY, including trembling, pacing, sweating, and using VERBAL FILLERS.

**behavioral mimicry, 216–17** The tendency for PEOPLE to mimic the emotional expressions of people around them.

behavioral strategies for anxiety, 32–35

**behaviors, 84–85** Actions and habits that outwardly express a person's VALUES and ATTITUDES.
    audience analysis, 84–86, 85*t*

beliefs
    attitudinal causes, policy change and, 390–91
    confirmation bias and, 147
    motivated reasoning and, 147
    persuasion and, 380–81
    social location and intersectionality, 10–12
    as topics of informative presentations, 368–69
    unconscious beliefs, 85–86, 85*t*
Berliner, Emile, 318

**bias, 167** An ATTITUDE or motive that creates an unfair or unjustified preference.
    anchoring bias, 158
    confirmation bias, 147
    informative presentations and, 350–51

Black Lives Matter, 180–81, 217–18
Black population, code-switching and, 243

**blocking, 446** Standing in the way of group progress when you don't agree with group decisions.

Blunt, Martin, 136
body positivity, 198–99
Bolden, Charles, 412
Bong Joon-ho, 414
books, source citations style, 174

Bottoms, Keisha Lance, 49
Bouguettaya, Zakaria, 434

**brain plasticity, 42** The constant changes our brain makes to incorporate new experiences.

**brainstorming, 117–20,** 118*f* Generating many possible ideas and solutions by suspending judgment.
    topic choice and, 117–20, 118*f*

breathing, mindful, 70
broadcast media, consolidation in, 319
Burke, Tarana, 392–93

# C

**call-and-response, 217** Calling your AUDIENCE to repeat a series of phrases after you.

**callback, 406** Revisiting your opening lines in your final words.

cameras, video recordings and, 330–32
Cannell, Sean, 331

**captions, 295** Textual explanations that highlight an image's important features.

catalog, library, 161–62

**categorical pattern, 187–88,** 363, 364, 368 Organizing MAIN POINTS into generally recognized types, groups, or sets.

**causal pattern, 189–90** Organizing MAIN POINTS into causes and effects.

**causation, 146** A special type of CORRELATION, where one thing leads to another.

cause-effect patterns, 189–90, 361
causes
    attitudinal causes, 390–91
    structural causes, 390–91
celebration presentations
    award speeches, 411–15
    connective presentations, building of, 400–407, 401*f*
    eulogies, 418–21
    occasions for, 407–8
    speeches of introduction, 408–11

**concept, 368** An abstract idea—a VALUE, an ATTITUDE, a belief, or a theory.

as topic of informative presentations, 368–69

concise thesis statements, 127

**conclusion, 193** Closing remarks that indicate your presentation is ending, review your MAIN POINTS, and emphasize what you want your AUDIENCE to take away from your presentation.

connective presentations and, 401*f*, 406

crafting of, 197–201

cue the ending, 198–99

framing effect, 193

group presentations, 432–33

logical errors in reasoning, 144–47

preparation outline, drafting of, 206

primacy effect, 193

reasoning with evidence, 140–44, 141*f*

recency effect, 193

review of main points, 200

speaking outlines, drafting of, 210

takeaway, providing, 200–201

**confirmation bias, 147, 158** Our tendency to interpret new EVIDENCE in ways that support our existing beliefs.

research plan and, 158

conflict resolution, 429

in group projects, 445–49

conflicts of interest, 350–51

**confusing correlation with causation, 146** Assuming that one thing causes another when the two things occur around the same time.

Congress for the New Urbanism, 431

connective presentations

award speeches, 411–15

basic structure of, 406–7

building of, 400–407, 401*f*

eulogies, 418–21

occasions for, 407–8

speeches of introduction, 408–11

toasts, 415–17

video tributes, 417

connectivity conclusions and, 201

connectors, search terms and, 159–60

**connotative meaning, 240,** 240*f* The emotional association a symbol suggests. *See also* denotative meaning

**consensus, 444,** 444*f*, **445** Requiring the agreement of all the voting members to reach a decision.

**context, 14,** 14*f*, 16 The setting and circumstances that frame your speech.

adornment and, 275–76

brainstorming about, 117

Paxton Smith speech and, 124–25

purpose and, 122

reason for speaking and, 112–14, 114*f*, 116–17

speaking situation and, 17–18

standpoint and contribution of speaker, 52

style and purpose, 247–54

**contradicting gesture, 272** A GESTURE that indicates that we mean the opposite of what we're saying verbally.

**contribution, 51–52** A unique perspective that a speaker offers to a particular AUDIENCE, on a particular TOPIC, in a particular CONTEXT.

**contributors, 428** Group members who provide information, generate solutions, and take action on group tasks.

**controversy,** 346, **348–49** A debate or disagreement among different views.

disagreement of fact, 375, 375*f*

disagreement of personal action, 375*f*, 376–77

disagreement of policy, 375*f*, 377–78

disagreement of value, 375–76, 375*f*

finding the level of, 374–78, 375*f*

persuading about personal actions, 385–89

persuading about policies, 389–95

persuading about values, 382–84

persuading about facts, 380–81

conversations, audience analysis, 86–88

**copyright, 309** The right to control the use and distribution of creative works.

copyright laws, 309–12

**correlation, 146** An association or relationship between two things.

**countercontagion, 218** When PEOPLE respond with EMOTIONS different from the ones you express.

**credibility, 42,** 42*f*, **349–50** Your AUDIENCE's trust that you have the relevant experience, knowledge, VALUES, and identities to speak on a particular TOPIC.

    admit your limits, 77, 78–79

    citing sources, 170–76

    connective presentations and, 402

    ethics and, 50–53

    false authority, 144

    immediacy and, 261

    informative presentations and, 349–51

    initial credibility, 51

    introductions, developing, 195

    purpose and, 122–23

    restoring of, 53–56

    speeches of introduction, 409–11

    testimony, use of, 136–37

credits, legal issues, 309–12

**crisis, 228,** 229–30 A significant change in the characters or setting that requires a response.

**criteria, 383–84** Standards for judging whether something fits your VALUES.

criticism, listening to feedback, 73–74

**cross-fade, 333** A transition where one video clip fades out while another fades in.

**cross-modal perception, 68,** 68*f* Blending the spectrum of sensory inputs into a unified whole to create experience.

cue the ending, 406

culture

    adornment and, 276

    attitudinal causes, policy change and, 390–91

    code-meshing, 244–46, 244*f*

    code-switching, 243

    implicit ethics, 43

    language and, 240–46

    linguistic diversity, celebrating, 243–46

    linguistic privilege and marginalization, 242–43

    social location and intersectionality, 9–12, 9*f*

    speech communities, addressing, 241–42

# D

databases for source material

    academic, 162–63

    news, 163

data representations, 297–98

decision-making, group projects, 442–45, 444*f*

**deductive reasoning, 140–41,** 141*f* REASONING from a general PRINCIPLE to apply it to a specific case. *See also* inductive reasoning *and* analogical reasoning

deep breathing, anxiety and, 30, 30*f*

definitions, 355

**delivery, 260** The way you communicate the content of your presentation.

    audio recording, tips for, 326

    extemporaneous delivery, 279

    functions of effective delivery, 260–62

    impromptu delivery, 279–80

    live online presentations, 338–40

    manuscript delivery, 278–79

    memorized delivery, 278

    physical delivery, 266–76

    planning and practicing, 277–83

    of slide presentations, 307–8

    vocal delivery, 262–66

**demographic information, 86** Data that categorizes your AUDIENCE members' identities. *See also* psychographic information

**demonstration, 134–35,** 139*t* Giving your AUDIENCE the opportunity to directly observe an EVENT or PRINCIPLE for themselves.

    processes, informative presentations, 364–67

**denotative meaning, 240,** 240*f* What a symbol explicitly names or describes. *See also* connotative meaning

Depew, Chauncey, 318

Desir, Danielle, 316–17

de Waal, Frans, 300

**diagrams, 297** Visual representations of structures or PROCESSES.

> informative presentations and, 356–58, 357*f*

Dias, Marley, 2–3, 10–11

dictionary, pronunciation tips in, 266

digital public speaking. *See* mediated presentations

disability, individuals with

> social location and intersectionality, 9–12, 9*f*
>
> Stella Young's advocacy of, 214–15
>
> stereotypes and hate speech, 44–45

**disagreement of fact, 375,** 375*f* A disagreement about EVIDENCE gained through OBSERVATION, scientific method, or historical analysis.

**disagreement of personal action,** 375*f*, **376–77** A disagreement about what members of the AUDIENCE should do or how they should behave.

**disagreement of policy,** 375*f*, **377–78** A disagreement about what policies an organization or institution should adopt.

**disagreement of value, 375–76,** 375*f* A disagreement about whether something is good or bad, important or unimportant.

Discovery, 319

**disidentification, 229–30** Emphasizing differences in identities, experiences, and VALUES. *See also* identification

disinterest, overcoming, 101–2

dissolve fade, 333

distractions

> external, 67–70, 68*f*
>
> internal, 70–71

**distress tolerance, 32,** 34 The ability to manage stressful or ANXIETY-producing EVENTS.

diversity

> linguistic diversity, 241–46

online communities and, 320–21

> variety and, 260–61

division, overcoming, 105–6

**double vision, 48,** 49 Marginalized groups' understanding of the needs, VALUES, and culture of the PRIVILEGED identity group as well as their own.

dress, 275–76, 329–30

# E

**echo chamber, 63** A CONTEXT where PEOPLE only encounter others who express similar views.

education. *See also* informing and educating presentations

> social location and intersectionality, 9–12, 9*f*

Egerton, Marilyn, 272

**ellipsis, 249** Omitting a word or phrase clearly indicated by the CONTEXT.

embodied action, 5

**emotion, 216** An intuitive reaction based on experiences, BEHAVIOR, VALUES, and ATTITUDES.

> amplification and minimization, 231–34
>
> anger, evoking of, 219–21
>
> aspiration, evoking of, 225–26
>
> attitudinal causes, policy change and, 390–91
>
> compassion, evoking of, 222–23
>
> contagion and countercontagion, 216–18
>
> de-escalating audience's reactions, 227
>
> evoking with expression, 216–18
>
> evoking with reasoning, 219–27
>
> facial expression and, 274
>
> fear, evoking of, 221–22
>
> figures of speech and, 247–50
>
> happiness, evoking of, 226–27
>
> hate speech, stopping spread of, 224
>
> identification and disidentification, 229–30
>
> imitation and rejection, 230–31
>
> mood and, 261
>
> stories, use of, 227–34

**emotional contagion, 216–18** Our tendency to synchronize our emotional experience with the PEOPLE around us.

**extemporaneous delivery, 279** Delivering a presentation from an OUTLINE.

external distractions, 67–70, 68f

**eye contact, 274–75** The experience of being looked at directly in the eyes.
    delivery, planning and practicing, 280–83

# F

Facebook. *See* social media

**facial expressions, 274** Moving or shaping the face to communicate EMOTION or accomplish one of the six functions of GESTURE.
    delivery, planning and practicing, 280–83
    intimate distance and, 269–70, 269f
    personal distance and, 268–69, 269f
    public distance and, 267–68, 269f
    social distance and, 268, 269f

**facilitators, 429** Group members who promote discussion and seek input from all members.

facts, persuasion and, 375f, 380–81

"fake news," identification of, 166–70

**fallacies, 144–47** Logical errors in REASONING.

**false authority, 144** When a source's credentials are not relevant to their claims.

family, social location, and intersectionality, 9–12, 9f

Fauci, Anthony, 77

**fear, 221–22** The feeling that some future harm may come to you or someone you care about.

feedback
    actionable suggestions, 73
    delivery, planning and practicing, 282
    listening to feedback and criticism, 73–74

**figures of speech, 247–50** Linguistic patterns that emphasize particular meanings or feelings.

**filter bubbles, 63,** 164 Personalized ECHO CHAMBERS where web-based PLATFORMS only present us with content we will enjoy and engage with.

Finley, Ron, 201

fireside chats, 318

fixed factors, speaking situation, 16

flip charts, 301–2

Flores, Lisa, 278

Floyd, George, 49, 135

focus, use of presentation aids and, 292
    handouts, 303

**follow-up questions, 87,** 87t Questions that encourage respondents to elaborate on their previous answers.

fonts, text in presentation aids, 293–94, 293t
    in slide decks, 305–6

**formal authority, 427** Holding a recognized position in an organization.

formatting text, in presentation aids, 293–94, 293t

Foxx, Deja, 60–61

**framing effect, 193** Presenting the same information through a different lens changes AUDIENCE perceptions of that information.

framing of message, speaking situation and, 17–18

**freeloading, 446** Refusing to contribute to group tasks while receiving group credit or rewards.

# G

Gandhi, Mahatma, 24

gender
    social location and intersectionality, 9–12, 9f
    stereotypes and hate speech, 44–45

**general purpose, 120–21,** 121f Your overall aim to either inform, persuade, or connect.

**gesture, 271** Moving your body—especially your arms, hands, or head—to communicate meaning.
    accentuating gestures, 272–73
    adapting gestures, 273
    contradicting gestures, 272
    delivery, planning and practicing, 280–83
    eye contact and, 274–75
    personal distance and, 268–69
    public distance and, 267–68, 269

regulating gestures, 273
reinforcing gestures, 271–72
social distance and, 268, 269
substituting gestures, 271

González, X, 115
Google platforms, 320–21
Gorman, Amanda, 398–99
grammar, culture and standpoint, 240

**grand style, 247–50** LANGUAGE rich with vivid imagery, METAPHOR, and other FIGURES OF SPEECH. *See also* plain style *and* middle style

graphs, types and uses, 297–98
Greeks, ancient, 4, 42

**group disruptions, 445–46** Actions that claim personal power within a group at the expense of the group's collective goals.

group meetings and presentations
group conflict, mediating, 445–49
group decision-making, 442–45, 444*f*
group meetings, organizing of, 436–41, 438*t*
leadership, sharing of, 426–29
Lights for Liberty, 424–25
organizing and preparing presentations, 432–33
panel discussions, 430–31
practicing of, 434–36
presentation tasks, assigning of, 431–32
social leadership skills, 428–29
speaking situation, analysis of, 431
symposiums, 430
task leadership skills, 427–28
team presentations, 430

**groupthink, 442** Making decisions based on maintaining group harmony rather than critically evaluating ideas.

# H

habits, credibility and, 42*f*

**handout, 303** Any material a speaker gives an AUDIENCE for them to keep or use.

**happiness, 226–27** Satisfaction with yourself and your circumstances.

Hatch, Jonny, 325

**hate speech, 44–45,** 224 Any communication that attacks, dismisses, or demeans a person or a group based on who they are, including religion, ethnicity, nationality, race, color, gender, sexual orientation, disability, or any other aspect of their identity.

Hawking, Stephen, 5
hearing impairment, individuals with, 288–89
Hixon, Chris, 420
Hixon, Natalie, 420

**host, 336–37** A person who coordinates a live online EVENT and manages attendees.

household income statistics, 138–39
how-to videos, 135
humor
articulation and pronunciation differences, 266
figures of speech and, 247–50
gestures and, 272

**hyperbole, 250** Exaggerating something's importance, size, or degree.

# I

**identification, 52–53,** 53*f* Communicating shared identities, experiences, and VALUES. *See also* disidentification
connective presentations and, 401*f*, 402–3
emotion and, 218
stories and, 229–30

identity groups, 7, 8*t. See also* intersectionality
personal ethics and, 43–44

**identity-neutral language, 46, 47** Language that refers to a person or persons without marking them according to their actual or possible identity traits.

**identity publics, 97–98,** 100, 100*f*, 101, 101*t*
Groups defined by shared social, cultural, or political membership.

## M

Moricz, Zander, 252–53
Mos-Shogbamimu, Shola, 404

**motivated reasoning, 147** Using REASONING to protect your existing beliefs.

**motivational pattern, 190–91** Organizing MAIN POINTS into PROBLEMS and SOLUTIONS.

**multimodality, 291** Simultaneously using multiple modes of communication to accomplish the same goal.

multiple choice questions, surveys, 87, 88

**multitasking, 69–70,** 69*f* The attempt to perform more than one activity simultaneously.

muscle relaxation techniques, 30

# N

Nahua traditions, 4

**narrative, 228** An account of connected EVENTS; a story.

nationality
    social location and intersectionality, 9–12
    stereotypes and hate speech, 44–45
Navajo traditions, 4
needs, Monroe's Motivated Sequence and, 385
news databases, 163
newspapers, source citation style, 175
Nixon, Richard, 318
nonverbal communication
    adornment and, 275–76
    delivery, planning and practicing, 281–83
    gestures, 271–73
    posture, 270–71
    proximity and, 266–70

**normalization, 47** Treating the needs, VALUES, and culture of a PRIVILEGED group as the standard.

note-taking, 70–71
    informational interviews, 166
    research plan and, 156, 157*t*
numerical data, statistics, 138–39, 139*t*

Obama, Barack, 15, 71

**object, 363** A material thing that can be sensed and acted on.
    as topic of informative presentations, 363–64

**objectification, 363** Treating or discussing PEOPLE like OBJECTS.

**observation, 134** Knowledge formed by seeing, hearing, touching, or otherwise encountering something through the senses.

**occasion, 407** A specialized CONTEXT that defines your PURPOSE.
    award speeches, 411–15
    eulogies, 418–21
    speeches of introduction, 408–11
    toasts, 415–17
    video tributes, 417

O'Hara, Eureka, 65
Omar, Ilhan, 276
online presentations and platforms, 4
    addressing audiences online, 321–24
    audience analysis, 88–89
    audio presentations, creating, 324–28
    group presentations and, 436
    hate speech, stopping spread of, 224
    live online presentations, 335–40
    media culture, 318–21
    video presentations, creating, 328–35
online sources. *See* websites

**onomatopoeia, 248** Referring to something using the sound it makes.

**open-ended questions, 87,** 87*t* Questions that invite respondents to answer in their own words. *See also* closed-ended questions

**open posture, 270** Relaxed arms and feet shoulder-width apart. *See also* closed posture

**optimal pitch, 264** A comfortable PITCH in the middle of a speaker's vocal range.

# P

Psaki, Jen, 410

pseudo-academic sources, 164

**regulating gesture, 273** A GESTURE that helps us take turns with each other in a conversation.

**reinforcing gesture, 271–72** A GESTURE that repeats the meaning of your words.

rejection, stories and, 230–31

relationships, reasoning with audiences and, 149, 150. *See also* audience

relevance, personal experience testimony, 137

**reliability, 166** The consistency of information across multiple sources.

    evaluation of, 166–70

religion

    adornment and, 276

    social location and intersectionality, 9–12, 9*f*

    stereotypes and hate speech, 44–45

Render, Michael, 49

**research, 156** The systematic collection and analysis of information.

    academic databases, 162–63

    citing sources, 170–76

    gathering information, 158–61

    informational interviews, 164–66

    library catalogs, 161–62

    news databases, 163

    process for, 156–58, 157*t*

    reliability of information, 166–70

    search terms, 158–61

**research plan, 156,** 157*t* A map of the EVIDENCE you need and where to find it.

resistance, overcoming, 103–5

**resolution, 228–29** Where the characters and setting end up as a result of the ACTION.

**reversing effects, 146** Assuming that an effect can be undone simply by removing its cause.

rhetorical devices, 247–50

**rhetorical questions, 357** Questions that you ask and answer yourself.

**rhyme, 248** Repetition of sounds at the end of nearby words or phrases.

**rhythm, 264–65** A repeated pattern of sounds.

**risk distortion, 146–47,** 147*f* Misjudging the likelihood of a negative EVENT occurring.

Robbins, Tony, 71

Rohn, Jim, 71

Romans, ancient, 4

Roosevelt, Franklin, 71, 318

*Root, The*, 198–99

royalty-free licenses, 309–12

# S

sarcasm, gestures and, 272. *See also* humor

satisfaction, Monroe's Motivated Sequence and, 386–87

Satti, Moe, 434

**sayings, 401** Short, pithy statements sharing folk wisdom or advice.

Schwarzenegger, Arnold, 232–33

Sealy, Gabriela, 409

**search terms, 158** Words or phrases you enter into a catalog, database, or search engine to locate sources of information.

    strategies for use, 158–61

    web search engines, 163–64

**secondary source, 169–70** A source that reports the knowledge, experiences, or statements of others. *See also* primary source

security, for live online presentations, 337

self-perception, 147–51

self-presentation, 11–12

sensory descriptions, use of, 137

setting, use of stories and, 229–30

sexual orientation

    social location and intersectionality, 9–12, 9*f*

    stereotypes and hate speech, 44–45

Shah, Sarah, 299

shared values. *See also* values

    acceptance speeches, 413–15

    audience as a public, 96, 97, 101*t*

    conclusions, review of main points, 200

**team presentation, 430** A single speech prepared and delivered by a group.

Teams, online meetings with, 441

technology. *See also* audio recordings; video recordings
    for group meetings, 440–41
    group presentations, communication tools, 433
    for live online presentations, 336–38
    for online meetings, 441
    in presentation space, 304–5, 307–8

television, public speaking and, 6–7

**terminal credibility, 51** The lasting impression you leave on your AUDIENCE after your speech. *See also* initial credibility

**term of art, 159** A word or phrase that has a specialized meaning in a particular field or profession.

**testimony, 135–36,** 139*t* An account of an individual's OBSERVATIONS, knowledge, and experiences.
    informational interviews, 164–66

text, use in presentation aids, 293–94, 293*t*

theme, slide decks, 305–6

theory, as topic of informative presentations, 368–69

**thesis statement, 126–28,** 128*f* A complete, concise, and clear sentence summarizing the main idea of your presentation.
    connective presentations and, 402, 407
    informative presentations, framing and organizing, 359–69
    in introduction of presentation, 194, 195–96, 203
    research plan and, 156, 157*t*
    supporting evidence for, 134

Thunberg, Greta, 12–13, A-1–A-2

TikTok, 4, 135

**timelines, 298** Graphic representations of EVENTS in sequence.

**toast, 415–17** A short tribute to someone or something that traditionally ends with a celebratory drink.

**topic, 114** What your presentation is about.
    brainstorming for, 117–20, 118*f*
    choice of, 114–20

    events as, 360–61
    informative presentations, framing and organizing, 359–69
    informative presentations, topic selection, 346–47
    purpose and, 120–24, 121*f*
    thesis statement and, 126–28, 128*f*

Torres, Heather, 331

**totalizing, 44** Defining a person's whole identity based on a single aspect of their identity or experience. *See also* essentializing

town hall events, 77

transcendence stories, 55–56

transformation stories, 54–55

**transitions, 191–92** Bridges that transport your AUDIENCE from one part of your speech to the next.
    preparation outline, drafting of, 203–6
    in slide decks, 306–7
    speaking outlines, drafting of, 207–10
    video, editing of, 332–35

**trigger warning, 295,** 299 A warning that upcoming content may disturb your AUDIENCE.

tropes, 247–50

truncators, search terms and, 159–60

trustworthy sources, 136–37

Twitter. *See* social media

# U

**unconscious beliefs, 85** ATTITUDES and VALUES PEOPLE hold without being aware of them.
    audience analysis, 85–86, 85*t*

**universal design, 289** Considering diverse needs and abilities throughout the design PROCESS.

**unrepresentative example, 145** Drawing conclusions from a specific case or set of cases that do not adequately characterize the overall group, category, or PRINCIPLE.

**upright posture, 270** Straight spine with the chin up and shoulders slightly back.

usage, language, 240–41

rhythm, 264–65
of slide presentations, 307–8
volume, 262–63

**voice, 262** Non-linguistic modifiers that affect the meaning, EMOTION, and understanding of LANGUAGE use.

**volume, 262** A speaker's level of amplification; how loudly or softly they are SPEAKING.

# W

# Y

# Z

# Notes

## CHAPTER 1

1. *CBS Mornings*, "Teen Activist Marley Dias on Her New Mission for Racial Harmony," YouTube, January 30, 2018, https://youtu.be/sFCrU8j_1u4.

2. Heidi Stevens, "Marley Dias, the Brains behind #1000BlackGirlBooks, Is Touring with a Book of Her Own," *Chicago Tribune*, January 30, 2018, https://www.chicagotribune.com/columns/heidi-stevens/ct-life-stevens-tuesday-marley-dias-book-appearances-0130-story.html.

3. Cecil Blake, *The African Origins of Rhetoric* (New York: Routledge, 2009); Anjali Gangal and Craig Hosterman, "Toward an Examination of the Rhetoric of Ancient India," *Southern Speech Communication Journal* 47, no. 3 (1982): 277–91, https://doi.org/10.1080/10417948209372534; Xing Lu, *Rhetoric in Ancient China, Fifth to Third Century B.C.E.: A Comparison with Classical Greek Rhetoric* (Columbia, SC: University of South Carolina Press, 1998).

4. Kerry M. Hull and Michael D. Carrasco, eds., *Parallel Worlds: Genre, Discourse, and Poetics in Contemporary, Colonial, and Classical Maya Literature* (Boulder, CO: University of Colorado Press, 2012); Don Paul Abbott, "The Ancient Word: Rhetoric in Aztec Culture," *Rhetorica* 5, no. 3 (1987): 251–64, https://doi.org/10.1525/rh.1987.5.3.251.

5. Damián Baca and Victor Villanueva, eds., *Rhetorics of the Americas: 3114 BCE to 2012 CE* (New York: Palgrave Macmillan, 2010); Richard Morris and Phillip Wander, "Native American Rhetoric: Dancing in the Shadows of the Ghost Dance," *Quarterly Journal of Speech* 76, no. 2 (1990): 164–91, https://doi.org/10.1080/00335639009383912; Gerry Philipsen, "Navajo World View and Culture Patterns of Speech: A Case Study in Ethnorhetoric," *Speech Monographs* 39, no. 2 (2009): 132–39, https://doi.org/10.1080/03637757209375747.

6. Amy Drahota, Alan Costall, and Vasudevi Reddy, "The Vocal Communication of Different Kinds of Smile," *Speech Communication* 50, no. 4 (2007): 278–87, https://doi.org/10.1016/j.specom.2007.10.001.

7. This typology of publics is adapted from chapter 2 of Michael Warner, *Publics and Counterpublics* (Brooklyn, NY: Zone Books, 2002). We have updated Warner's three types to better reflect contemporary social and technological conditions.

8. Vivian M. May, *Pursuing Intersectionality, Unsettling Dominant Imaginaries* (New York: Routledge, 2015).

9. For a more detailed explanation of standpoint theory and its relationship to communication, see D. Lynn O'Brien Hallstein, "Where Standpoint Stands Now: An Introduction and Commentary," *Women's Studies in Communication* 23, no. 1 (2000): 1–15, https://doi.org/10.1080/07491409.2000.11517687, and the other articles in that issue. For a general introduction to standpoint theory, see T. Bowell, "Feminist Standpoint Theory," *Internet Encyclopedia of Philosophy*, accessed February 1, 2022, https://iep.utm.edu/fem-stan/.

10. "What Is Autism Spectrum Disorder?" *Centers for Disease Control and Prevention*, March 25, 2020, https://www.cdc.gov/ncbddd/autism/facts.html.

11. Bruce Y. Lee, "Greta Thunberg: Why She Called Aspergers Her Superpower," *Forbes*, September 27, 2019, https://www.forbes.com/sites/brucelee/2019/09/27/greta-thunberg-why-she-called-aspergers-her-superpower/.

12. This model of the speaking situation is an adaptation and extension of Lloyd Bitzer, "The Rhetorical Situation,"

*Philosophy & Rhetoric* 1, no. 1 (1968): 1–14, https://www
.jstor.org/stable/i40008864; and Richard Vatz, "The Myth
of the Rhetorical Situation," *Philosophy & Rhetoric* 6, no. 3
(1973): 154–61, http://www.jstor.org/stable/40236848.

13.   The Obama White House, "President Obama Speaks
at the White House Correspondents' Association Dinner," YouTube, April 30, 2016, https://www.youtube.com
/watch?v=l-5vD5YVLv8.

## CHAPTER 2

1.   "How Mariale Marrero Used YouTube to Conquer
Her Fear of Public Speaking," *Simply* (blog), May 22,
2017, https://www.simply-inc.com/blog-feeds/mariale
-marrero.

2.  Ale Russian, "Bilingual Beauty," *Time*, accessed February 1, 2022, https://time.com/collection/american-voices
-2017/4920781/american-voices-mariale-marrero/.

3.   ABC News, "Inside the Big Business of Being a Social
Media Influencer," YouTube, February 22, 2019, https://
www.youtube.com/watch?v=5SOFSjlU0fM.

4.  Shawn Lindsey, "Fear Factor: Why Public Speaking
Tops the List," *University of Houston Magazine*, Fall 2017,
https://uh.edu/magazine/2017-fall/making-an-impact
/fear-factor.php.

5.  Cara C. MacInnis, Sean P. Mackinnon, and Peter D.
MacIntyre, "The Illusion of Transparency and Normative
Beliefs about Anxiety during Public Speaking," *Current
Research in Social Psychology* 15, no. 4 (2010), https://crisp
.org.uiowa.edu/sites/crisp.org.uiowa.edu/files/2020-04
/15.4.pdf.

6.  Judee K. Burgoon, Douglas L. Kelley, Deborah A.
Newton, and Maureen P. Keeley-Dyreson, "The Nature of
Arousal and Nonverbal Indices," *Human Communication
Research* 16, no. 2 (1989): 217–55, https://doi.org/10.1111
/j.1468-2958.1989.tb00210.x.

7.  Ana M. Rossi and William J. Seiler, "The Compar-
ative Effectiveness of Systematic Desensitization and
an Integrative Approach in Treating Public Speaking
Anxiety: A Literature Review and a Preliminary Investigation," *Imagination, Cognition and Personality* 9,
no. 1 (1989): 49–66, https://doi.org/10.2190/VR76-9GEF
-JVBW-V5UB. This model has been complicated in some
research, demonstrating cliffs at high anxiety rather
than a curve, but the core principles of the model remain
unchanged.

8.   Luvvie Ajayi Jones, "Get Comfortable with Being
Uncomfortable," YouTube, January 2, 2018, https://www
.youtube.com/watch?v=QijH4UAqGD8.

9.  Allison Wood Brooks, "Get Excited: Reappraising
Pre-performance Anxiety as Excitement," *Journal of
Experimental Psychology* 143, no. 3 (2014): 1144–58,
https://psycnet.apa.org/doi/10.1037/a0035325.

10.   While different researchers divide anxiety into different dimensions, this three-dimension model is among
the most common. See Graham D. Bodie, "A Racing Heart,
Rattling Knees, and Ruminative Thoughts: Defining,
Explaining, and Treating Public Speaking Anxiety,"
*Communication Education* 59, no. 1 (2010): 70–105, https://
doi.org/10.1080/03634520903443849; and Tynessa L.
Gordon and Bethany A. Teachman, "Ethnic Group Differences in Affective, Behavioral, and Cognitive Markers
of Anxiety," *Journal of Cross-Cultural Psychology* 39, no.
4 (2008): 424–46, https://doi.org/10.1177%2F002202210
8318224.

11.   Jane L. Rygh and William C. Sanderson, *Treating
Generalized Anxiety Disorder: Evidence-Based Strategies,
Tools, and Techniques* (New York: Guilford Press, 2004),
1–2.

12.   Harvard Medical School, "2007. National Comorbid-
ity Survey (NCS)," 2007, https://www.hcp.med.harvard
.edu/ncs/index.php.

13.   Anthony Bateman, "Mindfulness," *British Journal of
Psychiatry* 201, no. 4 (2012): 297, https://doi.org/10.1192
/bjp.bp.111.098871.

14.   Stephanie Vozza, "These Navy SEAL Tricks Will Help
You Perform Better under Pressure," *Fast Company*, May
24, 2019, https://www.fastcompany.com/90354456/these
-navy-seal-tricks-will-help-you-perform-better-under
-pressure.

15.   Srini Pallay, "How Simply Moving Benefits Your Mental Health," Harvard Health Publishing, Harvard Medical
School, March 28, 2016, https://www.health.harvard.edu
/blog/how-simply-moving-benefits-your-mental-health
-201603289350.

16.   Jesús Montero-Marín, Sonia Asún, Nerea Estrada-
Marcén, Rosario Romero, and Roberto Asún, "Effec-
tiveness of a Stretching Program on Anxiety Levels of
Workers in a Logistic Platform: A Randomized Controlled

Study," *Atención Primaria* 45, no. 7 (2013): 376–83, https://doi.org/10.1016/j.aprim.2013.03.002.

17. Christa Smith, "3 Ways to Outsmart Your Inner Critic," *Psychology Today*, April 30, 2015, https://www.psychologytoday.com/us/blog/shift/201504/3-ways-outsmart-your-inner-critic.

18. Self-talk first gained public popularity in the 1980s with the work of Shad Helmstetter and has been widely parodied in popular media. Researchers in psychology and especially sports psychology have been documenting its benefits for decades. Multiple studies show that positive self-talk helps manage public speaking anxiety, including Xiaowei Shi, Thomas Brinthaupt, and Margaret McCree, "Understanding the Influence of Self-Critical, Self-Managing, and Social-Assessing Self-Talk on Performance Outcomes in a Public Speaking Context," *Imagination, Cognition and Personality* 36, no. 4 (June 2017): 356–78, https://doi.org/10.1177/0276236617708740; and David Shadinger, John Katsion, Sue Myllykangas, and Denise Case, "The Impact of a Positive, Self-Talk Statement on Public Speaking Anxiety," *College Teaching* 68, no. 1 (2020): 5–11, https://doi.org/10.1080/87567555.2019.1680522.

19. For meta-analysis and a summary of research on self-talk, see James Hardy, "Speaking Clearly: A Critical Review of the Self-Talk Literature," *Psychology of Sport and Exercise* 7, no. 1 (January 2006): 81–97, https://doi.org/10.1016/j.psychsport.2005.04.002; and David Tod, James Hardy, and Emily Oliver, "Effects of Self-Talk: A Systematic Review," *Journal of Sport and Exercise Psychology* 33, no. 5 (2011): 666–87, https://doi.org/10.1123/jsep.33.5.666.

20. Joe Ayres and Theodore S. Hopf, "Visualization: A Means of Reducing Speech Anxiety," *Communication Education* 34, no. 4 (1985): 318–23, https://doi.org/10.1080/03634528509378623; Joe Ayres and Tim Hopf, "Visualization: The Next Generation," *Communication Research Reports* 8, no. 2 (1991): 133–40, https://doi.org/10.1080/08824099109359885.

21. Alistair Foster, "Emma Watson: 'I Was So Terrified before My Speech at the UN That I Had to Be Scraped Off the Floor,'" *Evening Standard*, November 1, 2016, https://www.standard.co.uk/showbiz/celebrity-news/emma-watson-i-was-so-terrified-before-my-speech-at-the-un-that-i-had-to-be-scraped-off-the-floor-a3384126.html.

22. Paris Lees, "From the Archive: Emma Watson on Being Happily 'Self-Partnered' at 30," *Vogue*, April 15, 2020, https://www.vogue.co.uk/news/article/emma-watson-on-fame-activism-little-women.

23. Foster, "Emma Watson."

24. Sam Littlefair, "Emma Watson Talks Love of Meditation, Yoga, Buddhism," *Lion's Roar*, December 3, 2015, https://www.lionsroar.com/emma-watson-talks-love-of-meditation-yoga-buddhism/.

25. Amy Packham, "Emma Watson Admits Feeling Like an Imposter and Reveals How She Overcomes Anxiety and Self Doubt," *Huffington Post UK*, April 8, 2015, https://www.huffingtonpost.co.uk/2015/08/04/emma-watson-advice-self-doubt-_n_7932292.html.

26. Lees, "From the Archive."

27. Christine A. Padesky and Kathleen A. Mooney, "Strengths-Based Cognitive-Behavioral Therapy: A Four-Step Model to Build Resilience," *Clinical Psychology & Psychotherapy* 19, no. 4 (2012) 283–90, https://doi.org/10.1002/cpp.1795.

## CHAPTER 3

1. Caroline Framke, "How Jazz Jennings Changed the World for Trans Youth Simply by Being Herself," *Variety*, 2021, https://variety.com/2021/tv/features/jazz-jennings-i-am-jazz-trans-legislation-1234985248/.

2. Katie Muldowney, Ignacio Torres, and Alexa Valiente, "Transgender Teen and 'I Am Jazz' Star Jazz Jennings on Sharing the Final Steps of Her Transition Journey: Her Gender Confirmation Surgery," ABC News, October 15, 2018, https://abcnews.go.com/Health/transgender-teen-jazz-star-jazz-jennings-sharing-final/story?id=58513271.

3. Terra Dankowksi, "Jazz Jennings Speaks to Self-Acceptance and Survival," *American Libraries*, June 28, 2016, https://americanlibrariesmagazine.org/blogs/the-scoop/jazz-jennings-speaks-self-acceptance-survival/.

4. Human Rights Campaign, "Jazz Jennings at the 2015 HRC Foundation's Time to THRIVE Conference," YouTube, February 14, 2015, https://www.youtube.com/watch?v=QaTeqORW7aU; Johnny Diaz, "7 Questions with Jazz Jennings of TLC's 'I Am Jazz,'" *New York Times*, January 30, 2020, https://www.nytimes.com/2020/01/30/arts/television/i-am-jazz-jennings.html.

5. Thesaurus Linguae Graecae, "ἦθος [ethos]," *The Online Liddell-Scott-Jones Greek-English Lexicon*, http://stephanus.tlg.uci.edu/lsj/#eid=48064.

6. C. S. Green and D. Bavelier, "Exercising Your Brain: A Review of Human Brain Plasticity and Training-Induced Learning," *Psychology and Aging* 23, no. 4 (2008): 692–701, https://dx.doi.org/10.1037%2Fa0014345. For a brief introduction to this principle and its implications, see "Lifelong Learning and the Plastic Brain," University of Cambridge, November 19, 2014, https://www.cam.ac.uk/research/features/lifelong-learning-and-the-plastic-brain.

7. Michael Waltman and John Haas, *The Communication of Hate* (Pieterlen and Bern: Peter Lang, 2011), 34–35.

8. Waltman and Haas, *The Communication of Hate*.

9. United Nations, *United Nations Strategy and Plan of Action on Hate Speech*, May 2019, https://www.un.org/en/genocideprevention/documents/UN%20Strategy%20and%20Plan%20of%20Action%20on%20Hate%20Speech%2018%20June%20SYNOPSIS.pdf.

10. Dennis Baron, "A Brief History of Singular 'They,'" *Oxford English Dictionary,* September 4, 2018, https://public.oed.com/blog/a-brief-history-of-singular-they/; "How Do I Use Singular *They*?" MLA Style Center, March 4, 2020, https://style.mla.org/using-singular-they/; "Singular 'They,'" *APA Style*, September 2019, https://apastyle.apa.org/style-grammar-guidelines/grammar/singular-they.

11. Sherry K. Watt, "Difficult Dialogues, Privilege and Social Justice: Uses of the Privileged Identity Exploration (PIE) Model in Student Affairs Practice," *College Student Affairs Journal* 26, no. 2 (2007): 114–26, https://eric.ed.gov/?id=EJ899385.

12. Bob Pease, "Theorizing Normalization as Hidden Privilege," in *Normalization and Outsiderhood: Feminist Readings of a Neoliberal Welfare State*, ed. Siv Fahlgren, Diana Mulinari, and Anders Johansson (Sweden: Bentham Books, 2011), 69–79.

13. Abigail Brooks, "Feminist Standpoint Epistemology: Building Knowledge and Empowerment through Women's Lived Experiences," in *Feminist Research Practice: A Primer*, ed. Sharlene Nagy Hesse-Biber and Patricia Lina Leavy (Thousand Oaks, CA: SAGE Publishing, 2007), 53–82, https://dx.doi.org/10.4135/9781412984270.

14. Kimberle Crenshaw, "Mapping the Margins: Intersectionality, Identity Politics, and Violence against Women of Color," *Stanford Law Review* 43, no. 6 (1991): 1241–99, https://doi.org/10.2307/1229039.

15. Audre Lorde, "There Is No Hierarchy of Oppressions," *Interracial Books for Children Bulletin: Homophobia and Education* 14, nos. 3–4 (1983): 9, http://digital.library.wisc.edu/1711.dl/Literature.CIBCBulletinv14n0304.

16. Atlanta Police Department, "Press Conference—Protest 5-29-2020," YouTube, May 30, 2020, accessed August 22, 2020, https://www.youtube.com/watch?v=SN1TxJeFkHs.

17. Sarah Rose, "Black Community Leaders Weigh In on Killer Mike's 'Kill Your Masters' T-Shirt," GPB.org, June 3, 2020, https://www.gpb.org/news/2020/06/03/black-community-leaders-weigh-in-on-killer-mikes-kill-your-masters-t-shirt.

18. Caren B. Cooper, Jennifer Shirk, and Benjamin Zuckerberg, "The Invisible Prevalence of Citizen Science in Global Research: Migratory Birds and Climate Change," *PLOS One* (September 3, 2014), https://doi.org/10.1371/journal.pone.0106508; Brian Wynne, "Misunderstood and Misunderstanding: Social Identities and Public Uptake of Science," *Public Understanding of Science* 1, no. 4 (1992): 281–304; Roland Petchey, Jacky Williams, Bill Farnsworth, and Ken Starkey, "A Tale of Two (Low Prevalence) Cities: Social Movement Organisations and the Local Policy Response to HIV/AIDS," *Social Science & Medicine* 47, no 9 (1998): 1197–1208, https://doi.org/10.1016/S0277-9536(97)10020-X.

19. Kenneth Burke, *A Rhetoric of Motives* (Oakland: University of California Press, 1969), 19–36.

## CHAPTER 4

1. Reed Dunlea and Jamil Smith, "'My Experience Is My Expertise': Deja Foxx on Being a Presidential Campaign Staffer at 19, Influencers, and Sexuality in Politics," *Rolling Stone*, January 13, 2021, https://www.rollingstone.com/politics/politics-news/deja-foxx-acivist-kamala-harris-campaign-1112872/.

2. Dunlea and Smith, "'My Experience.'"

3. D'Shonda Brown, "Deja Foxx Is Running the World from Point A to Generation Z," Hypebae, September 16, 2021, https://hypebae.com/2021/9/deja-foxx-gen-z-girl

-gang-founder-activist-sex-education-reproductive-health-instagram-creator-interview.

4. In the Know, "Meet the Youngest Staffer Working on a Presidential Hopeful's Campaign," YouTube, January 31, 2020, https://www.youtube.com/watch?v=kLsMMATual0; Raven Ishak, "How a Gen Z Activist Is Eliciting Change in Her Youth Community," Hello Giggles, September 5, 2021, https://hellogiggles.com/lifestyle/deja-foxx-interview-gen-z-girl-gan/.

5. Margarete Imhof, "Listening Is Easy!? Looking at Critical Factors for Listening Performance," in *Communication as Performance and the Performativity of Communication: Proceedings of the 2014 International Colloquium on Communication*, ed., Kevin M. Carragee and Annette Moennich (Virginia Tech Libraries, 2016), 76–88, https://scholar.lib.vt.edu/ejournals/ICC/2014/ICC2014.pdf.

6. Elisabeth Noelle-Neumann, "The Spiral of Silence: A Theory of Public Opinion," *Journal of Communication* 24, no. 2 (1974): 43–51, https://doi.org/10.1111/j.1460-2466.1974.tb00367.x.

7. Cass R. Sunstein, *#Republic: Divided Democracy in the Age of Social Media* (Princeton: Princeton University Press, 2017).

8. Eli Pariser, *The Filter Bubble: How the New Personalized Web Is Changing What We Read and How We Think* (New York: Penguin Press, 2011).

9. Tim Chan, "Shangela and Bob the Drag Queen Dish on Ariana Grande, 'Queer Eye,' and Active Allyship," *Rolling Stone*, June 29, 2020, https://www.rollingstone.com/tv/tv-news/hbo-were-here-shangela-bob-drag-queen-interview-1021643/.

10. Kyler Alvord, "How the Drag Stars of HBO's 'We're Here' Are Making Lasting Change in Small Towns," Thrillist, June 11, 2020, https://www.thrillist.com/entertainment/nation/were-here-hbo-series-review.

11. Alvord, "How the Drag Stars."

12. Amy S. Ebesu Hubbard, "Perspective Taking, Adaptation, and Coordination," in William F. Eadie, *21st Century Communication: A Reference Handbook* (Thousand Oaks, CA: SAGE Publications, 2009): 119–27.

13. Dominic W. Massaro, "From Multisensory Integration to Talking Heads and Language Learning," in *The Handbook of Multisensory Processes*, ed. Gemma A. Calvert, Charles Spence, and Barry E. Stein (Cambridge, MA: MIT Press, 2004): 153–76. Section two of this handbook includes five essays that explore cross-modal or multisensory perception of speech.

14. Se-Hoon Jeong and Yoori Hwang, "Media Multitasking Effects on Cognitive vs. Attitudinal Outcomes: A Meta-analysis," *Human Communication Research* 42, no. 4 (2016), 599–618, https://doi.org/10.1111/hcre.12089; Reynol Junco, "In-Class Multitasking and Academic Performance," *Computers in Human Behavior* 28, no. 6 (2012), 2236–43, https://doi.org/10.1016/j.chb.2012.06.031; Zheng Wang and John M. Tchernev, "The 'Myth' of Media Multitasking: Reciprocal Dynamics of Media Multitasking, Personal Needs, and Gratifications," *Journal of Communication* 62, no. 3 (2012): 493–513, https://doi.org/10.1111/j.1460-2466.2012.01641.x.

15. William R. Klemm, "Learn to Breathe for Better Health," *Psychology Today*, August 28, 2019, https://www.psychologytoday.com/us/blog/memory-medic/201908/learn-breathe-better-health.

16. For examples, see Obama's second inaugural speech and his 2008 victory speech.

17. "Suze Orman Says Oprah Taught Her an 'Encyclopedia Version of Life,'" *Tell Me More*, National Public Radio, May 24, 2011, https://www.npr.org/2011/05/24/136612221/suze-orman-says-oprah-taught-her-an-encyclopedia-version-of-life.

18. Richard Feloni, "Tony Robbins Started Out as a Broke Janitor—Then He Saved a Week's Worth of Pay, and the Way He Spent It Changed His Life," *Insider*, October 4, 2017, https://www.businessinsider.com/tony-robbins-changed-his-life-at-17-years-old-2017-10.

19. Healthline, "Healthline Live Town Hall Featuring Dr. Anthony Fauci," YouTube, August 18, 2020, accessed February 20, 2022, https://www.youtube.com/watch?v=E2waiMF-X98.

20. Grace Panetta, "Dr. Anthony Fauci and Gov. Andrew Cuomo Are the Most Trusted Leaders in America on the Coronavirus Right Now. Trump Is Not," *Insider*, March 26, 2020, https://www.businessinsider.com/americans-most-trust-fauci-cuomo-on-coronavirus-response-insider-poll-2020-3.

## CHAPTER 5

1. Jahmal Cole, "It's Not Regular—Full Speech by Jahmal Cole," YouTube, January 22, 2019, https://www.youtube.com/watch?v=23qdEXQ5AXE.

2. Milton Rokeach, *The Nature of Human Values* (New York: Free Press, 1973), 5–10.

3. While scholars generally prefer the term *value hierarchies*, we have chosen "value priorities" as a more intuitive and accessible term. Rokeach (see Note 2) is credited with founding modern research on value hierarchies. For an example of their use in communication and argument, see Edward S. Inch and Barbara Warnick, *Critical Thinking and Communication: The Use of Reason in Argument* (Boston: Allyn & Bacon, 2002), 263–64.

4. This tweet and the replies are hypothetical examples created for illustration only. The tweet and replies were generated using Tweetgen (https://www.tweetgen.com/).

5. Ashley Hinck, "Ethical Frameworks and Ethical Modalities: Theorizing Communication and Citizenship in a Fluid World," *Communication Theory* 26, no. 1 (2016): 1–20, https://doi.org/10.1111/comt.12062.

6. ABC News, "Jon Stewart Slams Congress over Benefits for 9/11 First Responders," YouTube, June 11, 2019, https://www.youtube.com/watch?v=_uYpDC3SRpM.

## CHAPTER 6

1. Caroline Carter and Simon Cox, "Gaming with Joshua Wong," *1843 magazine, Economist*, April 29, 2020, https://www.economist.com/1843/2020/04/29/gaming-with-joshua-wong.

2. En Liang Khong and Joshua Wong, "Hong Kong's Angry Young Millennials: An Interview with Joshua Wong," OpenDemocracy, November 1, 2015, https://www.opendemocracy.net/en/hong-kong-angry-young-millennials-interview-with-joshua-wong/.

3. Laignee Barron, "Hong Kong Democracy Activist Joshua Wong Goes to Prison Vowing That His Fight Will Continue," *Time*, December 2, 2020, https://time.com/5916998/joshua-wong-prison-hong-kong/.

4. Joshua Wong quoted by Feliz Solomon, "Facing Jail, Democracy Activist Joshua Wong Says 'Hong Kong Is under Threat,'" *Time*, August 16, 2017, https://time.com/4902751/hong-kong-joshua-wong-interview-sentencing-democracy/.

5. Lloyd Bitzer, "The Rhetorical Situation," *Philosophy & Rhetoric* 1, no. 1 (1968): 1–14, https://www.jstor.org/stable/i40008864.

6. Emma González, "A Young Activist's Advice: Vote, Shave Your Head and Cry Whenever You Need To," *New York Times*, October 5, 2018, https://www.nytimes.com/2018/10/05/opinion/sunday/emma-gonzalez-parkland.html.

7. CBS Miami, "Passionate Speech by Marjory Stoneman Douglas Student Emma Gonzalez at Anti-Gun Rally," YouTube, February 18, 2018, https://www.youtube.com/watch?v=PQPr3iMTL98.

8. Martin Vassolo, "Cuban-American Teen Thrust into Gun Debate Is Allergic to Dogs and Political 'B.S,'" *Miami Herald*, February 23, 2018, https://www.miamiherald.com/news/politics-government/article201858354.html.

9. Guardian News, "Emma González's Powerful March for Our Lives Speech in Full," YouTube, March 24, 2018, https://www.youtube.com/watch?v=u46HzTGVQhg.

10. "Paxton Smith Speech at Lake Highlands Graduation," YouTube, June 1, 2021, https://www.youtube.com/watch?v=mrfe27VDuRA&t=264s.

11. "Lake Highlands H.S. Valedictorian Calls Out Texas 'Heartbeat Bill' during Commencement Speech," KDFW Fox 4, June 3, 2021, https://www.fox4news.com/video/940166.

12. Ella Malena Feldman, "Dallas Valedictorian Swaps Graduation Speech to Slam 'Gut-Wrenching' Texas Abortion Law," *Austin American-Statesman*, June 3, 2021, https://www.statesman.com/story/news/2021/06/03/dallas-high-school-valedictorian-slams-abortion-law-graduation-speech-paxton-smith/7523609002/.

13. Olivia Blair, "High School Student Changes Graduation Speech to Rally for Abortion Rights," *Elle*, June 4, 2021, https://www.elle.com/uk/life-and-culture/culture/a36627520/paxton-smith-abortion-speech-celebrity-reaction/.

## CHAPTER 7

1. "Edna Chavez—We Are the Future: Youth Leadership & Community Activism," Bioneers, 2018, https://bioneers.org/edna-chavez-we-are-the-future-youth-leadership-community-activism/.

2. Olivia Fleming, "Gabrielle Giffords and Edna Chavez Refuse to Be Silenced on Gun Control," *Harper's Bazaar*, October 8, 2018, https://www.harpersbazaar.com/culture/features/a23118433/gabby-giffords-edna-chavez-women-who-dare-2018-gun-control/.

3. Girl Up, "2020 Leadership Summit: The Future Is Now," YouTube, July 23, 2020, https://www.youtube.com/watch?v=DuhLrbxBBSA.

4. "Edna Chavez—We Are the Future," Bioneers.

5. Emily A. Shrider, Melissa Kollar, Frances Chen, and Jessica Semega, *Income and Poverty in the United States: 2020*, September 2021, https://www.census.gov/content/dam/Census/library/publications/2021/demo/p60-273.pdf.

6. Diana Adjadj, "Fraud—What Constitutes Fraud in California?" Diana Legal, December 26, 2019, https://www.dianalegal.com/fraud-what-constitutes-fraud-in-california-what-does-a-cause-of-action-for-fraud-by-intentional-misrepresentation-in-california-mean/.

7. Brianna Keilar and Catherine Valentine, "What's Killing Staff Sergeant Wesley Black? The VA Doesn't Want to Talk about It," CNN, March 6, 2020, https://www.cnn.com/2020/03/06/politics/homefront-burn-pits/index.html.

8. Burn Pits 360, "Statement for the Record before the Senate Committee on Veteran's Affairs, United States Senate, for a September 25, 2019 Hearing Entitled: 'Toxic Exposure: Examining the VA's Presumptive Disability Decision-Making Process,'" Senate Committee on Veterans' Affairs, September 25, 2019, https://www.veterans.senate.gov/imo/media/doc/9.25.19%20-%20BurnPits360%20SFR.pdf.

9. El Paso Matters, "El Paso Trans Advocate Testifies at Texas Senate Hearing," YouTube, April 12, 2021, 0:35, https://www.youtube.com/watch?v=7tvM7eWzT_I.

10. Pew Charitable Trusts, "Pursuing the American Dream: Economic Mobility across Generations," July 2012, https://www.pewtrusts.org/~/media/legacy/uploadedfiles/wwwpewtrustsorg/reports/economic_mobility/PursuingAmericanDreampdf.pdf.

11. Virginia Thomas and Margarita Azmitia, "Motivation Matters: Development and Validation of the Motivation for Solitude Scale – Short Form (MSS-SF)," *Journal of Adolescence* 70 (2019): 33–42, https://doi.org/10.1016/j.adolescence.2018.11.004.

12. Neal A. Halsey, Susan L. Hyman, and the Conference Writing Panel, "Measles-Mumps-Rubella Vaccine and Autistic Spectrum Disorder: Report from the New Challenges in Childhood Immunizations Conference Convened in Oak Brook, Illinois, June 12–13, 2000," *Pediatrics* 107, no. 5 (2001): e84, https://doi.org/10.1542/peds.107.5.e84; Anders Hviid, Jørgen Vinsløv Hansen, Morten Frisch, and Mads Melbye, "Measles, Mumps, Rubella Vaccination and Autism," *Annals of Internal Medicine* 170, no. 8 (2019): 513–20, https://doi.org/10.7326/M18-2101.

13. The foundational essay for this research is Paul Slovic, "Perception of Risk," *Science* 236, no. 4799 (1987): 280–85, https://doi.org/10.1126/science.3563507. As of 2021, more than four hundred subsequent articles and numerous books have extended on Slovic's research.

14. Aurelio Locsin, "Is Air Travel Safer Than Car Travel?" *USA Today*, accessed February 28, 2022, https://traveltips.usatoday.com/air-travel-safer-car-travel-1581.html.

15. Ziva Kunda, "The Case for Motivated Reasoning," *Psychological Bulletin* 108, no. 3 (1990): 480–98, https://doi.apa.org/doi/10.1037/0033-2909.108.3.480.

16. Tessa C. Andrews and Paula P. Lemons, "It's Personal: Biology Instructors Prioritize Personal Evidence over Empirical Evidence in Teaching Decisions," *CBE: Life Sciences Education* 14, no. 1 (October 13, 2017), https://doi.org/10.1187/cbe.14-05-0084; Walter Mischel, "Connecting Clinical Practice to Scientific Progress," *Psychological Science in the Public Interest* 9, no. 2 (2008): i–ii, https://doi.org/10.1111%2Fj.1539-6053.2009.01035.x.

17. Climate Collaborative, "ShiftCon Climate Summit: A Call to Climate Action," Vimeo, December 11, 2020, https://vimeo.com/489872134.

18. Climate Collaborative, "ShiftCon Climate Summit."

19. We Don't Have Time, "#WeDontHaveTime—Q&A with Jamie Margolin," YouTube, May 6, 2019, https://www.youtube.com/watch?v=gqfALeldO5s; We Don't Have Time, "When the Grown-Ups Are Busy Destroying the Future, the Young Must Step In and Rescue It," Medium, January 1, 2019, https://medium.com/wedonthavetime/when-the-grown-ups-are-busy-destroying-the-future-the-young-must-step-in-and-rescue-it-ac40337222e3.

20. TEDx talks, "Patriarchy, Racism, and Colonialism Caused the Climate Crisis," Jamie Margolin, TEDxYouth@Columbia, YouTube, June 14, 2019, https://www.youtube.com/watch?v=amGyIqIBzEk.

21. Jamie Margolin, *Youth to Power: Your Voice and How to Use It* (New York: Hachette Go, 2020), chapter 9.

22. See Adrian Bardon, *The Truth about Denial: Bias and Self-Deception in Science, Politics, and Religion* (New York: Oxford University Press, 2020).

## CHAPTER 8

1. Blair Imani, "What Is Intersectionality? Why Is It Important?" Get Smarter with Blair Imani, YouTube, February 23, 2021, https://www.youtube.com/watch?v=iRRGpF63TJ4.

2. TEDx talks, "Queer & Muslim: Nothing to Reconcile," Blair Imani, TEDxBoulder, YouTube, July 9, 2019, https://www.youtube.com/watch?v=8IhaGUlmO_k.

3. Bradley J. Adame, "Training in the Mitigation of Anchoring Bias: A Test of the Consider-the-Opposite Strategy," *Learning and Motivation* 53 (2016): 36–48, https://doi-org.pallas2.tcl.sc.edu/10.1016/j.lmot.2015.11.002.

4. Amanda Ross-White, Christina M. Godfrey, Kimberley A. Sears, and Rosemary Wilson, "Predatory Publications in Evidence Syntheses," *Journal of the Medical Library Association* 107, no. 1 (2019): 57–61, https://doi.org/10.5195/jmla.2019.491; Joeran Beel and Bela Gipp, "Academic Search Engine Spam and Google Scholar's Resistance against It," *Journal of Electronic Publishing* 13, no. 3 (2010), https://doi.org/10.3998/3336451.0013.305.

5. Mike Caulfield, "SIFT (The Four Moves)," Hapgood, June 19, 2019, https://hapgood.us/2019/06/19/sift-the-four-moves/. The superiority of SIFT over the older CRAAP method is noted in Allison I. Faix, "Source Evaluation Strategies for the Misinformation Age," *South Carolina Libraries* 5, no. 2 (2021), https://doi.org/10.51221/suc.scl.2021.5.2.1; and in Kat Phillips, "No, Bananas Don't Cure HIV, nor Will Garlic Cure COVID-19: Searching for, Assessing, and Consuming Health Information Online," *Journal of Consumer Health on the Internet* 24, no. 2 (2020): 175–85, https://doi.org/10.1080/15398285.2020.1755149.

6. Jackie Mansky, "The Age-Old Problem of 'Fake News,'" *Smithsonian Magazine*, May 7, 2018, https://www.smithsonianmag.com/history/age-old-problem-fake-news-180968945/.

7. Andrew M. Guess, Brendan Nyhan, and Jason Reifler, "Exposure to Untrustworthy Websites in the 2016 US Election," *Nature Human Behaviour* 4, no. 5 (2020): 472–80, https://dx.doi.org/10.1038%2Fs41562-020-0833-x.

8. Erik Wemple, "'Fox & Friends' Fails on Obama-Muslim Museum Connection: No Surprise Here," *Washington Post*, October 7, 2013, https://www.washingtonpost.com/blogs/erik-wemple/wp/2013/10/07/fox-friends-fails-on-obama-muslim-museum-connection-no-surprise-here/.

9. Caitlin Dewey, "Facebook Fake News Writer: 'I Think Donald Trump Is in the White House Because of Me,'" *Washington Post*, November 17, 2016, https://www.washingtonpost.com/news/the-intersect/wp/2016/11/17/facebook-fake-news-writer-i-think-donald-trump-is-in-the-white-house-because-of-me/; Louis Jacobson, "No, Someone Wasn't Paid $3,500 to Protest Donald Trump; It's Fake News," Politifact, November 17, 2016, https://www.politifact.com/factchecks/2016/nov/17/blog-posting/no-someone-wasnt-paid-3500-protest-donald-trump-it/; Ishamel N. Daro, "How a Prankster Convinced People the Amish Would Win Trump the Election," Buzzfeed News, October 28, 2016, https://www.buzzfeednews.com/article/ishmaeldaro/paul-horner-amish-trump-vote-hoax.

10. Laura Sydell, "We Tracked Down a Fake-News Creator in the Suburbs. Here's What We Learned," *All Things Considered*, NPR, November 23, 2016, https://www.npr.org/sections/alltechconsidered/2016/11/23/503146770/npr-finds-the-head-of-a-covert-fake-news-operation-in-the-suburbs; Erik Hedegaard, "How a Fake Newsman Accidentally Helped Trump Win the White House," *Rolling Stone*, November 29, 2016, https://www.rollingstone.com/culture/culture-news/how-a-fake-newsman-accidentally-helped-trump-win-the-white-house-110039/.

11. Jacob L. Nelson and Harsh Taneja, "The Small, Disloyal Fake News Audience: The Role of Audience Availability in Fake News Consumption," *New Media & Society* 20, no. 10 (October 2018): 3720–37, https://doi.org/10.1177/1461444818758715; Nic Fleming, "Fighting

Coronavirus Misinformation," *Nature* 583 (July 2, 2020): 155–56, https://www.nature.com/articles/d41586 -020-01834-3; Thomas J. Froehlich, "The Role of Pseudo-Cognitive Authorities and Self-Deception in the Dissemination of Fake News," *Open Information Science* 3, no. 1 (2019): 115–36, https://doi.org/10.1515/opis-2019-0009.

12. Corey Siemaszko, "InfoWars' Alex Jones Is a 'Performance Artist,' His Lawyer Says in Divorce Hearing," NBC News, April 17, 2017, https://www.nbcnews.com/news/us -news/not-fake-news-infowars-alex-jones-performance -artist-n747491.

13. Jane McGonigal, "The Game That Can Give You 10 Extra Years of Life," YouTube, July 9, 2012, https://www .youtube.com/watch?v=lfBpsV1Hwqs.

## CHAPTER 9

1. Carolyn Twersky, "Thandiwe Abdullah Is Leading the Next Generation of the Black Lives Matter Movement," *Seventeen*, December 1, 2020, https://www.seventeen.com /life/a34717855/thandiwe-abdullah-black-lives-matter -voices-of-the-year-2020/.

2. PYFC Santa Monica, "Thandiwe Abdullah, BLM, Speaks at the National Walk Out at Santa Monica City Hall 4-20-18," YouTube, https://www.youtube.com/watch ?v=CnNUPU0pzHE.

3. PYFC Santa Monica, "Thandiwe Abdullah, BLM."

4. "TIME's 25 Most Influential Teens of 2018," *Time*, December 10, 2018, https://time.com/5463721/most -influential-teens-2018/.

5. Kieran O'Mahony, *The Brain-Based Classroom: Accessing Every Child's Potential through Educational Neuroscience* (London: Taylor & Francis, 2020), chapter 8.

6. Dietram A. Scheufele, "Framing as a Theory of Media Effects, *Journal of Communication* 49 (1999): 103–22, https://doi-org.pallas2.tcl.sc.edu/10.1111/j.1460-2466 .1999.tb02784.x.

7. Robert G. Crowder, *Principles of Learning and Memory* (New York: Lawrence Erlbaum Associates, 1976).

8. Arrest data: Federal Bureau of Investigation, "Crime in the United States: 2014," https://www.fbi.gov/about-us /cjis/ucr/crime-in-the-u.s/2014/crime-in-the-u.s.-2014 /tables/table-29; incidence data: Centers for Disease Control and Prevention, "Alcohol-Impaired Driving among Adults—United States, 2012," *Morbidity and Mortality Weekly Report* 64, no. 30 (2015): 814–17, http://www.cdc .gov/mmwr/preview/mmwrhtml/mm6430a2.htm.

9. National Archives Foundation, "The Surprising Story of Deborah Sampson Gannett, a Soldier in the Revolutionary War," https://www.docsteach.org/activities/student /the-surprising-story-of-deborah-sampson-gannett-a -soldier-in-the-revolutionary-war.

10. W. E. B. Du Bois, *John Brown: A Biography* (Philadelphia: George W. Jacobs, 1909).

11. The Overexplainer, *Essence*, "'Body Positivity' Is a Social Movement That Celebrates EveryBODY," YouTube, September 1, 2019, https://www.youtube.com/watch?v= _xMvkdBcnPg.

12. "YouTube for Press," YouTube, accessed March 7, 2022, https://blog.youtube/press/.

13. Dorie Clark, *Stand Out: How to Find Your Breakthrough Idea and Build a Following around It* (New York: Penguin Random House, 2015).

14. Robert Glazer, "Want to Build a Following Online? Follow These 3 Steps," *Forbes*, February 27, 2019, https:// www.forbes.com/sites/robertglazer/2019/02/27/want-to -build-a-following-online-follow-these-3-steps/.

15. Peter Vanden Bos, "How to Build a Loyal Blog Following," *Inc.*, accessed May 23, 2022, https://www.inc.com /guides/2010/04/build-a-loyal-blog-following.html.

16. Jarrett E. K. Byrnes, Jai Ranganathan, Barbara L. E. Walker, and Zen Faulkes, "To Crowdfund Research, Scientists Must Build an Audience for Their Work," *PLOS One* 9, no. 2 (December 10, 2014), https://doi.org/10.1371 /journal.pone.0110329.

17. Bhavik Sarkhedi, "Eight Exceptional Skills Every Digital Marketer Must Have," *Medium*, August 2, 2021, https://bhaviksarkhedi.medium.com/eight-exception-al-skills-every-digital-marketer-must-have-58e2f- 818ca4e.

18. Cathrin Manning, "0 to 1,000 Subscribers on You-Tube: YouTube Tips That Helped to Grow My Beginner YouTube Channel," YouTube, June 13, 2019, https://www .youtube.com/watch?v=ELMCY5nsZqs&t=720s.

19. Cathrin Manning, "How Long It Takes to Get Monetized on YouTube: The Review Process, Google AdSense,

and More!" YouTube, July 22, 2019, https://www.youtube.com/watch?v=_eg3-6rM89Y.

## CHAPTER 10

1. Stella Young, "I'm Not Your Inspiration, Thank You Very Much," TED talk, YouTube, June 9, 2014, https://www.youtube.com/watch?v=8K9Gg164Bsw.

2. This definition is based on how psychologists generally define emotion. For example, see "emotion" in the American Psychological Association's *APA Dictionary of Psychology*, https://dictionary.apa.org/emotion.

3. Elaine Hatfield, John T. Cacioppo, and Richard L. Rapson, *Emotional Contagion* (Cambridge, UK: Cambridge University Press, 1994).

4. Multiple studies demonstrate the power of emotional contagion online. See Adam D. I. Kramer, Jamie E. Guillory, and Jeffrey T. Hancock, "Experimental Evidence of Massive-Scale Emotional Contagion through Social Networks," *Proceedings of the National Academy of Sciences of the United States of America* (*PNAS*) 111, no. 24 (2014): 8788–90, https://dx.doi.org/10.1073%2Fpnas.1320040111; Christy Galletta Horner, Dennis Galletta, Jennifer Crawford, and Abhijeet Shirsat, "Emotions: The Unexplored Fuel of Fake News on Social Media," *Journal of Management Information Systems* 38, no. 4 (2021): 1039–66, https://doi.org/10.1080/07421222.2021.1990610.

5. Call-and-response has deep roots in the civil rights movement, originating from African and African American musical traditions. See Keith Gilyard and Adam J. Banks, *On African-American Rhetoric* (New York: Routledge, 2018).

6. Jules Lobel and George F. Loewenstein, "Emote Control: The Substitution of Symbol for Substance in Foreign Policy and International Law," *Chicago Kent Law Review* 80, no. 3 (2005): 1045–90, https://ssrn.com/abstract=757208.

7. These emotions and strategies are drawn from Book II of Aristotle's *Rhetoric*. We have adapted them both for our current age and for the ways that modern public speaking differs from the forms of speech common in ancient Greece.

8. Riccardo Williams, "Anger as a Basic Emotion and Its Role in Personality Building and Pathological Growth: The Neuroscientific, Developmental, and Clinical Perspectives," *Frontiers in Psychology* 8, no. 1950 (2017), https://doi.org/10.3389/fpsyg.2017.01950.

9. Myisha Cherry, *The Case for Rage: Why Anger Is Essential to Anti-racist Struggle* (New York: Oxford University Press, 2021).

10. US Bureau of Labor Statistics, US Department of Labor, *TED: The Economics Daily*, "Women Had Higher Median Earnings Than Men in Relatively Few Occupations in 2018," March 22, 2019, https://www.bls.gov/opub/ted/2019/women-had-higher-median-earnings-than-men-in-relatively-few-occupations-in-2018.htm.

11. Data reflects 2020 numbers retrieved from the US Census Bureau's QWI Explorer, accessed May 15, 2022, https://qwiexplorer.ces.census.gov/.

12. N. Reed and R. Robbins, "The Effect of Text Messaging on Driver Behaviour: A Simulator Study," *Transport Research Laboratory*, published project report 367, 2008, https://www.racfoundation.org/wp-content/uploads/2017/11/texting-whilst-driving-trl-180908-report.pdf.

13. Patrick DeGrasse, "Teens Texting and Driving: Get the Facts and Statistics Here!" Arrive Alive Tour, March 7, 2018, https://arrivealivetour.com/teens-texting-and-driving-facts/#:~:text=94%25%20of%20teens%20acknowledge%20that,result%20of%20texting%20while%20driving.

14. DeGrasse, "Teens Texting."

15. Rachel L. Ruttan, Mary-Hunter McDonnell, and Loran F. Nordgren, "Having 'Been There' Doesn't Mean I Care: When Prior Experience Reduces Compassion for Emotional Distress," *Journal of Personality and Social Psychology* 108, no. 4 (2015): 610–22, https://doi.org/10.1037/pspi0000012.

16. Kosisochukwu Judith Madukwe, Xiaoying Gao, and Bing Xue, "What Emotion Is Hate? Incorporating Emotion Information into the Hate Speech Detection Task," in *PRICAI 2021: Trends in Artificial Intelligence, PRICAI 2021, Lecture Notes in Computer Science*, ed. D. N. Pham, T. Theeramunkong, G. Governatori, and F. Liu, vol. 13032 (Springer, 2021), 273–86, https://doi.org/10.1007/978-3-030-89363-7_21; Karin Sandell, "Gay Clowns, Pigs, and Traitors: An Emotion Analysis of Online Hate Speech Directed at the Swedish-Speaking Population in Finland," *Folklore* 74 (2018): 25–50, https://doi.org/10.7592/FEJF2018.74.sandell.

17. Karsten Müller and Carlo Schwarz, "Fanning the Flames of Hate: Social Media and Hate Crime," *Journal of the European Economic Association* 19, no. 4 (2020): 2131–67, https://doi.org/10.1093/jeea/jvaa045.

18. Rui Fan, Jichang Zhao, Yan Chen, and Ke Xu, "Anger Is More Influential Than Joy: Sentiment Correlation in Weibo," *PLOS One* 9, no. 10 (2014): e110184, https://doi.org/10.1371/journal.pone.0110184; Christopher A. Bail, "Emotional Feedback and the Viral Spread of Social Media Messages about Autism Spectrum Disorders," *American Journal of Public Health* 106, no. 7 (2016): 1173–80, https://doi.org/10.2105/AJPH.2016.303181; Jonah Berger and Katherine L. Milkman, "What Makes Online Content Viral?" *Journal of Marketing Research* 49, no. 2 (2011): 192–205, https://doi.org/10.1509%2Fjmr.10.0353.

19. Chris J. Vargo and Toby Hopp, "Fear, Anger, and Political Advertisement Engagement: A Computational Case Study of Russian-Linked Facebook and Instagram Content," *Journalism & Mass Communication Quarterly* 97, no. 3 (2020): 743–61, https://doi.org/10.1177/1077699020911884; Karen Gregory and Sava Saheli Singh, "Anger in Academic Twitter: Sharing, Caring, and Getting Mad Online," *TripleC: Communication, Capitalism & Critique* 16, no. 1 (2018): 176–93, https://doi.org/10.31269/triplec.v16i1.890.

20. Dag Wollebæk, Rune Karlsen, Kari Steen-Johnsen, and Bernard Enjolras, "Anger, Fear, and Echo Chambers: The Emotional Basis for Online Behavior," *Social Media + Society* 5, no. 2 (2019): 1–14, https://doi.org/10.1177%2F2056305119829859.

21. Elizabeth Suhay and Cengiz Erisen, "The Role of Anger in the Biased Assimilation of Political Information," *Political Psychology* 39, no. 4 (2018): 793–810, https://doi.org/10.1111/pops.12463.

22. Berger and Milkman, "What Makes Online Content Viral?"; Karen Nelson-Field, Erica Riebe, and Kellie Newstead, "The Emotions That Drive Viral Video," *Australasian Marketing Journal* 21, no. 4 (2013): 205–11, https://doi.org/10.1016%2Fj.ausmj.2013.07.003.

23. Ashton Kutcher, "The Twitter Guys," *Time*, April 30, 2009, https://content.time.com/time/specials/packages/article/0,28804,1894410_1893837_1894156,00.html.

24. Biz Stone, *Things a Little Bird Told Me: Confessions of the Creative Mind* (New York: Grand Central Publishing, 2015).

25. Happiness is one of the hardest emotions to define and most debated among researchers. This simplified definition is based on writings by positive psychologist Sonja Lyubomirsky, behavioral economist Daniel Kahneman, and the Dalai Lama.

26. George Kennedy, ed., *Progymnasmata: Greek Textbooks of Prose Composition and Rhetoric* (Leiden, the Netherlands: Brill, 2003).

27. Arnold Schwarzenegger, "Governor Schwarzenegger's Message Following This Week's Attack on the Capitol," YouTube, January 10, 2021, https://www.youtube.com/watch?v=x_P-OI6sAck.

## CHAPTER 11

1. Mary Robinson, "Xiuhtezcatl Martinez and Kelsey Juliana," Time 100 Next, *Time*, 2019, https://time.com/collection/time-100-next-2019/5718896/xiuhtezcatl-martinez-kelsey-juliana/.

2. Claire Martin, "Xiuhtezcatl Roske-Martinez, 14, Wants to Save the World," *Denver Post*, May 28, 2014, https://www.denverpost.com/2014/05/28/xiuhtezcatl-roske-martinez-14-wants-to-save-the-world/.

3. Coco McPherson, "Environmental Activist Xiuhtezcatl Martinez: A Teen on the Front Lines," *Rolling Stone*, July 19, 2017, https://www.rollingstone.com/culture/culture-features/environmental-activist-xiuhtezcatl-martinez-a-teen-on-the-front-lines-197672/; Caroline Steyer, "15-Year-Old Climate Activist Speaks to UN General Assembly," *Huffington Post*, July 2, 2015, https://www.huffpost.com/entry/xiuhtezcatl-speaks-to-un_n_7715192; Robinson, "Xiuhtezcatl Martinez and Kelsey Juliana."

4. "Xiuhtezcatl Roske-Martinez, Earth Guardians Speaks at UN Climate Reception—21 April 2016," YouTube, April 28, 2016, https://www.youtube.com/watch?v=8DgmEetWiHs.

5. Bioneers, "Xiuhtezcatl Martinez—Youth Leadership," YouTube, November 4, 2014, https://www.youtube.com/watch?v=El8pEQH-pls.

6. TEDxYouth, "Hip-Hop Environmental Activism: Xiuhtezcatl Martinez at TEDxYouth@MileHigh," YouTube,

May 14, 2014, https://www.youtube.com/watch?v
=o2V2yVkedtM.

7. Xiuhtezcatl, "Xiuhtezcatl feat. Jaden Smith—Boombox Warfare" (Official Lyric Video), YouTube, April 26, 2019, https://www.youtube.com/watch?v=5DA-w-_HZLo.

8. This definition of language combines some of the common psychological and sociolinguistic definitions while setting aside controversies among linguists about the exact nature and origins of human language. See also "language," *The APA Dictionary of Psychology*, https://dictionary.apa.org/language; and William O'Grady, John Archibald, Mark Arnoff, and Janie Rees-Miller, *Contemporary Linguistics: An Introduction*, 7th ed. (New York: Bedford/St. Martin's, 2017).

9. Louis Hjelmslev, *Prolegomena to a Theory of Language*, trans. Francis J. Whitfield (Madison: University of Wisconsin Press, 1963).

10. Walt Wolfram and Natalie Schilling, *American English: Dialects and Variation*, 3rd ed. (Hoboken, NJ: Wiley-Blackwell, 2016).

11. For examples, see April Baker-Bell, "'I Never Really Knew the History behind African American Language': Critical Language Pedagogy in an Advanced Placement English Language Arts Class," *Equity & Excellence in Education* 46, no. 3 (2013): 355–70, https://doi.org/10.1080/10665684.2013.806848; Delicia Tiera Greene, "'Switchin' My Style Up!' A Case Study of a Black Girl's Literacy and Language Practices across Three Contexts," in *Genders, Cultures, and Literacies: Understanding Intersecting Identities*, ed. Barbara J. Guzzetti (New York: Routledge, 2021), 121–34; Lauren Mason Carris, "La Voz Gringa: Latino Stylization of Linguistic (In)authenticity as Social Critique," *Discourse & Society* 22, no. 4 (2011): 474–90, https://doi.org/10.1177%2F0957926510395835; Yen H. Nguyen, "The Importance of Antiracism in Speaking Center Pedagogic Materials: 'Neutral' Is No Longer Neutral," *Communication Center Journal* 7, no. 1 (2021): 127–29, https://libjournal.uncg.edu/ccj/article/view/2206; Kathleen Turner Ledgerwood, "Interventions Foregrounding and Honoring Black Language in FYC from a HBCU/PBI Perspective," in *WPA: Special Issue: Black Lives Matter and Anti-Racist Projects in Writing Program Administration* 44, no. 3 (2021): 158–61, https://wpacouncil.org/aws/CWPA/asset_manager/get_file/604389?ver=2.

12. For more on the origins and rise of white mainstream English, see William R. Van Riper, "General American: An Ambiguity," in *Dialect and Language Variation*, ed. Harold B. Allen and Michael D. Linn (New York: Elsevier 1986), 123–35.

13. Marcyliena H. Morgan, *Speech Communities* (Cambridge, UK: Cambridge University Press, 2014).

14. Wolfram and Schilling, *American English.*

15. Michael Silverstein, "How Language Communities Intersect: Is 'Superdiversity' an Incremental or Transformative Condition?" *Tilburg Papers in Culture Studies*, no. 107 (2014): https://pure.uvt.nl/ws/portalfiles/portal/30479851/TPCS_107_Silverstein.pdf.

16. Chad Nilep, "'Code Switching' in Sociocultural Linguistics," *Colorado Research in Linguistics* 19 (2006), https://doi.org/10.25810/hnq4-jv62.

17. The concept of code switching has long been used in linguistics and second-language studies to refer to how multilingual speakers move between or mix multiple languages, in addition to switching between marginalized and privileged forms of English.

18. Vershawn Ashanti Young, Rusty Barret, Y'Shanda Young-Rivera, and Kim Brian Lovejoy, *Other People's English: Code-Meshing, Code-Switching, and African American Literacy* (Anderson, SC: Parlor Press, 2018); Rawn Santiago, Nchopia Nwokoma, and Jasmin Crentsil, "Investigating the Implications of Code-Switching and Assimilating at Work for African American Professionals," *Journal of Business Diversity* 21, no. 4 (2021): 72–81, https://doi.org/10.33423/jbd.v21i4.4750; Sina Saeedi and Elaine Richardson, "A Black Lives Matter and Critical Race Theory–Informed Critique of Code-Switching Pedagogy," in *Race Justice and Activism in Literacy Instruction*, ed. Valerie Kinloch, Tanja Burkhard, and Carlotta Penn (New York: Teachers College Press, 2019): 147–63.

19. Young, Barret, Young-Riviera, and Lovejoy, *Other People's English*; Lilia D. Monzó and Robert Rueda, "Passing for English Fluent: Latino Immigrant Children Masking Language Proficiency," *Anthropology & Education Quarterly* 40, no. 1 (2009): 20–40, https://doi.org/10.1111/j.1548-1492.2009.01026.x.; Christopher Boulton, "Black Identities inside Advertising: Race Inequality, Code Switching, and Stereotype Threat," *Howard Journal*

of *Communications* 27, no. 2 (2016): 130–44, https://doi
.org/10.1080/10646175.2016.1148646.

20. Anna-Kaisa Newheiser and Manuela Barreto,
"Hidden Costs of Hiding Stigma: Ironic Interpersonal
Consequences of Concealing a Stigmatized Identity in
Social Interactions," *Journal of Experimental Psychology*
52 (2014): 58–70, https://doi.org/10.1016/j.jesp.2014.01
.002; Jamila Lyiscott, *Black Appetite. White Food. Issues
of Race, Voice, and Justice within and beyond the Classroom* (New York: Routledge, 2019); Santiago, Nwokoma,
and Crentsil, "Investigating the Implications of Code-
Switching"; Antija M. Allen and Justin T. Stewart, eds.,
*We're Not OK: Black Faculty Experiences and Higher Edu-
cation Strategies* (Cambridge, UK: Cambridge University
Press, 2022).

21. For more on this, we recommend Lyiscott, *Black
Appetite. White Food.*

22. Vershawn Ashanti Young, "'Nah, We Straight': An
Argument against Code Switching," *JAC* 29, no. 1/2
(2009): 49–76, https://www.jstor.org/stable/20866886;
Young, Barret, Young-Riviera, and Lovejoy, *Other People's
English.*

23. Harlan Pruden, "August 4, 2020 'TWO-SPIRIT'
Turns 30!!" *Two Spirit Journal*, August 3, 2020, https://
twospiritjournal.com/?p=973; Samantha Mesa-Miles,
"Two Spirit: The Trials and Tribulations of Gender
Identity in the 21st Century," *Indian Country Today*,
updated September 13, 2018, https://indiancountrytoday
.com/archive/two-spirit-the-trials-and-tribulations-of
-gender-identity-in-the-21st-century.

24. Jamila Lyiscott, "3 Ways to Speak English," TED talk,
YouTube, June 19, 2014, https://www.youtube.com/watch
?v=k9fmJ5xQ_mc.

25. Jamila Lyiscott, "Why English Class Is Silencing
Students of Color," TEDxTheBenjaminSchool, You-
Tube, May 23, 2018, https://www.youtube.com/watch?v
=u4dc1axRwE4. We highly recommend this talk to every
teacher and student of speech, communication, English,
or speech pathology. See also her 2019 book, Jamila Lyiscott, *Black Appetite. White Food.*

26. The literature on levels of style sometimes uses the
terms *high*, *low*, and *middle*. We have chosen *grand*, *plain*,
and *middle* for three reasons. First, these terms are more
descriptive and intuitive. Second, *high* and *low* sometimes
imply value judgments, which would be inappropriate in
this context, as no one style is innately better than the
others. Third, we find them more fitting translations of
the original Latin and Greek.

27. Scholars familiar with rhetoric may recognize some
echoes of the various lists of master tropes. Our classifica-
tion deviates from the master trope lists of Giambattista
Vico, Kenneth Burke, and Harold Bloom for two reasons.
First, we used simpler terminology to aid the student.
Second, we include schemes, which are important figures
of speech but overlooked when focusing solely on tropes.

28. Martin Luther King Jr., "I Have a Dream," *Negro
History Bulletin* 31, no. 5 (May 1968): 16–17, https://www
.jstor.org/stable/24767162.

29. Abraham Lincoln, "Gettysburg Address," *Voices
of Democracy: The U.S. Oratory Project*, accessed June
1, 2022, https://voicesofdemocracy.umd.edu/lincoln
-gettysburg-address-speech-text/.

30. John F. Kennedy, "Inaugural Address," John F.
Kennedy Presidential Library and Museum, accessed
June 1, 2022, https://www.jfklibrary.org/learn/about
-jfk/historic-speeches/inaugural-address.

31. This line was spoken in 1969 by astronaut Neil Armstrong as he became the first person ever to set foot on the
moon. There is some debate as to whether he said "one
small step for man" or "one small step for a man," but he
is usually quoted as leaving out the "a" and most readers
will be more familiar with that form of the quotation.
For more, see Olivia B. Waxman, "Lots of People Have
Theories about Neil Armstrong's 'One Small Step for Man'
Quote. Here's What We Really Know," *Time*, July 15, 2019,
https://time.com/5621999/neil-armstrong-quote/.

32. This famous line is the opening to Charles Dickens's
classic novel *A Tale of Two Cities*. Less well-known is
the extended use of antithesis that follows it: "It was the
best of times, it was the worst of times, it was the age of
wisdom, it was the age of foolishness, it was the epoch of
belief, it was the epoch of incredulity, it was the season
of Light, it was the season of Darkness, it was the spring
of hope, it was the winter of despair, we had everything
before us, we had nothing before us, we were all going
direct to Heaven, we were all going direct the other
way . . ." Charles Dickens, *A Tale of Two Cities*, vol. I (New
York: Sheldon and Company, 1863), 7.

33. Alexander Pope, *An Essay on Criticism*, 2nd ed. (W. Lewis, 1713), 27.

34. The confusion over the meaning of *biannual* has become so common that many dictionaries recognize both meanings. See "biannual," *The Britannica Dictionary*, https://www.britannica.com/dictionary/biannual; "bi-annual," *The American Heritage Dictionary of the English Language*, https://www.ahdictionary.com/word/search .html?q=biannual.

35. Matt Lavietes, "Gay High Schooler Says He's 'Being Silenced' by Florida's LGBTQ Law," NBC News, May 12, 2022, https://www.nbcnews.com/nbc-out/out -community-voices/gay-high-schooler-says-silenced -floridas-lgbtq-law-rcna28429.

36. Tomás Mier, "His Principal Wants to Censor His Graduation Speech. This Gay Student Leader Won't Let It Happen," *Rolling Stone*, May 12, 2022, https://www .rollingstone.com/culture/culture-features/zander -moricz-dont-say-gay-bill-censorship-1352475/; Zander Moricz, "I am the youngest public plaintiff in the 'Don't Say Gay' lawsuit. I am my Florida high school's first openly gay Class President. I am being silenced, and I need your help," 8-part thread, Twitter, https://twitter.com /zandermoricz/status/1523800075142504449.

37. Zander Moricz, "Zander Moricz Grad Speech," You-Tube, May 22, 2022, https://www.youtube.com/watch?v= qpTVyozS7M0.

38. Nicole Curtis and Laura Zaccaro, "Florida High Schooler Who Says He Was Censored in Graduation Speech Speaks Out," ABC News, May 23, 2022, https:// abcnews.go.com/GMA/News/florida-high-schooler -censored-graduation-speech-speaks/story?id=84863588.

## CHAPTER 12

1. Jordan Raskopolous, "Living with High Functioning Anxiety," TEDxSydney, YouTube, July 26, 2017, https:// www.youtube.com/watch?v=JUedQ0_EGCQ.

2. Michael Zane Hackman and Kim B. Walker, "Instruc-tional Communication in the Televised Classroom: The Effects of System Design and Teacher Immediacy on Student Learning and Satisfaction," *Communication Education* 39, no. 3 (1990): 196–206, https://doi.org /10.1080/03634529009378802.

3. Dominic A. Infante, Andrew S. Rancer, and Deanna F. Womack, *Building Communication Theory* (Long Grove, IL: Waveland Press, 2003); Robert H. Woods and Jason D. Baker, "Interaction and Immediacy in Online Learning," *International Review of Research in Open and Distributed Learning* 5, no. 2 (2004): https://doi.org/10.19173/irrodl .v5i2.186.

4. Ronald P. Carver, "Effects of Increasing the Rate of Speech Presentation upon Comprehension," *Journal of Educational Psychology* 65, no. 1 (1973): 118–250, http:// dx.doi.org/10.1037/h0034783; Mary E. Reynolds and Jenny Givens, "Presentation Rate in Comprehension of Natural and Synthesized Speech," *Perceptual and Motor Skills* 92, no. 3 (2001): 958–68, https://doi.org /10.2466%2Fpms.2001.92.3c.958.

5. Barbara Krahé, Andreas Uhlmann, and Meike Herz-berg, "The Voice Gives It Away: Male and Female Pitch as a Cue for Gender Stereotyping, *Social Psychology* 52, no. 2 (2021): 101–13, https://doi.org/10.1027/1864-9335 /a000441.

6. Jeffrey C. Hahner, Martin A. Sokoloff, and Sandra L. Salisch, *Speaking Clearly: Improving Voice and Diction*, 6th ed. (Long Grove, IL: Waveland Press, 2013).

7. Edward T. Hall, *The Hidden Dimension* (New York: Garden City Doubleday, 1966); Kath Dooley, "A Ques-tion of Proximity: Exploring a New Screen Grammar for 360-Degree Cinematic Virtual Reality," *Media Practice and Education* 21, no. 2 (2019): 81–96, https://doi.org /10.1080/25741136.2019.1641005.

8. Mark L. Knapp, Judith A. Hall, and Terrence G. Hor-gan, *Nonverbal Communication in Human Interaction*, 8th ed. (Boston: Cengage Learning, 2013).

## CHAPTER 13

1. Deborah Vankin, "John Leguizamo on Theater: 'It Didn't Just Change Me, It Saved Me,'" *Los Angeles Times*, June 11, 2018, https://www.latimes.com/entertainment /la-et-tony-awards-2018-winners-htmlstory.html; Lulu Garcia-Navarro, "John Leguizamo on 'Latin History for Morons,'" *Weekend Edition Sunday*, NPR, December 15, 2019, https://www.npr.org/2019/12/15/788195270/john -leguizamo-on-latin-history-for-morons.

2. For more on the impacts of European colonization and the use of the term *genocide* to describe the mass

extermination of Indigenous people in the Americas, see Tai S. Edwards and Paul Kelton, "Germs, Genocides, and America's Indigenous Peoples," *Journal of American History* 107, no. 1 (2020): 52–76, https://doi.org/10.1093/jahist/jaaa008; and David Stannard, *American Holocaust: The Conquest of the New World* (New York: Oxford University Press, 1992).

3. Luz Rello and Ricardo Baeza-Yates, "The Effect of Font Type on Screen Readability by People with Dyslexia," *ACM Transactions on Accessible Computing* 8, no. 4, article 15 (2016), https://doi.org/10.1145/2897736; British Dyslexia Association, *Dyslexia Friendly Style Guide* (2018), https://www.bdadyslexia.org.uk/advice/employers/creating-a-dyslexia-friendly-workplace/dyslexia-friendly-style-guide.

4. Frans de Waal, "Moral Behavior in Animals," TEDxPeachtree, November 2011, https://www.ted.com/talks/frans_de_waal_moral_behavior_in_animals.

5. Creative Commons, "What We Do," creativecommons.org, accessed June 6, 2022, https://creativecommons.org/about/.

## CHAPTER 14

1. WOC Podcasters, "About WOC Podcasters," WOCPodcasters, n.d., https://wocpodcasters.co/about/.

2. Sheswanderful, "WITS Week: The Future of Audio with Pandora Music," YouTube, April 19, 2021, https://www.youtube.com/watch?v=T-0pW6CulpM.

3. Taylor Lorenz, "Podcast Groups Aren't Just about Podcasts," *New York Times*, January 15, 2020, https://www.nytimes.com/2020/01/15/style/podcast-facebook-groups.html; *Podcast Business Journal,* n.d., https://podcastbusinessjournal.com/.

4. Sheswanderful, "WITS Week."

5. Bethany Hawkins, "Ep 9 Being a Thought Leader with Danielle Desir," Chatting over Chowder by Crackers in Soup, YouTube, March 1, 2021, https://www.youtube.com/watch?v=aoR9S6r7RlI.

6. Sheswanderful, "WITS Week."

7. Paul Charosh, *Berliner Gramophone Records: American Issues, 1892–1900* (Westport, CT: Greenwood Press,1995): xvii.

8. Melvin L. DeFleur, *Mass Communication Theories: Explaining Origins, Processes, and Effects* (Oxfordshire, UK: Routledge, 2016), chapter 11.

9. Melvin L. DeFleur, *Mass Communication Theories,* chapter 12.

10. Katja Friedrich, Till Keyling, and Hans-Bernd Brosius, "Gatekeeping Revisited," in *Political Communication in the Online World: Theoretical Approaches and Research Designs,* ed. Gerhard Vowe and Philipp Henn (Oxfordshire, UK: Routledge, 2016), 59–72; Gabriel Weimann and Hans-Bernd Brosius, "A New Agenda for Agenda-Setting Research in the Digital Era," in *Political Communication,* ed. Vowe and Henn, 26–44.

11. Riverside.fm Team, "Podcast Statistics and Trends (& Why They Matter)," Riverside.fm, September 22, 2021, https://riverside.fm/blog/podcast-statistics.

12. For example, Saron Yitbarek, "The Ultimate Podcasting Hack: Record in Your Closet and Use Two Pillows," Medium, June 2, 2018, https://medium.com/@saronyitbarek/the-ultimate-podcasting-hack-record-in-your-closet-39a478f4d89a; "Record in My Closet?" Reddit, discussion thread, 2020, https://www.reddit.com/r/podcasting/comments/gp95kl/record_in_my_closet/.

13. Brooke Auxier and Monica Anderson, "Social Media Use in 2021," Pew Research Center, April 7, 2021, https://www.pewresearch.org/internet/2021/04/07/social-media-use-in-2021/.

14. L. Ceci, "Average YouTube Video Length as of December 2018, by Category," Statista, August 23, 2021, https://www.statista.com/statistics/1026923/youtube-video-category-average-length/.

15. Ezra Fishman, "How Long Should Your Next Video Be?" Wistia, July 5, 2016, https://wistia.com/learn/marketing/optimal-video-length.

16. Think Media, "How to Make YouTube Videos on Your Phone (Beginners Tutorial)," YouTube, August 13, 2019, https://www.youtube.com/watch?v=am7kaAerVCQ.

17. Jouelzy, "Storytime: Bishes in the Forest," YouTube, February 21, 2019, https://www.youtube.com/watch?v=HBlE9Ay8pr8.

## CHAPTER 15

1. Mary Louise Kelly, "North Korean Defector Hopes to See Loved Ones Again—But Remains Skeptical," *All Things Considered*, National Public Radio, May 1, 2018, https://www.npr.org/sections/parallels/2018/05/01/607375723/north-korean-defector-hopes-to-see-loved-ones-again-but-remains-skeptical; Maeve Shearlaw, "'How I Escaped from North Korea'—Hyeonseo Lee's Story Live," *Guardian*, July 3, 2015, https://www.theguardian.com/world/2015/jul/03/north-korea-escape-hyeonseo-lee-live.

2. Hyeonseo Lee, "About Me," hyeonseo-lee.com, n.d., http://www.hyeonseo-lee.com/eng/about-me_27652.shtml; "Oslo Freedom Forum, May 12–14, 2014" Oslo Freedom Forum, n.d., retrieved from the Internet Archive Wayback Machine, https://web.archive.org/web/20140421115035/http://www.oslofreedomforum.com/pdfs/OFF14Speakers.pdf.

3. TED, "Hyeonseo Lee: My Escape from North Korea," YouTube, March 20, 2013, https://www.youtube.com/watch?v=PdxPCeWw75k.

4. To compare how this question is approached with an informative vs. a persuasive purpose, see Michael Siegel, Craig S. Ross, and Charles King III, "The Relationship between Gun Ownership and Firearm Homicide Rates in the United States, 1981–2010," *American Journal of Public Health* 103, no. 11 (2013): 2098–105, https://dx.doi.org/10.2105%2FAJPH.2013.301409; and National Rifle Association Institute for Legislative Action, "Crime | Criminal Justice: Gun Ownership and Crime Trends," October 2020, https://www.nraila.org/get-the-facts/crime-criminal-justice/.

5. Wired UK, "Jim Al-Khalili: Quantum Mechanics Could Help Us Understand the Question of Life," YouTube, January 25, 2019, https://www.youtube.com/watch?v=kk-fHeoJmCY.

6. Mark Phelan, "2020 Ford Explorer's New Tires Fix Themselves, Representing a Coming Trend for Drivers," *Detroit Free Press*, June 29, 2019, https://www.freep.com/story/money/cars/mark-phelan/2019/06/29/ford-explorer-self-sealing-tires/1599083001/.

7. NASA/JPL Edu, "How Many Decimals of Pi Do We Really Need?" EDU News, Jet Propulsion Laboratory, California Institute of Technology, March 16, 2016, https://www.jpl.nasa.gov/edu/news/2016/3/16/how-many-decimals-of-pi-do-we-really-need/.

8. Angela Walters, "Beginner Friendly WEAVE IT BE Lattice Quilt (with Walking Foot Quilting!)," Midnight Quilt Show, YouTube, March 21, 2018, https://www.youtube.com/watch?app=desktop&v=dRS6J-sTNu8.

## CHAPTER 16

1. Richard C. Paddock, "After Fighting Plastic in 'Paradise Lost,' Sisters Take On Climate Change," *New York Times*, July 3, 2020, https://www.nytimes.com/2020/07/03/world/asia/bali-sisters-plastic-climate-change.html.

2. Melati Wijsen and Isabel Wijsen, "Our Campaign to Ban Plastic Bags in Bali," YouTube, February 19, 2016, https://www.youtube.com/watch?v=P8GCjrDWWUM; Melati Wijsen and Isabel Wijsen, "It's About Time We Start Listening, Acting & Changing," TEDxLausanne Women," YouTube, January 23, 2017, https://www.youtube.com/watch?v=Y6Z5eOv6Nnk; Melati Wijsen, "A Roadmap for Young Changemakers," TED Countdown, YouTube, December 23, 2021, https://www.youtube.com/watch?v=SfROjZlyg7o; United Nations, "Melati and Isabel Wijsen—World Oceans Day 2017," YouTube, June 8, 2017, https://www.youtube.com/watch?v=QsUhTneXLLc; World Economic Forum, "The Disposable Society | DAVOS 2020," YouTube, September 12, 2020, https://www.youtube.com/watch?v=YAbY7-ni07Q; World Economic Forum, "The Plastic Revolution | Isabel Wijsen," YouTube, August 15, 2019, https://www.youtube.com/watch?v=8xJrt0reXlg.

3. For example, Connect4Climate, "Melati and Isabel Wijsen Inspire Young People to Action #SaveOurOcean," YouTube, June 27, 2017, https://www.youtube.com/watch?v=YQO2aCy_XiE. Melati Wijsen's Instagram profile can be found at https://www.instagram.com/melatiwijsen/. Isabel Wijsen's Instagram profile is at https://www.instagram.com/isabel.wijsen/.

4. More information about Youthtopia and its online classes can be found at its website: https://www.youthtopia.education/.

5. This tendency for audiences to hold closely to their existing values, attitudes, and behaviors is well documented in the research on social judgment theory. For more, see Muzafer Sherif and Carl I. Hovland, *Social Judgment: Assimilation and Contrast Effects in Communication*

and *Attitude Change* (New Haven, CT: Yale University Press, 1961).

6. We have based this section on stasis theory, as developed by the ancient Greek philosophers Hermagoras and Aristotle. We have modified the standard form to suit contemporary speaking situations by collapsing definition into fact and splitting personal action out from policy.

7. "'Radio Mullah' Sent Hit Squad after Malala Yousafzai," *Express Tribune*, October 12, 2012, https://tribune.com.pk/story/450639/radio-mullah-sent-hit.

8. Nobel Prize, "Malala Yousafzai: Nobel Peace Prize Lecture 2014," YouTube, January 10, 2020, https://www.youtube.com/watch?v=c2DHzlkUI6s.

9. We adapted this method of persuading about facts from Thomas Kuhn's paradigm shift model. See Thomas S. Kuhn, *The Structure of Scientific Revolutions* (University of Chicago Press, 1970).

10. Mayo Clinic Staff, "Red Wine and Resveratrol: Good for Your Heart?" Mayo Clinic, January 14, 2022, https://www.mayoclinic.org/diseases-conditions/heart-disease/in-depth/red-wine/art-20048281.

11. GBD 2016 Alcohol Collaborators, "Alcohol Use and Burden for 195 Countries and Territories, 1990–2016: A Systematic Analysis for the Global Burden of Disease Study 2016," *The Lancet* 392, iss. 10152 (2018): 1015–35, https://doi.org/10.1016/S0140-6736(18)31310-2.

12. "Alcohol and COVID-19: What You Need to Know," World Health Organization, 2020, https://www.euro.who.int/__data/assets/pdf_file/0010/437608/Alcohol-and-COVID-19-what-you-need-to-know.pdf; "Alcohol and Public Health: Frequently Asked Questions," Centers for Disease Control and Prevention, April 19, 2022, https://www.cdc.gov/alcohol/faqs.htm; "The Risks of Drinking Too Much," National Health Service, May 23, 2019, https://www.nhs.uk/live-well/alcohol-support/the-risks-of-drinking-too-much/.

13. GBD 2016 Alcohol Collaborators, "Alcohol Use and Burden."

14. Alan Houston Monroe, *Monroe's Principles of Speech* (Northbrook, IL: Scott Foresman, 1943).

15. Ulrich Schmidt and Horst Zank, "What Is Loss Aversion?" *Journal of Risk and Uncertainty* 30 (2005): 157–67, https://doi.org/10.1007/s11166-005-6564-6.

16. Antonia Abbey, Mary Jo Smith, and Richard O. Scott, "The Relationship between Reasons for Drinking Alcohol and Alcohol Consumption: An Interactional Approach," *Addictive Behaviors* 18, no. 6 (1993): 659–70, https://doi.org/10.1016/0306-4603(93)90019-6.

17. "Alcohol Facts and Statistics," National Institute on Alcohol Abuse and Alcoholism, March 2022, https://www.niaaa.nih.gov/publications/brochures-and-fact-sheets/alcohol-facts-and-statistics; Lydia Saad, "Majority in US Drink Alcohol, Averaging Four Drinks a Week," Gallup, August 17, 2012, https://news.gallup.com/poll/156770/majority-drink-alcohol-averaging-four-drinks-week.aspx.

18. GBD 2016 Alcohol Collaborators, "Alcohol Use and Burden."

19. "Alcohol Consumption Is the Sole Cause of 85,000 Deaths Annually in the Americas, PAHO/WHO Study Finds," Pan American Health Organization, April 12, 2021, https://www.paho.org/en/news/12-4-2021-alcohol-consumption-sole-cause-85000-deaths-annually-americas-pahowho-study-finds.

20. "Dietary Guidelines for Americans, 2020–2025: Executive Summary," US Department of Agriculture, n.d., https://www.dietaryguidelines.gov/sites/default/files/2021-03/DGA_2020-2025_ExecutiveSummary_English.pdf.

21. Aisha Harris, "She Founded Me Too. Now She Wants to Move Past the Trauma," *New York Times*, October 15, 2018, https://www.nytimes.com/2018/10/15/arts/tarana-burke-metoo-anniversary.html.

22. Alyssa_Milano, "If you've been sexually harassed or assaulted write 'me too' as a reply to this tweet," @Alyssa_Milano, Twitter, October 15, 2017, 4:21 p.m., https://twitter.com/Alyssa_Milano/status/919659438700670976.

23. Colleen Walsh, "Challenge of Archiving the #MeToo Movement," *Harvard Gazette*, August 11, 2020, https://news.harvard.edu/gazette/story/2020/08/challenge-of-archiving-the-metoo-movement/.

24. Tarana Burke, "Me Too Is a Movement, Not a Moment," TEDWomen 2018, November 2018, https://www.ted.com/talks/tarana_burke_me_too_is_a_movement_not_a_moment/transcript#t-367754.

25. Jane Kolodinsky, Jean Ruth Harvey-Berino, Linda Berlin, Rachel K. Johnson, and Travis William Reynolds, "Knowledge of Current Dietary Guidelines and Food Choice by College Students: Better Eaters Have Higher

Knowledge of Dietary Guidance," *Journal of the Academy of Nutrition and Dietetics* 107, no. 8 (2007): 1409–13, https://doi.org/10.1016/j.jada.2007.05.016.

## CHAPTER 17

1. Amanda Gorman, "Using Your Voice Is a Political Choice," TED, November 2018, https://www.ted.com /talks/amanda_gorman_using_your_voice_is_a_political _choice.

2. Text of Gorman's inauguration poem, "The Hill We Climb," is available at Lian Parsons, "History Has Its Eyes on US," *Harvard Gazette*, January 20, 2021, https:// news.harvard.edu/gazette/story/2021/01/amanda -gormans-inauguration-poem-the-hill-we-climb/. Video of her presentation is available at Denver7–The Denver Channel, "Amanda Gorman Reads a Poem at Inauguration," YouTube, January 20, 2021, https://www.youtube .com/watch?v=cNFAICB8vxw.

3. Gorman's Super Bowl poem, "Chorus of the Captains," can be found as text at Shanna McCarriston, "Super Bowl 2021: Read the Transcript of Amanda Gorman Poem 'Chorus of the Captains,'" CBS Sports, February 7, 2021, https://www.cbssports.com/nfl/news/super-bowl-2021 -read-the-transcript-of-amanda-gorman-poem-chorus -of-the-captains/. Video of her presentation is available at NowThis News, "Amanda Gorman Recites 'Chorus of the Captains' at Super Bowl LV," YouTube, February 7, 2021, https://www.youtube.com/watch?v=-ejbSCjg2qo.

4. Adam Gabbatt, "'An Inspiration to Us All': Amanda Gorman's Inaugural Poem Stirs Hope and Awe," *Guardian*, January 20, 2021, https://www.theguardian.com/us -news/2021/jan/20/amanda-gorman-poem-biden -inauguration; CBS News, "Amanda Gorman Makes History as Youngest Known Inaugural Poet," January 21, 2021, https://www.cbsnews.com/news/amanda-gorman -inaugural-poet-the-hill-we-climb/.

5. This model is loosely adapted from the advice for encomia (speeches of praise) offered by the ancient Greek rhetorician Hermogenes of Tarsus. See George A. Kennedy, *Progymnasmata: Greek Textbooks of Prose Composition and Rhetoric* (Leiden, NL: Brill, 2003).

6. George Szalai and Scott Roxborough, "Oscars: How Many People Watch the Ceremony Worldwide?" *Hollywood Reporter*, February 23, 2016, https://www .hollywoodreporter.com/news/oscars-worldwide-tv -audience-867554.

7. Oscars, "Bong Joon Ho Wins Best Director," YouTube, March 11, 2020, https://www.youtube.com/watch?v =ekMl5VHBH4I.

8. David Sims, "The Best Speech of Oscars Night," *Atlantic*, February 10, 2020, https://www.theatlantic.com /culture/archive/2020/02/bong-joon-ho-showed-oscars -can-still-be-magic/606319/.

9. "Rosa Parks Memorial Service," CSPAN, October 31, 2005, https://www.c-span.org/video/?189655-1/rosa -parks-memorial-service.

10. For the full lyrics to this traditional folk song, see "Riddle Song," Songs for Teaching, n.d., https://www .songsforteaching.com/folk/riddlesong2k.php.

## CHAPTER 18

1. Casey Smith, "'Close the Camps': Lights for Liberty Vigil Protests Treatment of Migrants at the Border," *IndyStar*, July 13, 2019, https://www.indystar.com/story /news/local/indianapolis/2019/07/13/lights-liberty-vigil -protest-treatment-migrants-border/1705875001/.

2. Erica Chenoweth, Tommy Leung, Nathan Perkins, and Jeremy Pressman, "The Anti-Trump 'Lights for Liberty' Events Might Be the Most Significant Protests You've Never Heard Of," *Washington Post*, July 31, 2019, https:// www.washingtonpost.com/politics/2019/07/31/anti -trump-lights-liberty-events-might-be-most-significant -protests-you-never-heard/.

3. "About Us," Lights for Liberty, n.d., https://www .lightsforliberty.org/about-us; "Content+Downloads," Lights for Liberty, n.d., https://www.lightsforliberty.org /downloads.

4. "Lights for Liberty: Plaza Fiesta," Facebook, n.d., https://www.facebook.com/events/426317611554788 /?active_tab=about.

5. This and other details about this event can be seen in the video posted by an attendee: Debbie Sumner, "Debbie Sumner Was Live," July 12, 2019, https://www.facebook .com/1360855908/videos/10219747272256552/.

6. While this is a common division in small group theory, we have drawn our inspiration for this section from J. Dan Rothwell's *In Mixed Company: Communicating in Small Groups and Teams*, 10th edition (New York: Oxford

University Press, 2019). We have simplified Rothwell's typology and adjusted it to better fit the way groups operate in group meetings and presentations.

7.  Shark Tank Australia, "The Highest Earning Business in Shark Tank History? | Shark Tank AUS," February 13, 2021, https://www.youtube.com/watch?v=_N326-JdKgg.

# Credits

## PHOTOS

**Frontmatter: Page ix:** Monica Schipper/Getty Images for We Day; **p. x (top)**: Craig Barritt/Getty Images for Beautycon NYC; **p. x (bottom)**: Reuters/Danny Moloshok/Alamy Stock Photo; **p. xi (top)**: Leigh Vogel/Getty Images for MoveOn; **p. xi (bottom)**: Meredith Goldberg/ZUMA Press/Newscom; **p. xii (top)**: Frédéric Marie/Alamy Stock Photo; **p. xii (bottom)**: Craig Barritt/Getty Images for Glamour; **p. xiii**: Cindy Ord/Getty Images for GLAAD; **p. xiv**: Earl Gibson III/Shutterstock; **p. xv (top)**: The Bureau of Educational and Cultural Affairs (ECA) of the US Department of State; **p. xv (bottom)**: Robin Loznak/ZUMA Wire/Alamy Live News; **p. xvi (top)**: Brendon Thorne/Getty Images; **p. xvi (bottom)**: JM11/Joseph Marzullo/WENN/Newscom; **p. xvii**: Danielle Desir; **p. xviii**: Saumya Khandelwal/Hindustan Times via Getty Images; **p. xix (top)**: Nyimas Laula/The New York Times/Redux; **p. xix (bottom)**: Rob Carr/Getty Images; **p. xx**: Steve Eberhardt/ZUMA Wire/Alamy Live News.

**Chapter 1: Page 2:** Monica Schipper/Getty Images for We Day; **p. 6 (left)**: Kashif Javed/Alamy Stock Photo; **p. 6 (right)**: NASA/Paul E. Alers; **p. 7 (left)**: US Air Force photo by Staff Sgt. Caleb Pavao; **p. 7 (right)**: Dennis Van Tine/Geisler-Fotopres/Alamy Live News; **p. 13**: Jemal Countess/UPI/Alamy Stock Photo; **p. 15**: White House; **p. 17 (left)**: Reuters/Mike Blake/Alamy Stock Photo; **p. 17 (right)**: AP Photo/Tom R. Smedes.

**Chapter 2: Page 22:** Craig Barritt/Getty Images for Beautycon NYC; **p. 26**: TED; **p. 33**: CNN; **p. 34**: Wavebreak Media Ltd./Alamy Stock Photo.

**Chapter 3: Page 40:** Reuters/Danny Moloshok/Alamy Stock Photo; **p. 49**: Atlanta Police Department; **p. 54 (left)**: Reuters/Albert Gea/Alamy Stock Photo; **p. 54 (right)**: UPI/Jim Ruymen/Alamy Stock Photo.

**Chapter 4: Page 60:** Leigh Vogel/Getty Images for MoveOn; **p. 64**: Living Room Conversations; **p. 65**: HBO Max; **p. 67**: Hero Images Inc./Alamy Stock Photo; **p. 73**: Melting Spot/Alamy Stock Photo; **p. 76**: UPI Photo/Gary C. Caskey/Alamy Stock Photo; **p. 77**: Healthline.

**Chapter 5: Page 82:** Meredith Goldberg/ZUMA Press/Newscom; **p. 87**: Tetra Images, LLC/Alamy Stock Photo; **p. 89**: GoFundMe; **p. 91 (top)**: Tweetgen; **p. 91 (inset)**: Jacob Lund/Shutterstock; **p. 91 (bottom)**: Tweetgen; **p. 93**: Cathrin Manning; **p. 94**: Audiense; **p. 98 (left)**: Bernd Wustneck/dpa/Alamy Live News; **p. 98 (right)**: Edwin Rodriguez/SPP Sport Press Photo/Alamy Live News; **p. 102**: World Politics Archive (WPA)/Alamy Stock Photo; **p. 104**: ABC News.

**Chapter 6: Page 110:** Frédéric Marie/Alamy Stock Photo; **p. 115**: Guardian News; **p. 117**: Sue Dorfman/ZUMA Wire/Alamy Live News; **p. 119**: horst friedrichs/Alamy Stock Photo; **p. 123**: ZUMA Press, Inc./Alamy Stock Photo; **p. 125**: Tim Rogers.

**Chapter 7: Page 132:** Craig Barritt/Getty Images for Glamour; **p. 135 (left)**: Jake Lyell/Alamy Stock Photo; **p. 135 (right)**: Level Nine Productions; **p. 136 (left)**: Al Seib/Pool/Abaca Press/Alamy Stock Photo; **p. 136 (right)**: Bob Collet/Alamy Stock Photo; **p. 138**: Mark Wilson/Getty Images; **p. 143**: El Paso Matters; **p. 149**: AP Photo/Elaine Thompson.